Dr Bryce Rankine was born in South Australi
of Adelaide (BSc 1945; MSc 1953), Californ
After four years as a bacteriologist with F.H. F
1950 he joined the CSIRO wine research ;
Research Institute, which eventually became the Australian Wine Research Institute. For the next twenty-seven years, he carried out research and extension for
the Australian wine industry. In 1978 he joined Roseworthy Agricultural College
as Head of the School of Viticulture and Oenology and later was appointed Dean
of the Faculty of Oenology. He retired in 1986 and is now a consultant for the
Australian wine industry, and until 1995 was Executive Director of the Australian Society of Wine Educators. He has published over 200 scientific and
technical papers and seven books. In 1986 he was appointed a Member of the
Order of Australia and has received various other honours and awards. He lives
in Adelaide and is still involved with the wine industry.

MAKING GOOD WINE

BRYCE RANKINE

WITH AN INTRODUCTION BY

MAYNARD A. AMERINE
Professor Emeritus of the University of California at Davis
and Former Chairman of the Department of Viticulture and Oenology

MACMILLAN
Pan Macmillan Australia

First published 1989 by The Macmillan Company of Australia
Reprinted 1990, 1991, 1992, 1993, 1994, 1995, 1996, 1997,
1998 (with additional material), 1999, 2001, 2002 (twice)
This revised Macmillan edition published 2004 by Pan Macmillan Australia Pty Limited
St Martins Tower, 31 Market Street, Sydney

National Library of Australia
Cataloguing-in-publication data:

Rankine, B.C. (Bryce Crossley).
Making good wine.

ISBN 1 4050 3601 X

1. Wine and wine making – Australia. 2. Wine and wine
making - New Zealand. 3. Wine and wine making – Amateurs'
manuals. I. Title.

663.2

Typeset in 11/13 Times by Post Pre-press Group
Printed in Australia by McPherson's Printing Group

The information in this book is given in good faith and is correct to
the best knowledge of the author. However, the author cannot
accept responsibility for errors which may arise from the
interpretation of the information provided.

Papers used by Pan Macmillan Australia Pty Ltd are natural, recyclable products made
from wood grown in sustainable forests. The manufacturing processes conform to the
environmental regulations of the country of origin.

To present and future winemakers, students, and all who seek to know more about good wine and how to make it.

*Go thy way, eat thy bread with joy,
and drink thy wine with a merry heart*

Ecclesiastes, 9, 7

Contents

Introduction

The twentieth century has seen greater technological advances in winemaking than any previous period. The quality of the raw material—grapes—has been improved with healthier varieties better cared for, careful control of the time of harvest, and more rapid crushing following harvest. The winery itself has been completely redesigned, with efficient equipment which contributes less undesirable metals. Both the vineyard and the winery are now in the hands of well-trained professionals.

The goal, of course, is to make the best possible quality of wines from the available material. With the increasingly high costs of grapes, losses in quality or quantity of wine produced must be kept to a minimum. World-wide, the wine-drinking public has come to expect and demand wines of impeccable colour and clarity with the appropriate aroma and, in some cases, an aged bouquet. Anything less is not tolerated.

This book is primarily intended for young winemakers, especially those in Australia and New Zealand. It offers detailed advice on the raw material, how to design and equip a winery, describes the various types of wine and how they should be produced, stabilized and cared for. The chapters on prevention of oxidation, malo-lactic fermentation and clarification will be particularly useful, not only to young but also experienced winemakers. Sensory evaluation and the various laboratory procedures are given their proper attention. The legal aspects of winemaking in Australia and New Zealand will be of interest to winemakers everywhere.

In a way this is a coming-of-age, a technical book covering all aspects of winemaking for Australian and New Zealand winemakers. It will be of great day-to-day service for them and winemakers everywhere will profit by it.

Maynard A. Amerine

St Helena, California
October 1988

Acknowledgements

This book is the outcome of over fifty years spent in the Australian wine industry in research, winemaking and extension, as well as in training students at Roseworthy Agricultural College for technical and marketing positions in the industry. The information comes from a variety of sources: personal experience in research and extension at the Australian Wine Research Institute and elsewhere over many years, published papers in the world oenological literature, instructional material presented to wine course students at Roseworthy Agricultural College, discussions with winemakers and other colleagues in Australia and New Zealand, and considerable overseas experience.

I am greatly indebted to my late friend, Emeritus Professor Maynard Amerine, formerly Chairman of the Department of Viticulture and Enology of the University of California at Davis and a world authority on wine, for kindly writing the Introduction—he has contributed as possibly has no other person to the technological advancement of winemaking, and I have greatly valued my association with him over the past thirty years.

Grateful acknowledgement is made to all those friends and colleagues who have contributed directly or indirectly to the writing of this book, and I am indebted to the following for their contributions to and/or constructive criticism of parts of the manuscript: David Armstrong of Penfold Wines Pty Ltd; Chris Astley of Dominant Chemicals Pty Ltd; Michael Brajkovich of Kumeu Vineyards, New Zealand; Dr Bryan Coombe of the Waite Agricultural Research Institute; Brian Croser of Petaluma Pty Ltd; Robin Day, Geoff Kurtz, Geoff O'Grady and Jeff Virgo of G. Gramp & Sons Pty Ltd; Jim Fraser of the New Zealand Department of Health; Bill Hardy, Tim James, Brian Walsh and their colleagues of Thomas Hardy & Sons Pty Ltd; Ross Jenkins, Ian McKenzie and Warren Randall of B. Seppelt & Sons Pty Ltd; Tom John of Wibeso; Alex and Geoff Johnston of A.C. Johnston Pty Ltd; Iain Johnston of W. E. Ware & Co.; Dr Tony Jordan, formerly of Oenotec Pty Ltd; Tim Knappstein of Tim Knappstein Wines; Dr Terry Lee and his staff (and my former colleagues Dr Chris Somers and Dr Patrick Williams) at the Australian Wine Research Institute; Peter May and his colleagues of Industrial Supplies Pty Ltd; Roger Macmahon, Ian Paton and their colleagues of J.B. Macmahon Pty Ltd; Professor Ray Molloy of the South Australian Institute of Technology (who kindly read and commented on the whole text); Dr Paul Monk of Intek; Ron Potter of A & G,

Griffith; Geoff Nettelbeck and his staff at the Australian Wine and Brandy Producers Association; Geoff Schahinger of C.A. Schahinger Pty Ltd; Dr Richard Smart and his colleagues in New Zealand; Richard Stevens and his staff at the Australian Wine and Brandy Corporation; my former colleagues at Roseworthy Agricultural College, particularly Andrew Ewart and Patrick Iland; Chris Weeks, formerly of Consolidated Co-operative Wineries Ltd; Ray White of White Refrigeration Pty Ltd in Adelaide and his associate Ben Adamson of Refrigeration Engineering Pty Ltd in Sydney; Chris Winnall of Adelaide Cooperage Pty Ltd; and to many others. Various suppliers to the wine industry have kindly provided illustrations and details of their equipment. The section on the New Zealand wine industry is based in part on documents written by Arthur Clarke, Geoff Kelly and Richard Smart.

I am particularly grateful to my wife, Ellaine, for her help with typing, her encouragement, tolerance and constructive criticism, and for her uncompromising attitude towards procrastination. Our daughter Jenny kindly helped read the page proofs. The errors that remain are mine and suggestions for improvement would be gratefully received.

Bryce Rankine
Adelaide, South Australia

Foreword

Wine has captured the interest of Australians and New Zealanders as never before. The annual *per capita* consumption in both countries has steadily been rising, and many new wineries are appearing. The community is far more knowledgeable about wine than formerly, and wine and food clubs flourish.

This book is intended for professional and amateur winemakers, students, wine lovers and buffs who want to know more about wine and winemaking. I hope all these people will find it readable. It explains all that is necessary to give an understanding of the principles as well as the practices of winemaking, and to highlight the remarkable nature of the product.

The wine industries in both countries have changed dramatically over the past forty years—from fortified appetiser and dessert wine production to table wines. In Australia about 98 per cent of all wines produced are now table wines, containing less than 14 per cent by volume of alcohol. This change has brought with it the emergence of many new wineries, most of them small and concentrating on the production of table wines. The total number of wineries in Australia stands at about 1625 (the exact number fluctuates), of which 67 per cent crush less than 100 tonnes of grapes annually. Most of the wine is produced by the larger wineries, of which 12 produce over 80 per cent of the total Australian production. Although 67 per cent of the smallest wineries collectively crush less than 3 per cent of the total tonnes crushed, they are nevertheless important in adding variety and individuality to the wine scene.

The large wineries are generally well equipped and operated, and make a wide range of wine types of consistent quality. On the other hand, many of the small wineries have been established by enthusiastic men and women from outside the industry, who need to acquire the technology. Consequently, the quality of their wines is variable and their costs higher.

Up to now there has been no book written specially on winemaking for Australian and New Zealand conditions. This book is intended to fill this need, and may also have application in other countries. It stems in part from articles written over some years in *Australian Grapegrower and Winemaker* and elsewhere, which have been updated and augmented with considerable new material. It has drawn heavily on published Australian and overseas technical oenological papers.

It is sometimes said that winemaking is simple and natural, and so it is, but the results of 'natural' winemaking without understanding the process and principles involved can be vinegar! Winemaking takes skill and understanding, and knowing when and when not to carry out particular operations. I hope that this book will fill a need in both the Australian and New Zealand wine industries, and will help to maintain the high quality which we have come to expect from their products.

How to use this book

This book is directed at several groups of people; winemakers and intending winemakers, students, and those interested in wine who want to know more about it and the way it is made. Accordingly, readers requiring specific information on winemaking operations should refer to the sections dealing with them, whereas those seeking more general information should start at the beginning and omit the sections which enter into more detail than they require. The first chapter is intended to give the broad picture of winemaking in Australia and New Zealand, with a brief background of the industries, together with a consideration of the role of the oenologist, and a review of general winemaking procedures.

Those intending to establish a winery are referred to the sections dealing with winery establishment and layout, and when ready to do so can delve into the chapters dealing with its operation. The concept of quality control pervades the text, because this is the essence of winemaking. Chapter 21 on the detail of quality control, diagnosis of faults and laboratory procedures is intended to furnish the necessary technical procedures.

This book does not deal with viticulture and the reader should consult the appropriate texts, because the potential quality of the wines is established in the vineyard, and carried to fruition in the winery.

1 Wine industry background

In presenting a book on winemaking for Australians and New Zealanders it is important to include the background to the respective industries, so that the contents can be placed in proper perspective.

Australia

The Australian wine industry is as old as white settlement in this country. Vines were introduced into Australia as part of the 'Plants for the Settlement' by the First Fleet in 1788. Hitherto, no indigenous grape vines capable of producing wine existed. The industry has advanced tremendously, particularly over the past fifty years, and has now achieved international recognition for the quality of its wines. The renowned British wine expert Hugh Johnson counts Australian red wines among the best wines in the world today, and various overseas wine authorities and the results of international wine expositions attest to the overall high standard of Australian wines on an international basis. Australia is currently seventh in the world on the basis of wine production (after France, Italy, Spain, United States, Argentina and Germany) according to the OIV in its latest figures in 1999, producing 851 million litres out of a world total of 28,144 million litres or 3 per cent.

Historically, grape production has followed several phases since the early days of the industry, when Gregory Blaxland in 1822 won the silver medal at the Royal Society of Arts in London for Australia's first wine exports—a quarter pipe of red wine made at his vineyard at Parramatta. Phylloxera was introduced from overseas in the 1870s, but did not become widespread as in Europe. The first major increase in vine plantings (on their own roots) from 7000 to 25,000 hectares occurred with the establishment of irrigation at Mildura by the Chaffey Brothers in the 1880s. A further increase in plantings to 45,000 hectares occurred after World War I with the post-war soldier-settlement blocks on the Riverland in South Australia. The most recent increase in vine plantings took place in the 1990s and 2000s with the development of new cool winegrowing regions, mainly in south-eastern South Australia and Victoria. The area of vines in Australia in 2001 was 148,000 hectares producing 1,423,950 tonnes, 85 per cent being used for winemaking. The production of grapes for wine in 2001 was 1,139,000 tonnes, for drying 90,241 tonnes and for table and other uses 64,686 tonnes.

The annual *per capita* consumption of wine has likewise increased dramatically. For example, in 1966–7 the *per capita* consumption was 6.8 litres per year, while in 1998 it had increased to 20.4 litres. This should be viewed in relation to the *per capita* consumption of the major world winemaking countries—which have shown the opposite trend. Over the same period the *per capita* consumption of wine in France has decreased from 117 to 59 litres, Italy from 109 to 52, Portugal from 109 to 50, and Argentina from 86 to 41.

Of the total production of grapes crushed for wine the current distribution by states, expressed as a rounded percentage of the total crush, is as follows:

South Australia	45 per cent
New South Wales	35 per cent
Victoria	17 per cent
Western Australia	3 per cent
Queensland and Tasmania	<1 per cent

The main winegrowing areas in order of the percentage of the total tonnage of grapes crushed for winemaking are as follows:

Riverland, South Australia	28 per cent
Murrumbidgee Irrigation Area, New South Wales	12 per cent
River Murray irrigation, Victoria and New South Wales	29 per cent
Barossa Valley, South Australia	12 per cent
South-east of South Australia	6 per cent
Adelaide and Southern Vales, South Australia	7 per cent
Hunter Valley, New South Wales	2 per cent
Clare, South Australia	2 per cent

Remarkable changes have also occurred in the types of containers in which wines have been packaged for sale. Over a period of 22 years to 2000—the longest period over which such statistics have been available—the proportion of wines sold in bottle (mainly 750 millilitres) has increased from 36 per cent to 40 per cent, wines in glass containers over 1 litre (mainly flagons), have decreased from 27 per cent to 4 per cent, and bulk wine sales have decreased from 9 to 3 per cent. On the other hand, the soft pack (multilayer collapsible bag-in-box) has increased from 28 to 48 per cent, and its introduction in that form in 1971 (initially by Wynn Winegrowers Pty Ltd with other companies following), has been responsible for a spectacular increase in wine sales in this type of package.

Exports of Australian wine have been a continuing part of the industry from the earliest times. In the last 15 years wine exports have risen considerably, and in 2000 stood at 62 per cent of total production.

Some of the most notable advances in the wine industry have taken place in viticulture, with the introduction of extensive drip and microjet irrigation, vineyard mechanisation and the planting of grape varieties more suited to the production of table wines. About one thousand mechanical grape-harvesters are in operation during vintage, frequently at night so as to harvest the grapes at their coolest temperature to retain freshness and fruit flavour. Grape vines are now being pruned mechanically and all vineyard operations are becoming increasingly mechanised. Increased plantings of classical vintages, such as Chardonnay, Sauvignon Blanc, Riesling, Traminer, Chenin Blanc, Semillon, Cabernet Sauvignon, Shiraz, Merlot and Pinot Noir, have resulted in the production of many table wines of outstanding quality.

The last twenty years have seen an increase in plantings of these quality varieties in new areas, not previously planted to vines. Such vineyards are mainly in cool climates and destined for the production of quality table wines. Examples are southern Victoria and New South Wales, south-eastern South Australia, Tasmania and the south-west of Western Australia. Most of these plantings are outside of the phylloxerated area in northern Victoria and southern New South Wales, and the vines are planted mainly on their own roots. However, an increasing tendency is to plant on rootstocks selected for nematode and drought resistance.

Major advances in wine technology have taken place over the last forty years, resulting in Australia emerging as one of the world's most technologically advanced wine industries. These advances are in part the subject matter of this book, and include pre-fermentation treatment of grape juice for white wine, involving partial or complete clarification, with temperature and oxidation control with cooling and inert gases, more rational use of sulphur dioxide and other antioxidants, together with greater overall quality control in making, stabilisation, maturation and bottling. A greater understanding of malo–lactic fermentation has enabled many wineries to successfully inoculate dry red wines with selected bacterial cultures to bring about this fermentation, rather than relying on its chance occurrence. In addition, acidity adjustment and control are widely practised, and the introduction of carbonic maceration is providing a further range of interesting and unusual red table wines.

Many wineries at considerable expense have increased their usage of European and American oak cooperage, usually 200 to 300 litres cask capacity, and have combined this with temperature control in the oak-maturation cellars. Filtration advances have centred on the use of diatomaceous earth and membrane filtration with a reduction in the use of plate and frame pad-filters. Membrane filters used in the industry are now cylindrical columns in single- and multi-column housings, and filtration is frequently preceded by centrifugation. The use of ultra- and tangential micro-filtration is beginning to appear.

These technical developments are now enabling consistently high-quality wines to be made, and it is likely that further advances in wine quality will come more from developments in the vineyard, including selected grape varieties in cool-climate regions, than from wine-making technology.

Various amalgamations and changes in ownership have taken place. Tolley

Scott & Tolley Ltd was acquired in 1961 by the Distillers Company Limited of Scotland; G. Gramp & Sons Pty Ltd by Reckitt and Colman Pty Ltd of the United Kingdom in 1970, and later by a management buy-out in 1988; Lindemans by Philip Morris of USA in 1971; Wynn Winegrowers Ltd by the New South Wales brewers Tooheys in 1972; Saltram & Stonyfell by Dalgety Australia Ltd in 1972 and later by Seagrams in 1978. Since 1973, no fewer than thirty-six large and small wineries have changed ownership. Important recent examples are Penfolds Wines Pty Ltd acquired by the NSW brewers Tooth & Co Ltd in 1976, and later in conjunction with Kaiser Stuhl (Barossa Cooperative Winery Ltd) by the Adelaide Steamship Company in 1980. This enlarged company acquired Wynn Winegrowers Pty Ltd in 1984, and later Tolley, Scott & Tolley Ltd and the Loxton Cooperative Winery and Distillery Ltd in 1987, with the result that Penfolds Wines (now Southcorp) is the largest winemaking company in Australia. In 1981 Renmano Wines Cooperative merged with Berri Cooperative Winery to form Consolidated Cooperative Wineries Ltd, and in 1985 B. Seppelt & Sons Pty Ltd was acquired by the South Australian Brewing Company Ltd. In 1987 the Stanley Wine Company Pty Ltd in Clare was acquired by Thomas Hardy & Sons Pty Ltd, and in 1988 G. Gramp & Sons Pty Ltd was the subject of a management buy-out with the new management now centred in South Australia. These ownership changes are ongoing and for further information see the *Australian Wine Industry Directory* (Winetitles, 2003).

As a result of these changes it is estimated that approximately 80 per cent of all wine made in Australia is now produced by 12 companies, although there are approximately 1,625 wineries in Australia. Of these approximately 75 per cent crush 200 tonnes or less of grapes per year, and represent only about 3 per cent of the total grape crush. They are nevertheless important in adding individuality and some outstanding wines to the industry.

Changes have also taken place in the organisation of the Australian wine industry. The Australian Wine Board (formed in 1929 as the Wine Overseas Marketing Board) became the Australian Wine and Brandy Corporation in 1981. Some rationalisation of functions has occurred between the Corporation and the industry trade association, the Australian Wine and Brandy Producers Association Inc. (formed as the Federal Viticultural Council of Australia in 1918 and now called the Winemakers' Federation of Australia Inc.). A new Small Winemakers Forum was formed in 1984. The winegrape growers have a national body, the Winegrape Growers Council of Australia Inc., formed in 1986, which represents the six state bodies, the largest of which is the United Farmers and Stockowners of South Australia Inc. Winegrape Section, also formed in 1986. A new technical society, the Australian Society of Viticulture and Oenology, was formed in 1980, which in conjunction with the Australian Wine Research Institute (1955) presents a national grape and wine conference every three years, and regional conferences and seminars at more frequent intervals.

The following list of selected events in the Australian wine industry indicates the kinds of key developments from the first edition of this book in 1989 to 2003.

1989
562,942 tonnes of grapes crushed for winemaking
Domestic wine sales 309 million litres
Exports 41 million litres valued at $121 million
Australian Wine Foundation formed
Australia's first degree course in viticulture commenced at Roseworthy
    College
Australian Grape and Wine Marketing Centre established at the University
    of South Australia

1990
530,638 tonnes of grapes crushed for winemaking
Domestic wine sales 300 million litres
Exports 38 million litres valued at $112 million
Winemakers' Federation of Australia Inc. (WFA) formed from the
    Australian Wine and Brandy Producers Association (founded in 1918)
WFA launched its national wine/health policy
Label Integrity Program inaugurated by the Australian Wine and Brandy
    Corporation (AWBC)
Inaugural Maurice O'Shea Award presented to McWilliams Wines Pty Ltd
    announced with Max Schubert as foundation recipient

1991
417,314 tonnes of grapes crushed for winemaking
Domestic wine sales 296 million litres
Exports 57 million litres valued at $168 million
Grape and Wine Development and Research Corporation formed
Australia Council of Viticulture formed
Co-operative Research Centre for Viticulture formed on the Waite Campus
    of the University of Adelaide
Inaugural convention of the Australia Society of Wine Educators
Roseworthy College merges with The University of Adelaide to become the
    Roseworthy Campus of the University

1992
564,010 tonnes of grapes crushed for winemaking
Domestic wine sales 314 million litres
Exports 78 million litres valued at $234 million
Establishment of the Australian Wine Export Council

1993
544,487 tonnes of grapes crushed for winemaking
Domestic wine sales 311 million litres
Exports 103 million litres valued at $289 million
Geographical Indications Committee established (AWBC)
Establishment of Register of Protected Names (AWBC)

1994
661,282 tonnes of grapes crushed for winemaking
Domestic wine sales 309 million litres
Exports 131 million litres valued at $359 million
EC/Australia Wine Agreement signed
Australia Journal of Grape and Wine Research established
First Wine Industry Outlook Conference organised at which Strategy 2025
    and Five-Year Plan were introduced (WFA)

1995
782,565 tonnes of grapes crushed for winemaking
Domestic wine sales 313 million litres
Exports 114 million litres valued at $381 million
Standards Drinks Labelling introduced (WFA)

1996
782,565 tonnes of grapes crushed for winemaking
Domestic wine sales 307 million litres
Exports 130 million litres valued at $471 million
Vision 2025 strategic plan released

1997
743,382 tonnes of grapes crushed for winemaking
Domestic wine sales 332 million litres
Exports 155 million litres valued at $596 million
Finalisation of all geographic indication zones

1998
870,627 tonnes of grapes crushed for winemaking
Domestic wine sales 340 million litres
Exports 193 million litres valued at $812 million
Establishment of Wine Industry Information Service (AWBC)

1999
1,076,207 tonnes of grapes crushed for winemaking
Domestic wine sales 348 million litres
Exports 991 million litres valued at $991 million

2000
1,111,137 tonnes of grapes crushed for winemaking

Domestic wine sales 369 million litres
Exports 288 million litres valued at $1,352 million
Commenced development of a web-based Wine Export Approval system
  (AWBC)

2001
1,391,123 tonnes of grapes crushed for winemaking
Domestic wine sales 384 million litres
Exports 339 million litres valued at $1,614 million
Australian Wine Export Council restructured
National Wine Centre opened in Adelaide
Formation of the New World Wine Producers Forum
First OIV World Congress in Australia held in Adelaide

2002
1,605,846 tonnes of grapes crushed for winemaking
Domestic wine sales 385 million litres
Exports 417 million litres valued at $2,000 million
Mutual Acceptance Agreement on Oenological Practices signed

2003
1,354,782 tonnes of grapes crushed for winemaking
Domestic wine sales 402 million litres
Exports 524 million litres valued at $2,391 million

The above is a short summary of selected wine industry developments intended to provide background for readers of this book. Much further statistical and other information is available from the Winemakers Federation of Australia, the Australian Wine and Brandy Corporation and other bodies, who work co-operatively on some issues. The information provided by these organisations for this book is gratefully acknowledged.

The Australian wine industry is attracting many new winegrowers who want to be involved in growing grapes and making and selling wines with a personal touch and flair. This finds considerable sympathy with consumers who can relate to an individual winemaker in a small winery, and small wineries have achieved an importance in the industry out of proportion to the volume of wine that they produce.

In considering the prospects for the industry it is necessary to be circumspect, since industry profitability depends on many factors, not all predictable. The industry is essentially based on the availability of suitable grapes and is thus subject to the vagaries of climate, and prone to periodic irregularities in production. Natural disasters, such as were experienced in the 1987 storm and frost damage in several important viticultural areas in South Australia, are likely to have a relatively long-term effect on the industry and be a reason for decreased grape supply and increased prices in 1988. In addition, some wines produced from red grapes require extended maturation and the producing companies must look well ahead in their planning to meet changing local markets and burgeoning exports. A change in the market, such as occurred with the greatly increased demand for white wines in the 1970s, cannot always be quickly met. Planting a new vine-yard, or grafting from one existing grape variety to another, to meet such a demand takes time. A new vineyard, for example, does not come into production until several years after planting, and full production may require six to ten years.

The quality of Australian wine is higher now than it has ever been in the his-tory of winemaking in the country—a fact widely appreciated by wine-lovers and the many wine and food clubs, and reflected in the considerable media inter-est in wine and the popularity of wine shows (of which over thirty are held annually), which have done much to raise wine quality. The industry and con-sumers alike are justifiably proud of Australian wine and actively promote its enjoyment in moderation as part of the national way of life. In 200 years the Australian wine industry has reached a healthy maturity.

New Zealand

Although New Zealand's wine industry is very small by world standards, it has had a colourful history, primarily stemming from developments in Australia. It began with the arrival of the Reverend Samuel Marsden, Chaplain to the Gov-ernment of New South Wales, who in 1819 planted at Kerikeri in the Bay of Islands 'about 100 grape vines of different kinds' brought from Port Jackson in New South Wales. He also planted vines at Waimate, north of Auckland, which Charles Darwin noted in his voyage on the *Beagle* in 1835. James Busby, one of the founding fathers of the Australian wine industry, also played a significant role in developments in New Zealand, both political and viticultural. He selected numerous cuttings of French and Spanish vines from European vineyards. Many were destined for the Sydney Botanical Gardens, some were used to establish Busby's vineyard in the Hunter River district of New South Wales, and the remainder were brought to New Zealand and in 1833 planted at the Bay of Islands. In 1840 Busby produced the first wine known to have been made in New Zealand—a light white wine in sufficient quantity to sell to the military.

The Marist religious order also brought vines to New Zealand which it culti-vated at Hokianga in the Bay of Islands, at Wanganui in the west coast of the North Island and Poverty Bay at Gisborne, before finally settling in Hawkes Bay in 1865. Much of the credit for this establishment and dissemination of the grapevine is due to Bishop Pompallier of Lyons, who had been appointed first Catholic Bishop of the South Pacific and landed in the Bay of Islands in 1838. Proof that Pompallier had grapevines with him exists on Futuna Island (part of the Wallis Group) where one of Pompallier's clergy, Father Peter Chanel, planted a vine that still lives today. Cuttings of this vine were brought to New Zealand in 1983 by Dr Richard Smart, and attempts are being made to identify the variety. The mission vineyard at Taradale, Hawkes Bay, remains today the sole remnant of the spread of grapevines by the Marist order and is regarded as the oldest vineyard in New Zealand under the same management.

In 1866 grapes were planted by a Spaniard, Joseph Soler, in Wanganui. He contended that New Zealand had the soil and climate to make good wines and that all that the growers needed was government encouragement, not bonuses. Soler proved the point by receiving overseas awards for his wine in Australia and London, the two principal export markets today. Later his nephew, Joseph Vidal, was to establish the largest vineyard in Hawkes Bay at that time, which today forms part of one of New Zealand's largest wine companies (Villa Maria-Vidals).

Phylloxera was first identified in New Zealand in 1885 and although efforts were made to exterminate it, the pest was widespread around Auckland by the early 1890s. It was about this time that phylloxera also appeared in the major viticultural areas of central and north-west Victoria in Australia.

In 1892 the Department of Agriculture was formed and in 1894 the New Zealand Premier, Richard Seddon, obtained from the Premier of Victoria the services of the Italian viticulturist Romeo Bragato. Government officials escorted Bragato throughout the country to assess viticultural potential and advise on the control of phylloxera. His verdict on the potential of New Zealand was favourable, particularly in Hawkes Bay, Wairarapa, Otago and Nelson.

He introduced rootstocks into New Zealand but apathy in the industry over their use led to phylloxera epidemics recurring each time the industry entered a new expansion phase. In 1901 Bragato was appointed New Zealand's first government viticulturist and headed a viticulture division in the Department of Agriculture. Under his supervision the Viticulture Research Station at Te Kauwhata, south of Auckland, was developed. In 1908 a Te Kauwhata red wine received a gold medal at the Franco-British Exhibition in London.

In 1906 Bragato produced a book, *Viticulture in New Zealand*. His recommendations of rootstocks were of particular note, especially those relating to 101–14 and other low-vigour rootstocks for fertile soils. Many of these low-vigour rootstocks were lost over the intervening years and have recently been re-imported to assess their potential.

In 1902 the Corban family winery began at Henderson just north of Auckland, and by 1906 there were 220 hectares (ha) of vineyards planted in the country, increasing to 268 ha by 1909. In this year Bragato resigned; the rise of prohibition quelled further development of the wine industry, and the viticulture division of the Department of Agriculture was abolished. In 1908 the prohibitionists scored their first victories as wine districts in Henderson and Masterton voted against the sale of alcoholic beverages, which led to the Masterton vineyards being removed.

During World War I the wine industry languished due to the lack of labour and prohibition depriving wineries of sales outlets, and by 1923 the area of vines had decreased to 71 ha. However, by 1938 following the depression, the vineyard area had risen to 216 ha, of which half was planted to table grape varieties. Expansion was also assisted by an increase in market protection by the government, by increasing the duty on still wines imported from South Africa and Australia.

The advent of World War II saw further rapid expansion as the demand for alcoholic beverages increased, and the vineyard area during the war increased to about 450 ha. During this period the industry turned heavily towards fortified wine production to satisfy demand, using sugar and water to achieve an 'acceptable product'. The use of more reliable French–American hybrid varieties, such as Seibel 5455, 4643, 5409, 5437 and Baco 22A, assisted in the production of these wines. Their other advantages as 'direct producers' became a liability as phylloxera once more began to affect vineyards planted to these varieties in the early 1950s. Following the war the momentum in the industry once more subsided, but was stimulated in 1956–8 by the deterioration of overseas currency reserves and the imposition of severe import controls, plus an assessment of the industry by a government select committee which recommended licensing of restaurants, more outlets for the sale of New Zealand wine, a reduction in the minimum quantity of wine for sale down to one bottle, and the abandonment of restrictions on sales from wineries in unlicensed districts.

By 1965 the vineyard area had increased to 500 ha, mainly devoted to hybrids, in the traditional areas of Henderson and Hawkes Bay. By 1968 plantings had increased to 660 ha, and the 1970s saw the industry participate in the world-wide 'planting boom', as the liberalisation of sale of wine, tariff protection for the industry, and an increased consumption of table wine, as distinct from fortified wine, stimulated rapid growth.

In 1970 the vineyard area rose to 1500 ha and led to the development of new viticulture regions such as Gisborne, where pastoral farmers were attracted into growing grapes on a contract basis. Of significance in this expansion was the planting of vinifera varieties instead of hybrids, as consumers became more quality conscious. Hawkes Bay also participated in this growth with new developments on more fertile soils previously used for processed vegetables and other crops. By 2000 the area under vineyards had risen to 13,637 ha, more than 27 times that of 1960. Gisborne continued to expand to become the second most important area after Henderson. White vinifera varieties comprised the bulk of the expansion, led by Mueller Thurgau and Palomino, with plantings of Pinotage, Cabernet Sauvignon and Chardonnay. In this period the development of further new regions in Marlborough and Canterbury took place and the Montana wines Brancott Estate vineyard in Marlborough was to become New Zealand's largest vineyard. Almost all the new vine plantings since 1970 were ungrafted cuttings, and thus susceptible to phylloxera.

The need to unify the wine industry and plan future growth led to the formation of the Wine Institute of New Zealand in 1975. Funding to operate this organisation came from a government levy on all winemakers. Shortly afterwards the grapegrowers formed their own organisation, the New Zealand Grape Growers Council, members of which today supply 80 per cent of New Zealand's wine grapes. By 1980 the vineyard area had increased to 4850 ha with over half yet to come into production. Mueller Thurgau, Palomino, Chenin Blanc, Traminer, Cabernet Sauvignon and Chasselas were the major varieties. The Henderson area relinquished its lead to become fourth behind Gisborne, Hawkes Bay and Marlborough. However, growth of the industry was to cease by 1983, due to fears of a downturn in consumption as a result of increased taxation and other factors. In 1983 a very dry season coupled with a record yield from Gisborne/Hawkes Bay resulted in oversupply, and brought with it the return of phylloxera as a problem on East Coast vineyards, previously thought to be free. With over 80 per cent of New Zealand's vineyards susceptible to attack these two effects (a surplus of grapes and fears of widespread phylloxera damage) led to the government assisting growers with a vine removal scheme in 1986 which saw 25 per cent of the national vineyard area removed.

However, despite the gloom in the industry, New Zealand's reputation as a cool-climate producer of high-quality wine became more prominent in Australia and the United Kingdom. This was led primarily by smaller winemakers in Marlborough, Hawkes Bay and Auckland with wines made from Chardonnay and Sauvignon Blanc. Today, the high quality of these New Zealand wines has led to restored confidence in the industry and the beginning of another growth phase in premium varieties. New Zealand's vineyards and wineries are among the most modern in the world, with new technology being readily accepted by the industry. For example, no other country has a higher rate of use of mechanical harvesting.

The 1989 vineyard area stood at 4500 ha, a reduction from the 6000 ha planted in 1985, due to oversupply and the government vine removal scheme. In Gisborne and Hawkes Bay almost all vineyards are planted on deep fertile soils with resulting high vigour and canopy shading problems. Marlborough vineyards are on shingle soils, while the traditional area around Henderson has vines growing on heavily leached clays. Most vines are trained on vertical trellises to accommodate mechanical harvesting, by which over 80 per cent of the crop is picked. Shoots are positioned vertically by a series of adjustable wires, then trimmed during summer.

Cane pruning is widely used, although more growers are endeavouring to reduce operating costs and improve canopy exposure by spur pruning, mechanical pruning and alternative shoot positioning techniques, such as Scott-Henry (Smart-Henry). Row spacings are commonly 3 metres and vines spaced 2 metres within the row.

The maritime humid climate encourages a high disease rate, requiring an intensive protective spray schedule for downy mildew, bunch rots, powdery mildew and anthracnose. Up to ten sprays per season are common, and botrytis resistance to dicarboxymides has recently appeared. Weed control is primarily by under-row herbicides and inter-row shallow cultivation. Irrigation is only used to any degree in Marlborough on dry stony soils. In 1983 about 80 per cent of New Zealand's vineyards were grown from cuttings and susceptible to phylloxera. A severe drought in that year, coupled with a record yield, saw severe damage in many Gisborne/Hawkes Bay vineyards and stimulated the use of grafted replants, along with economic restructuring that began with the wine oversupply. Major rootstocks used are 1202, 5BB and SO4 with increasing interest in low-vigour rootstocks, such as 101–14, Riparia Gloire and others.

The industry is now entering a minor replanting phase, again with the encouragement that wine exports have brought since 1985. Alternative sites with lower autumn rainfall and less fertile soils to produce better grape quality are being explored. New areas, such as Wairarapa, Otago, Nelson and Waiheke Island, are developing new quality standards for the industry.

Viticultural research is primarily carried out by the Ministry of Agriculture and Fisheries, although small programmes are undertaken at Lincoln College and Marlborough Research Centre. Several DSIR divisions are involved in studies of grapevine pests and diseases and vine physiology. The MAF effort is centred at Ruakura Agriculture Centre in Hamilton. Experimental vineyards are located at Te Kauwhata, Rukuhia, Gisborne and Hawkes Bay. Currently, the major research emphasis is in the area of vine improvement, reflecting the need to replant large vineyard areas due to phylloxera. These efforts include clonal selection and evaluation, virus indexing and elimination, importation and ampelography. Other research areas are in canopy management, especially the development of new trellis systems and associated machinery. Rootstock and scion evaluation, pruning levels, acid soil studies and vine physiology are also being researched. Future research areas will include bulk wine grape production aimed at minimising costs, and 'organic viticulture'. Government research efforts are being re-examined with the introduction of the 'user pays' principle. To date, there has been no provision of sustained industry funding to support research services, and their future extent is uncertain.

In the oenological area, 1980 marked the turning point in the emergence of New Zealand wine on the international scene. By then enough of the appropriate varieties were planted and bearing to ensure continuity of production. In the same year, the introduction of more restrictive Food and Drug regulations tightened up winery practice, particularly with respect to water addition. The yield of wine per tonne of grapes fell to 1265 litres for the 1980 vintage, and has since decreased to 770 litres in 1985 and 1986.

The aim prior to World War I to produce quality table wines was disrupted by phylloxera, prohibition and the world depression, which resulted in few vinifera vines surviving. The criteria at that time became disease resistance and yield. Labrusca varieties, such as Isabella (and its local clonal selection Albany

Surprise), and hybrid varieties, such as Baco 22A, Baco No. 1 and various Seibel hybrids, became prominent. Most of their production went to fortified wines.

The 1940s and 1950s saw reawakening of interest in table wines, but this was a time of austerity and import controls, and the legacy of the hybrid era was not to be shaken off for another twenty years. Although the quality of table wines made from hybrids was inferior, a generation of winemakers had grown up accustomed to their high yields, and unfamiliar with the flavours of the classic vinifera varieties.

Thus, as the move back to vinifera-based table wines developed in the 1960s and early 1970s, initial emphasis was on heavily cropping varieties, such as Chasselas, Chenin Blanc, Mueller Thurgau, Palomino and Pinotage. Of these, only Mueller Thurgau and Chenin Blanc have emerged as successful and enduring varieties.

In Hawkes Bay, Tom McDonald developed a red wine (Bakano) based on Cabernet Sauvignon. Private lots of red wine made from this variety had been made by both Corban and McDonald over the years, but the release of McDonald's 1965 McWilliam's Cabernet Sauvignon on a commercial scale indicated the quality of wine which could be made. Unfortunately however, the industry was preoccupied with Germanic-style white wines, and this message was not sufficiently heeded. Also, at that time more than 70 per cent of all wine was fortified.

The fifteen years from 1965 to 1980 were marked by the development of other varietal table wines, as the production of fortified wines decreased. McDonald also produced an outstanding Chardonnay in 1967, the importance of which was not sufficiently appreciated at the time. Corbans introduced a Pinotage in 1967, and Babich followed with a Pinotage/Cabernet in 1970. Nobilo in 1970 produced fine wines from Cabernet Sauvignon and Pinotage.

Through the 1970s the trend towards table wines increased, though still with emphasis on the Germanic-style white wines. Montana's Bernkaizler Riesling was produced in 1974, and Mueller Thurgau had by now become the main variety for the popular 'Riesling' label. Montana began planting in the South Island, locating vineyards in Marlborough in 1973–4. These vines were the first in New Zealand to be planted in a new region as a result of climatic and soil evaluation, rather than family propinquity or tradition. The following year Montana released their first Cabernet Sauvignon from the 1973 vintage—until then high-quality Cabernets were not readily available.

In 1976, in Gisborne, Irwin produced a remarkable Gewürztraminer, the first of a line to make both Matawhero and New Zealand noted for the variety. In Auckland, Nobilo produced outstanding red wines from Cabernet Sauvignon, Pinotage and Pinot Noir, which tended to set the pattern for New Zealand reds, and in the following year produced an excellent Chardonnay. In 1980 Montana produced the exceptional Marlborough Sauvignon Blanc, with strong varietal flavour.

It became clear that the future for fine table wines in New Zealand lay in the varietal wines from classical French varieties. The ratio of table to fortified wines has moved in favour of table wines, which represented 75 per cent in 1982.

Meanwhile, following McDonald's achievements with Cabernet Sauvignon in Hawkes Bay, the first of a series of fine Cabernet Sauvignon/Merlot blends emerged from the Te Mata Estate in 1982. In the same year a St Helena Pinot Noir from the newly established Canterbury district proved to be more Burgundian in style than any wine so far made in New Zealand. Quality wines from Merlot were produced in 1983 by both San Marino of Kumeu and Matawhero. Rhine Riesling wines showing strong varietal flavour were produced in 1983 by Corbans and Montana. Also in 1983 the first oaked or fumé version of Sauvignon Blanc was made by Coopers Creek, and the success of Cook's Chardonnay dispelled any doubts about the future for that variety in New Zealand. In 1984 the Wairarapa district returned to wine production after a gap of seventy-five years.

In 1985, the format of the National Wine Competition was upgraded to bring procedures more into line with overseas (particularly Australian) practice. Coincidentally, excellent vintages in 1985 and 1986, coupled with a reduction in the litreage of wine obtained per tonne of grapes processed, assisted in producing wines of international quality. The increase in wine quality achieved in 1985 and 1986, just twenty years after the pivotal 1965 Cabernet Sauvignon was made, indicated the quality development in the industry, and both whites and reds have blossomed. The first examples of botrytised Riesling styles have appeared, and interest in producing *méthode champenoise* wines has increased, though more progress is needed. Climatically, New Zealand is well placed to make classic sparkling wines close in style to the French model.

Looking ahead, a new generation of graduate winemakers is increasingly reshaping the industry. Some are New Zealanders, rather more are Australians, mainly trained at Roseworthy Agricultural College, and others draw their qualifications from California, Germany, Switzerland and France. From that breadth of experience a stronger and more diverse industry is expected to emerge, spanning both islands of the country, and reflecting the range of temperate viticultural climates to be found between Kumeu and Matakana in the north and Marlborough and inland Otago in the south. These districts span nine degrees of latitude—the same as that from the Mosel south to approximately Rioja or Tuscany—and hence offer considerable potential by European standards.

There is no doubt that New Zealand will be producing more white wines from Chardonnay, Sauvignon Blanc, Riesling and Gewürztraminer to command world attention. For red wines, the best areas have the capability to produce wines with deep and complex fruit flavours. Already this is shown by the best wines, and Cabernet Sauvignon, Merlot and, hopefully, Pinot Noir will form their basis. Over its relatively short history the New Zealand wine industry has come a long way.

The role of the oenologist

To many people interested in wine, the oenologist—one who has a knowledge of the science and principles and practices of wine and winemaking (from the Greek *oinos*, wine)—is synonymous with the winemaker, and the difference between the two terms is sometimes blurred. Winemaking is the practical part of the oenologist's activities, and is mainly what this book is about. But a winemaker may have no formal qualifications, which is the hallmark of the oenologist. To illustrate this, the winemaking course at Roseworthy Agricultural College led to the qualification of Bachelor of Applied Science in Oenology or Wine Science— not winemaking. We are going to examine the role of the oenologist, as distinct from the more narrow technical activities of the winemaker, because this is important to students planning to enter the wine industry in a technical capacity.

Oenology is now a well-recognised professional career. It attracts young men and, in recent years, young women, intending to be part of the Australian and New Zealand wine industries. Indications of the wine industry's importance are clearly shown by the number of new wineries and in annual sales. Winemaking is simple in principle, but with today's need for reasonably priced wines of consistent quality the oenologist needs to have a high level of educational and technical competence.

The demands of modern winemaking, which include an understanding of viticulture and the many requirements of a winery, may not always be appreciated by students and new oenologists. The modern oenologist needs to be as educated as possible (using the word in the broad sense), as well as being instructed in the various winemaking operations. This involves a considerable range of attainments, as we shall see.

As an oenologist one should be technically and academically competent, have a discriminating and trained palate, an appreciation of wine types and quality, be able to manage staff, and have some knowledge of management, costing and marketing. Technical competence needs to extend beyond the field of winemaking, maturing and bottling. The wines made must be of a style and quality which will sell, and in a large company one is guided by the marketing department which should anticipate trends in market demand.

Besides this, the oenologist should have the basis of a sound, broad professional education and keep abreast of current technical developments. One should read technical literature regularly and have a reading knowledge of an appropriate foreign language, such as French or German. One should be aware of the importance of, and be able to carry out, effective quality control on wine, winemaking and packaging materials, and should be able to conduct technical in-service training of the winery cellar staff. A further requirement is a sound knowledge of engineering as it relates to winery operations and equipment, and an understanding of the appropriate legal requirements.

The oenologist should enjoy drinking wine and have a clear understanding of what constitutes quality and the differences between wine styles. One should also have the ability to communicate well, both in writing and in speaking to groups of winemakers and to members of the public. One should try to gain experience as a wine judge or an associate on a judging panel, and should miss no opportunity to advance the understanding of this subject.

A competent oenologist is a valuable person, for in his or her hands lies the power to produce either consistently good wines from sound grapes or mediocre or even poor wines suitable only for distillation. Also, when the occasion demands, there is a need to produce acceptable wine from imperfect grapes. With the level of technology now existing and the complexity of wine styles and types made, the skills of the oenologist are becoming increasingly important. Astute winery managers are well aware of this fact, and skilled oenologists are usually well paid. This is as it should be, since a mistake involving spoilage or contamination of a large volume of wine can be expensive.

Technical training and competence

Educational requirements for oenologists have increased considerably over recent years. In the past, formal training at the diploma level or experience without formal qualification were accepted as adequate. But with improved technology and recognition of the need for training beyond just the practices of winemaking, the scope of oenological training has expanded considerably.

To meet the requirements of a modern wine industry, which is becoming technologically more complex, the oenologist's technical competence needs to extend beyond the field of actual winemaking, maturing and bottling. One needs to understand the principles and have some working knowledge of the operation of pumps, motors, general engineering, refrigeration, fluid transfer, electronics, welding and the various other activities encountered. Some oenologists recognise that they are almost as much chemical-process engineers as winemakers.

Indeed, future generations of oenologists may well be required to have some formal understanding of chemical engineering, food technology and electronic operation, since computers and programmable controllers are becoming increasingly used. In the past, some oenologists have considered winemaking as a skill distinct from that applied in food and beverage technology, but in fact it is but one aspect of this broad field. While the oenologist is a key technical person in the winery, a need also exists in large companies for other qualified technical people, such as chemical engineers, chemists and microbiologists. These people should have a sound oenological background, and for all senior technical appointments, working experience overseas is desirable.

Tasting

The oenologist needs to have a discriminating and trained palate—otherwise one has no business being an oenologist! In fact, they should have their palates tested before enrolling in the oenology course. Tasting tests are now available which will help assess tasting ability and identify palate attributes and deficiencies. In oenological education, considerable time is spent in sensory evaluation, in which students assess and identify the strengths and weaknesses of their own palates. They learn to understand the importance of proper tasting and quality evaluation. For example, if a student (or oenologist) has a reasonably good palate but cannot smell sulphur dioxide, then this is not the student's fault. At least the student is aware of this deficiency and can then rely on someone else on the tasting panel who can smell sulphur dioxide.

It is an important function of the oenologist to maintain the quality of wines once they are made and to recognise the incidence of spoilage. This requires a sensitive and discriminating palate. Cases have occurred where the wines in a winery were largely spoilt by bacterial action without the oenologist appreciating the fact. He only tasted the wines of his cellar and failed to recognise that he was operating with an infected cellar.

A tasting panel is essential in every winery, and the oenologist is expected to organise and operate it. All panel members should be tested for their relative abilities, and the panel should work as a team, desirably with coded wines both from their own winery and from their competitors. Tasting should be carried out daily or at least at frequent intervals. Experience in judging at wine shows is beneficial. These shows usually have provision for winemakers to serve as stewards or associates in order to gain experience in assessing wine quality and in judging procedures. This activity is a valuable contribution to the wine industry, and oenologists should take advantage of it wherever possible. Wine shows in Australia are important in establishing and maintaining quality standards, and the oenologist needs to have a clear concept of the requirements of each class of wine in which wines are exhibited. If one cannot find time to be involved in judging, either as a judge or as an associate, then one should study the requirements of the various classes carefully and if necessary discuss them with members of the judging panel.

Quality control

This involves the whole range of operations from planting the grapes or even selecting the vineyard site through to the packaged wine. In fact, winemaking in the broad concept is the proper operation of quality control (as will become evident in this book), and involves not only regular analytical checks and tastings but also control of the wide range of winemaking and packaging materials. The role of the winery laboratory is becoming increasingly important. The oenologist should be competent to design, equip and operate the winery laboratory to carry out the basic quality-control tests and checks, and to instruct others in their operation. The laboratory is an essential part of technical operations and quality control and, depending on the size of the winery, it should not be beneath one's dignity as an oenologist to spend some time in the laboratory on non-routine investigations. While oenologists are not usually trained in research procedures, they can save their company much money by intelligent trouble-shooting. It should be within the scope of the oenologist to diagnose a haze or other condition trouble in wine, apply the appropriate corrective measures and then alter procedures so that the problem does not occur again.

Technical literature

The science and technology of winemaking is advancing quickly, and the oenologist may have difficulty in keeping abreast of developments. This is particularly the case in areas remote from other wineries and out of contact with other oenologists. Accordingly, there is a need to be aware of the sources and availability of relevant technical and scientific literature, as well as all of the other kinds of information necessary to keep informed. The best way to maintain and improve technical competence is to read as much as possible of the technical literature and to have key textbooks and pamphlets at hand. Much of the world's oenological literature is published in languages other than English, and one should, therefore, develop a reading knowledge of at least one oenologically important foreign language.

In view of this dependence on technical literature, the oenologist should own and regularly read key reference books as well as encourage the company to establish a technical library. A regular budget item should provide for the purchase of new technical books and journals, which should be available to all technical staff. Some wineries understandably have certain processes or blends which they prefer to keep confidential. Generally speaking, however, few secrets exist in winemaking which have not been published. Claims made periodically by wineries that a particular process is a secret to their company are usually made in ignorance of what is already published in the oenological literature.

Understanding marketing requirements

The oenologist needs to have understanding and knowledge beyond the field of winemaking, maturing and bottling. Wines must be made which the consumer will buy. There is no advantage to be gained from making a top-quality wine if it cannot be sold for some reason or other. In this respect, the oenologist must collaborate with management and the marketing organisation, be aware of what types and styles of wines are selling and what are the expected trends, and arrange the winemaking programme accordingly. There is an interdependence between the oenologist and the marketing personnel, who in turn are the servants of the great and sometimes unpredictable master—the buying public.

Recent developments in both the Australian and New Zealand wine industries, including acquisition of wineries by large companies with sometimes little or no previous involvement in wine, have indicated the changing nature of the industry. Winery management in the major companies is now strongly market-orientated, and one needs to appreciate this situation. In large organisations, the oenologist is guided by marketing personnel and management as to what types and quantities of wine should be made and under what types of labels and packaging they will be sold. One may well be given considerably less latitude for individual expression than in former years. Professional contributions and satisfactions are based on a capacity to produce what the market requires at a price which the customer can afford. Accordingly, one's skill as an oenologist and the

WINE INDUSTRY BACKGROUND □ **19**

knowledge of the sales organisation must complement each other. Both must be guided by management, so as to balance their contributions and maintain the viability of the business. The oenologist may be situated in a known quality-producing area where all the wines simply must be good, or may be in a new or lowly area as yet unrecognised for its virtues. Either way a product saleable in the market place must be produced. The key word is saleable, because the company may fail even when producing high-quality wines if such wines cannot be sold.

Reception of new ideas
The oenologist should be encouraged to question and constructively criticise traditional winemaking practices. Traditional winemaking in a sense of following what father or grandfather used to do is rapidly disappearing. We are in the age of innovation and experimentation with, in some cases, way-out ideas. For example, the use of ultrasonics in the mundane role of bottle-washing may help to do the job better than the usual cleaning procedures. One should never be afraid to try a new idea, so long as it is economically feasible. Various new developments in winemaking are all the results of new ideas, and it is salutary to reflect that at some stage or other someone said that they would not work!

In the past, the oenologist had to be the all-round person with competence in all fields of winemaking and viticulture. With the growing size of wineries and the complexities involved in the various winemaking processes, it is also desirable for the oenologist to develop special competence in a particular field. In large wineries, specialisation is usual where there is a division of function and responsibility, and modern winemaking is becoming more and more the field of the specialist. In a small winery, however, the oenologist must of necessity be versatile.

Oenologists in small wineries
Since there are many small wineries in Australia and New Zealand and new ones continually being established, the importance of the oenologist to them should be emphasised. The proportion of faulty wines produced in small wineries is greater than that in large ones, which reflects in part the competence of the oenologist. One may be the owner of the winery or an employee, but to be successful one should meet the following criteria:

- Be familiar with all of the technology relevant to the efficient operation of the winery.
- Pay attention to detail—even automatic machinery does not remain so for long without attention.
- Maintain tidiness and sanitary conditions.
- Do not give in to adversity, because the path to success in a small winery is seldom smooth.

Viticulture competence

The oenologist is dependent for final wine quality on the quality and maturity of the raw material—the grapes—and should understand grape composition and condition and the various viticultural factors which affect it, so as to liaise with and advise the grapegrowers. Effective vineyard management is, therefore, an essential part of successful winemaking. Desirably, vineyard management should be in the hands of either a viticulturist with a good knowledge of winemaking or an oenologist with a good knowledge of viticulture. The present Australian distinction between winemakers and grapegrowers is largely unknown in Europe, where the *vigneron* (wine-grape grower) grows grapes as part of the total activity of winemaking. Too often, the commercial grapegrower is concerned only with maximum yield, without serious consideration of what happens to the grapes after they leave the vineyard.

The oenologist should be concerned with the quality of the grapes purchased, and should spend time in the vineyards and in consultation with grape growers. The large plantings of vineyards by winemaking companies is an indication of the need for close control of the growing, quality and maturity at harvest of grapes by the winemaker.

Management functions

Some newly qualified oenologists seeking their first job in a winery seem to expect that an oenology qualification should enable them to become winery manager in a short time. However, it is not that easy, although admittedly in recent years some oenologists have had rapid promotions, due largely to industry expansion and a shortage of trained personnel. The young oenologist first has to demonstrate technical competence to the employer. After this, promotion depends on other factors, such as opportunity, a knowledge of management and costing techniques, ability to control and encourage staff, a suitable personality and some luck. If one has aspirations in this direction then train accordingly, because the top jobs involve management, financial acumen and staff control. After all, jobs go (or should go) to people who are best qualified to hold them. An important attribute is common sense, a rather uncommon virtue which tends to prevent one making too many mistakes and yet still be an achiever.

Oenologists sometimes do not appreciate that a board of directors is not really concerned with science and the technical complexities of winemaking. It is concerned with money, profitability and the cost of operations, and one should keep this in mind when dealing with management. Management generally leaves the technicalities of wine production to the technical people, but the cost and profitability of the operation is the province of management. A wise oenologist will spend some time studying the economics of production in order to be able to talk to management along these lines. To repeat, there is no point in making fine wines if the winery goes bankrupt in so doing. One should recognise that in a winery of any size policy comes from management, technical control from the technical staff (of which the oenologist may be the whole or an integral part), product requirements from the marketing department, routine administration from the executive staff, and the actual winemaking operations are carried out by the cellar staff.

In-service training can improve efficiency at all levels by increasing each group's understanding of the significance of their respective jobs. Technical in-service training in the winery should be in the hands of the oenologist. Such training is important for two reasons: it increases the efficiency of the cellar staff because they understand more about their respective jobs, and it also gives them confidence in the capabilities of the oenologist—who should have an under-standing attitude to people, appreciate other points of view and be ready to accept new ideas. To get along with people is an important attribute, whether or not the oenologist aspires to management.

Legal aspects

The oenologist must be aware of and abide by a variety of laws and regula-tions—local, state and federal. This involves knowing the requirements of the food legislation, what additives and processes are lawful, hygiene, sanitation and health requirements, legislation relating to labelling, safety, fortification, spirit storage and so on, as well as the entitlements and union requirements of the staff. In comparison with some other winemaking countries, the Australian wine-maker is not unduly burdened with legal requirements, but it is likely that these will increase with time.

Terms and units

Like most industries the wine industry has its jargon terms and units, and we are going to meet these as we go on. In order to enable the reader unfamiliar with them to feel at home, the most common terms and units are summarised below.

Metric. Since the industry is metricated the standard practice is (mainly) to use metric units, and those most relevant are set out below together with their conversions to other units. The metric system has the advantage of being able to be converted from one unit to a larger or smaller unit by means of decade or multidecade prefixes e.g. conversion of millilitres to litres.

Increase by factor of	Prefix	Symbol
10 or 10^1	deca	–
100 or 10^2	hecto	h
1,000 or 10^3	kilo	k

Decrease by factor of	Prefix	Symbol
10 or 10^{-1}	deci	d
100 or 10^{-2}	centi	c
1,000 or 10^{-3}	milli	m
1,000,000 or 10^{-6}	micro	µ

Mass is a measure of the quantity of matter and is closely related to its weight, except that weight depends on gravity whereas mass is constant. Examples are as follows:

1 microgram (1 µg)	=	10^{-6} grams
1 milligram (1 mg)	=	10^{-3} grams
1 kilogram (1 kg)	=	10^{3} grams or 1000 grams
1 tonne (1 t)	=	1000 kilograms or 2204 pounds
1 pound (1 lb)	=	0.454 kilograms or 454 grams
1 ton (US)	=	2000 pounds or 907 kilograms
1 ton (imperial)	=	2240 pounds or 1016 kilograms

Length

1 micrometre (1 µm)	=	10^{-6} metre
1 millimetre (1 mm)	=	10^{-3} metre
1 centimetre (1 cm)	=	10^{-2} metre
1 kilometre (1 km)	=	10^{3} metres or 1000 metres
1 metre (1 m)	=	39.37 inches

Area

1 hectare (ha)	=	10,000 square metres or m^2
	=	2.48 acres
1 acre	=	0.405 hectares

Volume

1 microlitre (1 µL)	=	10^{-6} litre
1 millilitre (1 mL)	=	10^{-3} litre
1 hectolitre (1 hL)	=	10^{2} litres or 100 litres
1 kilolitre (1 kL)	=	10^{3} litres or 1000 litres
1 gallon (1 gal) imperial	=	4.54 litre
1 gallon (US)	=	3.78 litres
1 pound per cubic foot	=	0.016 grams per millilitre
1 hectolitre	=	22 imperial gallons
1 fluid ounce	=	28.35 mL

Concentration. This is usually expressed as grams per litre, which is the same as milligrams per millilitre.

Concentration = weight of dissolved substance
                          volume of solution

1 gram per litre	= 0.1 per cent w/v
	= 1 pound per 100 imperial gallons
1 milligram per litre (mg/l)	= 1 part per million (ppm)
10,000 milligrams per litre	= 1 per cent w/v

Density is the mass of a substance divided by its volume, and is usually written in grams per millilitre (g/ml or gmL^{-1}). *Specific gravity* is the density of the sample divided by the density of water.

Baumé (Bé)—see later in text for details. This French hydrometric measurement of density was originally a measure of salt in brine. The degree Baumé approximates to the potential alcohol resulting from complete fermentation of the juice from mature grapes.

| 0° Bé | = 1.000 specific gravity |
| 10° Bé | = 1.075 specific gravity—or approximately 10 per cent by volume potential alcohol. |

Another Baumé scale for liquids lighter than water exists but is not used in the wine industry.

Brix (Balling) is an hydrometer measurement used in the sugar industry. The Brix reading is the number of grams of cane sugar in 100 grams of solution at a temperature of 15.6° C. *Balling* is identical.

| 1° Brix | = 0.56° Baumé |
| 1° Baumé | = 1.80° Brix |

Note that the sugar in grape juice is invert sugar—a mixture of glucose and fructose. Sucrose is present only in low concentration.

Oechsle. This Swiss hydrometer scale is an alternative expression of specific gravity.

Oechsle = (specific gravity – 1) × 1000
e.g. 85°Oe = 1.085 SG.

Although this scale is based on specific gravity, it does not indicate either approximate sugar content or potential alcohol content of the wine. Brix is the Oechsle value divided by 4 and 2.5 deducted.

100°Oe = 13.1° Baumé or 23.6° Brix

Acidity in grapes and grape juice consists mainly of tartaric and malic acids, which together comprise more than 90 per cent of the total acidity. During fermentation other acids are formed—succinic, lactic and others—and malic acid may disappear due to bacterial action (malo-lactic fermentation).

Acidity is expressed in two ways:

• *Titratable acid*—sometimes incorrectly called total acid—and expressed as grams per litre of tartaric acid. In France, it is expressed as sulphuric acid, which is 0.653 of the value expressed as tartaric acid, i.e. a wine with a titratable acidity of 6.0 grams per litre as tartaric acid would have a value of 3.9 grams per litre as sulphuric acid. The titratable acidity is obtained by titration with standard alkali to a near-neutral endpoint of pH 8.4, or 7.0 in France. Usual values for titratable acidity in wine are 4 to 8 g/l.
• *pH* (not Ph or PH). This term takes into account the activity or acid strength of the acids as well as their concentration. The term pH refers to the quantity of hydrogen ions in the wine. The overall range is 0 (highly acid) to 14 (highly alkaline) with 7 representing neutrality. Australian wines have pH values between approximately 3.0 and 4.0, which represents a ten-fold difference in active or real acidity.

2 Grape development and composition

Grape berry development

To make good wine, one must know the raw material—the grapes. Otherwise the winemaker is akin to a blind painter. The really competent winemaker spends as much time as possible in the vineyard following the development in ripeness and taste of the grapes, as well as in the other vineyard operations. In recent years, wineries have increasingly recognised the importance of the vineyard and viti-culture in general.

The composition, quality and, in some cases, the type of wine are largely determined by the composition of the grapes at maturity. This final composition is affected by the grape variety and site, the vine canopy and its microclimate, soil-related factors, such as nutrients, water and root growth, and development of the grape berry and of the shoot which bears it.

The 'average' vine bursts in Australia about 22 September (plus or minus about thirteen days); flowering takes place about 30 November (plus or minus about twenty-six days); veraison (the beginning of ripening when the berry starts to change colour) about 6 February (plus or minus about eleven days); and the grapes are ripe about 2 March (plus or minus about fifty-four days). Variations in these dates are due to the factors listed above. Thus, the average time from flowering to ripeness is 167 days. To take an example, Shiraz at Roseworthy Agricultural College flowers in the first week of September and is ripe at the beginning of March—a total of about 180 days. Chardonnay, on the other hand, is about two weeks earlier throughout. The average period from flowering to vintage for four major varieties in five viticultural areas in Australia has been measured as 122 days (plus or minus twenty-six depending on grape variety and season).

Berry development characteristically follows a double-sigmoid or S-shaped curve, which can be divided into three periods:

1 The berry initially undergoes rapid cell division and growth, and acid accumulates but little or no sugar. This is the green stage.

2 Then the growth rate decreases markedly and the berry 'rests' until veraison, at about sixty days after flowering.

3 At veraison the berry starts to soften and accumulate sugar, acids degrade and colour begins to appear in the skin of pigmented varieties. The berry expands by increasing in cell volume, and flavour and aroma compounds build up.

4 Finally the berry begins to dehydrate due to water loss while still on the vine. This is utilised for the production of late-picked and fortified wine styles.

Ripeness is not a precise concept since it depends on the purpose for which the grapes are to be used. The concept of ripeness has changed greatly over the past thirty years in both Australia and New Zealand, with the swing from dessert (fortified) wines requiring high sugar in the grapes to table wines requiring less sugar and more acid. As an example, grapes considered ripe for dessert wine at 26° Brix (14.4° Baumé) would be over-ripe for table wine, which may require only three-quarters of this sugar content.

The grape is unusual among fruits in the high level of sugar which it produces. Essentially two sugars are involved: d-glucose or dextrose and d-fructose or lae-vulose. These differ considerably in sweetness with fructose being much the sweeter—a 15 per cent solution of fructose is equivalent in sweetness to a 22.8 per cent glucose solution or a 17.8 per cent sucrose (cane or beet sugar) solution. In other words, if the sweetness of fructose is expressed as 100 units, glucose is 66 and sucrose 84. Consequently, the proportion of fructose is significant since it influences the sweetness more than glucose. During ripening glucose accumulates earlier than fructose, but by the time the berry is ripe the proportion is usually about 1:1, although this can vary from 0.7 to 1.4. In very ripe grapes the fructose concentration exceeds that of glucose. Chardonnay and Pinot Blanc are examples of high-fructose varieties, and Chenin Blanc and Zinfandel high glucose.

The main acids of the ripe grape are L-(+)-tartaric and L-(−)-malic, which together comprise more than 90 per cent of the total acidity—normally in the range of 5 to 8 grams per litre. Citric acid comes next but in much lower concentration (0.1 to 0.5 grams per litre), followed by many other acids in smaller amounts. As far as the acid taste is concerned, tartaric and malic acids are more or less equivalent—when compared according to their acid strength tartaric is more acid, but when compared according to titratable acidity malic is more acid. In many threshold tasting tests at Roseworthy Agricultural College using the same concentrations of both acids, tartaric emerged as having a marginally more acid taste than malic.

Tartaric acid is uncommon in plants whereas malic occurs widely. As the berry grows both tartaric and malic acid increase in concentration until veraison, then both decrease as the sugar accumulates, with malic decreasing at a more rapid rate. Warm temperature increases the rate of malic acid breakdown, and generally a variety will be higher in acid at the same sugar concentration in a cool climate. Examples of high tartaric-acid varieties are Riesling, Sultana and Palomino, and high-malic varieties are Malbec, Pinot Noir and Chenin Blanc.

The different parts of the grape bunch at harvest vary considerably in their percentage by weight of the total bunch, for example:

stems 2–8 per cent
skin 5–20 per cent

flesh 74–90 per cent
seeds 0–6 per cent

Small berries, such as Cabernet Sauvignon, have relatively less flesh and more skin and seeds.

The stalks have a pH between 4 and 5, due to low free acid and high potassium. Their sugar content is less than 1 per cent and they contain between 0.5 and 3.5 per cent polyphenols by weight; these are the leucoanthocyanins and catechins, which have a harsh astringent taste and may be responsible for up to 20 per cent of the tannin in harvested grapes. The seeds contain up to 50 per cent of similar tannins, and can be the major source of them in wine. Seeds also contain bitter grape-seed oils. The skins contain considerable sugar, generally about 80 per cent of the level in the flesh. Black and white grape varieties contain about the same amounts of the non-pigmented tannins, but the skins of the black varieties contain about twice the total phenolics of the whites, because of the pigmented anthocyanins present. Approximately 10 per cent of the total phenolics of the grape berry of white varieties are contained in the skin, whereas the equivalent figure for black varieties is 65 per cent. The varietal flavour components of the berry occur both in the skin and the flesh of the berry. The waxy bloom of the skins is important because it contains fatty acids and sterols which stimulate yeast and bacterial growth. The degree of maceration, temperature, alcohol concentration and duration of skin contact influences the amount and rate of extraction of the various constituents.

The flesh consists of very large cells filled with sap, which provides the bulk of the free-run juice after crushing and draining. The flesh has the lowest pH (3.0 to 3.8) of all of the bunch components, indicating the high free acid-to-potassium ratio with much of the potassium being in the skins. The flesh usually contains less than 5 per cent of the phenolics of the grape berry. The implications of all this will appear as we study the winemaking processes.

Assessing grape ripeness in the vineyard

It is widely accepted that the basic quality of a wine is established in the vineyard, and assessment of grape ripeness and soundness on the vine is an essential part of winemaking. However, this is easier to say than to do, since we are dealing with many separate and variable individual vines, and sampling presents rather special problems. As it happens, considerable information has recently become available on the sources of variation of grapes on the vine, which is necessary to know before a reliable sampling procedure can be devised.

• The most important source of variation is the individual vine, so that the sampling method should include as many vines as possible. Since a vineyard contains upwards of 1200 vines per hectare there is a lot of walking to do!

- Next is the individual bunch on the vine, so that bunches from different positions on the vine and different degrees of shading should be sampled on a regular and predetermined pattern.
- Finally, and third in importance, is the position of the grape on the bunch, so that if berries or twigs are sampled, rather than individual bunches, they should be obtained successively from different parts of the bunch.

To ensure that these sources of variation are each taken into account, the vineyard should be sampled as follows:

1 Divide the vineyard into areas of about 2 hectares (5 acres), since these are of a manageable size for sampling.

2 Do not include end-vines or perimeter rows in the sampling unless the vineyard is quite small (such as when the perimeter vines are more than about 10 per cent of the total). These vines are normally atypical and can bias the sample.

3 Sample one vine in every ten by walking along each alternate row and taking at random one bunch, a twig from a bunch or one or two berries from different parts of the bunch, from vines from the row on the left then from the row on the right in sequence. This involves walking between each alternate two rows of vines in a zigzag fashion, taking samples from each row alternately and ensuring that both shaded and exposed bunches are sampled in proportion to their extent. In this way alternate rows are sampled from alternate sides of the vine and from different areas within the vine.

In sampling it is important to obtain a composite sample which accurately represents the state of ripeness of the vineyard at the time. By the above method, it is possible to obtain a sample which is within 1° Brix (0.6° Baumé) of that of the total crop after harvest. If this precision cannot be achieved then the sampling must be altered or intensified until it can be. There is no way that a brief stroll through the vineyard with a hand-held refractometer, sampling a berry here and there, can provide a reliable assessment representing the state of ripeness of the vineyard. To achieve this one must do a lot of walking and sampling.

It should be stressed that the *number of individual samples* and not their size is the important point. Bunch sampling results in a large and heavy composite sample, and twig or berry sampling is more convenient and easier to handle. For example, if berry sampling is used, and assuming that 10 per cent of the 1500 vines per hectare are sampled, the composite sample size for two berries from different parts of each vine is 300 berries per hectare. This is a minimum sample size. Twig sampling is rather better than individual berries, without providing an unduly heavy sample.

When the composite sample is obtained, it is juiced in a simple fruit-juicer, tasted, and the sugar, acidity and pH measured, recorded and plotted on a graph to show the progressive change with time in the stage of ripeness of the grapes in the vineyard. It is important to sample at several intervals before ripeness, so that a smoothed graph can be constructed and extrapolated to the desired stage.

Botrytis on grapes

Botrytis mould or rot on grapes can be desirable or undesirable, depending mainly on the climate. When it is desirable it is referred to as noble rot (a translation of the French *pourriture noble* or the German *Edelfaule*). Noble rot is a remarkable fungal infection occurring on grapes in various parts of the world. It is responsible for the tremendous complexity and flavour of many of the world's great sweet table wines, e.g. Sauternes and the sweet wines of Barsac in France; the Auslese (selected picking of infected bunches), Beeren-auslese (selected picking of infected berries) and Trocken-beeren-auslese wines (selected picking of dried infected berries) of Germany; and the Hungarian Tokay.

The mould responsible is *Botrytis cinerea* which forms a blue-grey film on the grapes. It is responsible for two separate effects—one desirable and the other not.

If the humidity is initially high (more than 90 per cent) for a maximum of 24 hours the botrytis spores will germinate and the mould will grow on and into the skin of the intact berries. If infection is then followed by a period of low humidity (60 per cent or below) when the temperature is between 20 and 25°C the berries will become shrivelled like raisins and acquire a 'botrytised' flavour without an associated caramelised taste. The juice is sweeter because of the water loss from the berry, which concentrates the sugar and the grape and botrytis flavours, and the wine resulting from fermentation of the grapes can be of remarkable quality.

However, if the weather is continually too wet and humid, the grapes will split and become spoilt with an infection of botrytis and other damaging moulds, yeasts and acetic acid bacteria growing on the released sweet juice of the berry. The condition is known as bunch rot and results in mouldy and acetic wine of poor quality.

Let us consider the first and desirable effect of this infection. Besides concentrating the juice, the botrytis infection imparts a special flavour of its own, which is highly prized—making such wines among the most expensive in the world. The wines are very sweet and do not ferment to dryness. Typical analyses are 12 to 14 per cent alcohol and 5 to 15 per cent sugar (good years result in higher sugar levels). An antibiotic, botryticin, is also produced by the mould, and its presence appears to prevent subsequent yeast growth in the sweet wines—sweet wines made from botrytised grapes do not referment as readily as wines from normal grapes. The mould also excretes other metabolic products, such as glycerine, which influence the composition and taste of the wine. In fact, the level of glycerine can be as high as 3 per cent, instead of less than 1 per cent as in normal wines.

When botrytis occurs in a vineyard not all of the grapes are infected equally, and the most botrytised grapes are selected to make the sweetest wines. This is particularly so with the Beeren-auslesen and Trocken-beeren-auslesen wines of Germany. In Sauternes, the great years coincide with a high incidence of *pourriture noble*. In hot dry vineyard areas of Australia the necessary climatic conditions for occurrence of noble rot occur less frequently. However, it is possible to spray grapes in the vineyard with spores of botrytis, which will infect the grapes if the humidity is sufficiently high. This is not always successful, due more to the microclimate than the availability of botrytis spores. I have made botrytised wines by spraying sound harvested Semillon grapes with botrytis spores, storing them in a temperature- and humidity-controlled room until infection was apparent, then making the grapes into wine. The wines had the typical rich botrytis character and sweetness. This process has also been used commercially in California—the grapes are placed on trays, sprayed with spores of the fungus and covered with plastic film for 24 hours to maintain high humidity. They are then stored below 75 per cent relative humidity at 20–22° C for 1–2 weeks. The resulting musts are usually over 17° Baumé and the wines show noble rot character.

One needs to be careful with such a procedure by ensuring that the berries are initially sound, because the conditions encouraging botrytis infection are also conducive to production of volatile acid by acetic-acid bacteria. Indeed, many of the classical Sauternes have high volatile acid. In areas where botrytis infection results in bunch rot, care should be taken to prevent such infection, rather than hope that noble rot will develop.

The problems associated with the production of botrytised sweet white table wines are unsatisfactory climatic conditions for botrytis infection and growth, presence of spoilage organisms, high volatile acidity and bound sulphur dioxide in the wine, and poor filterability, due to polymers produced by the mould. Moreover, the production of these wines is costly, the yield of fruit is lowered by as much as 75 per cent and the juice yield per tonne can be as low as 180 litres per tonne.

However, the rewards for making the botrytised wines justify the care needed to produce them, and some superb wines ranking with the great botrytised wines of the world are now being produced in Australia and New Zealand.

Grape temperature

This section of the text is concerned with Australia, where we have known for a long time that the hot climate in much of the winemaking areas presents special problems in making table wines. An important aspect is how this heat influences the temperature of grape loads arriving at the winery, and temperatures of subsequent winemaking operations and storage. The facts are as follows.

Daily temperature during the vintage season in most grapegrowing areas in Australia fluctuates considerably between day and night—termed the diurnal variation (see Fig. 2.1). Maximum temperature is usually between noon and 4 p.m. and minimum between midnight and 4 a.m. The temperature difference between the hottest and coldest periods in twenty-four hours can exceed 20°C.

Figure 2.1

Fig. 2.1: Daily fluctuations in temperature of grapes on the vine, Adelaide, February 1976 Courtesy Dr F. D. Morgan

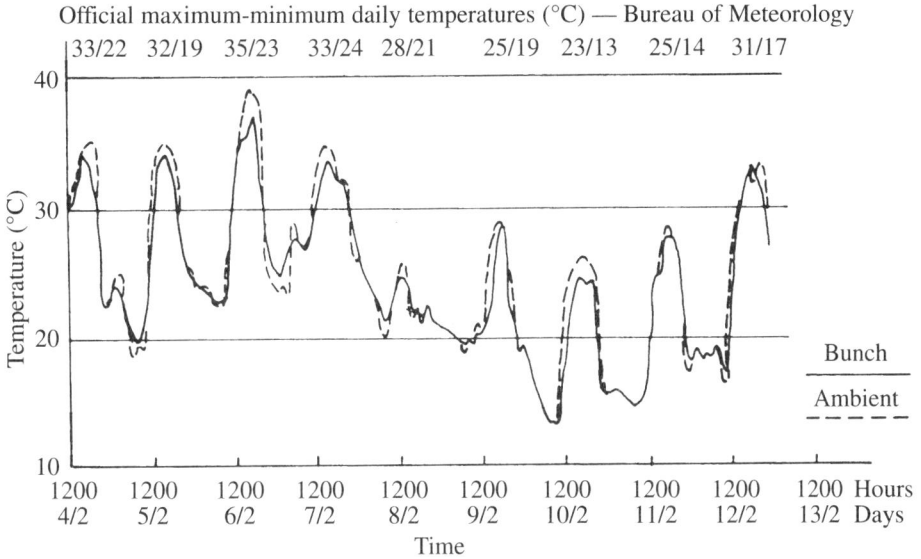

Official maximum-minimum daily temperatures (°C) — Bureau of Meteorology

33/22 32/19 35/23 33/24 28/21   25/19 23/13 25/14 31/17

Grapes on the vine not exposed to the sun closely follow this diurnal temperature change. They lag behind by perhaps half an hour or so, but show the same extremes of temperature as the surrounding air. If the grape bunches are directly exposed to the sun they will be hotter than the air in the vine canopy and the bunches shielded from the sun.

Accordingly, the temperature of a bunch of grapes when picked is close to or at that of the ambient temperature in the vine canopy. If a vineyard is harvested rapidly, as with machine harvesting, and the grape loads allowed to stand either in the shade or in the sun, the temperature of the load will not change much. This is because grapes have such a high specific heat, meaning that they tend to maintain their temperature for a long time. They heat up slowly but when hot retain their heat. The bottom of a load of grapes is usually marginally hotter than the top.

It is not surprising, then, that the temperature of grape loads is quite closely correlated with the time of harvesting—the hotter the day, the hotter will be the bunches at harvesting. The range of temperatures of grape loads, therefore, depends essentially on the prevailing temperature at the time of day of harvest—and can range from about 5 to 40°C, depending on the region and time of day.

Must and juice temperature is closely correlated with grape temperature. In other words, crushing and pumping the must into a drainer or other vessel does little to influence its temperature, unless cooling is carried out. The implications of all this are profound. Hot grapes are the major heat load in the winery and lowering the temperature of hot grapes is a costly undertaking. The alternative is to use natural night cooling, and with the advent of mechanical harvesting this has become a reality. Winemakers who have carried out night harvesting do not need to be convinced about its effectiveness as a means of obtaining cooler grapes. The amount and cost (both capital and operating) of refrigeration required to lower the must or juice temperature to desirable levels is considerable, and indeed this large expenditure on refrigeration is one of the major differences between Australian and cold winemaking countries. In Germany, for example, white grapes can be crushed and left overnight or even longer on skins with little ill effect and possibly some advantage, but the air temperature may be 5°C. Underground cellar temperatures in Germany average 11 to 14°C and are fairly constant over the year.

We are concerned here with one of the most important and significant oenological factors in Australian winemaking—temperature control, which we will be considering in detail in Chapter 8. The high temperature of grape loads is a major contributor, fermentation and storage temperature another. The advent of cooled wineries is with us in Australia and we will see further developments in this area, enabling wine in cask and bottle to be stored at a cool temperature. But a knowledge of the temperature of grape loads and ways of dealing with it is essential in modern winemaking.

3 Winery establishment and layout

Before considering the practical aspects of winery establishment and layout, it is necessary to consider the broader issues. Establishing a winery is attractive and exciting, and potential winemakers can become quite emotionally involved in such decisions. In view of the amount of money involved, as we shall see, establishing a winery can represent a major financial commitment.

We should first of all briefly consider the wine market, and make the point that wine marketing is exceedingly competitive—there are over 12,000 labels offered to the consumer, far more than can be displayed in any one retail outlet. Furthermore, imported wines are available at fairly competitive prices. Accordingly, competition is fierce and is likely to continue to be so, as the wine industry becomes polarised with large companies merging and gaining extra strength. The imposition of sales tax of 20 per cent (10 per cent in August 1984 and a further 10 per cent in August 1986) and licence fee, as well as the burgeoning cost of grapes, places an additional burden on all wineries, where costs are already high.

Approximately 54 per cent of all Australian wine is sold in bag-in-box, marketed by the larger companies. The quality of bag-in-box wines in relation to value for money is generally very good, and has been largely responsible for the dramatic increase in sales to the present level of 20.4 litres per head annual consumption. Only about one quarter of all Australian wine is sold in 750 mL bottles, and this is the highly competitive area in which small wineries normally operate.

The points which are important for small wineries are as follows.

Successful marketing is of key importance, particularly if the winery is in an area not yet recognised for its attributes or in an established area where the winery is not known. Wine show results can guide the winery on the perceived quality of its wines, and medals and awards can be used in promotion. However, the quality of the wines is of little avail if the products are not marketed successfully. Experience has shown that the consuming public will not beat a path to the door of every new small winery in sufficient numbers to ensure rapid commercial success.

It is important to ensure that the enterprise has realistic *financial planning and management*. This involves proper budgeting, stock and inventory control, an awareness of when and when not to spend money, good accounting practices, understanding of taxation and other aspects. Most technical operations have a financial component, and should be considered in that light. It is wise to employ a professional consultant who is aware of these financial considerations. It is tempting to establish the winery with the latest equipment, but over-capitalisation with expensive equipment used only at vintage can be financially disastrous. It is important for the prospective proprietor (and spouse if relevant) to write down the basic objectives of the project—both winemaking and financial—then have these checked by a qualified accountant who can 'think small'. There is no purpose in endeavouring to build a little empire which the project cannot sustain.

Before establishing a winegrowing enterprise the project must be thoroughly and realistically *researched* beginning at the selling end. One needs to decide on the wine styles for which a market exists or can be developed. Then decide whether these wines can be obtained without the costs and problems associated with establishing a vineyard and winery, providing that the appropriate licensing laws permit. Perhaps leasing or renting an existing facility and buying the grapes may be more economical. Then seek good practical and financial advice from qualified people. While small winemaking is a way of life, an accountant can show that today's establishment costs, high prices for premium grapes, marketing problems, government take-outs (licence fee, sales tax, fringe benefits tax etc.), hidden costs of employing labour on a seven-day week and so on, are unlikely to result in a commensurate financial return.

When *establishing a vineyard* important and expensive decisions must be made on a wide range of matters, such as purchase of land, choice of grape varieties, rootstocks if any, soil and its management, training and trellising, water needs and so on. Vineyard establishment costs, including trellising and drip irrigation but excluding the cost of the land, are currently about $50,000 per hectare and about 20 hectares (more or less) are needed for a viable winemaking enterprise. This already amounts to $1,000,000—buying grapes may well be the better way, especially in times of surplus.

The *quality of wines* from small wineries is generally *less consistent* and less predictable than that of wines from larger wineries. The main reason for this is lower technical competence, with sometimes lack of appropriate facilities. Winemakers have an obligation to know *all* of the relevant technology, which imposes great demands on the individual. Assistance from a competent consultant can be of value here. The winemaker may also be the vineyard and winery manager and be in charge of quality control and marketing. These demands on small winemakers make education and acquisition of relevant knowledge of critical importance.

The kinds of *wine faults* encountered by small wineries fall into several broad categories:

- Variable quality at sometimes quite high prices—examples are excessive extraction in reds, poor balance, lack of varietal character, immaturity and so on.
- Oxidation resulting in poor colour, lack of aroma and fruit flavour.

- Microbiological faults resulting in volatility, yeastiness and other taints, arising from the growth of spoilage yeasts and bacteria.

Thus the financial, marketing and technical challenges facing the small winery are considerable. Some small wineries have achieved success, particularly in viticultural areas recognised for their distinctiveness, but in most cases they have had good financial backing. As a way of life winegrowing has much to recommend it, and this is of course an attractive inducement. Historically, few people who have established small wineries close down their operation voluntarily, but many of them say that because of the work involved and low return on capital invested they would not do it again.

Practical aspects

It is important that the winery is properly conceived and designed to fulfil its anticipated needs. A sound principle in winery design is to size the equipment and facilities to meet the maximum anticipated grape intake, and to pick the grapes when they are ready to be picked—not, as can happen, when undersized equipment is ready to handle them. The following points should be considered regarding siting and construction.

- Availability of adequate electric power, preferably 415 volt supply. This can be expensive in remote areas. The capital cost of 415-volt supply is higher than 240 volts but running cost is cheaper.
- Availability of an assured supply of water of acceptable composition and quality. Since an adequate supply of water is sometimes a problem, it is sensible to plan and operate the winery on the basis of minimum water usage, particularly since disposal of waste water may be an even bigger problem. Mains water with high suspended solids may be unsuitable for certain tasks, such as washing filters and back-washing ion-exchange columns, and other sources of higher-quality water may be necessary. If mains water for general washing-down is not available other provisions need to be made, since a small winery normally uses about 250,000 litres per year. A useful rule of thumb for calculating water usage in a winery is 10 litres of water for every 1 litre of wine.
- Ensure convenient road access to the winery, avoiding steep gradients and sharp corners which may hinder truck access. Proximity to rail transport may be an advantage. If the winery site is away from a main road, make sure that it is well signposted (these must conform to regulations and should include business hours).
- Allow adequate manoeuvring space for vehicles around the winery, and parking space for staff and visitors. Provision for outdoor barbecue and related facilities may be desirable.

- Ensure the availability of labour and materials for construction, operation and repairs.
- Select a reasonably level, well-drained site, with soil capable of bearing the load of the winery and its contents. North–south orientation is desirable to prevent excessive heat loads on the building, and western-facing windows and skylights should be avoided for this reason. The site needs to be free from flood and fire risk, landslides, seepage etc. Level ground is desirable but not essential, as slopes may be used with advantage for siting crushers and tipping bins. The winery may be built on two or more levels, but this interferes with movement of hoses, pumps, filters etc. and is usually less workable. Levelling sloping land is expensive. Where possible it is good practice to operate on one reinforced concrete slab floor with a slope to facilitate drainage (about 1 in 100 is usual) but without box gutters with gratings. A good drainage system is essential and is sometimes overlooked.
- Include the availability of telephone, telex and fax services, and computers.
- Allow for adequate insulation, since heat loads are excessive in the warmer viticultural areas of Australia. Examples are sisalation, foam spray, evaporative and refrigeration cooling. Cooling of the winery building may be desirable, so that all operations are carried out below approximately 20°C.
- Conformity with local and state government regulations regarding industrial sites, noise, effluent disposal and related matters.
- Old buildings are sometimes available and can be excellent sales attractions. However, they can be costly to renovate and inefficient as wineries, due to unsatisfactory design, lack of space and drains or multilevels.

Financial considerations

Setting up a small winery with suitable buildings and equipment is expensive. Typically, the capital required for the buildings and equipment to process 150 tonnes of grapes and store the resultant wines up to the stage of bottling, is currently over $1,000,000, including offices, laboratory, cellar-door sales and its associated bottled-wine storage. This excludes the land, payment for the grape crop, working capital for requisites, bottling and of course marketing costs. The initial investment costs to the stage of earning an income is currently of the order of $1 million. A 150-tonne winery requires a minimum of approximately 600 square metres of floor area, depending on the types of wine being made and assuming contract bottling is to be carried out elsewhere. A way to reduce initial costs is to have the grapes crushed and juiced at another winery by contract, saving the cost of a tipping bin, crusher, must pump and press.

The proportion of white to red wine made is important, in view of the significant swing in Australia in recent years towards table wines. Although white wines are still quantitatively more important, red wines are increasing in popularity. The industry now produces predominantly table wines, rather than fortified dessert and aperitif wines of former years. Consumer demand for table wine is currently about three parts white to one part red. Red table wine is normally bottled at about eighteen months of age, and requires 2 litres of storage for every 1 litre made, since it is stored for one more year.

Small wineries making only white wine are continually asked for red wine, indicating a desirable grape crush at present of approximately 75 per cent white and 25 per cent red, with a small amount of red being made in the first year of operations and sold two years later. This proportion of red and white varieties depends on various factors, including the region in which the winery is situated. Opinions may differ as to the most desirable proportion, but it is unwise at present to make more red than white wine, except in areas of recognised red wine pre-eminence and with a prearranged market for the wine.

In planning the operations of the winery the following points should be considered:

• What varieties and tonnages of grapes are to be used and when and from where are they to be sourced?
• What types and styles of wine are to be made?
• What winemaking processes are to be employed?
• Are the wines to be bottled at the winery or by contract?
• What sales programme is envisaged? This relates particularly to provision for cellar-door sales facilities. How does this fit into the range of quality and pricing structures in the market?

All of these considerations influence the layout and equipping of the winery. In general terms, the total storage capacity of the winery producing both white and red wines must be between one and a half and twice that required to contain the annual crush, but the exact capacity varies from winery to winery. In the case of a 150-tonne crush, with one tonne of grapes requiring approximately 700 litres of storage capacity for the raw product (compared with about 600 for the finished product), the total storage capacity required is of the order of 200,000 litres or the equivalent of nearly twice the annual crush. These figures are intended to indicate the order of magnitude of storage required rather than be a precise figure, because of the wide variation between wineries.

The types of storage likewise differ. Most is in stainless-steel tanks of a range of sizes, usually from about 10,000 litres downwards. These combine fermentation and storage, which for white wines presents no problem but for red wines the tanks need to be able to handle skins. This means that the tanks require some means whereby the skins can be removed after fermentation. Colour extraction is usually carried out by pumping the fermenting juice over the skins, with or without some type of heading-down boards. When stainless-steel tanks are used as fermentation vessels a head space of about 30 per cent is needed to allow for foaming and working the skins.

Oak storage is an important and expensive part of winemaking. It is wise to standardise on one size of cask—hogsheads of 300 litres, puncheons of 500 litres, or barriques of 220 litres approximate capacity. The proportion of oak casks to other storage vessels depends on the wines to be made and whether the casks are to be used for fermentation as well as storage. The usual ratio is from about 20 to 50 per cent wood storage, but this varies considerably.

It is wise to have a modular operation, which in a winery of 150 tonnes crush is usually 4 to 7 tonnes, or 2800 to 4900 litres. This is based in part on the pressing operations, which can be a bottleneck. At least three pressings per day, each lasting about 2 to 3 hours, is usual where the press also serves as the drainer. The size of the stainless-steel tanks relates to this module. It is more economical to work a longer day than to duplicate capital equipment for the relatively short vintage season.

Fittings, unions and hoses

An important part of winery establishment and operation is the way grape juice and wine are transported about the winery, and Australia has a problem relating to the kinds of pipes, hoses and fittings to be used. In its development the industry has not standardised on uniform hose and pipe fittings and unions, with the result that various types are used and the situation is confused. For many years the wine-thread or Whitehill fitting has been predominant, particularly in South Australia, where it was developed in 1892 by Joseph Whitehill as a modification of the British Whitworth thread. The Whitehill is not interchangeable with other threads, is not recommended for permanent installations and cannot be cleaned in-place. As time passes it is being replaced by the British Standard Milk (BSM) fitting, although several thousand wine-thread adaptors and couplings are supplied to the industry each year.

The BSM fitting was developed by APV in England. It is also known as the RJT (rubber joint thread), APV or simply 'milk'. It is defined in British Standard 1864–1952 and Australian Standard 1528, part 2, 1976, where it is called the recessed ring joint type (RJT). The BSM thread is emerging as the standard in Australian wineries, since it is already widely used as well as being the standard thread in the milk, brewing, fruit-juice and pharmaceutical industries. However, it is not recommended for permanent CIP installations unless the optional CIP O-ring seal is fitted. A modified fitting—BSM modified CIP kleerkut—has recently been introduced to improve the hygiene of the BSM union. It is suitable for permanent assembly and can be cleaned in-place. An improvement on the standard BSM fitting is the PHU or Pedco Hygienic Union, which has the male part, liner and gasket modified to give a smooth bore with no crevices. The New Zealand Kleanflow is similar to the BSM, using the same thread-form.

Certain other fittings, such as the Triclover Tri-Clamp System, produced by the Ladish Corporation in the United States, are available but not all of the components are made in Australia and are expensive, being more than double the cost of the comparable Wine-Thread and BSM. However, Triclover is a fitting without a screw-thread, consisting of two tapered unions compressing a moulded gasket and held together by a clamp, and thus has an advantage in sanitation. It is widely used in the United States and Japan, and is suitable for permanent assembly and cleaning in-place. Kamlock fittings are also used on must-hose connections to provide a quick convenient coupling without the necessity of tools. They are not suitable as permanent couplings and require manual cleaning. At the present stage in development, it would seem a sensible choice in setting up a new winery to standardise on the BSM fittings.

Various other fittings are used overseas, but are usually replaced on arrival with Australian fittings, such as BSM. Most of the winery equipment from Europe comes with DIN 11851 (Deutsches Institut für Normung) fittings, which are hygienic and suitable for permanent assembly and CIP. They require a special tool for assembly and disassembly. BSP fittings (British Standard Pipe) are commonly found on service connections where the union is intended to be permanent. It is not an hygienic fitting as the joint does not use a gasket. The BSP threads are routinely used for water, air and gases. Fittings on Swedish and certain other equipment, such as centrifuges, are IDF/ISO (International Dairy Federation/International Standards Organisation) or ISS (International Sanitary Standard), which is similar to DIN. The 3A Bevel-Seat Union is the most common fitting in the USA food industry, and employs an ACME square-section thread.

The metals used in the construction of such fittings were formerly brass or bronze. In France, for example, there are still some copper-containing fittings, but in Australia they have been superseded by stainless steel, thereby avoiding the haze problems created by the use of copper. In fact, a little brass or bronze contact with the wine is not undesirable, since it reduces or removes hydrogen sulphide, which has become more prevalent with the introduction of stainless steel. Such copper-containing fittings become black inside with use, due to deposition of copper sulphide arising from the chemical reaction between copper and hydrogen sulphide. This deposit is insoluble and helps to remove hydrogen sulphide from the wine.

In the past hoses were normally reinforced food-grade rubber, with thick reinforced walls for suction and less robust thinner walls for delivery. In general, these hoses were satisfactory and widely used, but were both heavy (particularly suction) and expensive. As suitable reinforced plastic hoses became available they began to supersede rubber in small wineries where the usage rate was low. Improved technology of manufacture has made the costs of both types of hoses more competitive, with the outcome that rubber hoses continue to be employed where heavy use is involved and plastic for lighter duties. The lightweight reinforced plastic hoses have some problems, especially if used for delivery, such as pin-holing, instability to ultraviolet light (except for the red hoses which are UV-stable), greater susceptibility to mechanical damage, a tendency to crack or split when very cold wine is passed through them (such as after cold stabilisation), and a lower recommended working pressure than rubber. They have a weight advantage but a shorter life expectancy. For regular and predetermined transfers self-draining fixed stainless-steel lines are best.

In spite of metrication the sizes of fittings and hoses are still sometimes referred to in British measurements, and for small wineries 2 inch (50.8 mm) internal diameter is normal. The size depends on the volume of product to be handled in unit time, and different sizes may be employed for different purposes. Must lines present a special case, because of the need to pump an heterogeneous mixture of skins, juice, stems and seeds. In this case the wider the diameter, the better the pumping operation with lower internal friction, and the less chance of blockage. Three-inch must lines are desirable as a minimum, whereas 1 or 1½ inch lines and fittings, as well as 2 inch, may be used for wine transfer.

A wide range of valves exists. The wine industry adopted diaphragm valves initially, but these are being superseded by butterfly valves because of the greater cost of diaphragm-valve replacements. The handle position on a butter-fly valve gives an instant indication of open, part-open or shut, and is quick to operate. Butterfly valves are suitable for liquids without suspended solids, but do not handle grape stalks, skins and seeds well. Ball valves are not desirable because of the liquid retained in the annulus of the ball, which presents a sani-tation problem. Larger wineries tend to use air-actuated and other remote controls where possible, instead of manual operation, and diversion or multipass valves allow greater flexibility than is afforded by butterfly valves. All fittings are normally constructed in type 316 stainless steel.

Major suppliers to the beverage industries, such as Alfa Laval and APV-Bell Bryant, offer the BSM fittings as standard, while the wine-thread, BSM conver-sions from one thread to another specifically for the wine industry, plus valves and hoses, can be obtained from equipment suppliers.

Variable-capacity wine tanks

The wine industry has long made use of stainless-steel tanks for wine storage. These are usually made of type 316 stainless, less so type 304, and have been a boon to the industry. However, they are of fixed capacity and ullage or head space can be a prob-lem, because of the difficulty of storing table wine in full vessels of fixed capacity to prevent exposure to air with possible resultant oxidation. Inert gas has been one answer by replacing the oxygen in the ullage space with inert gas, or floating edible oil or plastic sheets on the surface of the wine. Variable-capacity tanks which avoid the problems of ullage space are thus an interesting alternative. They are now avail-able and should be mentioned in this section on winery equipment.

Variable-capacity tanks have been used for many years in the oil and gas storage industry, but the methods of sealing the movable lids have been different and not applicable to an oxidisable beverage, such as wine. The key to successful operation is in the seal between the lid and the wall of the tank. Variable-capacity stainless steel tanks for wine were developed by Spokane Metal Products, Spokane, Washington, USA, in 1982. Other companies advertise such vessels, such as J.B. North-West Engineering, Portland, Oregon. However, A. & G. Engineering of Griffith, who built the Australian tanks, obtained the seals from the Spokane company, and advise that they are available in three diameters—122, 168 and 229 centimetres.

Variable-capacity tanks were first installed in the Mountadam winery built by David and Adam Wynn in Eden Valley, South Australia. They are 1.7 metres in diameter, 3.6 metres high and hold 8700 litres or approximately 10 tonnes of grapes. The tanks stand on legs with a large lower door and a racking valve. The tank floor has an 8° slope to assist in removing skins when the tanks are used as red fermenters. The top is open and the lid can move up and down inside the tank in the same manner as a piston in a cylinder. It can also be lifted out of the tank and swivelled aside so that it is out of the way, and the tank can then be used as an open-topped fermenter, if required. A wire rope and ratchet handle enable the lid to be raised, lowered or swivelled. The tanks are constructed of stainless steel 1.6 mm thick and designed to be multipurpose to permit fermentation of red must and storage of fermented wine.

The sealing procedure of the lid to the wall of the tank is ingenious, and is the key to successful operation. Attached to the rim of the lid is a black food-grade inflatable rubber tube, similar to a large bicycle tyre. When deflated the lid can move freely up and down in the tank, but when inflated to 25 pounds per square inch gauge pressure (psig) the rubber tube seals closely to the wall of the tank and fixes the lid securely so that one can walk on it when the tank is empty. Compressed nitrogen for inflation is provided by a gas cylinder, and a pressure regulator built into the system limits the available pressure to 25 psig.

The advantages of such a tank are readily apparent—variable-capacity, multi-purpose use, ease of operation and hygiene. These tanks are new to the industry and represent an innovative concept which should have considerable application in wineries.

Programmable controllers

At first sight a discussion on programmable controllers may seem strange in a book on winemaking, but because of their economic and practical advantages in winery and bottling operations, they are becoming a necessary part of a modern winery and are now regarded as essential in automating industrial processes.

Programmable controllers can be described as digitally operated electronic devices with a programmable memory for storing and giving instructions to carry out a wide range of control functions. They were first introduced in 1970 and have been continually refined as newer microprocessors and integrated circuits have become available. Programmable controllers (PCs) are sometimes called programmable logic controllers (PLCs), which is a registered name by one of the manufacturers, so we will refer to them by the former name. Following their introduction, programmable controllers were rapidly applied to industrial control as replacements for permanently wired ('hard-wired') relay control panels, mechanical timers, counters, stepping controllers and others. When the control requirements of this former system changed it was usually not economical to rewire the panels, and often new ones had to be designed and purchased.

This need greatly stimulated the development of programmable controllers, which were capable of being programmed and reprogrammed without the extensive changes required in the former systems when such programme alterations were required. The important feature is that programmable controllers are essentially reprogrammable if the requirements change. They are not only less expensive but an essential part of automation, which is playing an increasing role in the wine industry's future. Following their development, programmable controllers were immediately accepted into the automotive industry and since then have been used widely in industry generally. As an indication of their importance, sales have increased by approximately 30 per cent per year.

Programmable controllers thus take the place of other control devices, such as relays, electric timers, counters and mechanical controllers, which are subject to mechanical wear, contact welding faults, solenoid burn-out and short circuiting. They cannot be reprogrammed without major change.

In discussing programmable controllers it is desirable to avoid the technical jargon associated with them. One of their important features is that they can be programmed, reprogrammed and maintained by ordinary staff. They have a number of advantages over the equipment which they replace. They operate more efficiently in areas with electrical noise, under high temperatures, and in the presence of mechanical shocks. They are essentially designed for an industrial environment but may need a regulated power supply. They have the advantages of reliability, low maintenance, small physical space, are capable of being programmed to meet changing control requirements, often less expensive than the equivalent permanently wired systems, and more flexible and reusable.

Programmable controllers have certain elements of a microcomputer, including the terminology associated with them. A simple programmable controller has several basic functions:

- A removable digital programmer which can serve many units. Also many small programmable controllers have built-in programmers.
- A central processing unit with its associated microprocessor, memory storage and power supply, normally 240 volts AC. All the relays, timers, counters and wiring used for logic control are within the programmable controller. There are also additional features available, such as data logging and memory, which can be used for preparing operational reports and progress readouts.
- Various input and output modules which accept from and give signals to sensors, switches, solenoids, starters, pilot lights and so on. These input and output modules interface the low voltages used in the programmable controllers with the

voltages actually used in switching etc. The internal operations normally operate on a few volts, and the outputs are flexible but usually 240 volts AC or DC.

The essence of the programmable controller is the central processing unit which receives a range of input data, carries out logical decisions based on a stored programme (which can be varied at will), and then drives various output operations. As an example,·let us take the example of a requirement to control the temperature of a number of fermentation tanks during vintage. These tanks are fitted with temperature sensors and are connected to a refrigeration line with valves, with the sensors and valve actuators connected to the input and output terminals respectively of the controller. A dedicated microprocessor controls a simple linear actuator to open and shut the array of valves. The controller is programmed to accept the temperature inputs from each of the tanks, and to ensure that they are within the programmed limits by carrying out the appropriate mathematical computations to control the operations of the valves admitting refrigeration to the tanks.

It is thus possible with a simple device of this kind to programme the temperature of fermentation tanks as a group or independently, and to change these requirements at will. Other operations can be incorporated, such as activating stirrers on a programmed time sequence and so on. The cost of the programmable controller, including the time taken to install them, is usually considerably less than that of the equipment which it replaces.

As we can see, programmable controllers offer important advantages in a wide range of winery processes. These range from quite simple controls, such as switching a pump on and off and the example given above, to complicated controls, such as the automation of a bottling or bag-in-box packaging line. There are many examples of the use of programmable controllers in the wine industry, such as:

- automated ion-exchange operations
- waste and effluent water treatment
- refrigeration plants
- grape crushing equipment
- desulphiting plants
- tank level/pressure sensing and control
- flow control
- waste and energy management
- automatic blending

Another important point is the ability of programmable controllers to facilitate the acquisition of important management information. Typically, a number of programmable controllers can be linked (called networking) to a more sophisticated information-processing device, such as a microcomputer. So that in addition to actually running the equipment or process more reliably, it can also record throughputs, wastage and so on.

4 Winemaking procedures

In this chapter, we will be dealing with the integrated procedures employed to make the various wine types produced in Australia and New Zealand. Because of the wide range of wines produced, often in the one winery, the technical requirements of Australian winemakers go beyond those of their European counterparts. Accordingly, the procedures are set out in a chronological sequence, and then later chapters will go into the detail necessary to understand both the principles and the practices of each operation.

Dry white table winemaking

One of the most important advances in the Australian and New Zealand wine industries in recent years has been the dramatic improvement in the quality of white table wines—so much so that both industries are now largely white table wine producers and the quality of these wines has never been higher. The reasons for this are listed below, and constitute a much greater understanding of the essentials of the white winemaking process.

We have reached the stage where white table winemaking has become predictable—more so than dry red wines, the making of which is still somewhat empirical. This remarkable improvement in the quality of white wines has been due to the following factors:

- Better grape varieties, such as Rhine Riesling, Chardonnay, Sauvignon Blanc, Traminer, Semillon and Chenin Blanc.
- Greater control over the maturity and soundness of the fruit.
- The use of cooling during the winemaking operations to conserve aroma and flavour.
- Prevention of oxidation by carrying out all operations under inert gas at low temperature.
- Minimum handling of the must and wine.
- Careful control of pH, free sulphur dioxide and ascorbic acid.
- Efficient overall quality control.

These factors will be discussed in detail.

In making dry white wines, as in all winemaking, the composition and soundness of the grapes is of major importance, since this dictates the quality of the wines resulting from them. The ripeness of the grapes at harvest depends on the type of wine to be made, but normal maturity is between 10 and 12.5° Baumé (18 and 22.5° Brix). Wines from some varieties, such as Chardonnay, can benefit from more mature fruit.

From the time that the grapes are harvested the modern approach is to employ reductive oenology, rather than the oxidative practices used in making dessert wines. Reductive oenology is essentially centred on preventing access of the must and wine to air to avoid oxidation, coupled with effective temperature control.

The grapes at harvest should be cool, preferably in the range of 8 to 16°C. In warm areas this is best achieved by harvesting mechanically at night when the ambient—and thus the grape—temperature is coldest. If not, must cooling is required. At harvest it is wise practice to add 50 to 75 milligrams per litre of sulphur dioxide as potassium or sodium metabisulphite, together with 50 to 100 milligrams per litre of ascorbic acid, as either the acid itself or as sodium erythorbate (which contains 81 per cent of ascorbic acid).

The grapes are preferably crushed in a roller crusher which destems before crushing. On occasion they may be pressed without crushing, as in Champagne production in France, to obtain the best quality free-run juice low in phenolics. This gives a greater yield of high-quality juice. Tartaric acid may be added at this stage, if required, to ensure that the pH of the juice is in the range of 3.0 to 3.4. Pectin-splitting enzymes may also be added to hasten the yield of drained juice. The activity of these mixed enzymes is strongly temperature-dependent (at 10°C they have between 15 and 25 per cent of their activity, at 20°C between 25 and 35, at 30°C between 40 and 60 per cent) and their optimum temperature is 45 to 50°C. At 60°C they rapidly lose their activity and at 80°C are ineffective. Consequently, a conflict exists between the winemaker's desire for cool temperature for grape-handling operations and the need for efficient activity of the pectin-splitting enzymes. The enzymes should accordingly be added as soon as possible after crushing to allow the longest period of time for them to act.

Some varieties benefit from skin contact between the juice and the grape skins, the length of time depending on temperature. There is no point in specifying the length of time of skin contact without indicating the temperature at which this takes place. Depending on the grape variety, skin contact can be up to about 18 hours at 5 to 10°C. The higher the temperature, the more astringent phenolics and tannins are extracted, and skin contact is of greatest value when employed on quality grapes from cool regions.

The must is then drained, preferably under carbon dioxide, at a temperature not exceeding 15°C, and the skins pressed, with an addition of 20 to 50 milligrams per litre of sulphur dioxide at the pressing stage. The pressings may or may not be added to the free-run juice, since the quality of wine made from free-run juice is normally higher than that from pressings.

The juice may then be clarified to an extent depending on the winemaker's preference. This clarification ranges from none at all, as is used in making white burgundies in France, through settling cold overnight (*débourbage*), in which the suspended solids are reduced to between approximately 1.0 and 2.0 per cent, to clarified juice which is settled with pectic enzymes and the supernatant then centrifuged and/or earth-filtered to contain below 0.5 and sometimes below 0.1 per cent suspended solids. These operations should be carried out below 15°C, and in general the cooler the better.

The juice is then inoculated with a selected pure yeast culture, grown under aerobic conditions to ensure a high yeast-cell count (preferably over 200 million cells per mL) and sterol content. At the same time an addition of 100 to 200 milligrams per litre of diammonium phosphate may be added as supplementary inorganic nitrogen to inhibit the possible subsequent formation of hydrogen sulphide during fermentation, and to assist in obtaining complete fermentation of the sugar. Some winemakers add a B-group vitamin mixture at this stage as a yeast nutrient to assist in the fermentation of highly clarified juice.

Fermentation is normally carried out between 10 and 16°C, with occasionally some winemakers preferring a lower temperature. The rate of fermentation with a given yeast strain depends on the temperature, which is the normal means of controlling the fermentation rate. The reduction in sugar content during fermentation is approximately linear and desirably between 0.4 and 0.8° Baumé (0.7 and 1.4° Brix) per day.

Bentonite may be added during fermentation at a rate dependent on the protein content of the juice, in order to avoid bentonite fining as a separate subsequent operation. The juice of some grape varieties, such as Chardonnay and Sauvignon Blanc, may be fermented in oak casks, depending on the style of wine required, and subsequently matured in cask after fermentation.

After fermentation, the wine is allowed to settle and is then racked under carbon dioxide to remove the gross lees. With some varieties, such as Chardonnay, this may be delayed for weeks or even months and malo-lactic fermentation may take place. At racking, sulphur dioxide is added to provide between 20 and 35 milligrams per litre free, depending on the pH of the wine, which should be between pH 3.1 and 3.4. The higher the pH the more free sulphur dioxide is required. It is good practice to add 100 milligrams per litre ascorbic acid (or the equivalent amount of sodium erythorbate) at the end of fermentation, followed by additions of between 25 and 50 milligrams per litre before each subsequent handling or movement of the wine. It is essential to have free sulphur dioxide present when ascorbic acid is added. In considering the various additives one should be aware of restrictions placed on wines exported to certain overseas countries, and the Wine Export Grid prepared by the Australian Wine and Brandy Corporation should be consulted.

Cool temperature and prevention of exposure of the young wine to air are of pre-eminent importance in white winemaking, together with the minimum handling of wine. When the various batches of wine so made are blended to form a uniform bulk, this is cold-stabilised by chilling to between minus 4 and plus 2°C and adding potassium bitartrate crystals if rapid stabilisation is required.

The chilled and stabilised wine is then racked from the crystalline tartrate deposit under inert gas. In all operation involving cold wine it is essential that the wine should not be exposed to air, especially during pumping, since the solubility of dissolved oxygen is much greater in cold than warm wine. At this stage the wine is analysed for pH (desirable range 3.0 to 3.4), free sulphur dioxide (15 to 30 milligrams per litre depending on pH), ascorbic acid (50 to 100 milligrams per litre) and reducing sugar (to suit the style of wine), and is then ready for bottling.

An example of a flow chart for the various procedures involved in making white table wines is shown in Fig. 4.1.

Sweet white table wines

In recent years the popularity of sweet white table wines has increased considerably, due to the greatly improved quality of these wines, resulting from improvements in winemaking technology, particularly filtration. This made the wines more attractive, especially to women. In the past, these wines were conserved by large doses of sulphur dioxide, which rendered them less palatable and did not always prevent yeast refermentation. With the advent of sterile filtration these wines could be made with much less sulphur dioxide and thus retain higher quality. Sweet white table wines can be made in two ways.

1 Use grape juice which is very high in sugar, so much so that the sugar cannot be fermented to dryness and the wine remains sweet. This is the case, for example, with the sweet wines of Sauternes and Barsac and the Auslesen, Beeren-auslesen and Trocken-beeren-auslesen wines of Germany. The sweetness in the must is the result of the growth of *Botrytis cinerea* on the grape berry, resulting in desiccation of the berry and the increased sugar content arising from this, as well as production of other and desirable flavouring constituents. The degree of sweetness is related to the extent of infection with the mould, and in both Australia and New Zealand botrytis infection is becoming more common, with the result that many excellent wines in the style of those listed above are being made. This was discussed in Chapter 2.

In addition, very sweet musts can be obtained without the help of botrytis by allowing the grapes to over-mature on the vine, with or without cane-pruning to assist desiccation, by making use of the hot climate in the warmer grapegrowing areas. Such wines remain sweet after fermentation to an extent dependent on the sweetness of the grapes. They normally require acid addition to obtain an harmonious balance of sweetness to acidity. In New Zealand, sugar can be added and the reader is referred to the section on chaptalisation in Chapter 5. In Australia, the addition of sugar is not permitted unless the wines are sparkling or flavoured.

Fig 4.1: Flow chart for white table winemaking

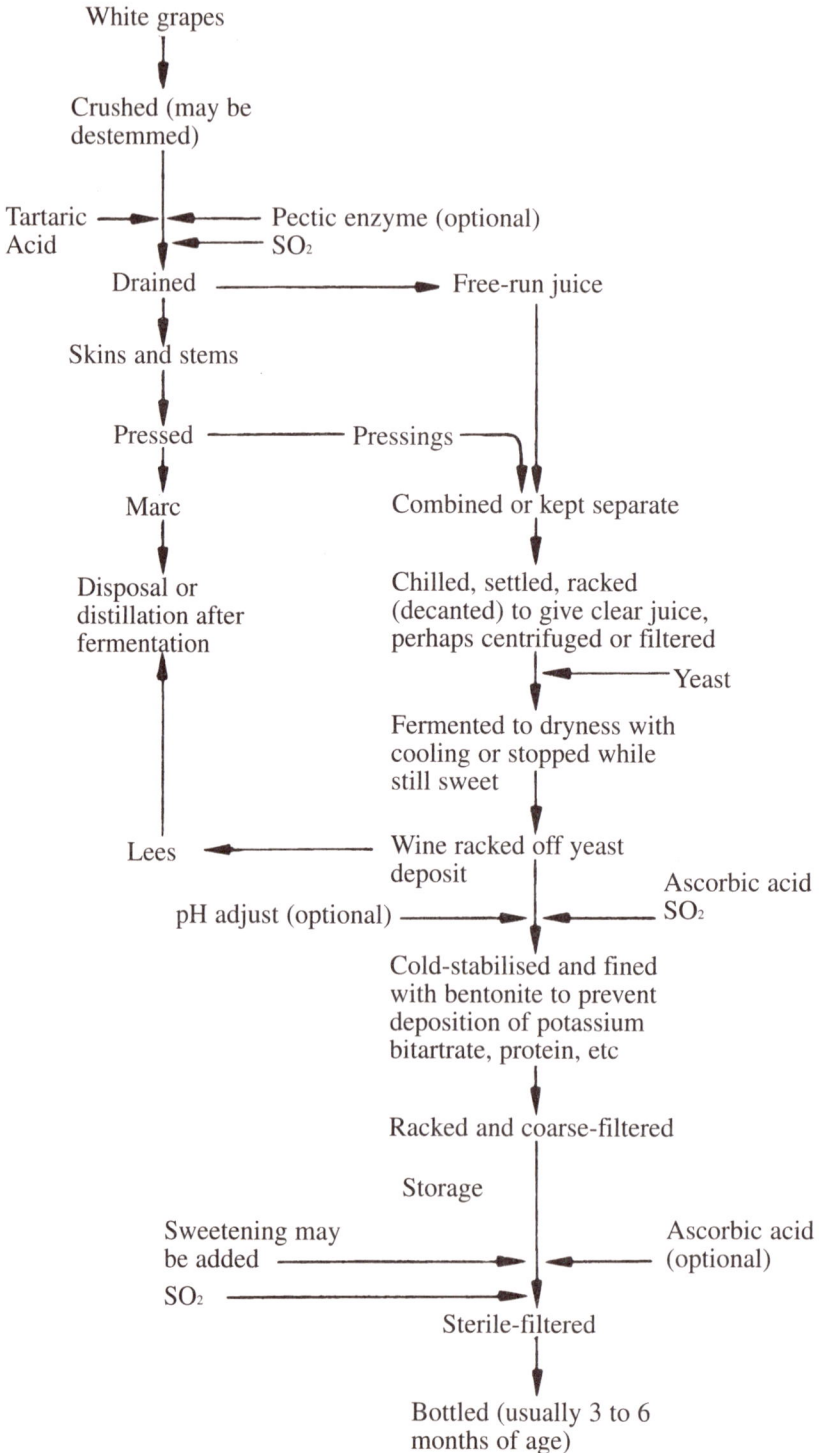

White grapes

Crushed (may be destemmed)

Tartaric Acid ——→ ←—— Pectic enzyme (optional)
←—— SO₂

Drained ————————→ Free-run juice

Skins and stems

Pressed ———————— Pressings ——

Marc   Combined or kept separate

Disposal or distillation after fermentation

Chilled, settled, racked (decanted) to give clear juice, perhaps centrifuged or filtered

←— Yeast

Fermented to dryness with cooling or stopped while still sweet

Lees ←———————— Wine racked off yeast deposit

Ascorbic acid
pH adjust (optional) ————→ ←—— SO₂

Cold-stabilised and fined with bentonite to prevent deposition of potassium bitartrate, protein, etc

Racked and coarse-filtered

Storage

Sweetening may be added ————→ ←—— Ascorbic acid (optional)

SO₂ ————————————→

Sterile-filtered

Bottled (usually 3 to 6 months of age)

2 Allow the juice to ferment to dryness normally, then stabilise and sweeten the wine with single-strength or concentrated grape juice before bottling. An alternative is to sweeten the wine before stabilisation, then bottle as soon as possible afterwards. The wine made in this way is prone to refermentation of the added sugar, but modern technology and sterile filtration prevent this from happening. In this way, the sweetness of the wine can be more precisely controlled than by fermenting a very sweet must, although better wines are normally made by the latter method. The grape juice used as the sweetening material is best conserved under refrigeration, since it is prone to fermentation. Concentrated grape juice is normally about 68 to 72° Brix, and can be stored at room temperature for short periods.

An important point is how to define sweetness in these wines. This relates to marketing as well as production. Sweet table wines are made in a wide range of sweetness from nearly dry (about 1 per cent of reducing sugar) to very sweet, such as 20 per cent sugar.

The definition of a dry wine from the viewpoint of setting a standard for exhibitors in wine shows in Australia is 7.5 grams per litre or 0.75 per cent reducing sugar. This definition has been set by the Wine Committee of the Royal Agricultural and Horticultural Society of South Australia. At least two natural grape sugars are involved, viz. glucose (dextrose) and fructose (laevulose), and, as we have seen, these differ in sweetness with fructose being considerably sweeter. During yeast fermentation glucose is usually fermented more rapidly than fructose, since most wine yeasts are glucophiles rather than fructophiles— a property which relates to the differential permeability of their cell membrane to these two sugars. This means that as the sugars are fermented the proportion of fructose usually becomes greater in relation to glucose, and the wine appears sweeter than a simple sugar analysis (which measures both sugars as one) would indicate. This is why sweet white wines, such as Sauternes styles, taste so sweet. Also, when the wine becomes nearly dry, such as 7.5 grams per litre reducing sugar, the sugar is largely the sweeter fructose.

If the Baumé measurement of a white table wine reads 0°, for example, it contains approximately 30 grams per litre or 3 per cent sugar. However, this figure is not precise because it depends on the alcohol content of the wine as well as the amounts of other soluble solids apart from sugar. The relationship is not linear and higher Baumé figures approximate to about 18 grams per litre of sugar for each Baumé degree. If one takes into account the alcohol content of the wine the relationship is somewhat more precise but still rather approximate. Some wines measure below 0° Baumé, such as dry sherries, where the alcohol content is high and the soluble solids low.

The only way to assess the sugar content in wine accurately is to measure it by one of the various chemical or physical methods available. The Lane and Eynon method involving copper reduction in alkaline tartrate solution is commonly used and the results are fairly precise. Chemical limit tests are also available, such as Dextrocheck or Clinitest, which give an approximate indication of sugar content.

Various terms are used in Australia to indicate to the consumer that the wine is sweet, such as late harvest, late-picked, Moselle and Sauternes (from the French) and Spätlese, Auslese, Beeren-auslese and Trocken-beeren-auslese (from the German). However, these terms are imprecise in that they only indicate the approximate sweetness of the wine, and different winemakers use them in different ways.

So how can the consumer know the sweetness of a wine of this type? What could be of benefit would be a small scale or chart on the label to indicate the amount of sugar which the wine contains. On the basis of the above discussion, a scale of 0, 2, 4, 6, 8 and 10 would seem appropriate to represent the actual sugar content in per cent, and would perhaps be useful in assessing a particular wine from a dietary viewpoint. The sweetness of the wine in question would be indicated on the scale, and the consumer could perhaps be guided by an indication in words and with colour the approximate relationship of sugar content to sweetness.

Taste	*Suggested scale*
dry	0
slightly sweet	1–2
medium sweet	2–5
sweet	5–8
very sweet	8–10

The number of times consumers ask how sweet is this or that wine indicates that the subject is important, and that this suggestion may be worth taking further.

Dry red table wines

In our present state of knowledge, red winemaking is still something of an art, in comparison with white winemaking where results are more predictable. The reason for this is that the composition and quality of red wine depends on a greater number of variables in the winemaking process than whites, such as time and temperature of the juice on skins during fermentation, various methods of colour extraction, the extent and type of wood aging, and more handling of the wine. The difference between red and white winemaking relates essentially to the grapes. In red (black) grapes of the kind grown in Australia and New Zealand (*Vitis vinifera*) the colour resides in the vacuoles of the cells just under the skin of the berry, and not in the pulp.

The colour consists of anthocyanins, which are the natural pigments in many of the flowers in our gardens. Those in grapes are the anthocyanidin monoglucosides, i.e. each anthocyanidin molecule is linked to a sugar molecule which affords it greater chemical stability. The anthocyanidins are malvidin (the main grape pigment), peonidin (occurring mainly in peonies), petunidin (petunias), delphinidin (delphiniums) and cyanidin (cornflowers). All of these pigments are closely related to each other chemically and their colours are influenced by pH and other factors. Some coloured tannins are also present and their concentration and molecular size increases as the wine ages, until in old wines they become so large that they deposit as bottle crust.

Let us assume that we are making a dry red table wine from Cabernet Sauvignon. The maturity at which the grapes are harvested depends on the style of wine intended and the fruit flavour present in the grapes. A ripeness of 10 to 14° Baumé (18 to 25° Brix) is usual, which results in a wine containing between about 10 and 14 per cent alcohol by volume. The riper the grapes, the heavier is the wine in body and (generally) in flavour, as well as the higher in alcohol. Red wines are normally made from grapes ranging from about 10 to 14° Baumé (18 to 25.2° Brix).

The wine after malo-lactic fermentation should have a pH value in the range of 3.3 to 3.6. The pH of the grapes is not a very reliable index of the final pH of the wine, because winemaking processes change the pH. For example, during the alcoholic fermentation the skins are continually being extracted by being in contact with the fermenting juice, resulting in a rise in pH because of the alkaline components, mainly potassium, sodium, calcium and magnesium, extracted from the skins. Accordingly, at the crushing stage it is more useful to work on the titratable acidity of the must than the pH, although neither gives a precise indication of the final acidity of the wine. The most important parameter is the fruit flavour of the grapes, since acidity can be adjusted.

We must assume that the grapes are sound and moderately cool. They are then destemmed and crushed (preferably in that order) and the stems discarded. The winemaker may include stems in the fermentation, but this is not usual because of their greater content of astringent phenolics. The crushed and destemmed must is then pumped to a fermentation vessel and tartaric acid may be added, together with a small quantity of sulphur dioxide, such as 50 milligrams per litre, followed by a selected yeast culture. The tendency now is to restrict or delete sulphur dioxide addition in favour of a higher yeast inoculum.

Then follows the empirical process of colour extraction on skins, which may be carried out in various ways.

1 Punching down the floating skins (the cap) at regular intervals during the fermentation so that they mix with the fermenting juice. This is applicable to small-sized fermentation vessels and efficiently extracts the skins. Mechanical devices can be used for this purpose.

2 Pumping over by taking the juice from under the cap of skins and irrigating the skins in an intermittent manner. Various systems of irrigation of skins have been developed, and the Algerian Ducellier system is probably the most interesting. It is

Fig. 4.2: Ducellier system

1 Fermenting must

2 Port for introducting must

3 Open juice fermentation space

4 Cooled fermenting juice

5 Valve for release of carbon dioxide

6 Cooling column for fermenting up-flowing juice

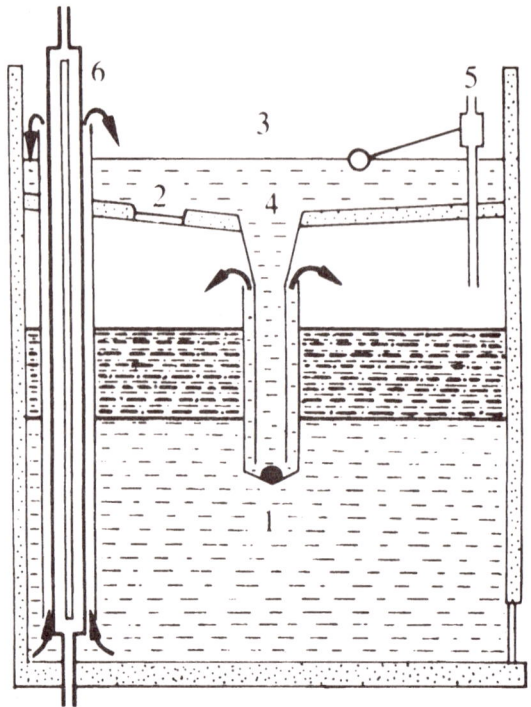

used in Australia and called the autofermenter (see Fig. 4.2). This system allows fermenting juice to be sprayed on a regular basis over the cap of skins in an atmosphere of carbon dioxide, and consists of a tank with an upper and lower section. The lower section holds the fermenting must under an inert atmosphere of carbon dioxide, while the upper section holds the fermenting juice which is forced up by the pressure of carbon dioxide generated by fermentation. When the upper section is full a release valve opens and the juice descends quickly through a central tube and sprays over the mass of skins in the lower section. This process enables rapid extraction of colour and can be operated on a semicontinuous basis. The system does not operate properly unless the bottom tank is full.

3 Submerging the skins with head boards so that the skins are in constant contact with the juice. In the past this was carried out in open-top concrete tanks, but now most heading-down is carried out in vertical stainless-steel tanks with a central riser tube to permit the fermenting juice to rise up under carbon-dioxide pressure and flow over the floating mass of skins under the head boards.

4 Use of specifically designed red-wine fermenters such as the Rototank or its more recent development, the Vinomatic. Several versions of this equipment have been developed, the most recent consisting of an horizontal cylindrical stainless-steel tank, which can rotate about its long axis with entry and delivery at one end. Inside the tank is a spiral flange which moves the skins in one direction or the

other, depending on the direction of rotation. After the colour has been extracted, the fermenting juice is drained off via an internal perforated screen, and the skins discharged through the central outlet in one end of the cylinder. The best analogy of the vinomatic operation is the rotating concrete delivery vessels mounted on the back of delivery trucks. When the direction of rotation is one way the concrete keeps mixing in the vessel, and when the direction of rotation is reversed the concrete is carried to the central outlet on the delivery end of the tank by the internal spiral flange.

5 Heat extraction of colour—this is dealt with in Chapter 5.

Temperature control is difficult when an insulating cap of skins is present, because the maximum temperature of the mass is in the centre of the bottom layer of the floating skins, and may be as much as 10°C higher than the temperature of the juice beneath it. Consequently, the temperature of fermenting red wine is the temperature of the juice under the cap of skins. The best wines are usually made when this juice has a temperature of between 15 and 25°C. Pinot Noir requires a somewhat higher temperature. Sometimes a lower temperature than 15°C is employed, but this results in a considerably slower fermentation. As a general rule, a reduction of 10°C halves the rate of fermentation.

During fermentation, winemakers sometimes add oak chips or shavings to impart oak complexity. This must be carefully done since harsh flavour and oxidation can result, and the best results are obtained by addition during fermentation, when the oxidation reduction potential is low (less than about 150 millivolts). Such addition is never a satisfactory replacement for oak-cask maturation.

Pressing takes place when the winemaker considers that the required amounts of colour, flavour and tannin have been extracted. This varies from about two days after commencement of fermentation until two or three weeks after its completion, depending on the style of wine required. In Bordeaux, for example, the wine is left on skins for one to two weeks after the fermentation has finished. For winemakers in new areas or with new grape varieties some experimentation with time on skins may be necessary. The pressed wine can be blended with the drained wine or kept separate, depending on the style of wine required. After pressing, the wine is left to ferment to dryness—between 1 and 2 grams per litre of reducing sugar, consisting of non-fermentable pentoses.

About this stage the wine usually undergoes malo-lactic fermentation, especially if a culture of *Leuconostoc oenos* is added early in the fermentation. Where this bacterium is endemic in the winery its addition is not usually required, and malo-lactic fermentation usually occurs naturally. In cool areas where the acidity is high malo-lactic fermentation is particularly desirable, and results in a distinct softening of the wine. In fact, the pH may rise by as much as 0.4 of a unit if the malic acid content of the grapes is high. The normal pH increase is between 0.5 and 0.4. At this stage the wine is preferably not yet in wood, and it is desirable for the malo-lactic fermentation to take place now rather than later. The wine can be given a light fining of bentonite at this stage, such as 0.2 to 0.4 grams per litre, or egg-white, one to three egg-whites per 100 litres, to settle the suspended material, and the acidity adjusted, if necessary, with tartaric acid (not citric) to between pH 3.3 and 3.6.

The wine is then wood-aged in *Quercus* oak barrels for a period of between a few months and about eighteen months, depending on the wine, the age, size and type of oak and the temperature. The normal barrels are hogsheads (300 litres), puncheons (475 litres) and barriques (225 litres), in about that order of use in Australia. Barriques are preferred in New Zealand. The proportion of French (mainly *Quercus robur*) and American (*Quercus alba*) oak used varies with the price. At the time of writing American oak is cheaper, but small wineries use mainly French oak (predominantly Nevers). The barrels are filled, hit a few times with a rubber mallet to dislodge air bubbles, and topped up and rolled so that the bung is at about 30 degrees to the vertical. Small oak casks tightly bunged and rolled do not need to be topped up between rackings. The temperature of barrel aging should be between 15 and 22°C. Racking is important in red winemaking to clarify the wine from the lees and allow limited aeration. Without a centrifuge, two or three rackings are necessary before the wine can be filtered.

After cask aging, the wine is blended, tasted again (every movement or treatment of the wine is checked by tasting), analysed, filtered and lightly sulphited if necessary, then bottled. Sterile filtration is not required, providing that the wine is sound, free from fermentable sugar and has completely undergone malolactic fermentation (less than 0.1 grams per litre of malic acid). Bottle-aging under cool temperature (15 to 20°C) improves the quality, but is expensive for small wineries with cash flow problems.

As can be seen, there are various ways to make dry red wines, and the flow chart in Fig. 4.3 will serve as an example.

Production of white wine from red grapes

In some parts of the world white wines are routinely made from red grapes as, for example, in the production of Champagne in France from Pinot Noir and Pinot Meunier, in which whole grape bunches are pressed without crushing. Juice obtained by this process is either uncoloured or varying shades of pink, and white sparkling wine is produced routinely from such grapes.

The amount of colour in the berries of red grapes is influenced by various factors:

• Grapes variety—these vary widely in the amount of colour in the berries at maturity.
• Crop level—generally the larger the crop, the lesser the colour.
• Stage of ripeness—generally the riper the crop, the more intense the colour.
• Berry size—generally larger berries have less colour.

Fig. 4.3: Flow chart for dry red winemaking

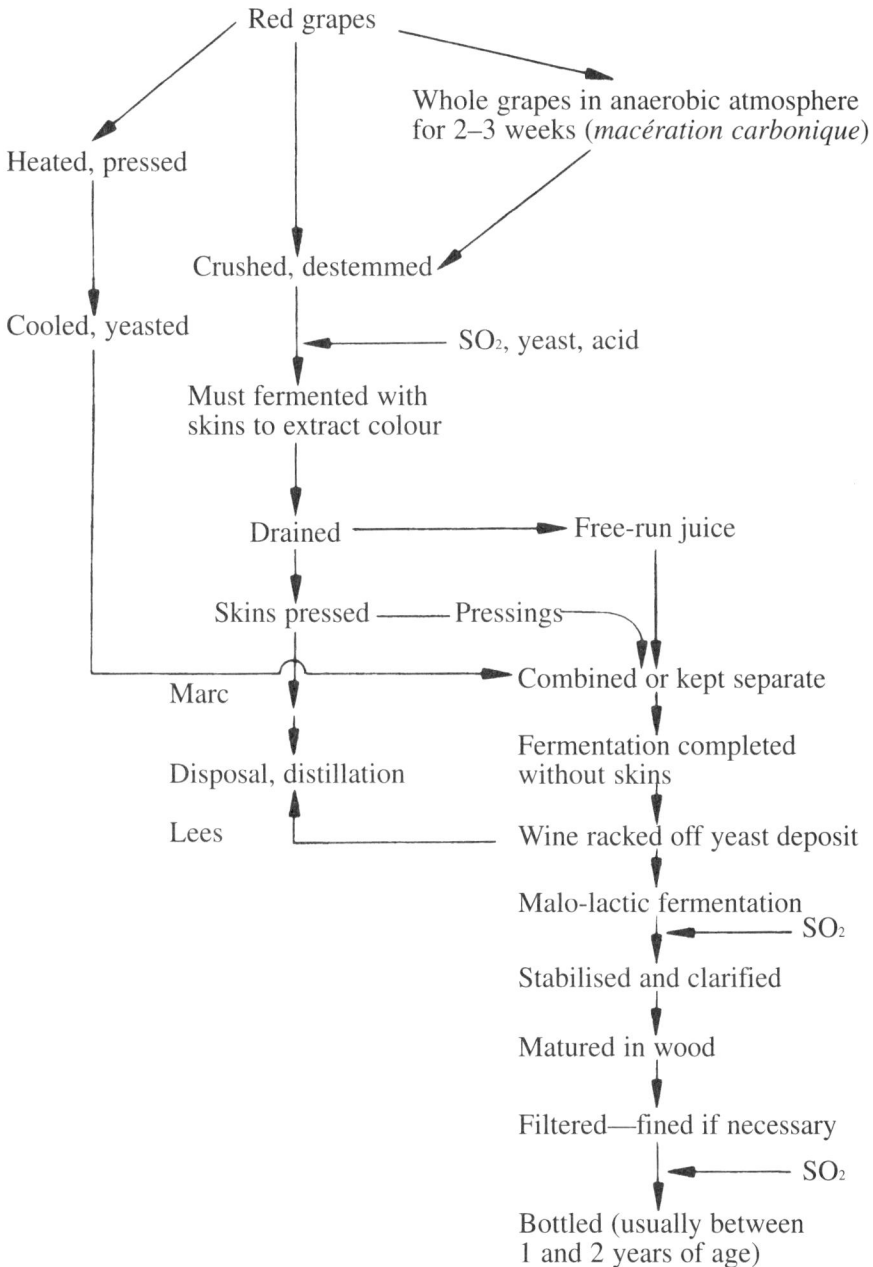

Red grapes

Heated, pressed

Whole grapes in anaerobic atmosphere
for 2–3 weeks (*macération carbonique*)

Crushed, destemmed

Cooled, yeasted

SO₂, yeast, acid

Must fermented with
skins to extract colour

Drained ⟶ Free-run juice

Skins pressed ⸻ Pressings

Marc

Combined or kept separate

Disposal, distillation

Fermentation completed
without skins

Lees

Wine racked off yeast deposit

Malo-lactic fermentation

SO₂

Stabilised and clarified

Matured in wood

Filtered—fined if necessary

SO₂

Bottled (usually between
1 and 2 years of age)

- Soil and climate—both can influence the amount of colour present and more colour is developed in cool climates. In very cool climates, such as Germany, pigment production is reduced because of inadequate maturity. The year can have a variable influence.

The amount of colour in the juice and the subsequent wine is likewise influenced by various factors:

• Time elapsing between harvesting and crushing, and the temperature of the grapes.
• Time on skins after crushing—up to a certain point the longer the time of contact with the skins, the more colour is released in the juice.
• Presence of sulphur dioxide—the effect here is complicated in that sulphur dioxide encourages colour extraction from skins and bleaches the colour temporarily.
• Presence of various finings and cold stabilisation.
• Phenoloxidase activity—tending to brown the wine.

The most important treatment to remove colour is the use of active carbon. There are many carbon products on the market and they vary considerably in their effectiveness in removing the anthocyanin pigments from juice or wine. This means that wine treated with carbon may turn pink in time as anthocyanins are released from their combination with sulphur dioxide. Other treatments can be used to marginally reduce the colour of red wines, such as addition of bentonite, PVPP, gelatin and other finings, but these cannot be relied on to produce a white wine from red wine.

White wines made by carbon treatment of red grapes are quite variable in quality and can be useful wines. At least one wine has reportedly won a gold medal, but this quality is unusual. The wines are normally blended with white wine and used as a sparkling wine base or as standard white wines. The procedure is not regarded as a desirable long-term practice for producing quality wines.

We are not referring here to pink or blush wines, which are carefully made to retain a pink colour in the wine. An example is the recent growth of pink sparkling wines, which have created a place in the market and can be of excellent quality.

Sparkling wines

Sparkling wines are those surcharged with carbon dioxide. They do not include the slightly effervescent or spritzig wines. Sparkling wines at present comprise about 9 per cent of the total annual sales of wine produced in Australia. The demand for bottle-fermented sparkling wine, which is regarded as the finest quality, has doubled in the last four years, and there is currently much interest in its production.

The Food Act and regulations in the various Australian states recognise and define three types of sparkling wine:

• Champagne. This wine must be produced by the traditional method of fermentation in a bottle of less than 5 litres capacity and aged on the yeast deposit for not less than 6 months. The word 'champagne' (and other European place names) cannot be used for wines designated for export.

- Sparkling wine. This is a wine which by complete or partial fermentation of the sugar content has become surcharged with carbon dioxide and to which sugar and wine spirit may have been added.
- Carbonated wine. This is a wine to which carbon dioxide has been added from any source, other than by its own fermentation, in excess of 100 kilopascals gauge pressure.

The grape varieties used to produce the various types of sparkling wine depend on the price of the product and the price and availability of the variety. In the production of quality sparkling wines made by fermentation-in-bottle, the classical varieties in Champagne are Pinot Noir, Chardonnay and Pinot Meunier. In Australia other varieties such as Semillon, Ondenc, Sultana, Chenin Blanc, Muscadelle, Pedro Ximenez, Palomino, Colombard, Crouchen, Riesling and Trebbiano are also used, as well as red grapes, such as Shiraz, Grenache and Cabernet Sauvignon. These grape varieties at maturity are required to produce delicate and firmly acid wines which have a fruity aroma and flavour (although not necessarily varietal) complementing the bouquet and flavour developed by the secondary fermentation and storage on yeast.

The most desirable grape varieties being developed in Australia for quality bottle-fermented sparkling wines which are to be matured in bottle are Chardonnay and Pinot Noir grown in cool localities. The use of Pinot Meunier is debatable—it is used as a 'softener' in France but this is less relevant here. The lack of high-quality Pinot Noir is more important, particularly when compared with Chardonnay. Many wines made from these classical varieties tend to be disgorged and sold prematurely.

The bulk-fermented and carbonated wines are usually intended for quick maturation and are made from a range of varieties, such as Muscat Gordo Blanco, Crouchen, Sultana, Semillon, Trebbiano, Shiraz and Grenache. They are produced in a wide range of styles, from light vinous character to strong muscat flavour with sugar levels varying from 10 to 80 grams per litre. To balance this sweetness they require an acidity of between 6 and 8 grams per litre and must be clean and delicate.

In France, sparkling burgundy is a lighter style with less sweetness, and is made from Pinot Noir. The sugar content of the grapes at harvest is normally between 11 and 13° Baumé (19.8 and 23.4° Brix). The same wine style in Australia requires a soft, fruity base wine with tannin in the middle palate rather than at the finish. The grape varieties best suited for this style are Shiraz (by far the main variety) and Pinot Noir, and for blending into quick-maturing styles Cinsaut and Grenache.

Fermentation-in-bottle

These wines can be made in two ways, viz. *méthode champenoise* and transfer. The first is essentially the classical French method of making sparkling wine in Champagne, and involves the following operations:

1 Pressing the grapes at 9 to 11° Baumé (16.2 to 19.8° Brix) without crushing, which minimises colour pick-up from red grapes and tannin from the skins of white grapes. The aim is to extract the juice from the grapes with minimum maceration of the fruit. In Champagne the best-quality *cuvée* (blend of base wine) is restricted to about 510 litres of free-run juice per tonne. A desirable pH for Chardonnay juice in Australia is 2.9 to 3.3 with a titratable acidity of 9 to 11 grams per litre.

2 Settling (*débourbage*) involving clarification of the juice with removal of the solids by racking, followed if necessary by centrifuging or filtration. The suspended solids are normally less than 0.2 gram per litre.

3 Fermentation with the use of a selected yeast at between 11 and 14°C. In France, chaptalisation by the addition of sugar (sucrose) is permitted by law. Fermentation is usually complete in 10 to 14 days, and bentonite at a rate of 0.1 to 0.25 gram per litre is added during the primary fermentation, together with 50 to 100 milligram per litre of diammonium phosphate.

4 Blending (*assemblage* and *coupage*) involving racking and blending wines from different varieties and areas to produce the required style of base wine.

5 Fining (*collage*) usually with isinglass or gelatin.

6 Cold stabilisation.

7 Sugar addition (*tirage liqueur*) involving the addition of cane sugar at a level of 19 to 26 grams per litre, depending on the alcohol content and pressure required—the higher the alcohol and the greater the pressure required, the more sugar needs to be added. For example, to obtain a pressure of 600 kPa (6 Bar, 87 psig or 6.0 atmospheres gauge pressure) 23 grams per litre of sugar are required in a base wine containing 9 per cent of alcohol, and 26 grams per litre for a base wine containing 12 per cent. The wine at this stage normally contains between 9 and 11 per cent by volume of alcohol with a pH of 2.9 to 3.3. Details are set out in the table below:

Alcohol % v/v	Sugar (grams per litre) required to obtain		
	5.0 atm	*5.5 atm*	*6.0 atm (gauge)*
9	19	21	23
10	20	22	24
11	21	23	25
12	22	24	26

For most purposes the following approximations relating to pressure of carbon dioxide at 20°C, can be used:

1 volume = 1 atmosphere = 1 Bar = 100 kilopascals = 14.5 pounds per square gauge pressure = 2 grams of carbon dioxide per litre.

8 Yeast addition (*levurage*) involving the addition of a selected yeast (see below).

9 Bottling (*tirage*) in which the wine with tirage liqueur (sugar and wine) and yeast added is bottled, crown sealed and stored.

10 Stacking (*entreillage*) in which the bottles are stacked horizontally for a period of time ranging from six months up to several years, depending on the quality of the wine, at a temperature of 12 to 15°C.

11 Shaking (*rémuage*) in which the bottles are stacked on to shaking tables (*pupitres*), settled then twisted back and forth a few turns daily during a period of several weeks to bring the yeast deposit down against the crown seal of the inverted bottle.

12 Removal of sediment (*dégorgement*) in which the wine in the neck of the bottle is chilled to about minus 24°C, the bottle then inverted right-way up, the crown seal removed and the frozen plug of yeast blown out of the bottle by the pressure of carbon dioxide.

13 Sweetening (*dosage*) and topping up (*remplissage*) in which the loss of volume resulting from removing the frozen yeast sediment is made up by both the addition of a uniform quantity of expedition liqueur (sugar dissolved in the base wine in a concentration of between 63 and 75 per cent), and more of the same wine. The expedition liqueur may also contain other constituents, such as brandy up to about 5 per cent by volume, sulphur dioxide up to 50 mg per litre, ascorbic acid up to 100 mg per litre, citric acid up to 500 mg per litre, copper up to 0.5 mg per litre and metartaric acid up to 100 mg per litre. Originally 'brut' on the label meant without expedition liqueur and therefore dry. Nowadays, wines labelled 'brut', 'extra sec' or 'extra dry' contain a dosage of 1 to 2 per cent sugar or 10 to 20 grams per litre, and 'sec' or 'dry' contain 2 to 4 per cent.

14 Corking (*bourbage*) usually with an agglomerate cork with one or more discs of high-quality cork in contact with the wine.

15 Wiring (*muselet*) in which a wire cap is tied over the cork to prevent it from blowing out.

16 Shaking to mix the viscous expedition liqueur with the wine.

17 Washing to clean the outside of the bottle.

18 Dressing (*habillage*), which consists of placing the foil cap over the *muselet* and securing it in position, and labelling.

Primary fermentation

The following now applies to Australian conditions. The wine should be made with as much care as possible to retain flavour and aroma and to prevent oxidation. To assist in achieving this the juice and the wine should have a pH between 2.9 and 3.3. Sulphur dioxide is particularly effective at these pH levels and should be used sparingly with not more than 50 milligrams per litre added prior to fermentation. Addition of ascorbic or erythorbic acid (up to 50 mg per litre) may be made before fermentation but is more effective afterwards. The juice is best cold-settled with pectic enzyme and earth-filtered, and diammonium phosphate (200–400 mg per litre) is usually added.

To bring about the fermentation makers normally use a yeast strain selected specifically for fermenting the sparkling wine base, to ensure complete fermentation and absence of volatile acid and hydrogen sulphide. The temperature of fermentation should be controlled at 15°C or less to secure a Baumé reduction of half a degree per day, and towards the end of fermentation the wine allowed to warm to a maximum of 20°C to ensure fermentation to dryness.

Colour pick-up from red grapes, such as Pinot Noir, is minimised by maturity control at harvest and minimum skin contact during processing, and is removed by carbon (up to 1.0 gram per litre) or PVPP (up to 0.5 gram per litre). Bentonite (up to 1.0 gram per litre) is normally added towards the end of the fermentation and further assists in colour removal. After fermentation all operations should be carried out under inert gas. The wine is then partially clarified, usually by centrifugation, to remove the yeast deposit and then cold-stabilised. The free sulphur dioxide should be as low as possible, preferably less than 20 mg per litre.

Secondary fermentation

The yeast used is selected on the following basis:

- The ability to tolerate free sulphur dioxide and low pH at inoculation, which in conjunction with the alcohol already in the base wine is a rather lethal combination to the yeast.
- The ability to ferment the wine to dryness at 10 to 15°C under pressure of carbon dioxide of 6 to 7 atmospheres at an alcohol content of 10 to 11 per cent.
- The ability to flocculate after fermentation leaving the wine clear.
- Absence of off-odours, particularly hydrogen sulphide and volatile acidity, which are accentuated in the wine when it is charged with carbon dioxide.

The sugar addition is calculated to produce a desired pressure of carbon dioxide on the basis that approximately 4 grams per litre produces 1 atmosphere of carbon dioxide. The normal pressure in bottle-fermented sparkling wine is approximately 6 atmospheres (5.9 bar, 88 psig or 608 kPa), which is equivalent to 8.4 grams per litre of carbon dioxide at 20°C and requires the addition of 26 grams per litre of sugar to a dry wine containing 11 per cent alcohol.

The normal temperature of fermentation is between 10 and 16°C in Australia and between 11 and 14°C in the Champagne district of France. The duration of fermentation is related to temperature and is normally 4–6 weeks. The fermentation is required to go to dryness in bottle fermentation, and the alcohol produced by this secondary fermentation to yield 8 grams per litre of carbon dioxide is 1.0 per cent by volume.

The solubility of carbon dioxide in grams per litre relates to both pressure and temperature, as shown in the table below:

Pressure (atmospheres)	0°C	10°C	20°C
1	2.5	2.0	1.5
2	5.0	3.8	3.0
3	7.4	5.6	4.4
4	9.7	7.4	5.8
5	11.9	9.0	7.2
6	14.0	10.7	8.4

If the wine contains 6 volumes of carbon dioxide the gauge pressure varies with temperature as follows: 0°C 38 psig, 10°C 86 psig and 20°C 100 psig.

The primary fermentation reduces the quantity of yeast nutrients in the wine and it is usual to make an addition of 50 to 200 milligrams per litre of diammonium phosphate before the secondary fermentation. Yeasts require vitamins of the B group—biotin, inositol and thiamine—but since enough are normally present it is not usual to make an addition. Commercial vitamin preparations are available for this purpose, if required.

The yeast culture should be prepared with aeration to obtain the maximum percentage of viable cells, which in a wine–sugar medium is of the order of 100 to 150 million cells per millilitre. The volume of yeast suspension added should be such as to yield about 1 to 1.5 million cells per millilitre in the bottle.

After addition of sugar, yeast and nutrients the wine is bottled and sealed with a crown cap and the wine put away for fermentation and storage on the yeast deposit. Riddling agents may also be added, and comprise isinglass (5–60 mg per litre), bentonite (20–150 mg per litre), alginate (5–25 mg per litre) and tannin (5–50 mg per litre) in some combination. The bottles may be stacked horizontally or vertically, and the temperature of storage is normally about 15°C. When the bottles are ready for yeast removal, various methods may be used to shake the yeast down onto the bottom of the crown cap of the inverted bottle. This can be done by hand which is an expensive operation, since although one person can shake about 1500 dozen bottles per day each bottle has to be shaken twice per day for twenty days, and this currently costs in time at least a dollar a bottle.

Various mechanical devices and shaking tables have been evolved to carry out this operation mechanically. The 'gyro-palette', for example, has been developed to reproduce the manual shaking operation, and consists of a cage containing a pallet of inverted bottles which undergoes a pre-set series of movements to bring the yeast deposit down on to the bottom of the crown cap.

Disgorging

Disgorging is a skilful operation when carried out manually, but the normal practice is to chill the wine to between 5 and 10°C, then freeze the neck of the bottle in a calcium chloride bath at about minus 24°C. This freezes the yeast plug in a small volume of wine, and this plug is discharged when the cork is removed mechanically. After removing the yeast plug, the wines receive a dosage of sweetening, with sometimes citric and ascorbic acids and brandy spirit, as well as more of the same wine to top up the bottle. Sulphur dioxide up to 20 mg per litre free may also be added if the wine is to be conserved for a period before drinking. This is followed by corking, wiring on the cork, then washing and dressing the bottle if it is not going to be binned before labelling. The corks now used in Australia are usually 47.5 mm long by 30.5 mm diameter and consist of a body of agglomerated cork with two discs of high-quality cork at the end in contact with the wine. It is important to shake the bottle after the liqueur has been added since it is of greater specific gravity and will form a lower layer unless mixed.

The transfer system

The ultimate quality of any bottle-fermented sparkling wine is not the result of the method used in disgorging, but the quality of the base wine and the period of maturation on yeast lees. In Australia today most of the bottle-fermented champagne is disgorged by the transfer process. The origin of the transfer process is unclear, but appears to have been developed in the USA about the turn of this century.

In this process, the cold-stabilised base wine is fermented in bottle as for the *méthode champenoise*, and stored on its lees for a legal minimum of six months. At this stage the wine has a pressure of about 11 grams per litre of carbon dioxide at 20°C or 525 kilopascals. The bottles are then removed from their storage bins and placed on a conveyor, which transports them to the transfer machine (Winterwerb Streng). The contents of both wine and yeast cells are removed by inserting a hollow spear through the crown seal of the bottle, which is then inverted and 200 kilopascals of carbon dioxide overpressure applied to force the wine out of the bottle through a port in the base of the spear. It is then chilled in-line to a pressure tank, from which all air has been removed by filling it with water and replacing the water with carbon dioxide. The bottles are automatically decrowned and washed ready for refilling, and the excess carbon dioxide used to empty the bottles is compressed, sterile filtered and reused, with the result that once the process is underway there is no need for external gas.

After fermentation and storage of the wine on its yeast deposit, the cold wine is removed by centrifugation and/or earth-filtration into a second pressure tank, which has previously been filled with carbon dioxide to a pressure of 200 kilopascals. A further analysis is carried out to check the levels of free sulphur dioxide (20 to 25 mg per litre), pH (less than 3.2), residual sugar (as required), pressure (480 to 550 kilopascals) and temperature (about minus 2 to 0°C).

The tank contents are then chilled to about 0°C to maintain the dissolved carbon dioxide and the pressure is approximately 400 kilopascals. The expedition liqueur is placed in the tank before transfer, the quantity being calculated from the number of bottles to be filled and the sweetness of wine being produced. The liqueur is mixed with the wine by a built-in stirrer, and the wine then left to stand to enable the yeast to settle.

The final operation is to rebottle the wine in the absence of air. From the bottling tank the wine is sterile-filtered through a pad or membrane filter into the filling machine operating at a pressure of 400 kilopascals at 0°C. The machine prefills the bottles with carbon dioxide, venting the displaced air from the bottle to atmosphere, and the cold wine is run into the bottles which are then corked and dressed.

The transfer process has the advantages of the wine receiving a uniform dosage of sugar, bottling under uniform pressure, having a predictable production rate because of minimum handling, and saving of space in storage. It has the disadvantages of the transfer equipment being expensive, and the possibility of contact with oxygen if air is not excluded from the tanks before filling. The most effective way to eliminate air is to fill the tanks with water and blow out the water with carbon dioxide, thus ensuring an oxygen-free atmosphere.

Ageing of sparkling wine on yeast is regarded as an important part of the maturation process for wines fermented in the bottle, and is recognised by legislation in various countries. In France, for example, a storage time of twelve months is required for normal Champagne, three years for vintage Champagne and nine months for *crémant*. The autolysis process is complex and involves the liberation of many nitrogenous and other compounds by the yeast, as well as subsequent readsorption in some cases. During the primary fermentation these nitrogenous compounds are assimilated by the yeast. Subsequent autolysis is more rapid as the storage temperature is raised. The most rapid rate of autolysis is about 55°C and pH 5, and yeast strains differ in their proteolytic activity and autolysis rate. The addition of a prepared autolysate to the base wine has been carried out and can result in similar products to that obtained by normal bottle fermentation and storage, except when the autolysate is prepared from baker's yeast. Some wines prepared by addition of a prepared autolysate scored well when compared to wines made by the traditional process.

Tank fermentation

The tank or bulk process was developed by Eugène Charmat in 1910 in France, but has been so altered and improved that the present method bears little resemblance to the original. The process requires the use of pressure tanks capable of withstanding 6 to 8 atmospheres gauge pressure.

The base wine is prepared as for bottle-fermented sparkling wine, and has the following composition:

free sulphur dioxide	15–20 mg per litre
pH	3.2 or below
titratable acidity	7.0
reducing sugar	2.0 or less grams per litre

volatile acid   0.5 or less grams per litre
heat and cold stable

The base wine is then pumped into a pressure tank, which has been previously filled with water and emptied by displacing the water with carbon dioxide to eliminate air from the tank (other methods are not as effective). Sugar (20 grams per litre) and yeast (at least 2 million viable cells per millilitre) are added. The sugar is prepared as a concentrated syrup containing 700 grams per litre, and the calculated amount to provide 20 grams per litre is added. For 50,000 litres of wine the calculation is simply 50,000 multiplied by 20 and divided by 700, which equals 1430 litres. The yeast is a selected strain, usually *Saccharomyces cerevisiae*, and is propagated in a sterile base wine with added sugar and continuous aeration to achieve approximately 150 million cells per millilitre.

The wine then ferments to dryness (about 1.5 grams per litre of sugar) at 12 to 15°C in the tank with the relief valve closed so that the pressure of carbon dioxide builds up to approximately 500 kilopascals. It is then chilled by means of a cooling jacket to between minus 2 and 0°C. The pressure falls to about 400 kilopascals due to the greater solubility of carbon dioxide at that temperature. The yeast settles over a few days and this assists the subsequent filtration. During this time a second pressure tank is prepared free from air and pressurised to 200 kilopascals with carbon dioxide.

The wine is then centrifuged and earth-filtered to this second pressure tank which already contains the sweetening material or expedition liqueur. This consists of sugar, sulphur dioxide and ascorbic or erythorbic acid. The sugar added depends on the sweetness required in the wine, while the free sulphur dioxide level is adjusted to between 20 and 25 mg per litre. Acid (citric) may be added. The contents are mixed by a built-in stirrer to ensure uniformity, and the wine is maintained at minus 2°C. At this stage the wine is analysed for sulphur dioxide (free and total), residual sugar, acidity (pH and titratable acid), alcohol, heat and cold stability, ascorbate and viable yeast count. Final adjustments are made at this stage.

The wine is then delivered to the final filter of sterile pads or 0.45 micrometer pore-size membranes, by either the pressure of carbon dioxide (by adjusting the head pressure in the pressure tank to between 400 and 450 kilopascals) or a centrifugal pump capable of 200 kilopascals delivery pressure. Coupled with the head pressure in the tank of 200 kilopascals, this results in a delivery pressure at the filter of 400 kilopascals. The wine displacement from the pressure tank during emptying is replaced with carbon dioxide, not air.

The process involves three transfers, each into an air-free vessel. All transfer operations are carried out in the cold at 0°C or below, so as to retain the required level of dissolved carbon dioxide. Tank-process wines are usually white and have the following general composition:

Alcohol per cent by volume	10–11.5
Titratable acidity grams per litre	6–7
pH	3.0–3.3
Free sulphur dioxide mg per litre	10–20
Volatile acid grams per litre less than	0.5

Sweetness depends on the wine type and is usually between 10 and 30 grams per litre.

The tank process can be used to make sparkling wines continuously, a development pioneered in the Soviet Union. The process involves continuous addition of wine, yeast and liqueur, and the product is bottled continuously. As a matter of interest the deoxygenated base wine is heated to 40°C for 24 hours to increase the flavour and aroma (the original Charmat process included a heating stage for the base wine). The wines which I have tasted do not compare well with Australian wines made in batch-process tank fermentations, but since the base wines were not the same this comparison is scarcely valid.

Carbonation

Carbonation is the process used for producing inexpensive sparkling wines of the 'spumante' type. The procedure is as follows:

The base wine is carefully made as set out earlier, stabilised against cold, protein and other possible instability and filtered as if it were ready for bottling as a table wine. The analyses should be in the following range:

Free sulphur dioxide	25–30 mg per litre
pH	less than 3.3
Titratable acidity	6.5–8.0 grams per litre
Alcohol	approx. 10 per cent by volume
Sugar (as required)	40–100 grams per litre

It is then chilled at 0°C in a tank under carbon dioxide cover to avoid contact with atmospheric oxygen and passed through a carbonator (saturator), under the pressure of carbon dioxide required in the bottle. The carbonator is usually a long vertical cylinder in which the chilled wine and carbon dioxide are mixed counter-currently, with baffles to increase the turbulence and result in a more intimate contact of the gas with the wine. The flow rate, wine temperature and pressure of carbon dioxide are adjusted to obtain the desired pressure of carbon dioxide.

The wine may then either be sterile-filtered and bottled directly with a counter-pressure filler or passed to a pressure tank where it is stored with stirring for a few days then filtered and bottled. The latter encourages retention of the carbon dioxide in the wine.

Unfortunately, due to the need to keep costs down, many carbonated wines are not of high quality, and this usually reflects the quality of the base wine. For carbonated wines of poor quality the process usually receives the blame, and hence carbonation is seen as an inferior process. In fact, carbonation is a safe and reliable method for producing sparkling wines, providing that the base wines are clean and fresh, and the carbon dioxide used is free from taints. Oxidation and lack of freshness in the base wines is the most important problem in carbonated wines in Australia.

For further information on the various systems for producing sparkling wines, see *Sparkling Wines. The Technology of their Production in Australia* by David Armstrong, Bryce Rankine and Geoff Linton, Winetitles, Adelaide, 1994.

Bottle sizes
The following bottle sizes are used for sparkling wines:

Pint	375 mL
Quart	750 mL
Magnum	1.5 L
Jeroboam	3.0 L
Rehoboam	4.5 L
Methuselar	6.0 L
Salmanazar	9.0 L
Balthasar	12.0 L
Nebuchadnezzar	15.0 L

These bottles are coloured dark green, amber or brown to prevent the passage of ultraviolet radiation (wavelength below 300 millimicrons) into the wine, which results in undesirable flavour changes.

Fortified wines

Fortified wines are those which have alcohol added during making. In California they are referred to as dessert wines. Australia and New Zealand have a history of producing fortified aperitif (wines drunk before a meal) and dessert wines, and Australia in particular has made and does still make some of the finest of such wines in the world. With the increase in quality of table wines and their introduction in relatively inexpensive and convenient table casks, the market for fortified wines has greatly decreased. In 1960 a total of 66 per cent of all wines made in Australia were fortified, whereas in 1987 this figure was down to 12 per cent. A similar decrease has taken place in New Zealand.

The production of wines with added alcohol is widespread in warm wine-growing areas, particularly in the Mediterranean basin. The initial reason was to conserve sweetness in the wine by stopping the fermentation with added alcohol, hence the term fortified. However, the process of fortification and the type of alcohol used enabled special wines to be made, which now span a broad spectrum in types and sweetness. The alcohol content of such wines is usually between 17 and 19 per cent by volume. Surprisingly, it is possible to produce wines containing this amount of alcohol without fortification, by continued incremental additions of sugar during fermentation. This method is termed syruped fermentation and has been practised commercially in some cold wine-growing regions, such as Canada. However, technical and microbiological problems have restricted its continued use.

In producing fortified wines the climatic requirement is a hot, dry summer, which produces grapes with high sugar and low acid. The higher the sugar content, the less alcohol needs to be added, and thus the lower the production cost. Grape varietal characteristics are less important than in table wines, and high-yielding standard varieties are normally used. With the exception of a few varieties, such as the Muscats and Tokay, the flavours of these wines are developed by processing and oxidative maturation, rather than by the use of specific varieties. The sweetness of the grapes should be as high as possible, and grapes in excess of 14° Baumé are sought—in certain areas, such as Rutherglen, 20° Baumé is not uncommon.

Processing is straightforward and essentially oxidative. The grapes are harvested, sulphur dioxide added to about 100 milligrams per litre together with tartaric acid to correct any deficiency in acidity, and the grapes destemmed and crushed. The yeast strain used to conduct the fermentation is selected for its ability to ensure a rapid fermentation under warm conditions, to tolerate high sugar content in the must and not to produce off-flavours. Fermentation may or may not be carried out on skins, depending on the wine type (dry sherries are fermented off-skins), at temperatures ranging from 15 to 25°C. The must is normally allowed to ferment to between 8 and 10° Baumé (14.4 and 18° Brix), depending on the sweetness required in the final wine; then the partially fermented juice is drained off the skins and fortified. The pressings are usually added back to the juice. Some wines are produced from must which has not or scarcely begun to ferment, so that all of the sweetness is retained, but since more alcohol is required for fortification these wines are more costly to produce.

Bentonite may be added during fermentation to remove heat-unstable protein, but more usually it is added immediately after fortification, when the temperature is higher, as a result of the heat produced by the chemical reaction between the added alcohol and the wine. This higher temperature increases the effectiveness of the bentonite treatment. The wine is then racked off gross lees, tasted and its composition checked and pH adjusted to 3.4 to 3.8 and total sulphur dioxide to 50 to 80 ppm. The wine is then matured in used rather than expensive new oak casks, since obvious oak flavour and aroma are not normally required. Some of the very sweet dessert wines from Rutherglen made from Muscat and Tokay have higher pH values, because of the prolonged maturation of the grapes on the vine. Dessert wines normally require acid addition, which is best made before fermentation rather than afterwards. As a rule of thumb, an addition of 1 gram per litre of tartaric acid lowers the pH by about 0.1 of a unit. After maturation in casks (or in stainless steel or waxed concrete storage for the bulk wines) the wines are blended, and this is one of the skills associated with their making. Some winemakers blend wines of different years (as well as within years), since these tend to mature at different rates, and blending minimises these differences.

Sherry

The word sherry derives from the name of the town from whence the wine type originated—Jerez de la Frontera in the south of Spain, inland from Cadiz—and consists of a range of aperitif wines ranging in sweetness from dry to quite sweet. The Spanish terms *fino*, *amontillado* and *oloroso*, indicating increasing levels of sweetness and extract, are still used in Australia. From the viewpoint of a complex succession of microbiological events, cask maturation and complicated blending, flor sherry ranks as one of the world's remarkable wines. Its original production in Spain, and later in Australia and elsewhere, has resulted in distinctive wines conforming to a clearly recognisable style.

Flor sherry. The word flor derives from the Spanish term *la flor* (the flower), meaning the growth of a film on the surface of the wine, which is referred to by local winemakers as 'the flowering of the wine'. Originally flor sherry production in Australia closely reflected Spanish practices. The Spanish grape varieties Palomino (Listan) and Pedro Ximenez were planted, flor yeasts capable of growing on the surface of the wine in partially filled casks were imported from Spain from 1908 onwards, and some solera-blending systems (see below) were established. The main differences in production were the use of selected pure flor-yeast cultures instead of the naturally occurring microflora, and relatively little use of gypsum (calcium sulphate) for plastering to increase acidity. The wines conformed more or less to accepted Spanish styles. However, there was a difference—flor sherry was usually not the only wine type made in the winery. This meant that the winemaker and cellar staff had to divide their time among a range of wine types requiring different handling methods and microbiological control.

Consequently, some flor sherry was not as good as it should have been. The main faults were oxidation, bacterial growth and low flor character. At that time (1930s to 1950s), flor sherry was important enough to the Australian wine industry for a major investigation to be initiated into its production. The resulting investigation (by J.C.M. Fornachon) was a landmark—the process was dissected, and the principles and practices defined, with the overall result of better sherries, at a time when demand for the wine was high.

Australia has thus had a tradition of making sherries—dry, medium and sweet—and has made many outstanding wines. These are the hardest fortified wines to make, especially flor sherry. For this style of wine the grape varieties are best harvested at between 10 and 11° Baumé (18 and 19.8° Brix) to conserve natural acidity and balance, otherwise the resulting wine is too broad, flabby and coarse. The flor sherry base wine is clean, vinous and neutral, and is produced in the same manner as a dry white table wine, using free-run juice, minimal sulphur dioxide (less than 50 mg per litre at the crusher) and cool fermentation. Ascorbic acid should not be added since it prevents subsequent flor growth. The pH of the wine should be in the range of 3.0 and 3.4. The young wine is stabilised with bentonite, either during fermentation or after first racking, and the fermentation is carried out to completion at 10 to 18°C. The pressings are normally kept separate for use producing non-flor dry sherry.

Surface-film growth in cask. Flor sherry is made in three stages—the first being to produce the base wine, as set out above. The second is to grow the flor yeast as a surface film or as a submerged aerated culture on or in the lightly fortified base wine; and the third and final stage is to mature the finished and refortified wine in cask. For surface growth in casks, the wine is first lightly fortified to 15 per cent alcohol by volume with neutral rectified spirit (containing approximately 95 per cent of alcohol by volume), pumped into oak casks (usually hogsheads) leaving about 20 per cent ullage space, and then inoculated on the surface with a selected sherry flor yeast. The casks are lightly bunged with cotton wool to allow air transfer but to keep out vinegar flies, and allowed to stand at a constant temperature in the range of 15 to 22°C.

The Spanish process makes use of the *solera* fractional blending system of maturation, in which casks holding wines on flor are stacked in layers one above the other. Each layer contains wine of a different year, with the youngest on top, the next youngest immediately below it and so on. These soleras and their associated criaderas, or initial soleras, can comprise many stages and can be quite complicated in operation, and are best explained by using a simple three-stage solera as an example. Usually twice a year about one-third of the wine in each of the casks on the bottom layer holding the oldest wine on flor is removed and blended. This wine is then fortified to about 18 per cent alcohol by volume, sweetened if required with wood-aged fortified must or sweet sherry, and further matured in casks, usually in another solera system. The spaces left in this layer of casks are then filled with wine from the next and younger layer directly above, with some of each cask being distributed into all of the casks of the bottom layer. Then the spaces in these second-layer casks are filled in the same manner with wine from the top layer containing the youngest wine on flor. Finally, the spaces in the top layer are filled with freshly fortified base wine from the current vintage. The wines are all under the flor film and care is taken not to disturb the film more than necessary during these transfers.

The result of all these individual blending operations is a remarkably uniform final blend, and this careful and continuous blending is the main feature of the Spanish system. The amount of manual labour is considerable, and where the solera system is used in Australia, it is modified to omit the many individual transfers. The average age of the wine in the various stages becomes constant after some years, depending on the number of stages. The age of a wine in the final stage of a four-stage solera becomes constant after about ten years, while the wine in an eight-stage solera requires about twenty years. It is sad that the demand for this type of wine is decreasing to the point where its production is becoming uneconomical and some of the high-quality sherries of former years are no longer available.

Tank production by surface-film growth. To achieve faster film growth, an Australian development has been to grow the yeast film on the base wine in shallow tanks of about 2 metres depth, closed but for a small ventilation hole covered with fine wire mesh (to prevent entry of *Drosophila* or vinegar fly). The main purpose of the cover is to prevent loss of alcohol by evaporation. The base wine is a stabilised filter-sterilised dry white wine made from Palomino and/or Pedro grapes, with alcohol increased by fortification to 15.0 per cent by volume, and with a pH of 3.0 to 3.4 and total sulphur dioxide less than 50 milligrams per litre.

Flor yeast is sprayed on to the surface with an atomiser or layered from another established film, and allowed to grow for six to ten weeks at a temperature of 15 to 22°C. By this time the wine with a depth of not more than about a metre has achieved sufficient flor character, as assessed by tasting and measuring the acetaldehyde content, which should be between 150 and 300 milligrams per litre. It is then pumped away carefully into maturation hogsheads without disturbing the flor film, and a fresh batch of base wine introduced under the existing film. In some cellars the new base wine is reseeded with yeast.

Various designs are used for covering the shallow waxed concrete tanks, such as building removable sloping roofs or covers. During flor growth, condensate forms on the underside of the sloping roof, and runs down to the edge of the tank and then into the wine. If the roof is not sloped this condensate drops back on the surface of the film breaking its continuity. The alcohol content of the condensate is usually between 15 and 20 per cent by volume.

The wine removed from the flor film is then filtered, fortified, cask-matured, blended, sweetened if required with cask-matured sweet dessert wine, and bottled. The extent of such maturation and blending with other matured wine depends on the market and quality of wine desired. The wine produced is of good quality, but not generally as fine as that made by flor growth in cask.

Submerged-culture sherry production. Industrial fermentations commencing with surface-culture growth of microorganisms frequently develop into submerged aerated culture. This is so, for example, with antibiotic and vinegar production and now with flor sherry production, particularly in California where the bulk of flor sherry now made is produced by submerged culture. Conditions vary widely and the product can contain a very high level of acetaldehyde—up to about 1000 milligrams per litre. Such high levels are neither very palatable nor possibly healthy, and are blended with untreated wine to lower the level. The wines thus produced after fortification and some cask maturation have obvious flor character, but not the sherry character and maturity that comes from prolonged cask maturation under a flor film.

The base wine is prepared as described above and contains between 13.5 and 14.8 per cent alcohol by volume. It is placed in a closed vessel with a *Saccharomyces* yeast—interestingly, not necessarily a flor yeast—and aerated for a period which can range from one to six weeks, at a temperature which may or may not be controlled. Aeration procedures differ between producers and no standard practice appears to exist. In some cases the wine is mixed under air or oxygen pressure, or by using the hydrostatic head of a tall tank to give an average pressure of 12 to 15 psig in the wine. Cavitation systems, where oxygen pressure comes from the physical force of rotating propeller blades, have also been successful.

Submerged aerated yeast growth has the important economic advantage of rapid acetaldehyde accumulation, so that a distinctive wine can be produced quickly. The wines are refreshing and palatable with youthful flor character, but not as matured or rounded as sherries produced by surface film growth, which receive considerable cask maturation.

Column flor growth. Fornachon developed (but did not publish) a process for rapid accumulation of acetaldehyde by passing the base wine for sherry slowly down a stainless-steel column packed with oak chips in which flor yeast grew. It was, in effect, an immobilised yeast column, with adjustable aeration vents (covered with mesh to prevent insect entry) to control the extent of flor growth. The process is being used commercially in Australia with success. The incoming wine is cooled to about 12°C, because yeast metabolism in the column generates considerable heat, and acetaldehyde production of 150 to 300 milligrams per litre is usual. The wine is initially recirculated to establish the required microbiological conditions in the column, then one pass of the wine down the column is sufficient to develop the required flor yeast character on a continuous basis. The wine is then fortified and cask-matured without flor growth for a period which depends on market requirements.

Temperature of flor growth. Temperature has an overriding influence on flor growth, and failure to control it can result in significant reduction in quality through overheating. The optimum temperature range for flor growth is 15 to 22°C, and consistent flor temperature above this range results in poor and untypical wine. Temperature control is particularly relevant in the sherry percolation column, where the wine warms significantly due to the active yeast metabolism during its passage down the column. For this reason such columns are operated in temperature-controlled rooms and the wine is cooled before entry into the column.

Selection of flor yeast. In Australia, flor sherry is essentially made with a pure culture of a selected film yeast. Some yeasts are indigenous to Australia but most derived originally from Spain. The film yeast originally described by Marcilla, Alas and Feduchy in Spain as *Saccharomyces beticus* has been referred to in the literature as *S. bayanus, S. fermentati, S. cerevisiae* and by other species. It was probably the original flor yeast imported into Australia. Various species and strains of *Saccharomyces* can form a stable aerobic film on wine after conducting an alcoholic fermentation, but this ability is not related to their taxonomic classification.

Composition of flor sherry. Modern analyses have revealed the chemical complexity of flor sherry. More than a hundred volatile compounds have been identified resulting from flor growth, comprising substituted lactones, acetals, esters and acetamide derivatives, as well as aldehydes. The main characteristic compounds appear to be aldehydes and acetals. Glycerol decreases under film growth, and cyclic acetals of glycerol have been identified. Some of the ethyl esters of n-hexanoic, n-octanoic and n-decanoic acid formed by film growth may be significant in sherry aroma. The classical method of acetaldehyde measurement is also being superseded by the more rapid and specific enzymatic procedure.

Port

Port is a fortified sweet wine made from red grapes, and derives its name from Porto (or Oporto) in Portugal, near where the grapes (from about seventeen Portuguese varieties) are grown in the Douro valley and where the wine is blended and matured at Vila Nova da Gaia, a suburb of Porto on the southern side of the Douro River.

The varieties normally chosen in Australia for port production are Grenache, Shiraz, Mataro and Cabernet Sauvignon, together with some white varieties, such as Tokay (Muscadelle) to lighten the colour. These differ from those used in Portugal, probably because they are much more widely planted than the Portuguese varieties, and produce the quality of port required by the market. The best wines are made from very sweet grapes in excess of 14° Baumé. The procedure is to destem and crush the grapes, pump the must into open-topped or closed fermenters, add 50 to 80 milligrams per litre of sulphur dioxide, tartaric acid and a selected pure yeast culture, and ferment on skins with pumping over the fermenting must or using heading-down boards. (As a matter of interest the Ducellier process, described under red winemaking, is widely used for making port in Portugal.) Fermentation temperature is normally between 18 and 25° because, if lower, the colour and body of the wine is reduced. The wines are normally taken off-skins at about 9° Baumé and then fortified to approximately 18 per cent by volume to achieve a final sweetness of between 3.5 and 6° Baumé, depending on the style. Australian ports are sweeter than their Portuguese counterparts, which are usually between 3 and 4° Baumé.

Tawny ports are normally blends of wines from different years and matured in cask, and usually fortified with high-strength fortifying spirit. This extended cask maturation results in a lighter colour and complex aroma and flavour. Vintage ports (see below), on the other hand, consist of wines from a single year and are matured for a short time in cask and for a longer time in bottle. They are usually fortified with brandy spirit containing 80 to 83 per cent alcohol by volume, and in Australia are heavier in body and darker in colour than tawny ports.

Fortification on skins is an advantage because the added alcohol assists in extraction of pigment from the skins. The pressings may be added back to the wine in the case of vintage ports where high tannin is desired, or fermented separately to produce cheaper ruby ports for the bulk trade. After fermentation the wines are racked, fined with gelatin if required to remove excess tannin, and selected as to style. Tawny port is the more popular style in Australia and is matured in small oak under warm conditions, such as 20 to 28°C. The wines develop quickest in small wood, such as quarter casks and hogsheads, under hot conditions. When stored in large wooden vats, such as 2000 litre capacity, the wines tend to develop a stale, vatty character.

The pH of both tawny and vintage ports is adjusted to between 3.4 and 3.8 and the alcohol content between 17 and 19 per cent by volume. Sulphur dioxide is measured as total rather than free and is normally between 80 and 150 milligrams per litre. Young ports may be cold-stabilised to precipitate potassium bitartrate and unstable pigment.

Vintage ports are diverse in style and less popular than their tawny counterparts. The grape variety is usually Shiraz because of its bigger body and extract. It is normally fermented for a longer period before being fortified, in order to finish with less sugar in the range of 3.5 to 4.0° Baumé, which corresponds more to the sweetness of the Portuguese vintage ports. However, Australian vintage ports are generally more highly extracted, contain more tannin and colour, and are more robust. They are fortified with brandy spirit to 18 to 20 per cent alcohol by volume and have pH values of about 3.7. Some are not stored in wood at all, being bottled directly from stainless-steel storage. This retains freshness and the wines tend to avoid the big, jammy styles. They may be fined with gelatin to remove excess tannins and then bottled directly without filtration.

Ports in Australia are maintaining their appeal and some very fine wines are produced. These are mainly tawny ports, the best of which show great finesse, complexity and depth of character resulting from long cask maturation. Their vintage port counterparts, on the other hand, are of less appeal, since they are quite high in body and colour and frequently immature and less fruity.

Other fortified wines are produced from various varieties, such as Tokay, Madeira, Muscat and Verdelho, by the methods described above, and generally represent good quality with some outstanding wines. Most wineries produce these wines, partly as a legacy from the fortified wine era, and discovering them is one of the delights of the wine lover. In addition, flavoured fortified wines— the vermouths—are also produced from neutral grape varieties. The character of these wines lies in the complex herbal flavours which they contain, and makes them a popular aperitif style. The dried herbs or the extract of them are imported, usually from Italy, and consist of up to thirty separate ingredients. The vermouths as a group vary in sweetness from dry or nearly so to quite sweet, and from pale gold in colour to deep amber.

Fig. 4.4 gives an example of a flow chart for making sweet fortified wine.

Fig. 4.4: Flow chart for sweet fortified (dessert) winemaking

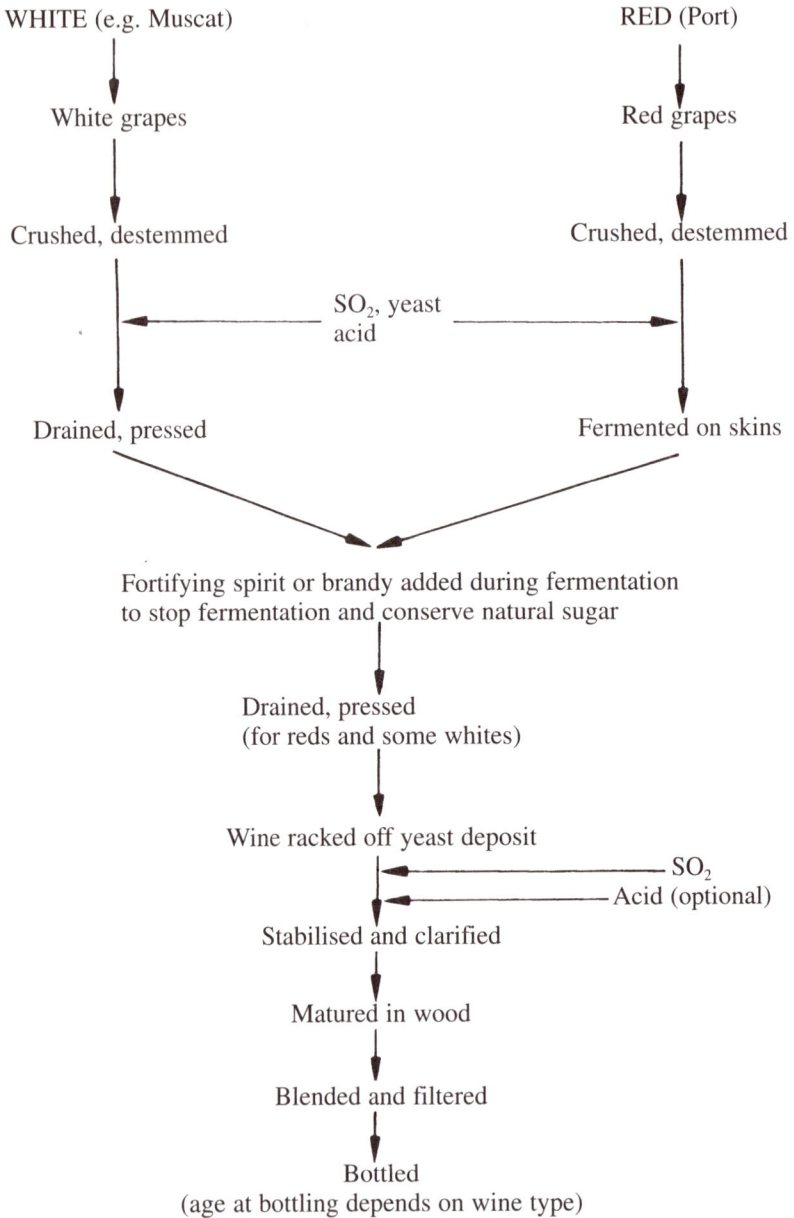

WHITE (e.g. Muscat)   RED (Port)

White grapes   Red grapes

Crushed, destemmed   Crushed, destemmed

SO$_2$, yeast
acid

Drained, pressed   Fermented on skins

Fortifying spirit or brandy added during fermentation
to stop fermentation and conserve natural sugar

Drained, pressed
(for reds and some whites)

Wine racked off yeast deposit

SO$_2$
Acid (optional)

Stabilised and clarified

Matured in wood

Blended and filtered

Bottled
(age at bottling depends on wine type)

Low-alcohol wines

In recent years there has been a demand for fermented beverages containing less than the normal content of alcohol. This applies particularly to wine and beer, and changes have been promulgated in legislation to define such products. The

Australian Food Standards Code 1985 gazetted by each state specifies two types of low-alcohol wines, in addition to normal wine which by definition contains not less than 80 ml per litre at 20°C (i.e. 8 per cent by volume). These are:

- Reduced alcohol wine—wine in which the ethanol content has been reduced by a means other than by dilution with water, so that it contains between 11.5 and 65 millilitres per litre at 20°C of ethanol.
- Non-intoxicating or dealcoholised wine—wine in which ethanol content has been reduced by means other than dilution by the addition of water to an amount not exceeding 11.5 millilitres per litre at 20°C.

The New Zealand Food Regulations 1984 specify low-strength fermented drinks containing not more than 1.7 per cent alcohol, as distinct from general alcoholic drinks which shall contain more than this figure. Other than this no minimum alcohol level for table wines is specified.

The legal requirements both in Australia and in countries to which Australia exports require that the wine must initially be fermented then the alcohol removed. The main problem in producing such wines is to retain the flavour while still removing the alcohol. We are concerned here with producing a low-alcohol wine from a normal wine, as distinct from producing low-alcohol wine from low maturity grapes or by arresting fermentation. One point about arresting fermentation is that the amounts of desirable esters and other flavour compounds produced by the yeast during fermentation are proportional to the amount of alcohol produced, and thus are reduced if the fermentation is arrested.

The main methods are vacuum distillation, and ultrafiltration and reverse osmosis.

Vacuum distillation. This involves distilling or concentrating the wine under vacuum by continuous flow and recovering both the distillate and the dealcoholised wine. The wine can then be blended with grape juice to increase the flavour. The high-vacuum low-temperature concentrators employing centrifugal, climbing or falling film evaporation are normally employed at a temperature of 30 to 40°C with a short contact time (a few seconds for the centrifugal concentrators). Also a distillation column operating under vacuum can be employed. The lower the temperature, the less flavour degradation of the wine occurs, and the shorter the heating time, the less is the possibility of undesirable hydroxy-methyl-furfural formation, which requires about 20 minutes at 80°C.

This high-vacuum low-temperature treatment enables efficient removal of the alcohol, which can then be incorporated into other products. From the viewpoint of wine quality this treatment is less severe than distillation at atmospheric pressure, in which the wine is exposed to a temperature of approximately 100°C for 20 to 30 minutes. The amount of volume reduction required depends on the amount of alcohol to be removed. As an example, to reduce a base wine containing 12 per cent alcohol by volume to 9 per cent about 8 per cent of the wine must be flashed off, but if the final alcohol required is 3 per cent by volume then about 45 per cent of the volume of the wine must be flashed off. For a wine with a lower alcohol content, such as 9 per cent, in order to reduce the alcohol to below 1 per cent by volume the wine needs to be reduced in volume by about 30 per cent. To remove all of the alcohol (as required by Muslim countries) the wine needs to be reduced in volume by about 60 per cent. Aroma recovery is desirable and is widely used in the concentration of fruit juices. The aroma volatiles are fractionally condensed at low temperature (between plus 5 and minus 30°C) to remove the alcohol and retain as much as possible of the volatile aroma compounds, which are then added back to the concentrated product.

Ultrafiltration and reverse osmosis. These processes have considerable potential for alcohol removal in which the alcohol passes through the membrane into the permeate, while the alcohol-reduced wine remains in the retentate. By using a membrane which allows passage of only the low molecular-weight molecules the alcohol (and other molecular-weight compounds) can be removed. Patents exist for producing low-alcohol beverages by dialysis under differential pressure, and claim to remove the alcohol without altering the flavour of the product. The most desirable membrane is one permeable only to alcohol and water.

One of the problems associated with low-alcohol wines is their proneness to microbiological spoilage, and this should be kept in mind. The techniques for preventing this from occurring are set out elsewhere in this book.

Yield of wine from one tonne of grapes

The yield of wine obtained from the grapes is important to wineries from the viewpoint of cost and efficiency of operations. This yield is dependent on many factors, particularly grape variety, state of maturity, climate, the extent of irrigation, methods of draining and pressing, and the volume of pressings added back to the wine.

The range of values for the yield of wine in litres from 1 tonne (1000 kg or 2204 lb) of grapes obtained in the Australian industry is given below:

White table wines	650–850 L
Red table wines	670–750 L
Dessert wines (excluding spirit added)	700–750 L

The total yield of juice obtainable with hard pressing is of the order of 750 to 850 litres per tonne, depending on winery area and variety. Final pressings are of the lowest quality. Highest yields are obtained from grapes grown in hot irrigated vineyards (such as the Riverland, Sunraysia and the Murrumbidgee Irrigation Area) from wineries specialising in extracting the maximum yield from Sultana (Thompson Seedless). For dry white table wines in quality areas about 500–550 litres of free-run juice are usually obtained from static drainers, and a yield of up to about 150 litres from presses of one kind or another. Because of the wide variation due to the factors listed above, precise averages are not very meaningful for the whole industry, although individual wineries may calculate such figures accurately. For example, for the 1987 vintage one winery obtained an overall average of 698 litres for white table wines and 722 litres for red table wines, but the range of values was considerable. In the production of premium quality table wines, yields of 650–730 litres for whites and 670–720 litres for reds are usual.

Relative percentages of the grape bunch as stalks, skins, seeds and pulp influence the yield of juice and wine, and are listed on page 27. These percentages vary with grape variety, climate, irrigation, method of vineyard training and technology employed.

Winery records

Wineries need to maintain records of their operations for technical, financial and legal purposes. The winemaker needs to know two types of information:

1 The present position in the winery:
- Location and volume of existing wines, including those on ullage.
- Contents, size and type of all wine containers—tanks, casks, etc.
- Details of operations which have been or are to be carried out on individual wines—additions, blending, filtration, fining, racking etc.
- Analytical and tasting records.
  2 Historical information on the winery's operations:
- Documentation on grape tonnage, juice yields, volumes after settling, losses and so on.

The accountant requires similar documentation to carry out the necessary costings and assess the financial implications and profitability of the operations.

Most wineries with a detailed recording system have two sections—one to indicate the whereabouts of all the wines and the content of all the storage vessels, and the other to record all aspects of the winemaking operations. The latter can be a large loose-leaf operations book. In small wineries the first of the two systems can be simple, because the winemaker is able to keep track of each wine and storage vessel. In larger wineries a more complex system is required, usually including a colour-coded wall display featuring the location, size and contents of all vessels. This may also include the proposed movements and/or treatments of the various wines.

The legal requirements relate to the use of brandy and fortifying spirit used in the production of fortified wines, which must conform to the requirements of the Department of Customs and Excise, and documentation required to assess the amount of levies and other legal payments required. These may be based on the tonnes of grapes crushed and/or the volume of wine sold.

There are various recording systems in use at present in different wineries, and this chapter highlights the need for such recording, but does not recommend any one system. It is not unusual for a large winery to use more than a hundred forms for various purposes in its winery operations, and these are usually in-house documents. A useful recording system was reported in the February 1974 issue of the *Australian Wine Brewing and Spirit Review*.

5 Grape and must handling procedures

It is important to understand the principles of winery operation. With respect to the various operations involved in grape-handling, it is helpful to understand the complex and rather compartmentalised nature of the grape berry, as depicted in Fig. 5.1.

Starting from the outside, the berry is covered with a rather impervious cuticle which keeps it intact and protects it from the weather, the waxy coating rendering the berry waterproof. Under the cuticle of the berry lies the epidermis layer and then the hypodermis or under-skin layer of cells. This hypodermis is important in winemaking, since the seven to eight layers of thick-walled cells

Fig. 5.1: Composite sections of a grape berry, including transverse section of (a) receptacle and (b) pedicel base.

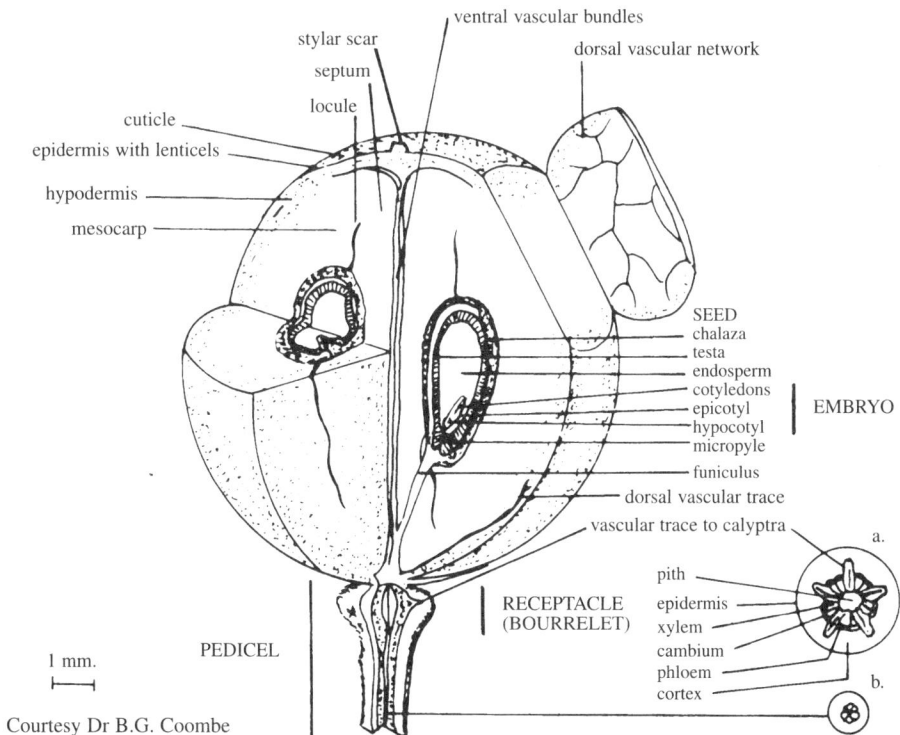

Courtesy Dr B.G. Coombe

79

which comprise it contain in their vacuoles the pigments responsible for colour in red wine, along with other important constituents. The cuticle, epidermis and hypodermal layers collectively make up the skin.

Below the hypodermis lies the flesh which occupies most of the volume of the berry. This is interspersed with a network of vascular bundles, and consists of very large irregular cells, of the order of 500 times the volume of the hypodermal cells. The sap of the berry comprises the juice and is mainly in the vacuoles of these large fragile cells, from which it is relatively easily released.

Near the centre of the flesh are the seeds, usually two, which act as a source of tannin in red wines, and which are partially extracted by prolonged contact of the skins and seeds with the juice during fermentation. The alcohol formed at the same time acts as a solvent to assist in extracting the seed tannins and phenolics into the must. The seeds contain the embryos for the reproduction of the vine, but this function of grape seeds is largely irrelevant to commercial viticulture and winemaking, other than when it is utilised for the breeding of new varieties.

The small skin and very large flesh cells consist of several parts viz. the cell wall, largely cellulose providing structural support for the cell, the cytoplasm between the vacuole and the cell wall, which is the site of much of the enzyme action necessary for cell function, and the plasma membrane which borders the cytoplasm and controls the passage of nutrients in and out of the cell. The nucleus of the cell is in the cytoplasm and is the site of genetic reproduction.

When the berry passes through the crusher the pulp cells are largely broken and release most of the juice. However, few of the hypodermal cells and none of the seeds are broken by this rather gross damage to the berry. When the crushed berry is drained, as in white winemaking, the juice continues to be released, giving rise to the free-run fraction.

When the drained berry is pressed most of the hypodermal cells are then broken, which give rise in large part to the pressed juice fraction. This is higher in astringent phenolics, cations (mainly potassium) and pH than the free-run juice, and for this reason may be kept separate by the winemaker. Skin contact with juice assists in extracting these and other flavouring constituents from the peripheral cells.

The walls of the berry cells are bound together by pectin, a long-chain gum-like binding material which also tends to keep the cells together in the juice after draining and pressing. To obtain clarified juice the pectin needs to be broken down by pectin-decomposing enzymes or pectinases, allowing the grape flesh and cell debris to settle. These enzymes occur naturally in small amounts in the berry but their clarifying action is slow and incomplete, so that juice settled naturally (*débourbage*) remains somewhat cloudy or opalescent. The pectin retains the cells and particles of grape flesh in suspension by virtue of its very long molecular chain length.

When a pectinase is added (various commercial preparations are available) the pectin is broken down more rapidly and can result in clear supernatant juice after settling. The most efficient temperature for pectin-splitting enzymes to function is about 45°C, but since this temperature is undesirably high from a winemaking viewpoint, clarification is carried out at lower temperature and hence more time needs to be allowed if clear juice is required.

In order to obtain maximum yield of juice the semipermeable membranes of the cells need to be broken, since they provide a barrier to free diffusion of the contents. Despite appearances, the cellulose walls themselves do not represent much of a barrier to the diffusion of solutes. These membranes are broken down by heat, sulphur dioxide and lipophilic solvents, such as alcohol. Consequently, release of anthocyanin (red and purple) pigments from the vacuoles of the peripheral cells into the juice is hastened by the alcohol arising from fermentation of the grape sugars. Heat alone, such as 70°C for 30 minutes, will release the vacuolar contents quite rapidly, and this is the basis of heat-extraction of colour for red winemaking. This is dealt with later in this chapter.

Consequently, in effect what the winemaker seeks is to destroy the semipermeable membranes enclosing the cells in the berry, and the practical procedures adopted are intended to do this. Many constituents are released, such as soluble grape proteins which reside mainly in the cytoplasm. If these proteins are not removed from the juice or wine by bentonite, proteolytic enzymes or heat, they can bring about protein haze in the bottled wine, one of the most serious 'condition' problems in winemaking.

Various other constituents may or may not be localised in the berry. Potassium, phenolics and pigments, for example, are mainly located in the small hypodermal cells—potassium largely and pigments wholly (except in those grape species which have red juices)—and thus the pressed juice is higher in these constituents than the free-run. Sugars on the other hand are present more in the pulp than the skin cells, and the proportion of glucose to fructose (the latter is sweeter) decreases as the berry matures. Acids are rather uniformly distributed throughout the berry. Flavouring constituents, such as the terpenes, are not necessarily resident in the skin as commonly believed, and grape varieties differ in the location of important terpenes between the skins, juice and pulp. For example, in Muscat Gordo Blanco and Frontignan, linalool is higher in the juice, whereas geraniol is higher in the skin cells.

Baumé, Balling, Brix and Oechsle

Over the years the Australian wine industry has made use of a range of hydrometer measurements for the density of must and wine. The usual measurements are Baumé and Brix, occasionally Balling and, more recently, Oechsle. New Zealand winemakers have mainly standardised on Brix. The origin of these terms and the ways in which they differ from each other are set out below.

Baumé
From the viewpoint of origin and usage in the Australian wine industry Baumé (sometimes incorrectly spelled Beaumé) is the most interesting measurement. It

was devised by Antoine Baumé entirely for a different purpose—the measurement of salt in brine. Baumé was born in Senlis, France, in 1728 and died in Paris in 1804. He was a Parisian pharmacist, being apprenticed in 1743, and supplied and manufactured drugs and equipment. He must have had wide interests, as he was the first large-scale producer of salammoniac or ammonium chloride in 1767, and won a prize in 1777 for the best furnaces and alambics for wine distillation. He developed his Aerometre (hydrometer) Baumé in 1768. However, the directions were not quite specific and the conditions for its use not easily reproducible, so consequently various Baumé scales appeared. This was eventually resolved with the outcome that two scales now exist—one for liquids heavier than water and one for lighter liquids.

For the heavier-than-water scale, which is of more interest to us, 0° Baumé corresponds to distilled water at 15°C and 10° Baumé corresponds to 10 per cent salt solution. Baumé originally defined 15° Baumé (Bé) as a solution of 15 parts by weight of sodium chloride in 85 parts by weight of water at 12.5°C or 10.0° Reaumur. For liquids lighter than water, 0° Baumé corresponds to a 10 per cent salt solution and minus 10° Bé to distilled water. For hydrometers calibrated at 20°C (modulus 145) they should read 0° Bé in distilled water at 20°C, which is the way of checking their accuracy.

Subsequently, it was discovered that, when applied to the juice from mature grapes, the Baumé degree corresponded fairly closely to the per cent by volume of alcohol which the grape juice would produce during fermentation. For example, a juice measuring 11° Baumé yields approximately 11 per cent by volume of alcohol when fermented to dryness. As a rule of thumb 1° Baumé in grape juice corresponds to 1.8 per cent soluble solids, most of which is sugar (glucose, fructose, and a little sucrose).

Balling

Karl Josef Napoleon Balling was a Czechoslovakian chemist (1805–1868). He worked in metallurgy, blast-furnace technology, sugar production and fermentation, and in 1839 developed the Balling hydrometer scale for measuring the concentration of sugar syrups. The degree Balling indicated the number of grams of cane or beet sugar in 100 grams of water at 15.6°C or 12.5° Reaumur.

Brix

Balling left his investigations incomplete. In 1854 Brix, an Austrian mathematician, produced from Balling's data a table from which a series of hydrometers could be made, which read directly the percentage of sugar in the syrup in tenths of 1 per cent from 0° to 75° Brix—that is, from 0 to 75 per cent of sugar. The Brix units are in almost universal use in the sugar industry today. When applied to grape juice the number of degrees Brix represents the percentage of soluble solids in the juice—and not the sugar content—although in juice from mature grapes sugar is the component present in largest concentration. Nowadays, most

Brix hydrometers are calibrated at 20°C, and a correction has to be applied when measurements are made at other temperatures. For every 1°C above 20°C the hydrometer reads 0.1° Brix low. In tropical regions a standard temperature of 27.5°C or 81.5°F may be used.

As a matter of interest, Brix was a mathematician who had nothing to do with the sugar industry and did no experiments—he simply worked on Balling's figures to produce the Brix tables which we use today.

Oechsle

This hydrometer term was introduced by Ferdinand Oechsle (1774–1852) in Pforzheim, West Germany, and is the most fundamental of all these measurements, as it relates directly to specific gravity. The degree Oechsle of a liquid such as grape juice is the specific gravity minus one multiplied by 1000, e.g. a must of 100° Oe corresponds to a specific gravity of 1.100, which happens to be equivalent to 13.1° Baumé or 23.6° Brix.

These four measurements are related to each other by a series of formulae, and are best compared in Table 5.1. A temperature correction is required if the readings are not measured at the temperature at which the hydrometer is standardised. For the Baumé scale the corrections are as follows: For each degree C above 20°C add 0.03° Baumé to the reading, and for every degree C below subtract 0.03° Baumé. The correction for Brix is 0.05°.

Pectin and pectolytic enzymes

When white grapes are crushed and drained, the juice is opalescent and sometimes quite cloudy. When it is allowed to stand overnight (*débourbage*) some of the larger suspended solids settle to the bottom of the vessel, and the juice becomes less cloudy. However, if a pectin-splitting enzyme is added after crushing, the juice clarifies to the extent that it may become quite clear, and a considerable deposit forms. What is happening is that in the untreated cloudy juice the suspended particles of grape flesh are held in suspension by pectins from the grapes. When these pectins are destroyed by pectin-splitting enzymes, the material held in suspension falls to the bottom leaving the juice clear.

Pectin is one of the important building components in plant cells, along with cellulose, hemicelluloses and lignin. In the grape berry pectin is found between the cells, as well as in the cell walls, and helps to keep the cells together in a structured position. As the grape berry matures the pectin is gradually hydrolysed by the naturally occurring pectolytic enzymes in the grape, and increases the softness of the fruit. The amount present in the ripe berry varies between 0.02 and 0.5 per cent.

Pectin is actually a range of related compounds consisting of anhydrogalacturonic acid residues, and includes protopectin, pectic acids and pectates. The basic pectin consists of a polymer of galacturonic-acid molecules each containing

Table 5.1: Comparison of measurements

D	Oechsle	Baumé	Brix Balling	D	Oechsle	Baumé	Brix Balling
1.051	51	7,0	12,5	1.091	91	12,0	21,7
2	52	7,1	12,8	2	92	12,1	21,9
3	53	7,3	13,0	3	93	12,3	22,2
4	54	7,4	13,2	4	94	12,4	22,4
5	55	7,5	13,5	5	95	12,5	22,5
6	56	7,6	13,7	6	96	12,6	22,8
7	57	7,8	14,0	7	97	12,8	23,0
8	58	7,9	14,2	8	98	12,9	23,2
9	59	8,0	14,4	9	99	13,0	23,5
1.060	60	8,2	14,7	1.100	100	13,1	23,7
1	61	8,3	14,9	1	101	13,2	23,9
2	62	8,4	15,1	2	102	13,3	24,1
3	63	8,5	15,4	3	103	13,5	24,3
4	64	8,7	15,6	4	104	13,6	24,5
5	65	8,8	15,8	5	105	13,7	24,8
6	66	8,9	16,1	6	106	13,8	25,0
7	67	9,1	16,3	7	107	13,9	25,2
8	68	9,2	16,5	8	108	14,0	25,4
9	69	9,3	16,8	9	109	14,2	25,6
1.070	70	9,4	17,0	1.110	110	14,3	25,8
1	71	9,6	17,2	1	111	14,4	26,1
2	72	9,7	17,5	2	112	14,5	26,3
3	73	9,8	17,7	3	113	14,6	26,5
4	74	9,9	17,9	4	114	14,7	26,6
5	75	10,1	18,1	5	115	14,9	26,9
6	76	10,2	18,4	6	116	15,0	27,1
7	77	10,3	18,6	7	117	15,1	27,3
8	78	10,4	18,8	8	118	15,2	27,5
9	79	10,6	19,0	9	119	15,3	27,8
1.080	80	10,7	19,3	1.120	120	15,5	28,0
1	81	10,8	19,5	1	121	15,6	28,2
2	82	10,9	19,7	2	122	15,7	28,4
3	83	11,0	20,0	3	123	15,8	28,6
4	84	11,2	20,2	4	124	15,9	28,8
5	85	11,3	20,4	5	125	16,0	29,0
6	86	11,4	20,6	6	126	16,1	29,2
7	87	11,5	20,8	7	127	16,3	29,4
8	88	11,7	21,1	8	128	16,4	29,7
9	89	11,8	21,3	9	129	16,5	29,9
1.090	90	11,9	21,5	1.130	130	16,6	30,1

a methoxy group side chain, and various sugars, such as galactose, mannose and arabinose. Pectin is not a uniform material—its molecular weight ranges from 10,000 to 400,000, equivalent to from 50 to 2000 galacturonic acid units. During fermentation, most of the pectins in the juice are broken down by the pectolytic activity of the yeast and the alcohol produced. A simple test consists of adding 4 to 5 volumes of alcohol and observing the gelatinous deposit formed, which indicates the presence of pectin in the juice or wine.

Pectin-splitting enzymes occur naturally in grapes, slowly breaking down the pectin and reducing the viscosity of the grape juice. In doing so they liberate galacturonic acid and methyl alcohol, and are the source of the latter in wine. However, they are normally not present in sufficient concentration in grapes to clarify the juice, and commercial preparations are frequently added to assist in obtaining a more rapid juice yield during draining and to assist in filtration. Commercial pectolytic enzymes are known under a variety of names, such as pectinases, pectolases, pectozyme and so on. These pectolytic enzymes are normally produced from fungi and are a mixture of several enzymes. Those of importance in grapes and wine are the endo-polygalacturonases, which break down the long-chain polymer in a random fashion, and the pectin methylestarses, which split off the methoxy groups with the formation of methanol.

The addition of commercial pectolytic enzymes is common in the processing of fruit juices generally, enabling a more rapid flow of juice of increased clarity, and many winemakers use them routinely. Their activity is strongly dependent on the pH of the juice and is most active in the range of pH 2.8 to 4.2. As the pH decreases (acidity increases) more of the enzyme is required. They operate in a temperature range of between about 8 and 55°C, with the optimum between 45 and 50°C. Within this range raising the temperature 10°C towards the optimum approximately doubles the reaction rate. The inhibitors of the enzymes are free sulphur dioxide, alcohol (particularly above about 17 per cent by volume) and fining with bentonite and tannin.

Crushing

The grape berry is a remarkably intact fruit capable of withstanding a range of physical conditions, such as rain, heat, some desiccation and even exposure to vacuum. As we have seen, this resistance is due to a firm epidermal or skin layer and a waxy resistant coating consisting mainly of oleanolic acid. Accordingly, to release its contents the berry needs to be physically deformed by uneven compression or shearing. Direct even compression, such as in a press cage, will break only a proportion of the berries. This pressing without crushing is used in the Champagne district in France to obtain white juice from red berries where the pigment is only in the skins. It is also used on occasion in various parts of the world to obtain the best-quality free-run juice from white grapes.

However, to release all of the juice the berries need to be crushed, using a crusher designed for the purpose.

Historically, grape crushers in Australia have been of the beater type, consisting of a fixed perforated stainless-steel cylinder in which metal or wooden beaters rotated lengthwise. These crushers were so designed that the grape bunches fed in from one end were destemmed, the broken grapes forced through the circular holes in the cylinder, and the stems ejected at the other end. This design was simple and effective—the straight beaters were at an angle to the axle to which they were attached, and this enabled them to break the berries at one end of the circular screen by shearing them against the holes. Then further along the screen the altered angle of the beaters relative to the screen lifted the stalks away from the screen and carried them to the discharge end. The crushers were thus obligatory destemmers. Examples are the Whitehill and Bagshaw grape mills—the Garolla, which is widely used in California, is similar except that the cylinder rotates.

The gap between the beaters and the screen was important in the operation of the crusher, and was adjustable by means of shims on the axle bearings. Beater crushers set for small-berried grapes usually needed adjustment to handle large berries and *vice versa*. The circular holes in the screen were best chamfered on the inner side to remove proud edges which may strip the stalks. Other types of perforations are also used. These beater crushers are still used but are being supplanted by roller crushers, which have a more gentle action and are more suitable for the production of table wines.

These roller crushers also feature optional destemming. They are available in several forms: rollers alone, rollers then destemmer or destemmer then rollers. The rollers consist of two, four or more horizontal fluted or grooved rollers made of solid moulded rubber, rubber-coated steel, stainless-steel or aluminium alloy, operated by gears and rotating towards each other. They are adjustable and set so that the grapes are crushed without breaking the seeds or grinding the stems. A recently introduced French design, the Demoisy, features rubber double-cone discs which have a diamond-shaped cross-section, and incorporates an integral must pump.

Destemming may take place before or after crushing and the former is better, since the stems are removed before the berries are broken. The destemmer consists of bars or fingers attached radially to a central rotating spindle inside a perforated cylindrical cage, which itself may or may not rotate. The grapes pass through the holes in the cylinder, while the larger stalks are carried out through the distal end. A good destemmer should completely remove the stems without damaging them nor impregnating them with juice, and not breaking the grapes. With roller crushers it is normally possible to crush without destemming by closing the connection to the destemmer.

Other crushers are available, such as vertical crushers and disintegrators, but are little used in Australia as they have not been shown to be suitable for making quality wine. They tend to pulverise the berry tissue excessively, and to induce frothing and air entrapment.

A must pump is part of the crusher assembly, and may or may not be integral with the crusher. Various pumps are used and it is now common practice to use a piston or serpentine pump, the latter with an open throat incorporating an archimedian-screw feed. Submerged suction is desirable so that the must pump only operates when must is available, thus avoiding pumping air and aerating the must.

Stalk disposal is carried out by either a stalk blower, operating on a vacuum created at the delivery end, or by a slat conveyor fitted with wooden, plastic or metal slats or nylon brushes. Both present sanitation problems. Stalk blowers are effective over a short delivery length only, and consume considerably more power than belts or conveyors. The stalks can be disposed of in the vineyard or washed to extract the residual grape sugar, which can be fermented to recover the alcohol. The crushing and stalk disposal area should be designed so that it can be cleaned and kept hygienic.

Draining and pressing

When grapes are crushed the juice in the pulp, and in any of the peripheral cells which are ruptured, slowly drains from the grape berry. The rate of juice removal depends on the time of draining, restrictions to the flow of juice, pressure, presence of added pectin-splitting enzymes and temperature. The quality of the juice and, in part, the yield are also influenced by the presence of sulphur dioxide, as well as absence of oxygen and presence of antioxidants, such as ascorbic or erythorbic acid.

Historically, and even to the present day, it has been customary and economical to use a grape press as a drainer before applying pressure. Traditionally, the vertical basket press has been used, and it remains a symbol of winemaking, but in recent years other types of drainers and presses have been developed to speed up the dejuicing operation and provide better quality juice. These are of several types.

Static drainers allow the crushed juice to drain through a perforated or slotted screen, either exposed to the air or in a partial carbon-dioxide atmosphere. Several variations of this type of drainer are in use, the most popular being the Miller static carbon-dioxide pressure drainer and the Lindeman modification. These have provision for breaking up the mass of drained skins by means of an internal horizontal rotating shaft with projecting fingers, and emptying by means of two internal horizontal contra-rotating archimedian screws.

Horizontal basket presses apply mechanical or hydraulic pressure from one or both ends. The basket can be rotated to facilitate both breaking up the compacted mass of pressed skins and emptying. The basket may be encased in a shield or cover so that draining and pressing can be carried out in a partially inert gas atmosphere. In this type of press the draining surface area becomes less as the pressing proceeds, since the mass of skins is compacted into a smaller volume.

McWilliams multipurpose vertical tanks, developed by McWilliams Wines Pty Ltd, operate on the principle of a hydrostatic head to facilitate draining. These tall (about 13 metres high) stainless-steel vessels are basically simple with no moving parts—the lower third (approximately) is lined internally with perforated stainless steel attached a few centimetres from the wall to serve as a draining surface. Many variations of static drainers exist, both with and without screens.

Potter drainer-fermenters in which a multipurpose vessel has the facility for draining crushed grapes before, during or after fermentation, and also can be used as a storage vessel. Draining is carried out through a central vertical cylindrical slotted stainless-steel screen, which can be removed for cleaning and when the vessel is used for storage.

Inclined dejuicers force the crushed grapes over an inclined cylindrical slotted screen by a slow-moving archimedian screw, which imparts a mild pressing action as well as draining. As with any equipment which operates by forcing crushed grapes over a screen, the drained juice contains more suspended solids.

Air-bag presses are based on the horizontal basket principle, in which a longitudinal inflatable rubber bag provides pressure from the inside of the mass. This type of press has the advantage that the draining surface area remains constant during pressing. Repositioning the mass of pressed grapes for repressing, and emptying the contents, are carried out by rotating the cage.

Tank presses drain and press the juice in a pressure vessel fitted with internal drainage channels, with the pressure being provided by an inflatable membrane attached to the internal wall. This press has the advantage of being able to be filled with inert gas, and the draining surface area remains constant throughout the draining and pressing operation.

McKenzie multistage continuous press, developed in South Africa, used the inflatable air-bag principle on an endless moving perforated belt. The pressing stations (usually four) operated simultaneously with the belt stationary. The mass of pressed grapes was then redistributed on the belt by rotating beaters while the belt moved to carry the mass to the next pressing station. The press is no longer available.

Horizontal screw presses combine a draining section as well as allowing fractions of pressed juice to be taken from different sections of the pressure cylinder. A back pressure at the solids outlet may be applied to increase the pressure on the skins. Such presses are usually fitted with some device for redistributing the mass of crushed grapes for further pressing, such as a bivalve.

Pumping

In earlier days wineries were sometimes built on the sides of hills to obtain the help of gravity in moving juice and wine. Grapes arrived and were crushed at the top and progressed through the winemaking operations arriving as wine at the bottom. While this system had the advantage of gravity it had practical disadvantages, and nowadays wineries are built on one or more levels, depending on the contour of the land, but not to utilise gravity specifically. Wine is moved by pumps with fixed and/or movable pipelines. Pumps used in wineries are based on several principles.

Centrifugal with non-flexible impeller. These are inexpensive and will pump large volumes, but will not self-prime and thus require a flooded suction. They lack versatility and will not pump lees, but can handle a few skins and seeds. In a small winery their place is usually as a large-capacity second pump. They are affected by airlocks and high carbon-dioxide gas content of the product, and are not normally reversible. They can be shut off at the outlet while still running, such as when delivering wine to a filler where the outlet is intermittent.

Centrifugal with flexible impeller. These are excellent on clean wine without suspended solids, but abrasive particles, such as diatomaceous earth, will rapidly wear the flexible rotor. They are lightweight, efficient, available in small sizes, self-priming, not affected by airlocks or high gas content of the product, and stop immediately the power is switched off. However, they will not handle high solids and cannot be run dry without damage.

Helical rotor pump with flexible stator—Mono type. These pumps are self-priming and can handle high solids with positive displacement, and are widely used to pump wine, lees and destemmed must. They can be fitted with an open or closed throat (the former enables them to accept crushed must), a by-pass and are reversible. They do not stop immediately the power is switched off, and must not be operated dry since this damages the rubber stator. They should be run with the outlet against the sealing gland, so that any leaks become apparent and air is not sucked into the pump. Generally they are very useful for cellar work.

Piston pumps. These have positive displacement, are self-priming, effective and shut off quickly. They will handle a reasonable amount of suspended solids, were formerly used widely as must pumps, and can be run dry for a short period without damage. However, they are seldom made completely of stainless steel, and are difficult to sanitise (having an air chamber which is not totally wetted), and may not pump without priming after a long period of disuse, as the piston buckets tend to dry out. They tend to be less used than formerly in winery operations.

Lobe and gear pumps. These have intermeshing lobes or gears which provide an even flow without surging. They can handle a wide range of viscosities, but are not designed for high solids. A by-pass can be fitted, they can be steam-sterilised and are good metering and bottling-line pumps.

A wide range of makes and models of pumps is available, and the selection depends on pumping requirements and the conditions under which the pump is required to operate. A pump expert should be consulted to ensure the correct selection. Besides cost, points to watch for are:

- Matching output with anticipated requirements.
- Sanitation and ease of cleaning.
- Maintenance requirements and availability of spare parts.
- Possible metal contamination of the product with iron or copper.
- Ease of operation, portability and versatility.
- Adequate pressure (especially with filtration).
- Optional extra fittings, such as bypasses and variable speed.

The pumps most widely used are the positive-displacement helical rotors for pumping juice and wine with suspended solids and without too much gas, and centrifugal pumps for rapid wine transfer and general duties with clear wine and juice.

Further information on bottling is given in Chapter 15.

Must and juice cooling

In view of the overriding importance of temperature control in most Australian wine-growing areas, coupled with the fact that grapes frequently arrive hot at the winery, it is important in making table wines to apply refrigeration as soon as possible in the winemaking process.

Must cooling is widely used in white winemaking, with the object of reducing the temperature of the must to between approximately 10° and 18°C, with a desirable average of about 15°C. In this range the cooler the better, but the cost of cooling needs to be balanced against the benefits derived. Some winemakers cool the must to lower temperatures, such as 2° to 10°C, for wines of special quality. White musts are cooled before draining or skin-contact to reduce the rate of oxidation of phenolics. Juice may also be cooled, sometimes to even lower temperatures, such as minus 2° to plus 4°C, in order to conserve it for later fermentation or as sweetening material for dry wines.

Because of the rapidity of enzymatic oxidation of crushed grapes, cooling is best applied as soon as possible after crushing, rather than waiting until the must is drained to obtain juice free from gross suspended solids. While it may be argued that refrigeration energy is used to cool skins and seeds which will eventually be discarded, the benefits of doing so outweigh the cost.

We must first consider the concept of heat loads. The level of heat in a system is measured in degrees C, while heat as energy is measured in joules (J) or kilojoules (kJ). The time taken to remove heat from must, juice or wine determines the size of the refrigeration plant. The capacities of the compressors, evaporators and condensers are all stated in units of energy per unit time, i.e. kilojoules per second. The alternative name for a kilojoule per second is a kilowatt (kW). With the change to SI units, the 'refrigeration ton' or ton R, and the horsepower (HP) are gradually being discontinued. The relationship is:

$$1 \text{ ton R} = 3.517 \text{ kW}$$
$$1 \text{ HP} = 0.746 \text{kW}$$

Similarly, the old unit of pressure, pounds per square inch gauge-pressure or psig, has been replaced with the Pascal (Pa) or kilopascal (kPa). One pound per square inch gauge-pressure equals 6.895 kilopascals gauge pressure.

The must-cooling load in kilowatts is the product of tonnes of grapes crushed per 24 hours and the required temperature drop in °C divided by 24. For example, to lower the temperature of 1 tonne of grapes from 30°C to 15°C requires 0.63 kW of heat to be removed. Alternatively, 1 kW of refrigeration can cool approximately 1.5 tonnes of grapes per day through 15°C, from say 30°C to 15°C or 35°C to 20°C.

The transfer pump is a source of heat by putting energy into the must to pump it through the cooler and its associated piping. This energy appears as frictional heat and has to be removed by the cooler. The heat load from the must pump, for example, is the nominal power of the motor driving the pump.

The remaining heat source is the heat transferred from the surrounding air to the must or juice through the piping. If the cooler is adequately insulated the heat gain is approximately 5 per cent of the calculated must or juice cooling load. If the cooler is not insulated it is necessary to add 15 to 20 per cent of the must cooling load. The cooler has to be designed for the total heat load, which is the sum of the must or juice cooling, the pump power and the heat from the surroundings.

The normal practice for must cooling is to pass the must through a tube-in-tube or spiral heat-exchanger against chilled brine or direct-expansion refrigerant immediately after destemming and crushing. Tubes of at least 100 millimetres internal diameter with detachable end-sections of large-radius return bends are desirable to reduce the chance of blockage by any stems which may have been left in the must after the destemming–crushing operation.

The cooling medium can be chilled water, a brine solution or a directly expanding refrigerant. Brine is the general name given to any secondary coolant, whether it is sodium chloride or calcium chloride solution, methylated alcohol, glycol or other coolant. Jacketed draining-tanks and fermenters are sometimes used for this purpose in small wineries as a batch process, but are relatively inefficient because the must is stationary and therefore heat transfer is slow. Once the temperature of the must is under control, subsequent handling operations and fermentation are facilitated.

For juice cooling, if the juice is to be cooled continuously in a heat-exchanger, the juice cooling-load in kilowatts is the product of the juice flow-rate in litres per hour and the required temperature drop in degrees C divided by 900. To this is added the minor heat loads of the electrical power of the pump and the heat gains from the surroundings. However, if the juice is to be cooled in a tank, the cooling load in kilowatts is the product of the volume of juice in kilolitres, the required temperature drop in degrees C and 1.1, divided by the time required to cool the juice in hours.

Although there is no pump to add to the heat load, the heat gain to the tank from the surroundings is greater than the comparable heat gain to a heat exchanger. If the tank is insulated with at least 40 millimetres of polyurethane the heat gain in kilowatts is the tank surface areas (walls and top) in square metres divided by 150. Alternatively, if the tank is uninsulated but inside an enclosed non-cooled winery, the heat gain in kilowatts is the tank surface area in square metres divided by 20. However, if the tank is uninsulated and outside exposed to hot northerly winds and the sun, the heat gain in kilowatts is given by the tank surface area divided by 6.

The thermal properties of must, juice and water are shown in Table 5.2.

Table 5.2: Thermal properties of must, juice, wine and water

	Temperature °C	Density kg/m³	Thermal conductivity W/m.°C	Specific heat kJ/kg°C	Dynamic viscosity mPa.s
Must	0	1095	0.48	3.65	25
	10	1090	0.49	3.70	15
	20	1085	0.50	3.75	10
	30	1080	0.51	3.80	7
Juice	0	1100	0.49	3.56	5.0
	10	1095	0.505	3.58	3.4
	20	1090	0.52	3.60	2.5
	30	1085	0.535	3.62	1.9
Wine	0	982	0.49	4.25	3.8
	10	978	0.50	4.30	2.6
	20	975	0.51	4.35	2.0
	30	972	0.52	4.40	1.6
Water	0	1000	0.569	4.21	1.75
	10	1000	0.587	4.20	1.30
	20	998	0.603	4.18	1.0
	30	996	0.618	4.18	0.8

Must pasteurisation

When compared with other industrial fermentation, such as brewing and antibiotic production, winemaking is not closely controlled from the microbiological point of view. The must is normally not sterilised, except for the addition of sulphur dioxide, and the use of a pure yeast starter-culture is based on the domination by this culture over the naturally occurring micro-organisms. This is one reason why many wines have microbiological faults. In brewing, on the other hand, the wort is boiled before pitching the yeast, and thus the fermentation is carried out in an effectively sterile medium.

The use of must pasteurisation for white wines enables much closer microbiological control. The must is lightly clarified then passed through a plate heat-exchanger against steam, where it is rapidly heated to about 87°C for 30 seconds and then cooled to 15°C. This high-temperature short-time heating brings about considerable destruction of the micro-organisms in the must, as well as oxidase enzymes and heat-unstable protein. Such treatment is particularly useful for musts from unsound grapes, which are high in oxidase enzymes.

From a winemaking viewpoint such heat treatment gives the winemaker considerably more control without damage to the must, because the heating is carried out in the absence of air and for a very short time. A disadvantage is the cost of the treatment, since considerable energy is required to raise the temperature of the must then reduce it again, although heat recuperation is employed by exchanging the heat must with incoming cool must.

Another use of heating must is to increase the flavour in the juice. This practice has been in use in Australia for many years, and is of particular benefit with aromatic grape varieties, such as Muscat Gordo Blanco. Work at the Australian Wine Research Institute has recently shown that the heat brings about formation of more of the flavouring materials from their precursors in the juice.

Conserving grape juice

Grape juice is conserved for several reasons, such as sweetening dry wines, storage for later fermentation, addition to other beverages as a sweetening material, and as a beverage.

In making sweet white table wines some form of sweetening is employed to obtain the desired amount of sweetness in the final wine, provided that the fermentation is not stopped before all the sugar in the juice has been fermented. While the latter method results in better-quality wine, the addition of sweetening material to a dry wine is easier to manage to be sure of obtaining the required level of sweetness. In New Zealand the addition of sugar or chaptalisation is permitted and is described at the end of this chapter. In Australia, sugar addition is not permitted (except for the production of sparkling and flavoured wines) and the winemaker needs to rely on other methods. The normal method in Germany and Austria, for example, is to use 'Süss-reserve'—unfermented or partially fermented grape juice containing a maximum of 8 grams per litre alcohol—which is produced commercially for the purpose.

Grape juice can be conserved in various ways.

Partially fermented grape juice conserved under a pressure of carbon dioxide, produced by the partial fermentation of the grape juice. This is the Swiss Boehi process (Adolf Boehi 1884–1925), which requires the use of robust pressure tanks capable of withstanding the high pressure. The grape juice is placed in the pressure tank, inoculated with yeast and allowed to ferment with the gas release valve of the tank closed. The accumulation of carbon dioxide generates sufficient pressure to stop the fermentation, and the sweet and lightly alcoholic juice, supersaturated with carbon dioxide, is stored in the tank until needed. Modifications to the original process are to impregnate the filter-sterilised juice with carbon dioxide from cylinders or with dry ice, without resorting to fermentation to produce it. Since the pressure generated by the carbon dioxide increases with temperature, the pressure tanks should be kept cool and not exceed 20°C. The pressure corresponding to 15 grams per litre of carbon dioxide at 10°C is 6.2 atmospheres, at 15°C 7.6 and at 20°C 8.5 atmospheres. The capital cost of the pressure tanks has made the process expensive, and it is being superseded by other methods.

Sterile-filtered juice. The vessels and fittings must be heat-sterilised, and care taken to ensure that no microbiological contamination takes place. The juice usually contains between 100 and 300 milligrams per litre of sulphur dioxide. This process results in high-quality juice, but the problem of possible yeast contamination always exists. Sorbic acid may be added to a level of 200 milligrams per litre, corresponding to 270 milligrams per litre of potassium sorbate. Cool storage is desirable.

Chilled clarified juice. The colder the storage temperature, the more stable is the juice, and temperatures range from about minus 4°C to plus 2°C. The juice may also be protein-stabilised by treatment with bentonite, and depectinised with pectolytic enzyme. The free sulphur dioxide content is maintained at 30 to 50 milligrams per litre with the pH as low as possible in the range of 2.9 to 3.2. This storage practice is widely used in Australia, and results in a quality juice in which varietal character, flavour and appearance are preserved. Since some yeasts (psychrophiles) can grow slowly at low temperature, the juice needs to be regularly monitored for yeast growth. The juice can be pasteurised beforehand to kill viable micro-organisms. In the tall stainless-steel vessels used for storage, a temperature gradient exists, with the warmest temperature at the top. Consequently, yeasts tend to grow in the upper layers of the juice and slowly grow down, requiring the juice to be continuously monitored and filtered from time to time during storage.

Pasteurised grape juice. Pasteurisation of grape juice was first carried out by Thomas B. Welch in the USA in 1869. It is now common practice, employing short-time high-temperature pasteurisation at 85°C for two to three minutes using a plate heat-exchanger. The juice is then cooled by heat recuperation, and stored at room temperature in stainless-steel vessels under a low level of sulphur dioxide, such as 100 mg per litre total, to reduce oxidation. After pasteurisation the juice is sterile and must be kept so, otherwise it will ferment. This means that all vessels, fittings and hoses must be heat-sterilised beforehand, and the juice must be regularly monitored for possible yeast growth.

Highly sulphited juice. This procedure has been in use for many years in Europe and the product is known as *muté*. In Australia the process is more recent (1975) and is referred to as 'brimstone'. By 1980 nine brimstone units built by

Fig. 5.2: Grape juice desulphiting process

Courtesy *Food Technology in Australia*

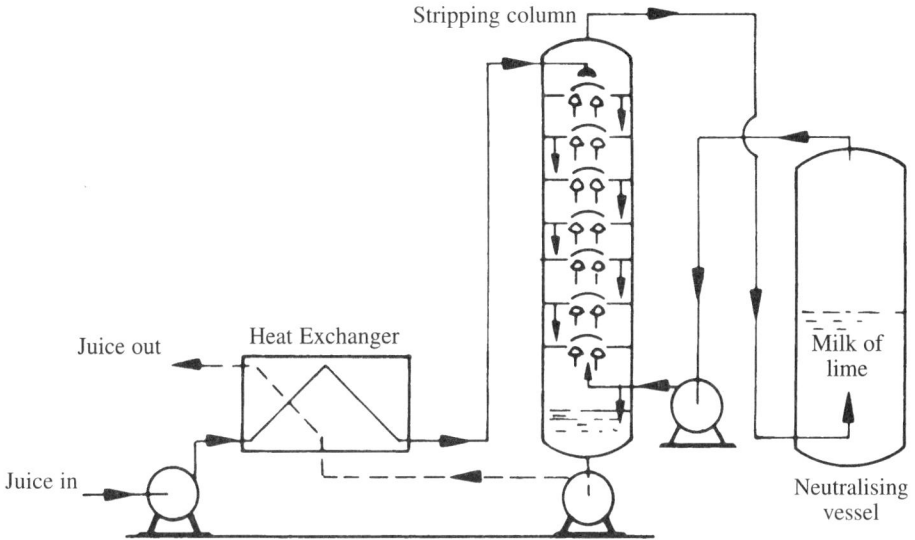

Stripping column

Juice out

Heat Exchanger

Milk of lime

Juice in

Neutralising vessel

A. & G. Engineering were in operation, and in 1981 12 per cent of the total Australian grape crush was sulphited in this way. The grape juice is protein-stabilised with bentonite, clarified and the pH reduced to approximately 2.7 by hydrogen ion-exchange. Sulphur dioxide is added to a level of between 1000 and 2000 milligrams per litre, and the juice stored at room temperature in stainless-steel vessels (type 316) until required.

It is then desulphited in equipment designed for the purpose. (See Fig. 5.2.) The sulphited juice is heated rapidly to approximately 110°C in the absence of air to liberate the sulphur dioxide, which at that temperature and pH is in the free form. The liberated sulphur dioxide is then removed in a fractionating column by hot nitrogen or steam under pressure and adsorbed in a calcium-hydroxide suspension. The calcium sulphite so produced is discarded. The juice remains in the fractionating column for a very short time (a minute or less), and the nitrogen or steam circulates in a closed loop. Removal of the sulphur dioxide is effective, with the amount remaining usually not exceeding 100 milligrams per litre. The flavour of the juice is somewhat altered, although not necessarily impaired, and the product is used to make bag-in-box wines. An addition of 0.5 to 1.0 milligram per litre thiamine is made before inoculating with yeast, because the process destroys the thiamine present in the juice.

Storage at low pH. High acidity (low pH of 2.2 to 2.4) coupled with approximately 50 mg per litre of free sulphur dioxide usually prevents yeast growth in filtered fresh grape juice, and this process can be used with care to conserve juice at ambient temperature for extended periods of time. The clarified and filtered juice is acidified by hydrogen ion exchange (described in Chapter 7), filtered through a membrane filter and stored in stainless-steel tanks. The quality of the juice is reported as fair and can be used after deacidification for preparation of yeast cultures and other uses. An addition of diammonium phosphate is desirable. The juice is likely to ferment if the level of free sulphur dioxide falls too much. The procedure is not designed for production of quality wines.

Fortified juice. When grape juice is fortified with grape spirit to about 10 per cent by volume the combination of alcohol and sugar prevents yeast growth, and the process has been used as a means of conserving juice. The product is known as mistelle or, in South Africa, 'jeropico'. It is used for sweetening dessert wines and vermouth, and can be wood-aged to enhance its flavour. It is not suitable for fermentation and is expensive because of the cost of spirit.

Concentrated grape juice. The introduction of modern high-vacuum/short-time concentrators has resulted in the production of grape juice concentrate of higher quality than was hitherto available, and this has found a place in sweetening dry wines. The product is approximately 68°C Brix, which corresponds to between 3.5 and 4.1 concentration. It is stable at ambient temperature, but tends to brown on storage and is best stored cool.

Sulphur dioxide

Sulphur dioxide is almost universally used in winemaking, and is one of the few compounds for which legal maximum limits exist (currently in Australia 250 to 300 milligrams per litre and in New Zealand 250 to 400 milligrams per litre, each depending on the sweetness of the wine with sweeter wines containing over 35 grams per litre of sugar having the higher figure). Sulphur dioxide is a remarkable compound, since it combines both germicidal and anti-oxidant properties, is relatively non-toxic, and an excess can be detected by smell. No other compound has been found which possesses all these characteristics and which may be legally added to wine.

Chemically, sulphur dioxide is quite reactive, and exists in wine in both free or uncombined and bound or combined forms. The free form consists of molecular or un-ionised sulphur dioxide, the bisulphite anion and the sulphite anion. The proportions of each of these three forms depends on pH, with the most acid wine having the most undissociated sulphur dioxide. Free sulphur dioxide includes all three forms, of which the undissociated or molecular sulphur dioxide moiety is the most germicidal, but at the pH of wine (3 to 4) the bisulphite form is the most abundant. The bound or combined form involves many compounds, especially acetaldehyde, with which it is very strongly bound. The many bound or addition compounds exist in equilibrium with one another in a complex fashion.

The free and bound portions together comprise total sulphur dioxide. Since the free sulphur dioxide is the more effective moiety, its measurement is much more important than that of total sulphur dioxide. As time goes on we may well speak in terms of molecular sulphur dioxide rather than the overall free portion as we do now, because of its great importance.

The amount of free sulphur dioxide required to preserve a wine is related to pH, since this influences the proportion present in the free form, and particularly in the most effective molecular form. Because more undissociated sulphur dioxide is present at lower pH levels, i.e. in the more acid wines, we need less free sulphur dioxide in such wines. At the present state of our knowledge we can only specify accurately the level of free sulphur dioxide in white wines. In red wines almost all of the free is in fact loosely bound to the anthocyanin pigments, and is released by the acidification of the wine during its measurement. Thus the amount of apparent free sulphur dioxide in a red wine is not a true figure in the chemical sense, but represents in part the amount of pigment in the wine. Nevertheless, it is a useful, if incompletely defined, concept in red wines.

The influence of pH on the percentage of molecular sulphur dioxide in the free moiety is given below in part (a) of the table.

It has been shown that a level of at least 0.8 milligram per litre of molecular sulphur dioxide is required in white table wine to inhibit the growth of bacteria and prevent oxidation. In order to achieve this level it is necessary to maintain the levels of free sulphur dioxide in milligrams per litre in the pH range 3.0–3.7 given in part (b) of the following table:

(a)	pH	Free SO_2	
		as bisulphite	as molecular SO_2
	3.0	94.0	6.0
	3.2	96.0	4.0
	3.4	97.5	2.5
	3.6	98.5	1.5
	3.8	99.0	1.0
	4.0	99.4	0.6

(b)	pH	Free SO_2
	3.0	13
	3.1	16
	3.2	21
	3.3	26
	3.4	32
	3.5	40
	3.6	50
	3.7	60

Consequently, it is not possible to specify standard levels of sulphur dioxide for all wines, since each wine type has to be treated separately. Recommended levels are as follows:

White table wines

pH 3.00 to 3.20	10 to 20 milligrams per litre free
3.21 to 3.40	20 to 30 milligrams per litre free
3.41 to 3.50	30 to 50 milligrams per litre free
Above 3.5	50 plus milligrams per litre free

Red table wines

pH 3.4 to 3.6   10 to 20 milligrams per litre apparent free sulphur dioxide or 50 to 150 milligrams per litre total, depending on pH and whether malo-lactic fermentation is or is not desired. To encourage malo-lactic fermentation, sulphur dioxide levels should be kept as low as possible.

White dessert wines

10 to 15 milligrams per litre free, 100 to 150 milligrams per litre total.

Red dessert wines

50 to 150 milligrams per litre total.

Sulphur dioxide is available in three main forms:

1 As *liquefied gas* which is metered into the must or wine as a liquid or as the gas above the liquid. Sulphur dioxide is a gas at normal temperature and pressure, so must be kept under pressure if to be used as a liquid. It is dangerous to handle. It has a boiling point of minus 10°C, 1 millilitre weighs 1.43 grams and 1 millilitre per 100 litres of must is equivalent to 14.3 milligrams per litre (parts per million). If the old British measurements are used, as with some old sulphitometers, 1 ounce per 100 imperial gallons is equivalent to 63 milligrams per litre.

Withdrawal of liquid sulphur dioxide from a pressure vessel in which it is stored creates a reduced temperature due to expansion of liquid to gas. If large quantities are withdrawn rapidly the expansion valve may freeze, requiring it to be heated. The pressure of the gas above the liquid at 20°C is 280 kilopascals per square centimetre or 40 pounds per square inch gauge pressure.

2 As *sulphurous acid or a solution of sulphur dioxide in water*. This is prepared by bubbling sulphur dioxide through chilled water, and its concentration can be measured by hydrometer, as set out in the following table:

Per cent by weight	SO_2 g/l	Specific gravity at 15°C
1.0	10	1.0056
2.0	20	1.0113
3.0	30	1.0168
4.0	40	1.0221
5.0	50	1.0275
6.0	60	1.0328

Usually a 6 per cent solution is prepared, and must be kept cold because sulphur dioxide continues to evaporate at a rate proportional to the temperature. For a 6 per cent solution the addition of 1 millilitre to a litre of juice or wine corresponds to 63 milligrams per litre.

3 As *salts of sulphur dioxide*. These are usually potassium or sodium metabisulphite and are the salts most rich in the gas. The potassium salt (commonly called PMS or meta) is hygroscopic and loses strength with time. When added to juice or wine it liberates approximately 50 per cent of its weight of sulphur dioxide in practice, although theoretically it should release 57 per cent. Addition of 60 milligrams to a litre of white juice or wine provides approximately 30 milligrams per litre of sulphur dioxide. One litre of a 5 per cent solution of potassium metabisulphite in cold water added to 1000 litres of juice or wine provides 25 milligrams per litre of sulphur dioxide.

Carbonic maceration

Carbonic maceration is a process for making table wines by preliminary storage of whole grape bunches in an inert atmosphere. It has received attention in Australia recently and many wines are being made by this process or some modification of it. It is mainly applied to red grapes but is also applicable to whites.

Historically, carbonic maceration has had an unusual beginning. In 1934 a French research team experimented to develop a new method for conserving fresh grapes during transport and storage between the vineyard and the consumer. Whole grape bunches were stored under carbon dioxide at about 0°C. After two months they were examined and found to be alcoholic, gassy and unfit for sale, but the flavour was found to be quite palatable. The grapes ended up by being crushed and made into wine, resulting in a pleasantly unusual wine. The credit for the first scientific investigation of carbonic maceration goes to Professor Michel Flanzy in southern France. The bulk of the developmental work was carried out by Flanzy, his son Claude, and Dr Pierre André of the Station de Technologie des Produits Végétaux, INRA, Montfavet, near Avignon, together with collaborators from Beaujolais, Burgundy and related areas, who formed the Group de Travail Macération Carbonique.

The success of their work is evident in the increasing use of the technique, initially in the Rhone Valley in France, then in other French wine-growing areas and overseas, including Australia. In developing their work the Group investigated achieving anaerobic conditions by the use of sulphur dioxide as well as carbon dioxide, deciding finally on the latter as the most appropriate means of excluding air from the stored grapes. The essential feature of the process is storage of whole grape bunches under anaerobic conditions in an atmosphere of carbon dioxide.

It is interesting to note that Pasteur in 1872 observed that storage of whole grapes under anaerobic conditions retained more of their flavour than when exposed to air. He predicted that this process may result in wines with special properties, perhaps with commercial advantage. However, he did not follow up this prediction and it was overlooked or forgotten for sixty years.

The process can be divided into four phases:

1 *Storage of whole grape bunches (not destemmed) in a closed vessel filled with carbon dioxide.* Grape varieties used for the process in southern France have little varietal character, e.g. Aramon, Carignan, Gamay and Grenache. Carbon dioxide may be generated by yeast fermentation of juice expressed by the weight of grapes above, or by addition from an outside source, or both. It is necessary to replace the air sufficiently that the spaces in the bunches are filled with carbon dioxide, or else growth of *Acetobacter* and other spoilage microorganisms may occur. To prevent this the oxygen content of the gas in the vessel should be below 0.5 per cent b volume. (Air contains 20.9 per cent oxygen.)

2 *The maceration phase in which the berries undergo internal anaerobic metabolism.* This is distinct from the alcoholic fermentation of the expressed juice by yeast and is chemically quite complex. The freshly harvested grapes in the vessel are alive and consume their own internal oxygen in a day or so. This enzymatic process within the living berry is termed intracellular fermentation or anaerobic metabolism, and lasts until the berry dies. Death of the grape berry is caused by accumulated alcohol (up to 2 per cent in the berry) or by bursting the skins due to the weight of grapes above it. The death of the berry marks the end of the important aroma-producing phase of carbonic maceration. It takes place at least five days after the grape depletes its oxygen supply, or at least eight days (depending on temperature) after the grapes enter the storage vessel. At 35°C death occurs after about eight days, at 25°C 10 to 12 days, while at 15°C it occurs after about two weeks.

During anaerobic metabolism the grape absorbs carbon dioxide from its environment, and this can reach 10 per cent of the berry's total volume at 35°C, 30 per cent at 25°C and 50 per cent at 15°C. This is followed by carbon dioxide release, associated with breakdown of malic acid into ethanol, sugars and other acids. At 35°C about half of the malic acid is consumed, with less at lower temperature. In addition, anaerobic metabolism increases the nutritional level of the must, mainly due to the increased amounts of amino acids, which are claimed to stimulate malo-lactic fermentation in carbonic maceration wines. On the other hand tartaric acid undergoes little or no change during the process.

After pressing, a rapid rise in temperature occurs due to yeast alcoholic fermentation of the sugars. Cooling needs to be available, because a rise in temperature is undesirable in fragrant wines of this type, which then should be handled as if they were white table wines.

3 *Pressing whole bunches without crushing.* The pressed juice is of higher quality than the free-run. Skins, seeds and stalks are discarded.

4 *Yeast alcoholic fermentation.* The pressed free-run juice is yeasted and fermented to dryness. Malo-lactic fermentation usually occurs either concurrently with alcoholic fermentation or shortly afterwards.

Red wines made by carbonic maceration have certain characteristics:

- Less colour and tannin than wines made from the grapes by normal vinification.
- A carbonic-maceration character engendered by three factors—aromatic compounds produced by anaerobic intracellular fermentation in the berry, the yeast alcoholic fermentation, and only minimal extraction of grape constituents by alcohol.
- An aroma reminiscent of cherries and strawberries is frequently observed. The nose is more aromatic and fresher, and because of low tannin levels, the palate has early maturity.

The implications of such compositional and quality differences, as compared with classical fermentations, are that the wines can be marketed earlier and assist in cash flow, caterers and merchants do not need to bin them, and decanting to remove deposit before serving is not required.

During carbonic maceration, between 1 and 2 per cent of alcohol by volume is formed within the berry, the level reaching a plateau in one to two weeks depending on temperature. Glycerol (about 2 grams per litre), methanol (about 50 milligrams per litre), acetaldehyde (about 20 milligrams per litre) are also produced, along with succinic, shikimic and quinic acids and other compounds in lesser amounts. In addition, polyphenols diffuse from the skin into the pulp.

Temperature has a profound effect on carbonic maceration, with the optimum being between 30 and 35°C. All of the changes in the constituents listed above take place more rapidly as the temperature rises, and accordingly the duration of the storage phase of carbonic maceration is closely related to temperature. There are various suggested periods of time and those most frequently used are listed above. However, this depends on the grape variety, its composition and other factors. One aspect which has slowed down the spread of the true carbonic maceration process is that few cellars are built specifically for the process. More storage space is needed with the requirement that whole bunches can be tipped directly into the tanks. Wineries designed solely for carbonic maceration are more expensive and less adaptable to other methods of winemaking.

In some wineries in southern France the horizontal stainless-steel fermentation vessels have been designed specifically for carbonic maceration, with an opening in the top of the tank for entry of the bunches and a large door in the bottom of the end of the tank to remove the grapes after the maceration process.

In spite of such limitations the use of carbonic maceration is becoming more common. It does not feature as yet in *appellation* wine in France as a specific process, but proponents believe that it should. In Beaujolais a form of carbonic maceration has been used for many years. Whole bunches are stored in tanks for up to one week. The weight of grapes releases enough juice to start a yeast fermentation and fill the tank with carbon dioxide. The grapes are then mixed with normally crushed grapes and allowed to ferment in the anaerobic conditions thus produced. The wines have an appealing freshness and the Primeur and Nouveau, released annually on 15 November and 15 December respectively, are much in demand on the Paris and United Kingdom markets. Beaujolais is sometimes referred to as being made by a semi-carbonic maceration, but is more precisely a blend of classical red winemaking and carbonic maceration. The proportions of the latter range from 50 to 80 per cent of the volume of the wine.

In Australia there are variations on the process, one of them being to pass the grapes through a roller crusher with the jaws set widely apart so that most of the grapes remain uncrushed. The mass is then yeasted and fermented so that the juice undergoes a yeast alcoholic fermentation, while the intact berries undergo the internal enzymatic breakdown described above. The mass is drained and the whole grapes and skins pressed, and the pressings returned to the fermenting juice. This is considerably easier to carry out than a true carbonic maceration process, while enabling some carbonic maceration flavour to be imparted to the wine.

An important aspect of carbonic maceration wines is that they live in bottle for more than the two to three months regarded as the life of Beaujolais Nouveau on the Paris market. This short life is because the wines are shipped to Paris in cask, spritzig, slightly cloudy but rarely through malo-lactic fermentation. They are consumed in two to three months and, if left to the following spring, the warm weather recommences the malo-lactic fermentation and the wines tend to deteriorate. However, if the wines are properly handled and bottled after undergoing malo-lactic fermentation, or alternatively protected against this occurring, they will last considerably longer in bottle.

Heat extraction of colour from red grapes

In the red grapes used for winemaking in Australia and the classical vinifera varieties used in New Zealand, the anthocyanin and tannin pigments are present in the skin, in the vacuoles of the surface layers of the cells, and the juice is not coloured. Certain hybrid grapes (little grown in Australia) have red juice. When the grapes are heated above about 50°C these peripheral cells are killed and the pigment is released into the pulp. If the grapes are then pressed the juice expressed is deeply coloured, and may be fermented as for white wine without skin contact. The higher the temperature, the more rapid is the release of pigment, and in practice a temperature of 60 to 75°C is used, with 20 to 30 minutes holding time to allow for diffusion of the released colour into the flesh of the berry.

Heat extraction of colour has been in operation for many years, and in eastern United States is standard commercial practice for making red grape juice. Commercial heat treatment of grapes for winemaking is about sixty years old, being initially used in Europe to handle mouldy grapes. In practice, several methods of heat treatment are available, differing in procedure but identical in principle. The grapes are crushed, some of the juice may be drained off and either the must heated or the separated juice heated and sprayed over the grapes. Heating should be rapid, since the activity of the various enzymes in the must (oxidative, pectolytic, proteolytic) is most rapid at 45 to 50°C, depending on the enzyme and pH. Therefore, the temperature should be raised above this level as rapidly as possible. The most effective method of doing this is with a swept-surface heat exchanger ('oenoheater'), which brings about rapid heating of the must without localised overheating.

Colour extraction from the vacuoles of the damaged peripheral cells into the juice by diffusion is accompanied by slowly mixing the hot must to facilitate pigment diffusion. The grapes are then pressed (usually continuously since the process lends itself to continuous operation), the red juice cooled, inoculated with yeast and fermented as if it were white juice. The resulting wine retains its purple colour in a stable form, but has less of the varietal character than that obtained by traditional (non-heated) fermentation. Heating also releases considerable grape pulp which renders the wine turbid. Addition of pectic enzyme during cooling of the juice aids clarification, because heating destroys the natural pectinase enzymes.

The process has both advantages and disadvantages. Advantages are continuous or semicontinuous operation, ease of handling the skins (no cap to plunge nor skins to remove from fermentation tanks) and rapid removal of the skins from the cellar in the same day. The process thus has considerable economic advantages. Disadvantages are that the heating equipment is usually only for the one purpose and thus lies idle for most of the year; the juice has to be cooled before fermentation; the wine requires more clarification; and it may differ in taste from that made from the same grapes by traditional fermentation. It does not (or should not) have a cooked taste. The process can be automated and equipment made by various makers is available. Production of dry white, sweet red and white dessert wines by heating the must has also been carried out in Australia for some years and results in big, full-flavoured wines, and the process is now established in Australia as one of the alternative winemaking procedures.

Freeze concentration of wine

This process operates on the principle that when an aqueous solution is partially frozen the water freezes first, leaving the remaining solution richer in solute or dissolved solids. A typical example is in the formation of sheet ice in salt water, in which the ice consists of relatively pure water, with the sea water surrounding it becoming proportionally richer in salt.

So it is with wine, in that when partially frozen and the ice removed, the wine becomes more concentrated—higher in alcohol, sugar, acids and all other solutes. The same principle is involved in making *Eis-wein* (ice-wine) from frozen grapes in very cold climates, such as Germany. The frozen grapes are pressed without warming to extract the concentrated juice, while the ice, representing a proportion of the water, is removed with the skins. The *Eis-wein* thus produced by fermenting the concentrated juice is prized for its greater sweetness and complexity.

The practice of freeze concentration is sometimes used in Australia to concentrate sweet white table wines to make them more sweet and luscious. One simple procedure is to immerse a cooling coil in the wine, on which a mass of ice freezes. The coil is then removed and the ice allowed to melt. This results in the wine being partially concentrated, and the colder the refrigerant in the cooling coil the more rapidly does the block of ice form.

Chaptalisation

Chaptalisation is the process of adding sugar to must or wine—a technique widely practised in cold winemaking countries. It derives from Jean Antoine Chaptal (1756–1852), a minister of the French Government who proposed it in 1801. Other names are *sucrage* in French, *Zuckerung, Anreicherung* and *Verbessrung* in German, *zuccheraggio* in Italian, and sugaring or sweetening in English-speaking countries. It is legal in cold winemaking countries where the musts are too low in sugar and too high in acidity.

The laws governing the addition of sugar are complex, and vary in different countries. In some regions permission may not be granted every year, depending on the climate at the time. It is legal in New Zealand, which is the reason for its consideration here, but is not permitted in Australia, although a case could be made for its use in poor years in Tasmania and perhaps in the coolest mainland areas. In Australia, sugar can be added to sparkling wine for the secondary fermentation, and to flavoured wines, coolers and brandy. The New Zealand Food Regulations (1984/262) permit the addition of the following sweeteners to must and wine: fructose, glucose, glucose syrup, sugar and syrup BP, with the addition of not more than 5 per cent of drinking water for incorporation.

In Europe, the wine-growing areas are ranked into five categories, based on latitude, by regulations established by the European Economic Community. Definitions are made for each zone as to the minimum natural alcoholic content which the must should yield for that type of wine, the total maximum alcoholic content after sugar addition, and the limits of sugar addition. Sugaring is normal in the most northern (coolest) zones, permitted only in unfavourable years in the intermediate zones and then in lesser amounts, and not permitted in the warmest areas. In Germany, the wines designated as *Qualitätswein mit Prädicat* cannot be sugared.

Crystalline cane sugar (sucrose) is normally used rather than beet sugar, except for red vintages in which no distinction is made. Brown sugar is avoided because of the molasses taste imparted. The rate of addition is determined by the desired final alcohol content in the wine and thus depends on the must. It is based on the fact that 100 grams of invert sugar produces between 45 and 48 grams per litre of alcohol during complete fermentation. To obtain an increase of 1 gram per litre of alcohol requires the addition of 2.4 grams per litre of sucrose, because in the inversion process of sucrose to glucose and fructose by the naturally occurring invertase enzyme in the yeast, the amount of invert sugar is 5 per cent higher than the amount of sucrose, due to the uptake of one molecule of water during inversion. To raise the level of alcohol by 1 per cent by volume (which is about the usual rate of increase) in white wines 17 grams per litre of sugar are required, and for red wines 19 grams because of loss of alcohol by warmer fermentation and pumping-over operations.

For white wines the free-run juice is normally sugared rather than the must, whereas in red wines the must is sweetened. This is often carried out in France in two parts, the first at the beginning of fermentation to give a boost and produce an additional rise in temperature to aid colour extraction, and the second towards the end of fermentation to maximise the extraction. Without the addition of sugar in Europe millions of litres of thin and poor wine would be produced. However, excess sugaring renders the wine too light in body and unbalanced, and this is a danger in the process. In extreme cases in the cold areas in Germany chaptalisation can amount to the production of as much as an additional 4.5 per cent alcohol by volume.

The sugar should be dissolved before addition, because if added directly to the must or juice in a tank it falls to the bottom and forms a sweet layer as it slowly dissolves. To treat a tank, the required weight of sugar is poured slowly into a small vessel into which must or juice is continuously run from the tank with stirring, and the must or juice with the sugar completely dissolved continually pumped back into the tank. Sugar addition is best carried out in one step before or at the beginning of fermentation when the yeast is most active. It must be remembered that sugar addition gives rise to a further temperature increase, which needs to be taken into account in assessing the cooling requirements for the fermentation. The addition of sugar to red wines before or during malolactic fermentation is dangerous, because of the possibility of lactic fermentation with its resulting flavour and quality impairment.

The following table gives the relationship between the must weight of low-sugar musts and the potential alcohol content of the resulting wine. It is based on German white musts and is of necessity approximate.

Oechslé	Brix	Baumé	Potential alcohol	
			g/l	% v/v
50	12.2	6.9	48	6.1
55	13.5	7.5	54	6.8
60	14.7	8.2	60	7.5
65	15.8	8.8	67	8.4
70	17.0	9.4	73	9.2
75	18.1	10.1	78	9.8
80	19.3	10.7	84	10.6

6 Microbiology and fermentation

Grape juice is a restrictive medium for microbiological growth. It is sweet (normally containing 18 to 24 per cent of sugar), acidic with pH normally between 3 and 4 and titratable acidity between about 3 and 8 grams per litre as tartaric acid, and contains added sulphur dioxide. Wine is more restrictive than grape juice because it contains alcohol (7 to about 20 per cent by volume). Therefore only those micro-organisms which can tolerate these rather restrictive conditions can grow. These comprise some of the yeasts and certain lactic and acetic bacteria. Moulds will grow in grape juice but not in wine, because they are inhibited by the alcohol. Many micro-organisms are present on the waxy bloom of grapes, which consists mainly of oleanolic acid, and these are selected naturally into those which can and cannot grow.

Louis Pasteur said that wine is one of the most healthful and hygienic of beverages, indicating that pathogenic or disease-producing bacteria cannot grow in wine. It is possible to isolate from the bulk wine some other harmless bacteria, such as spore-forming *Bacillus*, but these do not grow in wine in the same way as do the other micro-organisms mentioned above and simply exist in small numbers. They can occasionally be isolated from bulk wine and have no detectable influence on the wine. They are surprisingly alcohol tolerant, and can occasionally be isolated from brandy containing 38 per cent by volume of alcohol.

The natural micro-flora of grapes consists mainly of moulds with lesser numbers of bacteria and yeasts, and varies with climate and soil type. It is this natural micro-flora that spontaneous fermentations, as distinct from pure-culture fermentations, depend on. Due to the wide variability of microbial types found in the natural flora of the grapes from one region to another, and indeed from one vineyard to another, it is not possible to predict the success of a natural fermentation.

The yeasts which grow readily in grape juice are the fermenting yeasts, mainly *Saccharomyces* (sugar-loving) and these are now added as selected pure cultures, which are dealt with later in this chapter. Strains and spores of the *Saccharomyces* differ considerably in their tolerance to alcohol. Indeed, it is possible to obtain up to 18 per cent by volume of alcohol during fermentation, in which small additions of sugar are added at regular intervals. Thus, it is possible to make a fortified wine without the addition of fortification.

The bacteria are limited to only two groups:

1 *Lactic acid bacteria* which belong to the genera of *Lactobacillus* (long rods), *Leuconostoc* (short rods), and *Pediococcus* (spheres). Their main contribution is in malo-lactic fermentation and, occasionally, lactic spoilage.

2 The *acetic acid bacteria* or *Acetobacter* which are almost wholly spoilage organisms, producing mainly acetic acid (legal maximum limit 1.5 grams per litre in Australia and 1.2 in New Zealand) and ethyl acetate.

Thus we can see that relatively few genera of micro-organisms can grow in grapes and wine. In spite of the restrictive nature of both grape juice and wine, these organisms, if not controlled, can bring about serious reduction in quality of the wine if their growth is not desired. The specific aspects of these micro-organisms will be discussed later.

Yeast starter-cultures and their preparation

Historically, wine fermentations occurred spontaneously due to chance yeasts, and the results were frequently unpredictable. Pure cultures were first used for brewing in about 1890, and later for winemaking. It is interesting to note that Pasteur in his classic studies on fermentation did not work with pure cultures. Pure yeasts for winemaking became established in Australia in about 1950, having been used earlier for sparkling winemaking.

We are now able to define the attainable goals for the rational use of pure yeast cultures in the primary alcoholic fermentation as follows:

- Rapid onset of fermentation, enabling the effective use of fermentation vessels in the shortest time.
- Predictable and controllable fermentations.
- Absence of undesirable flavour and aroma.
- Efficient conversion of grape sugars to alcohol, leaving no residual fermentable sugar.
- Possibility of creating specific and desirable yeast flavours.
- Predictable flocculation characteristics under certain conditions, such as in sparkling winemaking.

With the above in mind it is clear why the use of pure-culture yeasts is widespread in the wine industry, and why it is one of the factors responsible for the general high quality of Australian and New Zealand wines. In themselves yeasts do not create quality, which comes from the grapes, but are important in preventing poor quality. However, yeasts can also be selected for flavour enhancement, which occurs with the production of greater amounts of the higher alcohols and esters. This is useful with neutral grape varieties, but is relatively short-term, such as six to twelve months, because the esters hydrolyse over time.

The sources of selected yeasts are research institutions in Australia and overseas, winery laboratories and commercial suppliers of dried preparations. Yeast strains should only be bought from reputable suppliers who monitor the strains for viability, contamination and mutation. Yeasts can be supplied on agar slants or in dried form. When the slants or freeze-dried (lyophilised) cultures are used, the winery needs to be able to build them up into pure starter cultures. This is done by a series of serial transfers in increasing volumes of sterile nutrient medium. The final sterile inoculum is then added to the bulk of the juice which is generally not sterilised. The procedure is as follows. (See also Fig. 6.1.)

With a flame-sterilised inoculating loop, transfer aseptically a small quantity of the yeast from the slant agar culture into about 100 millilitres of heat-sterilised diluted grape juice or other suitable medium. When an agar slant is used, new slants should be prepared from the parent culture and stored at 4°C in the refrigerator. These are the working cultures, and are used to avoid possible contamination of the parent culture.

Incubate this liquid culture at 25 to 30°C for 2–3 days until active fermentation is underway, indicated by cloudiness and gas production. This temperature is close to that for optimum growth of yeast (30 to 35°C), but above the optimum temperature for must fermentation.

Pour this culture aseptically into approximately 2 litres of sterile diluted grape juice containing about 50 milligrams per litre sulphur dioxide, and allow to ferment at the same temperature as the winery fermentations will be conducted.

Transfer this culture into 50 to 100 litres of sterile grape juice in a vessel equipped with an air sparge, so that the culture can be aerated during growth. This increases the number of yeast cells and enhances the production of sterols and fatty acids which encourage yeast growth.

Fig. 6.1: Pure yeast culture

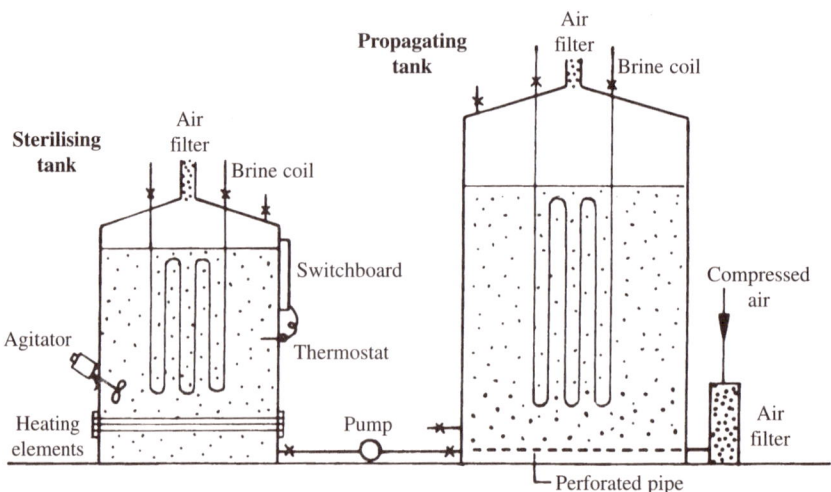

If a larger volume of yeast starter is required this culture is transferred into a larger yeast propagator fitted with an air sparge. This pure-culture fermentation is kept going by regularly drawing off the culture to inoculate the musts and adding fresh sterile grape juice. The propagator in the winery should be large enough to provide about one-tenth of the total quantity of must to be inoculated on a daily basis. The yeast is usually renewed at regular intervals, such as every two weeks.

At the peak of an aerated fermentation for production of the yeast starter the yeast cell numbers should be at least 300 million cells per millilitre. If less than this, the growth conditions are inadequate. It is important that the yeast used to inoculate a must contains high levels of ergosterol, lipids and the energy reserve materials glycogen and trehalose. Yeast is unable to grow for many generations without access to oxygen or ergosterol. The yeast strains used in winemaking have an absolute requirement for the B-group vitamins biotin, pantothenic acid, the grape sugar-alcohol inositol and nitrogen-containing compounds, such as amino acids. The latter can be replaced or supplemented with diammonium phosphate or ammonium hydroxide.

However, no vitamin deficiencies have been found in Australian musts, except in desulphited juice which is deficient in thiamine, and in concentrated juice which may be deficient in biotin. Insufficient amino acids may limit growth in some musts, and can result in the formation of hydrogen sulphide and a decrease in the amounts of higher alcohols and esters produced. This is the reason for the addition of diammonium phosphate to the must or juice before fermentation. For further details see the section later in this chapter on incomplete fermentation of clarified juice.

The number of cells required to inoculate a must is between 5 and 10 million cells per millilitre final concentration—the higher figure is for red must on skins. Therefore, it is desirable to count the cells in the propagating vessel to calculate how much starter culture to add. This count is best made with an haemocytometer slide under a microscope or by measuring the turbidity, although this is less accurate. In the fermentation of musts, as distinct from preparing the starter culture, the cell numbers at the peak of fermentation are between 80 and 160 million cells per millilitre. The clarity of the wine or the yeast starter culture gives some indication of the numbers of yeasts present, as shown by the following table:

Appearance of the wine	*Yeast cells per millilitre*
Brilliantly clear	1,000 (10^3)
Clear to brilliant	10,000 (10^4)
Slight haze	100,000 (10^5)
Light cloud	1,000,000 (10^6)
Heavy cloud	10,000,000 (10^7)
Opaque	100,000,000 (10^8)

If a commercial dried yeast preparation is used the manufacturer's directions should be followed, particularly as they relate to rehydration. This is normally carried out in warm water at 35 to 40°C for 30 minutes, and if this is not done the culture will be relatively ineffective. Various commercial dried yeast preparations are now available, and permit a more simple preparation of the yeast starter. The dried yeast can be added directly after rehydration to the must, or grown in a yeast culture generator and used in the same manner as a culture which has been grown from an agar culture. The viability of these commercial preparations can be checked by microscopic examination using a vital stain, such as methylene blue, which stains only the dead cells.

Mixed pure cultures are sometimes used, but a problem is to maintain the desired proportions in the mixture. Some yeasts tend to dominate others, due in some cases to a killer factor excreted by certain yeasts which prevent or restrict the growth of other similar yeasts.

Killer yeasts

Killer yeasts were first discovered in 1965 and considerable information is now available on this interesting subject. A number of yeasts from at least seven genera produce what are called killer toxins, either proteins or glycoproteins, which kill certain other yeasts. The presence of killer toxins is demonstrated in the same way as is the presence of antibiotic compounds released from certain moulds, by observing the inhibition of growth of one strain in the presence of another.

In this connection there are three kinds of yeasts, viz killer strains, sensitive strains which are killed by the toxins excreted by the killer yeasts, and resistant or neutral strains which are unaffected. Many killer proteins have now been identified, and these were originally classified into ten groups, known as K1 to K10. In fact, some recently identified toxins do not fall into these groups and it is apparent that the classification of the killer toxins needs to be widened.

The toxic activity is greatest in the range of pH 4 to 5 but it can still be apparent during wine fermentations at pH 3 to 4. It is associated with virus-like particles in the killer yeasts, and current studies are concerned with the genetics of killer toxin production. The toxins are stable up to approximately 30°C and more stable at lower pH than higher, usually being inactivated above about pH 5. It is interesting to note that dried yeast starter cultures with killer properties are obtainable commercially.

The killer characteristics are not effective in maintaining pure cultures, because a killer yeast when grown with other yeasts will only result in the death of certain of these which are shown to be sensitive, so a killer strain cannot be regarded as having a sterilising effect on the medium. The mechanism of the effect of killer yeasts in their inhibition of growth of sensitive strains has not yet been fully worked out, but one important point is that the presence of these killer toxins in beverages appears not to be harmful to the health of the consumer. Breweries, of course, are aware of killer yeasts but they try to avoid their use because of the possibilities of these organisms producing off-flavours in beer. Work carried out on the ecology of killer yeasts has shown that they exist in nature in larger proportions under warm conditions than cold, and are not resistant to European winter conditions. Also killer yeasts can apparently lose their killer factors on long storage.

Research currently is concerned with identifying the genetic characters in a range of yeast genera responsible for production of the killer toxins. Morphologically the killer yeasts are identical with normal yeasts, except that they may contain small virus-like particles in their cytoplasm. The initial hope that these strains would be able to conduct pure culture fermentations in the presence of contaminating micro-organisms, by virtue of the killer toxin eliminating the other micro-organisms, has not been found to be reliable.

Alcoholic yield from fermentation

The basis of calculation of the yield of alcohol from fermentation of the sugar in grape juice is that alcohol (ethanol) and carbon dioxide are the two major products, but not the only ones. During fermentation, sugar is broken down to alcohol and carbon dioxide and converted into a range of other secondary products, as well as being used by the yeast for growth. One kilogram of invert sugar (glucose and fructose) produces approximately 480 grams of alcohol in complete fermentation, depending on the temperature, aeration and type of yeast. The formula on which the yield of ethanol is based is that proposed by Gay Lussac in 1810, which is as follows:

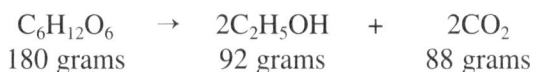

$$C_6H_{12}O_6 \quad \rightarrow \quad 2C_2H_5OH \quad + \quad 2CO_2$$

| 180 grams | 92 grams | 88 grams |

To take an example, grape juice containing 20.0 per cent sugar (measured as reducing sugar by chemical analysis) would produce by fermentation 96.3 grams of alcohol per litre or 12.20 per cent of alcohol by volume—the latter figure obtained by dividing the weight per cent of alcohol by its specific gravity (0.7893). This average value assumes minimum loss of alcohol by evaporation, a yeast which does not produce excessive quantities of other by-products, absence of aeration and cool fermentation.

However, sugar in must is usually measured by a hydrometer as degrees Baumé, Brix or Oechsle. For example, a must of 22.0° Brix corresponds to 12.2° Baumé, 1.092 specific gravity or 92° Oechsle. This hydrometer reading measures total dissolved solids, of which sugar from the must of mature grapes is the major part. Actual reducing sugar in white musts of mature grapes is the major part. Actual reducing sugar in white musts averages 2.0 per cent or 20 grams per litre less than the Brix reading, or 1.1 less than the Baumé reading. Red musts are somewhat higher, depending on the amount of pigment and other materials extracted from the skins during fermentation.

Thus, a drained white must of 22.0° Brix or 12.2° Baumé would contain on average 20.0 per cent of fermentable sugar, depending somewhat on the grape variety and the stage of maturity. On fermentation this would yield 12.2 per cent alcohol by volume. The relationship between Baumé and yield of alcohol varies with the Baumé level, and at 10 to 12° Baumé generally approximates to the same figure expressed as alcohol yield per cent by volume. This is why wine-makers work to a rule of thumb of 1° Baumé yielding 1 per cent alcohol by volume. But since the amount of reducing sugar in the must is not precisely indicated by the hydrometer reading, any calculation of alcohol yield based on the hydrometer reading of the juice must be approximate. The precise way is to measure the sugar content of the juice chemically and base the calculation on this figure as indicated above.

Incomplete fermentation of clarified juice

The occasional incomplete fermentation of clarified white juice is one of the nuisances of winemaking. The fermentation proceeds slowly and eventually comes to a stop with some sugar still remaining. The restarting of these 'stuck' fermentations is not always easy—involving reseeding with the same or a different yeast and possibly warming the juice. Having 100,000 litres of a stuck fermentation in the middle of vintage can be a problem.

The first time I encountered incomplete fermentation in white juice was in the 1950s, in pilot-plant fermentation in 1 to 5 litre lots of filter-sterilised grape juice for evaluating different strains of wine yeasts, where many of the fermentations stopped short of completion or fermented far too slowly. In part this was due to certain strains of yeast, since yeasts differ considerably in rate and completeness of fermentation. However, the problem was mainly caused by clarification of the juice. If the juice was not clarified it normally fermented to completion.

At that stage little information was available on this problem. The late Professor Schanderl of Geisenheim had encountered it and found that addition of inert particles helped in stimulating the fermentation. In the above studies on yeast evaluation such additions before fermentation resolved the problem and a range of seemingly inert solids was effective. These included diatomaceous earth, cellulose powder and bentonite.

There appear to be two reasons for the enhancing action of these solids. Certain solid particles occlude air (oxygen) by virtue of their structure. When diatomaceous earth suspended in wine is microscopically examined, the skeletal nature of the earth can be seen to occlude air bubbles in the claw-like structure of the individual particle, since they are in reality skeletal siliceous remains of diatoms. This air is available to the yeast cells resulting in an increased growth rate, which assists in synthesising sterols and encouraging survival of the yeast. However, the amount of air which can be occluded in this way is small, and another mechanism is involved. Particles have the ability to bind nutrients to their surface by hydrogen bonding. Many nutritional compounds required by growing yeast cells are attached in this way, and the yeast grows faster in proximity to such solids, and thus more cells are generated to promote complete fermentation. The same situation exists with opalescent or turbid grape juices, in which the particles of suspended grape flesh behave in the same way. Winemakers know that cloudy juices ferment better than clarified juices.

Yeast growth is related to the nutrient status of the grape juice, and we are learning more about this. Addition of diammonium phosphate to assist in preventing hydrogen-sulphide formation improves the nutrient status. The level of available nitrogen in Australian musts is low by European standards, so winemakers tend to add diammonium phosphate, usually at a level of 200 milligrams per litre.

Australian musts generally appear to contain adequate vitamins for yeast growth. Thiamine is the only vitamin which may be present in sufficiently low amounts as to limit yeast growth, and this usually occurs in desulphited grape juice. French data indicate that *Botrytis* growth on grape berries also reduces thiamine content in the must. If thiamine is limiting, yeast growth is slowed to a rate controlled by the yeast's ability to synthesise it. Biotin is also required by wine yeasts, but excess is present in grape juice and biotin deficiency does not appear to be a problem. Some winemakers add a nutrient preparation of vitamins together with diammonium phosphate, but insufficient information is available at present to indicate whether such a vitamin addition is warranted. It can do no harm.

Oxygen deficiency in the must results in poor fermentation. Oxygen is needed to build up cell numbers in the yeast starter, and ensure adequate synthesis of sterols and related compounds, which aid yeast growth and survival during fermentation. Therefore, the starter culture should be aerated before addition to must to ensure a high count of active viable cells. If oxygen is deficient in the must, as can occur when draining under carbon dioxide, for example, the lag phase between yeast addition and onset of fermentation is prolonged, and the delay is indicative of insufficient oxygen.

The significance of all this to the winemaker is that if clarified juice is to be fermented the yeast culture should be aerated before addition (a wide general precaution anyway), and addition of diammonium phosphate (about 200 milligrams per litre) and thiamine (about 1 milligram per litre) is desirable.

Recovery of volatiles from fermentation

Winemakers have long speculated that the carbon dioxide from wine fermentation may entrain sufficient amounts of desirable volatile compounds to justify being condensed and added back to the wine.

There is precedence for this view, in that aroma ('essence') recovery in the concentration of fruit juices is carried out commercially. However, the situation with wine is not analogous to fruit juice concentration, in that the volatile compounds in wine are entrained in quite low vapour concentrations (depending somewhat on the temperature of fermentation) in a great volume of carbon dioxide. They are thus much more difficult to condense, and very cold condensing temperatures are needed, such as that of liquid nitrogen at minus 196°C, rather than industrial refrigeration temperatures of perhaps minus 15°C.

If industrial refrigeration is used, the condensed product consists largely of water and alcohol, while the desirable aromatic compounds in quite low concentrations are largely uncondensed from the mass of carbon dioxide entraining them.

Fortification

This is related to the discussion in Chapter 4 of the making of fortified wines. Fortification is the process of adding highly rectified grape spirit or brandy spirit to must or wine before, during or after fermentation, so as to increase the alcohol level. The minimum alcohol level of fortified wine for sale in Australia under the State Food and Drug Acts is 17.0 per cent by volume and the maximum is 23 per cent, except for wines intended for export where the permitted level is 24 per cent by volume. Most fortified wine contains between 17 and 19 per cent alcohol by volume.

The Australian and New Zealand wine industries have a history of producing fortified wines, and as recently as 1965 more than half of the wines made in Australia were fortified. Many of these wines were and still are of outstanding quality on world standards, and have earned Australia an enviable reputation in this area.

The types of grape spirit used are either highly rectified fortifying spirit with an alcohol content between about 94 and 96 per cent by volume (SVR or *Spiritus Vinum Rectificatum*) or brandy spirit distilled at a strength of between 57 and 83 per cent by volume. Fortifying spirit is essentially high-proof alcohol with very few other constituents (congenerics) apart from water. Since alcohol and water form a constant boiling mixture at 96.4 per cent by volume, these cannot be separated by distillation, even with the most efficient distillation columns. To obtain fortifying spirit above this alcohol content, such as 100 per cent or absolute alcohol, the water must be removed as a ternary azeotrope by incorporating another compound, such as benzene, which preferentially combines with it and is separable by distillation. Brandy spirit, on the other hand, contains a number of congenerics, mainly higher alcohols, aldehydes and esters, which add to the complexity of the spirit, and thus to the wine to which it is added.

The addition of either of these spirits during fermentation, and followed by mixing, stops fermentation by inhibiting the growth of yeast. If the added alcohol is not mixed with the fermenting juice it will float on the surface, permitting fermentation to continue below. The sweetness of the resulting fortified wine depends on the sugar content of the must or juice at the time of fortification. The sweetest wine is obtained by fortifying must or juice without fermentation (mistella), while the driest is obtained by fortifying a dry wine.

Fortification is not a precise operation, because of the difficulty of accurately measuring the Baumé of fermenting must, as well as continued fermentation after draining the juice from the skins before alcohol addition. The use of a hydrometer reading during fermentation to measure the sugar content is misleading, since alcohol (specific gravity 0.789) causes the hydrometer to sink, thus indicating a lower apparent sugar content than is actually present. This results in the use of the term 'apparent Baumé' where both sugar and alcohol are present. The term 'obscuration' used in this context means the amount by which the true alcoholic strength is obscured by the presence of other dissolved constituents, such as sugar and caramel, which increase the reading of the hydrometer. The calculation of obscuration is based on the figure of 1.0 per cent of alcohol by volume being obscured by 0.26° Baumé or 0.47° Brix.

When fortifying spirit is added heat is produced, due to the chemical reaction between the alcohol added and the water moiety of the must or wine. This results in an expansion in volume. However, when this heat is removed, the volume of the fortified product falls to a level slightly below that of the combined volumes. This contraction in volume is usually sufficiently small to be ignored in practice.

In order to carry out a fortification the following information is required:

• the initial sweetness of the must or wine to be fortified expressed as degrees Baumé;
• the initial volume of the must or wine to be fortified and its alcohol content;
• the volume and the alcoholic strength of the neutral fortifying spirit or brandy spirit used;
• the volume of wine after fortification;
• the alcohol content of the wine after fortification.

In calculating the amount of alcohol to add and the stage of fermentation at which the additions are to be made, it is necessary to know the amount of alcohol in the must or wine and the Baumé (or Brix) degree at which the fortification should take place. When these are known the required volume of spirit of a given alcoholic strength can be calculated, using a formula based on the Pearson Square. The basis on which the calculations are carried out, together with an example, are set out below:

Must: 5,870 litres at 13.4° Baumé
Fortifying spirit: 95.0 per cent V/V alcohol.
Required: Wine containing 18.5 per cent V/V alcohol at 4.5° Baumé.
Question: How much fortifying spirit is required and when should it be added?

1 *Obscuration*—the *final* alcohol content multiplied by 0.26, on the basis that 1 per cent V/V alcohol obscures 0.26° Baumé
i.e. $18.5 \times 0.26 = 4.8°$ Baumé
Thus this alcohol content obscures 4.8° Baumé of sugar.

2 *Apparent Baumé* after fortification when corrected for alcohol obscuration give the *true or corrected Baumé*
i.e. the apparent Baumé of 4.5 plus the obscuration of 4.8 equals 9.3° Baumé
This figure is used to calculate the alcohol content produced by fermentation prior to fortification, on the basis that 1° Baumé produces 1 per cent V/V alcohol.

3 *Alcohol produced before fortification*
The initial Baumé minus the true or corrected Baumé expressed as alcohol as in (2) above
i.e. $13.4 - 9.3 = 4.1°$ Baumé
Thus 4.1 per cent V/V alcohol would be produced prior to fortification.

4 *Obscuration* of Baumé by the alcohol formed during fermentation, using the conversion figure of 0.26 in (1) above:
$4.1 \times 0.26 = 1.1°$ Baumé
Thus the alcohol produced by fermentation obscures 1.1° Baumé.

5 *Apparent Baumé at fortification*:
This is obtained by deducting the obscuration from the true or corrected Baumé
i.e. $9.3 - 1.1 = 8.2°$ Baumé
Thus the must should be fortified at 8.2° Baumé when it will contain 4.1 per cent V/V alcohol.

6 *Fortifying spirit addition*:
This is calculated using the Pearson-Square formula
$$X = \frac{V(C - A)}{B - C}$$
Where
X = litres of fortifying spirit required
V = litres of must or wine to be fortified
C = final alcohol content
A = alcohol content of must or wine at fortification
B = alcohol content of fortifying spirit
$$X = \frac{5870(18.5 - 4.1)}{95 - 18.5}$$
$$= \frac{84,528}{76.5}$$
$$= \underline{1105 \text{ litres of spirit}}$$

i.e. 1105 litres of fortifying spirit added to 5870 litres of fermenting must at 8.2° Baumé will result in 6975 litres (a reduction in volume of approximately 1.6 per cent actually takes place but which may be ignored) of wine 4.5° Baumé containing 18.5 per cent alcohol by volume.

7 Adjusting acidity in musts and wine

In the warmer areas of Australia the natural acidity of grapes tends to be low, in contrast to cool countries, such as New Zealand, where acid is frequently excessive due to the difficulty of obtaining sufficient ripeness in the grapes. Moderately high acidity or, more particularly, low pH, is essential for the production of balanced and harmonious table wines. If the grapes are too low in acid the must needs to be acidified in order to bring the pH into the correct range, which is set out below. Low pH (high acidity) has the following important advantages in processing and increasing quality:

- increases the antimicrobial and antioxidant properties of sulphur dioxide;
- encourages the growth of desirable micro-organisms;
- tends to inhibit microbial spoilage;
- encourages clarification of juices and wines;
- accentuates the fruitiness and balance of wines generally.

Accordingly, from the Australian viewpoint it is important to consider the ways by which acidity may be increased.

Acidification

The usual acid to add is L(+) tartaric acid, which is the naturally occurring acid in grapes. Addition of the racemic or DL-tartaric acid should not be made because of the resultant slow precipitation of DL-calcium tartrate. Addition of tartaric acid results in reduction of pH followed by precipitation of potassium bitartrate. However, this precipitation occurs after the acidity has been increased, so that the tartaric acid addition has already had its effect.

The addition of acid results in a pH reduction which is not directly related to the amount of acid added, because of the variations which occur in the buffering capacity of different wines. The largest decrease in pH occurs with the first part of the acid addition, as illustrated in the following practical examples:

- A dry red wine with a pH value of 4.04—progressive additions of 2 grams per litre of tartaric acid were made and resulted in reducing the pH successively by 0.34, 0.22, 0.16, 0.14 and 0.10.

- A dry red wine with a pH value of 3.72—the pH reductions for the same progressive additions were 0.24, 0.18, 0.14 and 0.11.
- For white wines the decrease in pH is greater because of lower potassium and the absence of pigments and other phenolics, which buffer the change in pH. For a dry white wine with a pH of 3.75 the same addition rates of tartaric acid resulted in progressive pH reductions of 0.35, 0.22 and 0.13.

It is not possible to establish an accurate rule-of-thumb for the amount of acid to be added, and the normal rate of addition ranges from 1 to 4 grams per litre. When citric acid was added to the above wines its effectiveness in reducing the pH was approximately 15 per cent less than tartaric. In addition, citric acid can be partly metabolised by yeast during fermentation, and by certain lactic acid bacteria to acetic acid. Furthermore, it is not permitted to be added to wines intended for export.

Malic acid can be used to reduce pH, but is not normally used for this purpose. Not only can it be partially metabolised by yeast during fermentation, but it also increases the malic acid level in the must and resultant wine. This means that when malo-lactic fermentation takes place the loss of malic acid can result in a large reduction in acidity of up to about 0.45 of a pH unit. Such an acid reduction can be detrimental to the quality of the wine, unless it is corrected by a further acid addition.

Plastering, or the addition of calcium sulphate (gypsum), results in an increase in acidity, by decreasing the pH without changing the titratable acidity. It is normal practice in sherry-making in Spain and results in precipitation of calcium tartrate and the liberation of hydrogen ions. It also tends to make the wine bitter and, for this reason and because of the slow precipitation of calcium tartrate, its addition is not usual in Australia and New Zealand.

The addition of acid to must and juice is much more important than its addition to wine, and winemakers need to establish rates of addition based on experience with their own wines. It is possible to set guidelines based on the level of pH reduction required. For grapes intended for dry red wines an addition of tartaric acid to the must to reduce the pH to between 3.2 and 3.4 is recommended. For white grapes a pH value of 3.1 to 3.3 in the must or juice is required. The tartaric acid addition is best made at the crusher, where the acid is weighed and dissolved in the minimum quantity of cold water and added to the grapes before crushing or to the must immediately afterwards. It is essential to add the acid as early as possible, and desirably before fermentation. The use of a minimum quantity of water to dissolve the tartaric acid is permitted by the Food and Drug laws.

Deacidification

Deacidification, or the reduction in acidity in the juice or wine, is carried out in cold climates where the grapes do not mature sufficiently and have too much acid and not enough sugar. Consequently, it is sometimes required in New Zealand but rarely in Australia. It is normal practice in cold European wine-growing areas, such as Germany and Switzerland.

The prevailing European procedure for deacidification is to add calcium carbonate or calcium carbonate-malate (double salt) to the must or wine, which brings about a precipitate of calcium tartrate or, in the latter case, combined calcium tartrate-malate, with a reduction in acidity. Potassium carbonate can also be used, and biological deacidification, in which the acidity is broken down with certain micro-organisms, is another alternative.

Calcium carbonate deacidification is based on the principle that 1 gram per litre of calcium carbonate precipitates 1.7 grams per litre of tartaric acid. The powdered calcium carbonate is mixed with a small volume of must and added to the bulk with continuous mixing. A slow precipitate of calcium tartrate takes place, and the resulting wine can be unstable for a period depending on the length of time that the calcium tartrate takes to deposit.

Double-salt deacidification has partially superceded the use of calcium carbonate alone. It was developed by Münz in Germany in 1960 and first used in 1965, a year characterised by very high acidity on the Mosel. It was designed to remove portion of both tartaric and malic acids (the two main acids) in the must, as an improvement over traditional deacidification by addition of calcium carbonate which removes only tartaric acid as insoluble calcium tartrate. In both procedures carbon dioxide is released. In the past the level of malic acid could only be lowered, and then only in the wine, by biological means, such as malolactic fermentation or by the use of certain *Schizosaccharomyces* yeasts which decompose malic acid. Neither of these two procedures are reliable in very acid wines.

Double-salt deacidification requires a specially prepared calcium carbonate containing a small proportion of calcium tartrate-malate. This product ('Acidex') is produced by C.H. Boehringer & Son, Ingelheim, Germany. When mixed with must to raise the pH value to 4.5 or above, both malate and tartrate anions combine with calcium to form the characteristic porcupine-like crystals of calcium malate–tartrate. This insoluble racemic compound consists of a ring structure, in which the tartrate and malate anions are bound to each other with two atoms of calcium, one at each end of the two molecules.

Rates of Acidex addition are based on the initial titratable acidity and that desired after deacidification. For 1000 litres of must the recommended quantities required are as follows:

Initial acidity g/l	12	15	15
Desired acidity g/l	8	8	10
Acidex addition kg	2.7	4.7	3.4
Must portion in litres	380	520	380

e.g. must containing 15 grams per litre titratable acidity (measured as tartaric acid) for deacidification to 8 grams per litre requires 520 litres to be gradually stirred into 4.7 kilograms of Acidex (not the other way around). After 15 minutes stirring the suspension is filtered and the filtrate added to the untreated balance of the must (480 litres).

Deacidification has been largely carried on white musts and the procedure is as follows:

1 Prepare the juice to the stage where it is ready for yeast inoculation prior to fermentation.

2 Measure its volume and titratable acidity and calculate the weight of Acidex to use from the manufacturer's table, examples of which are given above.

3 Add the stipulated portion of the must to the Acidex with continual stirring and check that pH is 4.5 or above. After 15 minutes filter or centrifuge then add the clear filtrate to the untreated balance of the juice.

Double-salt deacidification is more complicated than the simple calcium carbonate deacidification, because part of the must is over-deacidified, filtered and added back to the untreated must. However, deacidification is greater because portion of both malic and tartaric acid are removed.

Potassium bicarbonate deacidification. It is possible to bring about a reduction in acidity by the addition of either potassium bicarbonate or carbonate—the former is preferred as the more 'gentle' deacidification agent. The potassium combines with the tartrate anion and precipitates as potassium bitartrate while the bicarbonate disappears as carbon dioxide. This can be carried out before or after fermentation and an addition of 1 gram per litre will reduce the titratable acidity by 0.75 grams per litre as tartaric acid. The advantage of this treatment over calcium salt addition is that no calcium is involved (with the consequent problem of slow calcium tartrate precipitation); the pH is not raised higher than about 3.6, and the precipitation of potassium bitartrate takes place quickly. For this reason it is often the preferred method.

Microbiological deacidification. Some strains and species of the yeast genus *Schizosaccharomyces* have the ability to break down malic acid in wine and their use has been proposed for this purpose. However, they require another carbon source, such as sugar, and do not compete well with the more strongly fermentative *Saccharomyces*. In addition, they can also produce off-flavours, and their use is presently rather unreliable.

Adjusting acidity with ion-exchange

Ion exchange is a process which lends itself to wine technology. Its main use is in stabilising wine against potassium bitartrate crystallisation, and more recently in altering the acidity. For details of the principles and background of ion exchange see the section on the use of ion exchange to cold-stabilise wine in Chapter 10.

Ion exchange offers a practical means of increasing the acidity of juice and wine, as well as lowering the pH further than is achievable by the addition of tartaric acid (or other weak acid) to give the same increase in titratable acidity. When tartaric acid is added, both hydrogen ions and the weak base, the tartrate anion, are added, while with ion exchange hydrogen ions alone are increased in the wine with an equivalent decrease in the other cations—potassium, sodium, calcium and magnesium.

The procedure for hydrogen exchange is to charge the cation-exchange resin with hydrogen ions by regeneration with mineral acid, wash out the excess acid with water of low cation content, pass the clarified juice or wine down through the resin until the exchange capacity is exhausted, then backwash the column and repeat the process. The cations in the juice—potassium, calcium, magnesium and sodium—are taken up by the resin, and the equivalent quantity of hydrogen ions are released with consequent reduction in pH. For specific details of the operation of ion-exchange columns see the section in Chapter 10.

In the following discussion I will refer to wine, but the same procedure applies equally to juice, except that the pH reduction is normally less. During the exchange the pH drops sharply to between 2.0 and 2.2 and remains there until the resin is exhausted, then rises rapidly to its original value. The volume of wine which can be treated to the breakthrough or exhaustion point of the resin is between 10 and 20 resin-bed volumes for complete exchange, and the flow rate is between 6 and 12 resin volumes per hour. Calcium and magnesium are most strongly attached to the resin (along with traces of iron and copper, if present), followed in order by potassium, sodium and hydrogen ions. Thus, the hydrogen-charged resin will take up all the other cations and liberate the equivalent amount of hydrogen ions into the wine. Regeneration of the resin requires the replacement of potassium and the other cations on the resin with hydrogen ions, i.e. a reversal of the treatment process.

The divalent cations calcium and magnesium are held at the top of the resin column, while the monovalent cations potassium and sodium are in the lower layer. During acid regeneration, the monovalent cations are released first, followed by the divalent cations. The equipment and resin used for pH reduction are the same as that for sodium exchange for potassium-bitartrate stabilisation, especially in that no corrosible metals, such as brass, should be used.

The procedure for column operation, which requires a minimum depth of resin of about 75 centimetres, is to regenerate the resin with 6 resin volumes of mineral acid by slow up-flow for 30 minutes, so that the acid diffuses uniformly up through the resin. Then rinse with water by down-flow to remove the excess acid and drain the column. This rinsing takes about 6 resin volumes and lasts about 30 minutes. Then introduce the clarified juice or wine slowly from the bottom and, when the column is filled and air bubbles are removed, commence the treatment by down-flow at a flow rate of between 6 and 12 resin volumes per hour, stopping the flow when the breakthrough point indicating exhaustion of the resin (a rapid rise in pH) is reached. Drain the column and backwash the resin with 12 resin volumes of water to remove any suspended matter and to reset the resin bed ready for the next regeneration.

Various mineral acids, such as hydrochloric, sulphuric and nitric acids of accepted commercial quality, can be used for regeneration, and the choice is governed by cost, convenience of use and the resin manufacturer's recommendations. In Australia, sulphuric acid is the preferred regenerant on the basis of cost and convenience of use, and is normally used at a concentration level of between 3 and 5 per cent by volume and requiring about 6 bed volumes (5 per cent sulphuric acid contains 51 grams of acid per litre and is 4.5° Baumé or 1.032 specific gravity). Higher concentrations are avoided because of the possibility of calcium sulphate precipitation in the resin. Hydrochloric acid in 10 per cent solution (1 part acid and 2 parts water) and nitric acid (1 part acid and 9 parts water) can also be used, each requiring about 2 bed volumes, and the products of regeneration are all soluble. (10 per cent hydrochloric acid contains 105 grams of acid per litre and is 6.6° Baumé or 1.048 specific gravity; 10 per cent nitric acid contains 105 grams of acid per litre and is 7.5° Baumé or 1.054 specific gravity.) The purity of the acid used for regeneration is important, because a phenolic-like contamination, for example, can occur in the resin resulting from the use of hydrochloric acid stored in black recycled plastic containers.

The water should be the purest available, since any cations which it contains are bound by the resin and result in a reduced exchange capacity. Rinse water if high in dissolved salts can seriously reduce exchange capacity, and in such cases the water should either be treated beforehand by hydrogen-ion exchange or rain water should be used. If the resin contains a high level of calcium, and sulphuric acid in excess of 5 per cent is used as a regenerant and the regenerant flow is stopped for any reason, it is possible for the column to be cemented solid with calcium sulphate (gypsum).

If water containing suspended solids is used to rinse the column the resin bed then acts as a filter, with resultant inefficient operation and possible resin blockage and breakdown due to excessive pressure drop. Mains water in parts of Australia contains a high level of both suspended and dissolved solids, and should be clarified and treated before use. Rain water is preferable. Since aeration of the wine is possible due to the handling involved, the column and lines should be flushed with inert gas beforehand. It is important to remove air or inert gas from the resin bed by upflow of wine before treatment, otherwise channelling is likely to occur resulting in inefficient exchange.

Wine may be treated in two ways, either by treating a batch until the breakthrough point is reached, then blending this with untreated wine, or by treating the wine and passing it back into the same vessel which is kept stirred. Both methods are used commercially with pH monitoring. In the second method when the desired reduction in pH is obtained, the flow is stopped. If treated wine at about pH 2 is blended with untreated wine, an addition of 15 per cent by volume lowers the pH of the blend by about 0.2, depending on wine type and buffer capacity. Over-running the exchange capacity of the resin past the breakthrough point is another alternative.

The amount of wine which can be treated is between 10 and 20 resin volumes depending on the resin exchange capacity, efficiency of regeneration, wine composition and treatment procedure. Resin capacity is fixed by the volume and type of resin. The efficiency of regeneration influences how many exchange sites in the resin are occupied by hydrogen ions, and the state of the resin (amount of fouling, absorbed materials and so on). The composition of the wine and, in particular, the concentration of cations influences the volume which can be treated, and this depends on the particular wine. Finally, the procedures used to treat wine, such as purity of the wash water, correct flow rates and so on, are important if the best results are to be achieved.

When using the column to treat red wines, the resin becomes contaminated with pigments which are incompletely removed by the normal regeneration and washing procedure. If white wine is then passed through the column, some of the pigment may be released into the wine, so care is needed if the column is used for both red and white wines, and it is preferable to have two columns. Suspended materials can be absorbed onto the resin, reducing the number of exchange sites available and thus lowering the exchange capacity of the resin. The resin can be restored by treatment with 1 per cent formaldehyde, a 5 volume solution of hydrogen peroxide or a sodium hypochloride solution containing 3 per cent available chlorine. Storage of the resin when the column is not in use is best achieved by regenerating in the hydrogen form and storing under acidified water with 500 milligrams per litre sulphur dioxide, or brine or diluted fortifying spirit containing about 20 per cent alcohol by volume.

Hydrogen exchange has established itself as a useful procedure for increasing acidity without the addition of tartaric acid, which is both expensive and can result in formation of potassium bitartrate crystals. Both clarified juice and wine are treated, and the procedure is standard practice for pH reduction of juice prepared with high levels of sulphur dioxide, in which case the decrease in pH to about 2.8 or below converts sulphur dioxide largely into the molecular form, enabling its more effective removal by the desulphiting equipment. An important feature of ion exchange is its versatility, in that the same resin (sulphonic-acid bead-type cation exchanger) and equipment can be used for hydrogen exchange, mixed hydrogen and sodium, and sodium exchange. The first two increase acidity and all three render the wine stable to tartrate precipitation.

8 Wine-handling operations

Racking

Racking is the process of transferring juice or wine from one container to another, so that the clear supernatant is drawn off and the deposit left behind. It is similar in principle to decantation. The word 'racking' is wine industry jargon and stems from the Middle English *rakken*, which comes from old French Provençale *arraca* or *raca*, meaning the skins, stems and seeds of grapes.

At first sight the operation of racking appears quite simple but more is involved, as we shall see. Many deposits can exist in must and wine, such as particles of grape solids, yeast and bacteria, tartrate crystals, settled finings, metal and protein precipitates and the like. Their rate of settling depends on particle size, differences in specific gravity between the particles and the liquid, electrical charge (if any), temperature gradients in the vessel and viscosity of the liquid. The rate of sedimentation is described by Stoke's law, which defines the rate of fall of a small sphere in a viscous fluid.

Certain deposits settle quite firmly and are not readily disturbed when the supernatant liquid is removed. Examples are yeast lees, tartrate crystals and egg-albumen fining. Some deposits settle poorly and are easily disturbed, such as grape flesh in settle juice, bentonite and isinglass. Two of the problems of bentonite fining, particularly sodium bentonite, are the light flocculent deposit, which does not compact well and is readily disturbed, and its large volume.

In large stainless-steel tanks situated outside the winery a considerable vertical stratification in temperature usually exists (details are given later), and convection currents occur if the tanks are warmed on one side by the sun. This delays settling of flocculent finings and can result in inefficient racking. A further point with tall tanks is that the pressure resulting from the hydrostatic head of liquid keeps carbon dioxide in solution in the depth of the tank. When a wine is racked and the pressure reduced, the gas comes out of solution as bubbles and can disperse the settled finings.

Some small charged particles, with an approximately diameter of 1 micrometre and with a specific gravity close to that of wine, such as lactic acid bacteria (*Leuconostoc*, *Lactobacillus* and *Pediococcus*), tend to remain dispersed due to their charge effect and settle slowly. Racking such hazy wines can be ineffective unless the bacteria are settled by fining beforehand.

Fig. 8.1: A racking pipe and plate

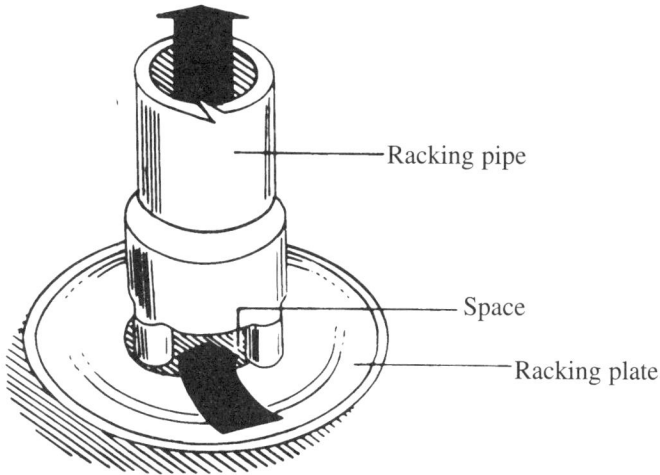

Racking pipe

Space

Racking plate

Useful points to observe when racking juice or wine are as follows:

- Use a sight glass in the suction line to the pump, illuminated by a light so that the clarity of the supernatant liquid can be observed as it is drawn off.
- Use a racking plate on the end of a rigid racking pipe (rather than a flexible hose) with a non-return valve. The racking plate (see Fig. 8.1) is usually a flat or slightly bowl-shaped sheet of stainless steel fixed so that a centimetre or so separates the end of the racking pipe from the plate, which is set at right angles to the pipe. This enables the liquid to be sucked into the pipe from a horizontal direction while the pipe is vertical. The non-return valve usually consists of a heavy rubber ball which fits into a seat in the pipe, and prevents backflow of liquid which may disturb the deposit when the pump is switched off.
- With deposits which are easily disturbed it helps to follow the wine down with the racking pipe with the aid of a light, so that the point of suction is kept just below the level of the descending wine. At the same time regulate the speed of the pump accordingly.
- For wines prone to damage by aeration ensure that all connections are airtight, and use inert gas in both the racked and the receiving vessel.
- Use of a rotatable short racking pipe permanently installed in a stainless-steel tank is a good idea. This pipe, which is bent at right angles inside the tank, is capable of being swivelled in the tank from the outside so that as the pipe is turned it follows the wine down to the level of the deposit. Large tanks usually have two, or sometimes more, fixed racking valves at different heights above the floor of the tank. Installation of a rotatable racking pipe about a metre long affords more flexibility to the operator during racking.

In handling white wines it is important to transfer them as little as possible, and racking is best combined with another operation, such as centrifugation or earth filtration. Racking cold white table wine in the presence of air into another vessel is not good practice, because atmospheric oxygen dissolves rapidly. However, red wines benefit by racking and the associated mild aeration. Bordeaux red wines are normally racked from one barrique to another several times during the first year after making.

Blending

The blending of wine is an important aspect of winemaking. Blending is essentially the process of mixing two or more wines for the following purposes:

- to achieve a certain wine style;
- to standardise a product;
- to obtain the best balance and complexity from wines from different grape varieties, areas and vineyards;
- most importantly, to improve the total quality of the various individual wines.

It is a process carried out widely in winemaking countries and results in better wines. The golden rule in blending is never to blend two or more wines unless the resulting blend is superior to that of each component.

The extent of blending ranges from little or possibly none in the case of small wineries to extensive blending in the case of certain dessert (fortified) wines. As an example, the great sherries from Spain are all blends of many individual components, and the secret of sherry-making resides largely in the skilful blending of these components. In fact, the process of fractional blending—the solera system—was developed in Spain to produce a highly standardised product. In French champagne production the *cuvée* (or base wine) is carefully blended to obtain the best flavour and acid balance from the blend of the grape varieties Pinot Noir, Pinot Meunier and Chardonnay. Pinot Noir provides the long palate flavour while Chardonnay contributes flowery aroma and Pinot Meunier complements the overall structure. So it is in producing the same and other wine types in Australia, where blending both in the vineyard and in the winery is usual. In fact, the most successful winemakers are generally the best blenders.

This is probably the place to lay to rest an erroneous assumption in the minds of some people, including wine writers from time to time, that blending is somehow improper, and blended wines are in some way adulterated and inferior to the individual components. This is incorrect, and the finest wines in Australia are blended to a greater or lesser extent. This is even true for wines made from grapes grown in the one vineyard, where the individual wines made in the various fermentation tanks are then blended to constitute the bottled product. A completely individual wine may have educational value in illustrating the type of wine resulting from the grapes in that particular vineyard at that time, but from the point of view of quality and palate appeal it may well be deficient in one or more aspects of its structure. Organisations involved in introducing appellation schemes to Australia need to be aware of this fact.

In the case of blending to a standardised wine there are many such wines in Australia marketed in large volume, with the requirement that the wines should not vary from one bottling to the next. We all know that various factors contribute to the characteristics and quality of a wine. For example, a particular year may result in a somewhat different wine from the same vineyard, depending on the amount of rain, temperature and other climatic factors. The yield of wine from a vineyard likewise varies. The wines in question are produced in such quantities that many vineyards are involved, with the wines resulting from them possessing different characteristics. Because of these variables it is normal practice with widely selling labels to blend a number of component wines to maintain continuity of style.

Many examples can be quoted of blending grape varieties to achieve special flavours or characteristics. The famous clarets from the Médoc, northwest of Bordeaux, are all blends of red grape varieties, mainly Cabernet Sauvignon, Cabernet Franc, Merlot and Malbec. This combination of varieties has been found over many years to give the best wine for the wide climatic variations experienced in that region, in which the varieties complement each other. As an example, Merlot in small proportion provides the softness and smoothness lacking in the middle palate of Cabernet Sauvignon.

In Australia, the two red varieties Cabernet Sauvignon and Shiraz complement each other to the extent that the blend is usually better than either of the two varieties separately—so much so that some consumers regard the name Cabernet-Shiraz as one variety. Another example is Traminer-Riesling, a blend of Traminer and Rhine Riesling which combines the desirable features of both varieties. Many other examples could be quoted.

Blending enhances the balance or harmony (drinkability) of the wine. A wine with too much or too little acid is unbalanced, in the same way as is a red wine with too much tannin. It is desirable to blend to correct these palate imperfections. This is an area of much importance to the winemaker, who seeks the ideal varietal and area mix, including the contribution of individual vineyards, as well as suitable oak maturation and so on.

Blending takes into consideration the various factors listed above, and the winemaker needs to have the end result clearly in mind when commencing a blend. In other words, haphazard blending is of little value. Furthermore, blending should not be a means of disposing of inferior or bad wine, which can contaminate or dilute the good wines resulting in a lower-quality blend. The golden rule stated at the beginning—the blend must be better than the individual components—should always apply.

From the winemaking point of view it is important to stabilise the blend rather than the individual components. The reason is that two (or more) stable wines when blended together can result in an unstable blend. The reasons for this can be complex, but a simple example will suffice. The cold stability of a wine depends on various factors, one of which is its pH. If two cold-stable wines with different pH values are blended, the pH change may be sufficient for the blend to be unstable.

Blending is a precise operation and is carried out initially in the laboratory with the range of component wines, measuring cylinders and tasting glasses. This constitutes the trial blend, which is compared with the components to ensure that it meets the requirements of the blend. This is essentially the skill and the art of the winemaker, who identifies the strengths and weaknesses of each component of the proposed blend, in order to make most use of them in the final blend.

Finally, the legal requirements must be kept in mind. These are quite specific in Australia, and state that a wine from a designated grape variety or region must contain at least 80 per cent of that variety or from that region. If the wine is a blend of two or more varieties, the order in which they appear on the label must reflect the proportions of each variety in the blend. Finally, the vintage date requires that at least 95 per cent of the wine must be from that vintage.

Cooling

Cooling has had a long history in winemaking. As early as the sixteenth century, it was noted that precipitation of tartrates by cold improved the wine. Artificial cold by refrigeration was developed in Italy and France before 1900. Similarly, the possibility of concentrating wine by partial freezing of the water had been postulated in the sixteenth century and developed from 1870. an early application of refrigeration was to assist '*dégorgement*' in Champagne production, the elimination of deposit of yeast which accumulates against the cork (later a crown seal) of the inverted bottle after fermentation in bottle. The neck of the bottle was (and is today) immersed in brine at about minus 20°C and the block of ice containing the yeast deposit blown out when the cork or crown seal was removed. The operation was a success when introduced in 1884 and fifteen plants were installed in the Champagne district by 1900.

Refrigeration was first used for cold stabilisation in the Australian wine industry at the Emu Wine Company at Morphett Vale in 1932. This plant was followed by others, and all installations for the next twenty years were used for cold-stabilisation. The first application of refrigeration for temperature control of fermentation was in the mid 1950s at G. Gramp & Sons Orlando winery in the Barossa Valley and Cinzano in Sydney, where cold brine was circulated through jackets around pressure fermenters. After a number of these brine-cooled pressure fermenters were installed, it was apparent that wines made in non-pressurised fermenters could also be improved by controlling the fermentation rate with low-temperature brine.

The first direct application of a refrigerant without an intermediate coolant, such as brine, was the use of flooded liquid ammonia in a swept-surface heat-exchanger (ultracooler) at Mildara winery in Merbein for cold-stabilisation in 1956. In 1960 the Berri Coop Winery (now Consolidated Cooperative Wineries Limited) installed a three-tube swept-surface heat-exchanger with flooded liquid ammonia, for cooling must directly from the crusher prior to fermentation. These swept-surface heat-exchangers became popular because of their versatility. The swept agitation not only promoted the precipitation of potassium bitartrate for stabilisation and helped keep the heat-transfer surface clean, but also increased turbulence and hence increased the cooling heat transfer.

In more recent years, the industry has investigated and installed simpler and cheaper evaporators into their refrigeration systems: shell-and-tube, tube-in-tube, jacketed tanks, skin cooling and immersion chillers. In the larger wineries screw compressors have been introduced, usually to provide base-load refrigeration with reciprocating compressors for light loads. Currently, we are witnessing the growth of programmable logic control (PLC) systems and computer control, where the controls for the refrigeration plant are incorporated into a master system, including crushers, centrifuges and so on, with print-out reporting.

Importance of temperature control
Controlled temperature is important in the production of fine table wines. Its influence begins when the grapes are ripening, and continues through fermentation, aging and bottling of the wine. Even high-quality grapes of the best varieties will not produce the best-quality wines if proper temperature is not maintained during the winemaking process. Temperature control is important in table wines to preserve quality, for the following reasons:

- High temperatures encourage oxidation, microbiological spoilage and instability.
- Desirable aroma and flavour compounds, as well as alcohol, are depleted by volatilisation under warm fermentation and storage conditions.
- Above about 38°C the yeast becomes sluggish and fermentation may stick with residual sugar.

Consequently, refrigeration has developed into one of the most important and essential requirements of Australian white winemaking. Its use extends from must and fermentation cooling to cold-stabilisation and, more recently, to cooling the whole winery. The main heat-load in the winery is the temperature of grapes, and together with must cooling, is of sufficient importance to be treated separately (see the sections on grape temperature in Chapter 2 and must cooling in Chapter 5).

Refrigeration
The amount of refrigeration required depends on the tonnage of grapes crushed, their temperature, other heat loads in the winery, the proportion of white wines made, and other factors. There is no simple relationship between winery size and

refrigeration requirement. As we have seen, hot grapes are the most important heat load, and their temperature may be as high as 40°C. If grapes can be cooled, such as by harvesting in the cool of the night, then the refrigeration requirement is considerably reduced. Calculations show that a reduction in the grape temperature of 10°C can achieve a reduction of 8.7 kilowatts (2.5 tonnes) of refrigeration per tonne of grapes per hour, by not having to use refrigeration for this purpose.

To take an example, assuming a winery crushing at an average rate of 20 tonnes per hour, yielding 750 litres of juice per tonne, and cooling the must from 30 to 10°C, a refrigeration capacity of approximately 350 kilowatts (100 tonnes) would be required. If the grapes were 10°C cooler on arrival at the winery, this would result in a saving of 175 kilowatts (50 tonnes) of refrigeration. Accordingly, the size of the refrigeration plant required for this purpose, without taking into account spreading the load by use of a brine tank or similar storage, would be reduced by approximately 50 per cent.

The type of refrigeration system depends on individual requirements. The most efficient system with the greatest cooling effect for a given power input is achieved by cooling the product directly with an evaporating refrigerant, separated only by a thin stainless-steel wall. Primary refrigerants are the working fluids of the refrigeration cycle, evaporating and condensing as they absorb and release heat. Although other refrigerants are available, primary refrigerants are usually R22 (one of the freons) and ammonia. Although the selection is a compromise between conflicting desirable properties, freon is generally used in small units and ammonia in large units. Ammonia is about 2 per cent more efficient than R22, and has a higher latent heat of vaporisation requiring less refrigerant to be circulated for a given heat load. Freon is non-toxic and odourless, whereas ammonia has a strong smell which indicates leaks. Ammonia is the cheapest refrigerant and is manufactured in Australia, while all the freons are imported. Many other factors have to be considered, such as the reaction of the refrigerant to the common contaminants—moisture, air and oil.

Many wineries use a secondary coolant, or 'brine' system which serves as a reservoir of cold to smooth out peak cooling loads. It is easily reticulated about the winery enabling alterations and extensions to be made more readily with cheaper and more flexible coolant piping and controls. As a brine system is less efficient than direct refrigerant (depending on the sizes of the brine/refrigerant evaporator and the wine/brine heat-exchanger) it is economically important to maintain the brine temperature as high as possible. The higher the average brine temperature, the greater is the refrigeration capacity and the lower the consumed power unit of refrigeration.

There is no secondary coolant suitable for all applications. Water is an excellent secondary coolant because of its cheapness and favourable thermodynamic properties, and is used in some wineries at about 2 to 5°C. However, it cannot be used for cold-stabilisation because of its high freezing point of

0°C. Dissolving salts (e.g. sodium or calcium chloride) or adding water-soluble liquids (e.g. ethyl alcohol, propylene glycol) lowers the freezing point of the 'brine' solution. Up to a certain point the more salt dissolved, the lower is the freezing point. As the salt content increases, the fluidity (viscosity), specific heat and thermal conductivity, and hence the heat transfer properties, all decrease. Hence, the stronger the solution, the greater the quantity which must be circulated for a given amount of cooling. A 20 per cent by volume ethanol brine having a freezing point of minus 10°C, together with a corrosion inhibitor, is used in many Australian wineries.

Refrigeration usage in Australian wineries has increased greatly in recent years and demand has changed. Cooling methods for white wine fermentation cover a wide range from simple, inexpensive skin cooling to expensive and efficient jacketed and insulated tanks with recirculated refrigerant, the temperature of the fermenting juice being sensed with a thermometer and the refrigerant flow controlled by automatic valves.

Skin cooling uses recirculated chilled water which flows down the outside of stainless-steel tanks to a catchment tray leading to a chilled water reservoir cooled by a refrigeration compressor. The rate of circulation of cold water over the surface of the tanks is approximately 1500 litres per metre of tank diameter per hour.

Other in-place heat exchangers are coils or double-sided plates of various design built inside tanks, either permanently or removable, or with part of the tank wall as a jacket, whereby only one side of the plate is used for cooling. The refrigerant brine is circulated through the plates, coils or jackets and the chilled wine or juice in the tank circulated either by carbon dioxide generated during fermentation or by mechanical stirring. Such cooling can readily be automated.

Alternatively, the must or wine can be passed through an external heat exchanger, such as an ultracooler, plate or tube-in-tube. These can be cooled directly with evaporating refrigerant, as is usually the case with ultracoolers, or with brine, as in tube-in-tube must chillers.

The refrigeration cycle

To remove the heat from wine, the refrigeration plant must provide a lower temperature than that of the wine, so that heat flows of its own accord from the higher to the lower temperature. This heat transfer causes the refrigerant liquid at lower pressure to evaporate or boil to a vapour in the heat exchanger or evaporator. All that is required is a liquid with an evaporating temperature lower than the temperature of the wine to be cooled. The rest of the refrigeration plant, viz. compressor, condenser and liquid feed valve, simply recycles the vapour back to a lower pressure liquid. Although the refrigerant may be released to the atmosphere after absorbing heat from the wine (e.g. liquid nitrogen cooling) it is usually retained in a closed circuit and cycles continuously.

The refrigeration cycle has four separate operations.

1 Vapour from the evaporator is drawn through the suction line into the compressor. Here the pressure and temperature are raised by compression, and the high-pressure high-temperature vapour is discharged to the condenser.

2 In the condenser, cooled water and air cools the vapour, reducing its high temperature to the 'saturation temperature' corresponding to the discharge pressure, and then condenses the saturated vapour at a constant temperature back into liquid. By the time the refrigerant reaches the bottom of the condenser, all vapour has been condensed to liquid.

3 Liquid is temporarily stored in a liquid receiver, and the warm-temperature high-pressure liquid then flows to the liquid feed valve. As the liquid passes through this valve, the pressure is reduced so that the temperature of the evaporating liquid falls below the temperature of the wine to be cooled. Some of the liquid evaporates as it passes through the valve and this is called the 'flash gas'.

4 In the evaporator, the heat from the wine passes through the evaporator walls and evaporates the liquid at a constant pressure and temperature. The vapour leaving the evaporator has the same temperature and pressure as the evaporating liquid. The circuit is thus complete and the cycle is repeated.

Hence, a refrigerator is a heat pump. It removes heat at a low temperature and discharges it at a high temperature. The two pressures existing in the refrigeration cycle are often called the 'low side' and the 'high side' or, referring to the compressor, they are called 'suction pressure' and 'discharge pressure'. For every pressure there is a unique temperature at which boiling (or evaporation) and condensation take place. Different refrigerants have different pressures corresponding to the same temperature, e.g. at minus 15°C ammonia has a pressure of 135 kilopascals (gauge or kPa(g)); R12, 81 kPa(g) and R22, 194 kPa(g), or, conversely, at atmospheric pressure or 0 kPa (gauge) ammonia has a temperature of minus 33.3°C; R12, minus 29.8°C and R22, minus 40.7°C.

As the sole purpose of refrigeration is the transfer of heat, it is more meaningful to refer to pressures in terms of their temperatures. Hence, we often refer to a 'suction pressure of minus 10°C' instead of the correct 'suction pressures of 190 kPa gauge' (i.e. 190 kPa above atmospheric pressure).

Fermentation heat load

Grape juice fermentation is an important source of heat, because fermentation is an exothermic reaction. The amount of heat generated by fermentation of a gram-molecule of sugar (180 grams) is 98.5 kilojoules (kJ). In other words, 1 kilogram of grape sugar (glucose and fructose) generates 545 kJ. Each per cent of sugar (1° Brix or 0.56° Baumé approximately) in the must generates enough heat during fermentation to raise its temperature by 1.3°C if no heat is lost. Thus, a must of 12° Baumé (21.7° Brix or 91° Oechslé) would generate sufficient heat to raise its temperature by 28.2°C. However, up to 20 per cent of this heat is carried away by the 35 to 50 fermentation volumes of carbon dioxide evolved, depending on the sugar content of the juice. The precise proportions of the total heat generated lost by each of these mechanisms depends on the size, shape and material of which the fermenter is constructed, the surrounding air temperature and the rate of fermentation.

The warmer the juice, the faster it will ferment. As an approximate rule-of-thumb, refrigeration requirements are of the order of 100 megajoules (MJ) per tonne of grapes crushed, or 110 MJ per kilolitre or cubic metre of 12° Baumé juice. This is, of course, strongly influenced by the initial temperature of the grapes. The peak fermentation rate is generally about 1.5 times the average. This value, multiplied by the volume of must fermenting, provides the maximum rate of heat generation. The heat transfer area of the jacket or external exchanger can then be calculated, after including the heat gained from the surroundings through the tank walls.

The rate of fermentation is temperature dependent and with white wines is usually adjusted to obtain a uniform Baumé reduction of between 0.5 and 1° per day. This corresponds approximately to a fermentation temperature of 10 to 20°C. Most white wines are fermented at between 12 and 16°C and most red wines between 18 and 24°C.

Fermentation cooling

The fermentation heat load in kilowatts is the product of the volume of the fermenting juice in kilolitres or cubic metres and the required degrees Baumé per day reduction. A reduction of 2° Baumé per day for red wines constitutes a heat load four times that of white wines fermenting at 0.5° Baumé per day. For example, 1 kilowatt of refrigeration can control 20 tonnes of white juice fermenting at 0.5 Baumé per day in an insulated tank, but 1 kilowatt can only control 5 tonnes of red must fermenting at 2° Baumé per day in an insulated tank. Alternatively, 1 tonR (or 3.517 kW) can maintain 35 tonnes of fermenting juice at a fermentation rate of 1° Baumé per day in an insulated tank.

The heat gains from the surroundings can be calculated as in juice cooling above. These have to be added to the fermentation heat loads to obtain the total load requiring cooling or refrigeration. If the tanks are not insulated and housed in a 75-millimetres-thick polystyrene insulated building where the air is cooled by refrigeration, the heat gain from the surroundings in kilowatts is the total surface area of the building (walls and roof) in square metres divided by 85. This is still a heat load on the refrigeration plant, although not generated by the fermenting juice. Cooling fermentations in a cooled insulated building also introduces additional heat loads. The greatest of these is the power of the fan motors, which all ultimately appears as frictional heat energy in the air. Other sources of heat are people (approximately 0.25 kilowatts each), lights (0.015 kilowatts per square metre), pumps and air leakage through gaps and doors. For further information on refrigeration refer to Ray White's book *Refrigeration for Winemakers*, Winetitles, Adelaide, 1989.

Control of wine storage temperature

Control of storage temperature is an important aspect of the post-fermentation handling of wines, particularly whites. Transfer of wine from the fermenter to a storage vessel, or from one vessel to another, generally results in partial saturation with oxygen, more so when the wine is not saturated with carbon dioxide. The storage temperature influences the rate of irreversible oxidative browning reactions, and for white wines at temperatures below ambient the oxidative rate is reduced to about one-fifth its value for each 10°C reduction in temperature. Similarly, the hydrolysis of carboxylic esters is more than halved for each 10°C reduction in temperature.

Thus, table wine from fermentation to after bottling should be stored at a controlled temperature in the range of 0 to 18°C. In general terms, the higher the quality of the wine the cooler should it be stored. Such control is simple when the wine is in tanks with individual temperature control, but less simple when in casks or bottles. This is the reason why wineries are now being cooled, so that every operation and type of storage is temperature-controlled. It should be emphasised that oxidative deterioration of wine is irreversible, and that cooling fermentations is only one step in the cooling regime required in modern winemaking.

For the refrigeration requirements of cold-stabilisation see Chapter 10. The thermal properties of must, juice, wine and water are shown in Table 5.2 in Chapter 5.

Temperature stratification in the winery

As we have seen, a knowledge and control of temperature is essential to good winemaking, especially in warm to hot areas. Cellar temperature varies widely in Australia and most areas are hot by European standards. For example, in Germany the cellar temperature is normally between 9 and 15°C, along with must temperature of 5 to 15°C. In Bordeaux, the temperature of red musts is normally between 15 to 25°C, with 30°C being exceptional. As we well know, the temperature regime in hot areas of Australia is considerably warmer than this and imposes severe loads on insulation and refrigeration.

In addition, the temperature in the winery and in wine in bulk vessels can vary considerably because of its natural vertical stratification. Many examples can be quoted, and typical cases are given below. Two examples of temperature stratification measurements at different heights in wineries are given to indicate the influence of height. The first is in a new winery insulated with reflective foil, with mean values over three days during vintage:

Height	Minimum	Maximum
0.8 m	17°C	23°C
4.5 m	18°C	25°C
8.0 m	18°C	30°C

The second is in a nearby winery without insulation over the same period. Both wineries are in the Southern Vales region in South Australia.

Height	Minimum	Maximum
0.5 m	22°C	24°C
3.7 m	23°C	29°C

In both of these wineries a diurnal variation was evident—the temperature rose during the day and fell during the night.

In the first winery the temperature stratification in an insulated area set aside for storage of wines in cartons on pallets, which showed no diurnal variation, was as follows (mean of seven days):

Height	Temperature
0.5 m	20 ± 1°C
3.7 m	25 ± 1°C

The implications of these data are clear—the natural vertical temperature gradients in wineries can be considerable and can influence the quality of wine significantly. The storage of packaged table wines at temperature above about 20°C has been shown to bring about a progressive deterioration in their quality. This is the reason why modern wineries now cool storage cellars exposed to this kind of temperature gradient.

Let us now consider the storage of wine in stainless-steel tanks, and the extent of temperature variation encountered. Wine stored in these tanks naturally stratifies in temperature with the warmest wine being at the top of the tank. The extent of this temperature gradient depends on the location of the tanks and whether or not they are insulated. In non-insulated tanks exposed to the sun the temperature gradient can reach and sometimes exceed 30°C from the bottom to the top of the tank. It is not uncommon to find a temperature of 20°C at the bottom of the tank and 40 to 50°C at the top. The temperature at the top shows considerable diurnal variation, whereas near the bottom it is fairly stable. An example of the temperature variation occurring in dry red wine at three depths over four days in non-insulated and insulated 91,000-litre tanks exposed to the sun in the Barossa Valley in March is given below:

Depth below surface in cm	Non-insulated °C	Insulated °C
10	20–43	23-33
50	26–38	29–30
500	25–26	24–25

It is important to bear in mind that the influence of the diurnal variation in temperature is to mix the contents of the tank. The hot wine at the top of the tank, which is now of lowered quality because of being heated, is cooled by the cooler night temperature. Being then of greater density, it sinks, and its place is taken by wine of lighter density from below. This means that the damaging effect of heat on the top layers of wine is transmitted to the bulk of the wine by natural convection, resulting in a reduction of quality in the bulk of the wine.

The significance of this temperature stratification on wine quality is obvious given the overwhelming evidence that to conserve the quality of white and red table wines, the temperature from crushing through making, storage and packaging to the point of sale of the bottled or cask wine should not exceed 20°C. Current Californian recommendations on the most appropriate storage temperature for aging table wines in bulk are 13 to 18°C. At lower temperatures settling and clarification are slower, as are flavour changes associated with aging. Above about 18 to 20°C loss of volatile aroma and flavour compounds, together with oxidation and browning reactions, occur more rapidly and cannot be easily controlled. In addition, loss of sulphur dioxide and microbiological growth are both greater. Many of the desirable aroma compounds are rather volatile, and as the wine warms they increasingly enter the vapour phase above the wine. If the vessel is not sealed more become lost to the atmosphere, with a resultant decrease in their concentration in the wine and a concomitant reduction in quantity.

9 Fining

Fining is a procedure for clarifying and purifying liquids, and when applied to wine means the addition of either natural or synthetic materials to clarify and stabilised the product. The French equivalent is *collage* and the German *Schönung*. Fining is a traditional process of clarification and in practice (but not in theory) essentially a simple operation, in which a material is mixed with the wine, allowed to settle and the clarified wine racked or decanted from the deposit.

Sound wines often settle to a clear or brilliant condition, but may take a long time to do so. To hasten the process fining is used, whereby the particles in suspension are carried down with the fining agent. However, fining is more than simple clarification, which can be achieved by filtration, in that it may involve stabilisation which is a separate and distinct action. An example is bentonite fining, in which the stabilising action in removing heat-unstable protein is more important than the clarification achieved.

The mechanisms of fining can be quite complex and are usually oversimplified. The simplest explanation is that of electrostatic attraction, whereby the fining carrying a particular electric charge reacts with wine constituents carrying the opposite charge and the neutralised combination precipitates. An example is the reaction between positively charged gelatin and negatively charged tannin.

Fining is empirical, in that the removal of a certain constituent is not directly related to the amount of fining agent added—the reaction between the two is more logarithmic than linear. Various other considerations also apply, such as temperature (bentonite fines better in warm than in cold wine); different molecular weights of both the fining material and suspended particles; the amount and effectiveness of mixing, and so on. Consequently, each fining operation should be preceded by a trial to establish the minimum fining rate which will achieve the purpose.

It must be borne in mind that fining materials can have an adsorptive action on flavouring compounds in the wine—bentonite in particular can adsorb sufficient of these materials to lower their amount in wine sufficiently to reduce the flavour. In addition, every movement of the wine can expose it to air unless this is specifically avoided, and the resulting partial aeration can lead to oxidation. Furthermore, the fining materials themselves are usually naturally occurring and of variable purity, and can contaminate the wine by virtue of their addition. An example is the iron content of bentonite, which may be high enough to render the fined wine susceptible to iron haze. Further, the sediment or lees left behind after racking the wine leads to loss of some of the wine unless an efficient lees filter of some sort is used. Thus, finings should be used only when necessary and at the minimum effective rates.

Gelatin

The addition of gelatin is made to reduce the level of tannin in astringent red wines and, less frequently, in white wines. It serves as a fining agent to improve the flavour of excessively astringent and bitter wines, and can be added in conjunction with other fining materials, such as bentonite, tannin or silica (kiesel) sol.

The dosage rate is 0.05 to 0.15 grams per litre, and the method of preparation is to hydrate the required amount of gelatin powder by mixing in cold water overnight, then warming to dissolve and adding to the wine with thorough mixing. The gelatin should have little colour and a neutral odour. Its gelling power is expressed in bloom number, which should be between 80 and 200. This number is a measurement of the resistance to deformation of a gelatin block set solid from a 6.7 per cent solution at 10°C for 18 hours. The bloom number indicates the ability of the gelatin to absorb water, usually between six and ten times its weight, and the greater the bloom number, the greater the binding capacity of the gelatin. The desirable molecular weight range for fining is between 15,000 and 140,000.

Gelatin has an isoelectric point of pH 4.7, well above the normal pH of grape juice or wine. Thus, it is positively charged in solution and reacts with negative-charged molecules, such as phenolics, by hydrogen bonding. It should be remembered that gelatin is a protein and as such can cause protein haze in wine if excess is added.

Isinglass

At first sight isinglass is a curious substance to add to wine, for which it is used to remove phenolics and bitter tannins. It is made from an unlikely source—the swim bladder of certain fish, such as the kingfish and threadfish of Saigon and Penang, and the catfish of Karachi and Brazil. The name derives from the air bladder of the sturgeon (from the German *Hausenblase*—the French *ichtyocolle* or fish glue is less specific) from which it was first made. The *Codex Oenologique International* defines its composition for use as a fining agent for wine as: humidity less than 18 per cent, ash less than 1.2 per cent of the dry weight, total nitrogen above 14 per cent and iron less than 100 milligrams per kilogram. Isinglass is mainly used to clarify beer after fermentation by settling yeast and other insoluble material. Its use in wine followed its brewery application.

The swim-bladder tissue consists almost entirely of collagen, a protein containing a high proportion of the unusual amino acid hydroxy-proline. The isoelectric point is 5.5, so that at the pH of wine (3.0 to 4.0), it has a net positive charge which electrostatically attracts negatively charged particles in wine. Sometimes other non-charged particles become entrained in the complex and these too will sink to the bottom. Once settled the finings stabilise the sediment, making it more resistant to disturbance during racking.

Isinglass is a rather difficult material to prepare. It must be completely dissolved, which is the main problem in its use. The traditional process involves a number of steps. The selected and dried swim bladders are cleaned, bleached and sterilised, then prepared in strips and shredded or ground. Newly developed milling procedures yield a product which dissolves more quickly, and the more finely divided the isinglass, the more easily does it dissolve.

By virtue of its chemical composition isinglass begins to denature at quite a low temperature (10°C), and thus should be stored as cool as possible. If isinglass is prepared hot it undergoes partial hydrolysis and the molecular weight is reduced from 140,000 to between 15,000 and 58,000. Its fining effectiveness is likewise reduced and it then acts in the same manner as gelatin.

Isinglass has the advantage that it can be used to fine white wines without unduly removing colour, as may occur when casein or gelatin are used. The amount of lees is small, usually less than 2 per cent when compared with other finings. Bentonite, for example, can produce up to 10 per cent lees. Isinglass removes more leucoanthocyanins but less condensed tannins than do gelatin and casein. Isinglass is regarded by many winemakers as the best protein fining, resulting in a brilliantly clear and 'softer' wine. Fining rates are low, usually 0.02 to 0.1 gram per litre, and the solubilised material should be added slowly to the wine with thorough mixing. (Beer fining rates are 10 to 20 milligrams per litre.) Isinglass is frequently used in conjunction with bentonite, with the bentonite added first. Tannin addition is not desirable and may jeopardise the fining action.

The fining procedure is as follows:

In a 250-litre vessel add 60 litres of fresh rain water, 500 grams of citric acid and 140 grams of potassium metabisulphite. Mix until dissolved. Continue mixing and sprinkle 1 kilogram of finely divided isinglass on to the surface and mix until uniformly distributed in the solution. Allow to stand overnight in the cool (15°C) so that a gel is formed. Next day make the volume to 200 litres with rain water with thorough mixing. Further standing and mixing can be beneficial. Rubbing through a silk screen helps to reduce particle size but this is tedious. This solution contains 5 grams isinglass, 2.5 grams citric acid and approximately 350 milligrams of sulphur dioxide per litre.

Assuming a fining rate of 25 milligrams isinglass per litre of wine, for 1000 litres of wine, 25 grams or 5 litres of the preparation are required. This should be added to the wine by slowly introducing into the inlet side of a pump circulating the wine in the vessel, and continuing circulating until all the isinglass is thoroughly mixed with the wine. The wine is then allowed to stand until clear and racked off the deposit.

Milk and casein

Milk fining is a traditional treatment for white wines to remove phenolic bitterness. It is essentially a protein fining, and is related in its action to gelatin, egg albumen and isinglass. The essential milk constituent is casein, a heteroprotein present as the calcium form. It does not precipitate by heat but does so in acid medium, as distinct from the other proteins mentioned. It is relatively insoluble in water but soluble in alkali—which is the reason why casein is made alkaline before adding to wine. As soon as it is added it is exposed to the acidity of wine and flocculates.

Casein fining is widely used in white table wines and sherries for softening the palate, removing bitterness, harshness and off-flavours, and lightening the colour. The decolourising power of different caseins is directly related to their formol titration values, a measure of free amino groups.

Several types of milk fining materials may be used—skim or whole milk, lactic casein and sodium caseinate. If whole milk is added to wine (at rates up to 1 litre per 100 litres) the cream tends to float on the surface, and for this reason skim milk (with the butterfat removed) is more frequently used. It is simply mixed with water and slowly added to the wine with mixing. Skim milk is more gentle in its action than the casein products, possibly because it avoids the dissolving and mixing problems associated with the latter.

Lactic casein is preferred by many winemakers but is sometimes difficult to obtain. It needs to be made alkaline to dissolve and this is achieved by dissolving in warm water with about one third of its weight of potassium carbonate. The normal rate of addition of lactic casein is between 0.05 and 0.3 grams per litre (50 to 300 grams per 1000 litres). A concentrated solution is prepared and added slowly to wine to give the required final concentration.

Sodium caseinate is more readily available and is already alkaline, so is more soluble but still somewhat difficult to dissolve. Accordingly, potassium carbonate is added to the warm aqueous sodium caseinate solution, which is then stirred and left overnight. The rate of addition is the same as for lactic casein.

Milk fining using lactic casein or sodium caseinate is, like bentonite, largely a mixing problem. The alkaline fining should be prepared in warm water, stirred thoroughly to eliminate lumps, and screened or sieved before addition to wine. The addition should be made slowly, preferably through a venturi on the inlet side of a pump circulating the wine in the tank. After the fining has settled the wine is racked or filtered. If the fining is added too quickly it coagulates and either floats to the surface or settles to the bottom as lumps, both of which are largely ineffective.

In order to save on handling operations casein fining may be used in conjunction with and before other treatments, such as cold stabilisation or bentonite.

Casein, either as lactic casein or sodium caseinate, is used mainly on white wines—for red wines gelatin is preferred. Casein is the only protein which can be used in high doses without risk of over-fining and giving rise subsequently to protein haze.

Egg-white or albumen

This protein fining is used to a limited extent to clarify and remove harsh tannin from red table wines. The proteins in eggs are mainly albumen with some globulin, and each egg white contains 3 to 4 grams of protein.

The procedure used is to break the eggs, separate the yolks and combine the whites (the yolks make great omelettes!). These are then made into a 10 per cent solution with 0.5 per cent sodium chloride, which assists in dissolving the protein. The solution is then introduced into the wine via the inlet side of a pump circulating the wine in a tank. The usual dose rate is one to three eggs per 200 litres of wine.

Alternatively, frozen egg-white can be used, at a dose rate of between 0.1 and 0.5 grams per litre. The frozen powder is thawed and made into a solution in dilute salt solution as above. Foaming should be avoided in preparation because this interferes with the fining process.

Polyvinyl-polypyrrolidone (PVPP)

Most of the various materials used for fining wines are traditional, deriving from natural sources and frequently variable in composition. Examples are bentonite, casein, egg white, gelatin and isinglass. It is not surprising, therefore, that in this age of polymer-chemistry synthetic materials with defined composition and more precise function are being developed for such purposes. PVPP falls into this category and is the first synthetic fining material for wine. It is used in white wines to absorb phenolics which lead to browning and pinking.

PVPP is the abbreviation for poly-vinyl-poly-pyrrolidone, and is the larger molecular-weight polymer of PVP or poly-vinyl-pyrrolidone. Chemically, both are based on 2-pyrrolidone—a 5-membered ring containing a nitrogen atom subtended by a vinyl sidechain. The polymer consists of many of these units joined together through the side chain. The main product used is Polyclar AT produced by the GAF Corporation in the USA. Various vinyl-pyrrolidone polymers exist and are used for widely different purposes, such as blood plasma substitutes, cosmetics, pharmaceuticals, adhesives, coatings, detergents and soaps, electrical components, fibres and textiles, lithography and photography, and paper and plastics.

The smaller polymer, PVP, is available in a range of molecular weights from 10,000 to 360,000, all of which are more or less soluble in water. PVP was first proposed for use in beer in the USA in 1954. By contrast, higher molecular-weight cross-linked PVPP, which was developed in 1961 by a polymerisation technique using alkaline treatment, is practically insoluble. It was introduced into Australia for wine in 1972. The description of PVPP by the makers is as follows:

> Insoluble, high molecular-weight polymer used for beverage clarification and stabilisation. Used in the finishing of beer to improve flavour, clarity, colour and foam properties. Provides complete chill-proofing without enzymatic treatment; adaptable also to combination with enzymes. Reduces storage time for filtration. Stabiliser for taste and colour in whisky, wine, vinegar, fruit juices and tea.

PVPP is used in wine as a rather specific absorbent for phenolic compounds, particularly in pressings, which lead to astringency and browning of white wines. It is also used to remove or prevent pinking, in which application it absorbs the phenolic precursors of pink pigments. Its binding action on leu-coanthocyanins, catechins, flavonols and phenolic acids (in that order) takes place through hydrogen bonding, by which the phenol links to the ketoimide group in the five-membered ring. Because PVPP is practically insoluble in wines it may be considered as a processing agent rather than an additive.

In comparison with other stabilising materials, such as nylon 66 and silica gels, PVPP has the advantage that it is more adsorptive to phenols and can be used in conjunction with other stabilisers, such as enzymes or gels. It is essentially a gentle fining, which specifically removes undesirable phenolics and does not decrease the aroma of the wine.

From the legal point of view PVPP is a permitted additive to wine, with a legal maximum of 100 milligrams of soluble material per litre in Australia and 60 milligrams in New Zealand. Soluble material from PVPP does not usually exceed 1.5 per cent, i.e., for a dosage of 500 milligrams per litre, a soluble residue of not more than 7.5 milligrams would be expected.

Since PVPP is expensive, large users such as breweries tend to recover used PVPP by filtration or centrifugation, followed by treating with 0.5 per cent sodium hydroxide, neutralisation and reusing—a process which may be repeated many times. Incorporation of PVPP into filter sheets also enables wine to be treated continuously, without having to add and then collect the residue. The removal of anthocyanogens is logarithmic—high initially and decreasing progressively during filtration. An example for beer stabilisation is 85 per cent removal of phenolics after commencement of filtration, 50 per cent after 3 hours and 30 per cent after 7 hours. The sheets can be regenerated by backwashing with warm water, then hot 0.5 per cent sodium hydroxide solution, neutralising with 0.5 per cent sulphuric or phosphoric acid, followed by a hot-water wash.

The method of use in wine is to mix the appropriate amount (as determined by a trial fining) of the white PVPP powder in wine, then adding with continual stirring to the bulk wine and maintaining mixing for one hour to ensure good contacts between the insoluble fining and the wine. The PVPP is then allowed to settle to the bottom and the wine racked off. Rates of addition to wine depend on the amounts of phenolics to be removed, and accordingly vary considerably from about 0.2 to 0.5 grams per litre.

Tablets (Unitest 50) are available from GAF for trial fining to determine the correct dosage to use in practice. A 50-milligram tablet in 500 millilitres of wine corresponds to a dosage of 0.1 gram per litre. The tablets are added to wine and allowed to stand with shaking each 15 minutes for one hour. The wine is then filtered and evaluated to assess the required dosage.

Silica sol

This relatively new fining material is also known as Kieselsol or Baykisol. Its purpose is to prevent overfining with protein finings, such as gelatin, and to hasten deposition of the fining—it is thus an auxiliary rather than an independent fining. It is an aqueous colloidal suspension of silicon dioxide which carries a net negative charge. In the presence of positively charged particles, such as gelatin or naturally occurring protein, electrostatic bonding takes place which initiates flocculation and settling. Positively charged silica sol has also been developed, and when used in conjunction with normal silical sol gives a sharper and more rapid fining than silica sol and gelatin alone.

Silica sol is supplied as an opalescent suspension in which the concentration of silicon dioxide is normally about 30 per cent. The rate of addition is firstly 0.03 to 0.1 grams per litre of gelatin then 0.06 to 0.2 grams per litre of silica sol, the materials to be added separately in that order with mixing in between. Silica sol allows a more economical use of gelatin and is more effective than tannin in clarification of wines using gelatin. The replacement of tannin by silica sol in the gelatin fining of white wines is recommended, since tannin may impart an astringent taste to the wine.

Combined silica sol and gelatin fining gives excellent clarity and a firmly compacted deposit, particularly in wines which are difficult to clarify, such as those made from botrytis-infected grapes. An added advantage is that overfining with gelatin is not possible because the silica sol removes the excess gelatin.

Fining trials

When fining wines it is important to use the minimum quantity of finings which will carry out the task—the reasons for this are given above. Wines differ in their composition and the amount of a particular fining required; therefore, a trial fining is necessary before the actual fining in the winery. In carrying out such a trial it is important to duplicate the winery conditions as closely as possible, particularly with respect to the temperature of the wine and the fining material used. If possible, the same fining preparation as used in the winery should be used in the trial.

Besides indicating the appropriate level of a particular fining to use, the fining trial indicates to the winemaker the time which the floccules take to appear, the rate of flocculation, the degree of clarity and the compactness of the deposit.

Bentonite

Place 100 millilitres of wine in a number of labelled bottles or stoppered graduated measuring cylinders to cover the range of bentonite levels chosen. An example is from 0.1 to 0.7 grams per litre or eight bottles, one being a control. Add to each bottle the required amount of bentonite from a stock suspension preserved with 200 milligrams per litre sulphur dioxide. Assuming that a 5 per cent suspension of bentonite prepared in hot water is to be used, to obtain an addition of 0.1 gram per litre in the 100 millilitres of wine 0.2 millilitres of the bentonite suspension is added. The additions are as follows: add 0, 0.2, 0.4, 0.6, 0.8, 1.0, 1.2 and 1.4 millilitres of bentonite suspension to the bottles labelled 0, 0.1, 0.2, 0.3, 0.4, 0.5, 0.6 and 0.7 grams per litre respectively. Mix well and allow to settle.

Observe the clarity and, if clear, decant some of each supernatant and heat in smaller closed bottles in a water bath or microwave oven at 80°C for 6 hours. If a haze forms after cooling, the bentonite dose rate is insufficient. Alternatively, add 1 millilitre of Bentotest reagent to each tube of clear supernatant and mix. The protein-unstable wines will form a haze, and the first tube which does not form a haze indicates the amount of bentonite to add to the bulk wine. If all tubes form a haze repeat the trial with a higher range of bentonite additions. The heat test is more appropriate to practical conditions, since the Bentotest can be too severe and lead to overfining.

Gelatin

A similar procedure to that for bentonite is carried out, using a range of gelatin additions of 0.0, 0.05, 0.1, 0.15, 0.20, 0.25, 0.30, 0.35 and 0.40 grams per litre. Assuming that a 5 per cent solution of gelatin (dissolved in hot water and allowed to cool) is to be used, add the following amounts to 100 millilitres red wine in labelled bottles: 0, 0.1, 0.2, 0.3, 0.4, 0.5, 0.6, 0.7 and 0.8 millilitres, which correspond to the range of concentration listed above. Mix well and allow to stand for an hour, then decant off enough of the clear supernatant to taste. The result will be a successive reduction in the tannin level in the wine, and the fining rate which gives the best tannin balance is chosen.

Isinglass, casein, egg albumen and PVPP

The same procedure as set out for gelatin is carried out, with the range of levels as listed in the text. The assessment of the correct fining level is made by tasting and visual examination, including colour removal. It is essential that the finings flocculate completely leaving a brilliant supernatant, since incorrect amounts or preparations can lead to the formation of protective colloids which can confuse the result.

10 Stabilisation

If wine is stored for long enough it will eventually become stable to precipitation and further change. However, the winemaker requires more rapid stabilisation than is attainable naturally, and formal stabilisation practices have now become established in winemaking. The concept of stability needs to take into account the quality of the wine and its maintenance, since stabilisation practices tend to lower quality unless they are carried out carefully.

It is possible to over-stabilise wine in an attempt to obtain stability under almost any conditions. It has been stated that certain wines have been stabilised to such an extent that they fell exhausted into the bottle. In other words, the stabilisation practices should be so designed as to provide a reasonable shelf-life, such as a minimum of one year in bottle, without damaging the wine. Consumers are aware that red wines, for example, may deposit precipitated pigment or bottle crust in the bottle over a period of time, and regard this not as a fault but as evidence of prolonged bottle maturation—and something to be prized accordingly. However, the appearance of potassium bitartrate crystals, for example, is not so easily accepted, nor is heat haze resulting from heat-unstable protein.

Accordingly, stabilisation practices are aimed at preventing these and other such faults, and the procedures and the principles relating to them are set out below.

Bentonite and protein stabilisation

At first sight it seems curious that a clay, such as bentonite, can be used to clarify wine and, more importantly, stabilise it against the precipitation of soluble grape proteins, which can occur when the wine is stored in a warm place. Bentonite is the most important fining agent used in Australian winemaking, and thus merits more attention than other fining materials. In recent years the attitude to bentonite has changed, and it is necessary to give the background to the process and highlight recent developments, as well as set out the procedures for its use.

Bentonite was first introduced into winemaking in 1934 by Saywell in California, although various kinds of naturally occurring earths, such as kaolin and Spanish clay, had been used previously. Its application in Australia followed soon afterwards and was established before World War II. Bentonite was not used in Europe until more recently—in Germany it was introduced in 1947 when the wines of that warm year showed marked heat haze due to unstable protein. European oenological textbooks published before about 1950 usually do not list bentonite as a fining material.

As a matter of interest the important and possibly unique properties possessed by bentonite give it considerable commercial value in various fields, such as decolourising oils, catalyst manufacture, bonding moulding sands, preparation of oil-well drilling muds, sealing of water storage dams—and wine clarification.

The term bentonite was first applied in 1898 to a particularly highly colloidal plastic clay of the montmorillonite group found in the cretaceous beds near Fort Benton in Montana, USA. Deposits have been found to occur in various parts of the world, including Australia, and are formed by deposition and alteration of volcanic ash in the presence of water. The deposits in Montana and Wyoming are of particular suitability for wine clarification, since they carry sodium as the dominant ion instead of calcium.

From the viewpoint of correct nomenclature, bentonite should be referred to as montmorillonite, but the use of the former term in winemaking is widespread. Montmorillonite is an embracing term for aluminium-silicate clays with a defined expanding crystal-lattice structure. The name, which was first suggested in 1847, derives from Montmorillon, east of Poitiers in France, where deposits once occurred but have now been exhausted.

Bentonite is basically an impure hydrated aluminium silicate, which when dispersed in water exists as exceedingly small flat plates or sheets about 5000 Angstrom units wide by about 10 Angstrom units thick (one Angstrom unit is one ten-millionth of a millimetre). The plates or sheets consist of layers of atoms in a defined order, and the composition of the plates, particularly in their content of silicon, aluminium and magnesium, differs in bentonites from different areas. These plates are negatively charged, and the charge attracts exchangeable cations, such as sodium, calcium or magnesium, which form a layer around the plate. These cations are not part of the permanent crystal structure but confer on bentonite its exchange capacity, which is about one milli-equivalent per gram.

Bentonite is usually about 90 per cent montmorillonite with the other 10 per cent consisting of feldspar, gypsum, calcium carbonate, quartz and traces of other minerals, such as heavy metals. The presence of particularly iron contamination should be checked, and limits for iron, arsenic, heavy metals calcium and magnesium are set out in the OIV *Oenological Codex*. It is these impurities which alter its colour, which in the pure state is almost white. The apparent specific gravity of the powder is about 2.8, depending on the state of fineness of subdivision, and hardness on Mohr's scale is 1 to 1.5, which is slightly harder than talc.

When bentonite is mixed with warm water in a 5 per cent w/v suspension, it forms a pale green–grey milky liquid, but as the concentration rises to 10 to 15 per cent, it forms a gelatinous paste. These thicker slurries exhibit the interesting phenomenon of thixotrophy—on standing they form a gel which becomes a fluid on shaking. This phenomenon is due to the presence of positive charges on the edges of the bentonite plates, which electrostatically attach to the negatively charged faces of other plates at an angle. A good sodium bentonite should remain dispersed in distilled water almost indefinitely, due to the negative charge on each plate repelling neighbouring plates.

When bentonite is soaked in hot water the plates separate to form this homogenous colloidal suspension. In this dispersed condition an enormous surface area is presented, of the order of 750 square metres per gram for sodium bentonite. The plates of calcium bentonite tend to clump together with consequent reduction in surface area, and the suspension tends to settle out and is less effective for fining, but which forms more compact lees. For this reason calcium bentonite is sometimes preferred over sodium, because of this low volume of lees and rapid rate of settling, even though it is much less efficient in protein removal and more expensive. Calcium bentonite comes from Europe, and sodium bentonite from Cudgen in Queensland is now being used along with that from the United States.

Kaolin, by comparison, swells only slightly and has a much smaller surface area of 20 to 40 square metres per gram and, consequently, is much less effective for fining. At least a ten-fold addition of kaolin is required to achieve fining comparable with sodium bentonite.

The colloidal property of sodium bentonite is of basic importance in oenology. It will adsorb nearly five times its volume of water and at full saturation occupies a volume of twelve to fifteen times its dry weight. On drying it shrinks to its original volume and this swelling and shrinking is reversible. It swells faster in hot water than cold, but swells only slightly in alcohol. Consequently, the bentonite suspension for addition to wine should be made in hot water rather than cold—and never in wine.

The essentially important factor of bentonite is its ability to adsorb proteins in grape juice and wine, and this is the basic purpose for which it is used in winemaking. This adsorption results from either electrostatic attraction between positively charged proteins and the negatively charged bentonite, or from adsorption of the protein molecules by hydrogen bonding. The charge on the protein molecule is dependent on pH of the juice or wine and is usually positive, the lower the pH, the more positive the charge.

The factors influencing protein removal are as follows:

- Correct type of bentonite—batches differ widely in their ability to adsorb proteins and this depends on the amount of swelling. The suspension in water should be stable and not settle out, indicating that the bentonite is fully swollen. Effective protein removal is related to the formation of light flocculent lees which are a feature of high swelling. One problem is that the wine contained in such lees needs to be recovered to reduce cost.
- The amount added—bentonite adsorbs part of the flavour of wine and consequently the minimum addition should be used. In fact, this is a good reason for avoiding using bentonite.

- The method of preparing the bentonite suspension—the addition of a prepared smooth creamy suspension of bentonite prepared in hot water is much more effective in protein removal than adding the same amount of bentonite directly to the wine. The aqueous suspension is best prepared in hot water with vigorous mechanical mixing, and allowing time for full hydration and swelling. When the suspension is stable and does not settle out it is fully swollen.
- Acidity of the wine—the more acid the wine, the more effective is the removal of protein, due to the increased positive charge of the protein molecules at low pH values. One fourth as much bentonite is required at pH 3.0 as at pH 3.6.
- Temperature—protein removal is more effective in warm than in cold juice or wine.
- Wine composition—while bentonite normally fines well in wine, poor fining frequently occurs in wine treated with cation exchange resin in the sodium form to stabilise against potassium bitartrate deposition. The reason is the reduction in the concentrations of the divalent cations in wine—calcium and magnesium—brought about by ion exchange which influences the ability of bentonite to flocculate. Accordingly, wine should be fined with bentonite before ion exchange.
- Water—it is advisable to use as pure water as possible, since a high level of calcium in mains water considerably reduces the effectiveness of bentonite.

Other important points are the amount of contamination of bentonite with metals, particularly iron, freedom from foreign odours or taints, the ability of the bentonite to form a stable suspension in water, and the method of addition. To ensure rapid mixing it is best to add the bentonite suspension on the suction side of a pump circulating the wine in a vessel. Bentonite treatment is a mixing problem, and this method of addition has been found to be an effective way of rapidly mixing the aqueous bentonite suspension into the wine.

The dosage required depends largely on the wine, the type of bentonite and its method of preparation. Consequently, a laboratory fining trial is necessary. Usually a fining rate of 0.3 to 0.8 grams per litre is adequate, but some wines made from protein-rich grapes, such as Muscat Gordo Blanco, may need a higher addition. A fining rate of 0.5 grams per litre, for example, corresponds to an addition of 5 litres of a 10 per cent smooth suspension in water to 1,000 litres of wine.

Addition of a complimentary fining, such as gelatin, assists in sedimenting the bentonite. Protein removal occurs quickly in wine. If mixing is rapid, the protein is removed in the first few minutes and the remaining time is spent waiting for the bentonite to settle. In fact, it is possible to fine wine with bentonite in-line if it is effectively mixed. The wine can then be centrifuged or filtered and stability achieved quickly.

The use of bentonite is decreasing, due to the high cost of lees recovery, reduction (usually) in aroma and flavour, a small increase in the sodium content of the treated wine (which could influence the export of the wine to the European Economic Community, where low sodium is specified), and the availability of other methods of clarification.

To the present, protein-splitting enzymes or proteases have not been completely effective in protein removal in wine, but when a protease becomes available which can operate rapidly and economically at the acidity levels of white table wines and without untoward side effects, this should result in reduced usage of bentonite.

We must be careful not to regard protein in wine as only one constituent. Recent findings with Muscat Gordo Blanco juice indicate many protein fractions, ranging in molecular weight from 31,000 to more than 500,000. The isoelectric points of the various fractions are similarly wide, ranging from 3.7 to 9.5, although most of the protein fractions lie within the narrow pH range of 3.7 to 4.7.

Cold-stabilisation

Young wine is usually saturated with potassium bitartrate and sometimes calcium tartrate, although the latter is not usually present in sufficient concentration to reach saturation unless the calcium content of the wine is high. When the wine is cooled the solubility limit of potassium bitartrate is exceeded and some comes out of solution as a crystalline deposit. When this happens to white wine in the bottle the deposit is unsightly and may be mistaken by the uninitiated for broken glass. Customers expect such wines to be free form deposit and, consequently, its prevention is essential.

Potassium bitartrate is present in the grapes, partially precipitates as argols during fermentation because of its lower solubility in alcohol, and is present in the young wine as a saturated or even a super-saturated solution in excess of its normal solubility. If the wine is cooled some potassium bitartrate slowly precipitates on the walls and floor of the storage vessel as argols (impure crystals of potassium bitartrate with pigment from the wine), until the saturated equilibrium at that temperature is reached. This slow precipitation can take weeks or sometimes months to reach the new equilibrium set up by the cooler temperature. If the wine is further cooled more potassium bitartrate precipitates until a further new equilibrium is reached. Calcium tartrate, if present, is also involved in this precipitation, but at a slower rate because its solubility is less influenced by temperature.

Several factors influence the rate of tartrate precipitation, viz.:

- nucleation or the number of tiny nuclei on which the crystals form and grow;
- diffusion, or the rate at which the dissolved potassium bitartrate contacts the growing crystals;
- crystal surface growth or the rate at which cold stabilisation occurs;
- the grape variety.

The amount of potassium bitartrate which will remain in solution depends on the following factors:

- Alcohol content—the higher the alcohol level, the less soluble is potassium bitartrate. This is the reason why masses of argols or impure potassium bitartrate are deposited during fermentation.
- Temperature—the cooler the temperature, the less soluble is the bitartrate.
- pH—at pH 3.6 or thereabouts, depending on the alcohol content, the proportion of the sparingly soluble potassium bitartrate in relation to the soluble tartaric acid and potassium tartrate is greatest. As the pH moves away from 3.6 in either direction the proportion of potassium bitartrate becomes less, although the total tartrate content remains the same, and the likelihood of precipitation becomes less. Because of this pH effect two cold-stable wines can result in an unstable blend. Therefore, the blend must be cold-stabilised and not the individual components.
- Potassium (and calcium) content—the addition of potassium or calcium renders the wine more cold-unstable.

The normal procedure for cold-stabilising wine before bottling to avoid unsightly precipitation of tartrate crystals in the bottle has been to chill the wine through a heat-exchanger to near its freezing point in the temperature range of about minus 2 to plus 2°C, store in an insulated vessel for between one and three weeks, then filter or rack while still cold. In very cold areas the same result can be achieved by opening the cellar doors to chill the wine naturally over winter.

Advances in technology have resulted in important changes to this cold-stabilisation process, particularly through a greater understanding of the principles of nucleation involved in the precipitation of potassium bitartrate in wine—the main compound involved in cold instability. The most important at present is the contact process.

Stabilisation by contact process

This process is an important development in the rapid cold-stabilisation of wines, and by virtue of saving considerable time has advantages over the traditional prolonged cold storage of wine. German researchers in a joint venture between the Seitz-Werke and the Henkel companies have found that wine can be cold-stabilised rapidly by stirring in contact with finely powdered potassium bitartrate crystals for 30 to 60 minutes at approximately 0 to minus 2°C. Potassium bitartrate present in the wine as a saturated solution at normal temperature crystallises on to the added crystals, which serve as the source of nucleation. The deposited crystals are removed, dried, ground and reused. The stabilised wine is then warmed against incoming wine in a heat-exchanger, and will be stable at temperatures down to that at which it was treated.

The small crystal size (less than about 40 microns and about the same particle size as finely powdered icing sugar) is necessary to expose sufficient surface area to act as the nucleation sites on which the potassium bitartrate in the wine can crystallise quickly. Only potassium bitartrate crystals can be used for seeding—other sharp-edged crystals do not produce the desired result. It is necessary to add a large number of very small crystals in order to provide sufficient surface area. In fact, 4 grams of finely powdered potassium bitartrate crystals (the recommended dosage per litre) has a crystal surface area of approximately 3 square metres. Crystallisation is rapid and complete in an hour or less in the stirred suspension, because the potassium bitartrate molecules in solution need only to travel a calculated average of 0.3 millimetres before encountering a crystal face on which to grow.

Furthermore, polymeric inhibitors of nucleation, which slow down the rate of conventional cold-stabilisation, have relatively little effect on the stabilisation time required by the contact process. The avoidance of this problem means that stabilisation by the contact process is more predictable. The deposited potassium bitartrate is reused by separating, drying and grinding, and the balance is available for sale as a winery by-product (cream of tartar) if a demand exists for it. Stabilisation is best carried out after final blending before bottling.

Cold-stabilisation of red wines by the contact process usually involves a brief preliminary chilling to remove cold-unstable pigments and tannins, otherwise gross contamination of the crop of potassium bitartrate crystals will occur. The length of time of pre-chilling depends on the wine and may require only 24 hours.

The contact process has considerable economic advantage, particularly for white wines, because the wine needs only to be cooled to the desired temperature for an hour or so, enabling continuous cold-stabilisation to be carried out with this process. For batch treatment the successive operations are as follows: chill the filtered wine against out-going wine to the desired stabilisation temperature, add 4 grams per litre of finely powdered potassium bitartrate crystals, mix for approximately one hour, and separate the deposited crystals by centrifugation.

Stabilisation by filtration

Another process employs stabilisation by filtration of the chilled wine, using a filter containing a bed of potassium bitartrate crystals, with a lower rate of seeding, such as 1 gram per litre, in the incoming wine. The crystals grow in the filter as the potassium bitartrate in the chilled wine deposits on the preformed crystals. The wine may be recirculated through the filter if required.

Stabilisation by crystal flow

A further process is crystal flow developed by the Alfa Laval company, in which tiny potassium bitartrate and ice crystals are generated in the wine by chilling in a scraped-surface heat-exchanger (as distinct from swept-surface), at about the freezing point of the wine. Three steps are involved:

1 Cooling the wine to its freezing point with agitation to induce formation of tartrate crystal nuclei.

2 Growth of the crystals in the suspension of ice and tartrate crystals.

3 Melting the ice crystals in a plate heat-exchanger to allow the tartrate crystals to be removed by filtration or racking.

The temperature to which the wine is chilled depends on the alcohol and solute composition and is usually about minus 5°C. The crystals act as nuclei for further crystal growth, without having to add seeding crystals, and the plant is easy to run as it is continuous and self-regulating, as distinct from the seeding process. This process relies on having a scraped-surface heat-exchanger, which is not a normal item of winery equipment at present. However, the normal swept-surface ultracooler can be modified to operate as a scraped-surface cooler.

The question may be asked as to which of these processes is the 'best' under our conditions, and it is likely that all three will find a place in our industry. Slow chilling and prolonged cold storage of wine to allow cold-stabilisation to take place is still being used, for the joint reasons of retaining quality and achieving cold-stability in the process. However, these recent developments are expected to save time as well as to lead to continuous operation. Quality-control tests for checking cold-stability are set out in Chapter 21.

Refrigeration requirements for cold-stabilisation

If the wine is to be cold-stabilised by initially chilling it through a heat-exchanger, the chilling requirement in kilowatts is the product of the wine flow rate in litres per hour and the required temperature drop in °C, divided by 850. To this must be added the minor heat loads of the electrical power of the wine pump and the heat gain from the surroundings, both calculated using the same procedures as set out in the section on must cooling in Chapter 5.

If the wine is to be cooled in a tank, the chilling load in kilowatts is the product of the volume of wine in kilolitres, the required temperature drop in °C, and 1.15, divided by the time in hours required to cool the wine. If the tank is insulated with 50 millimetres of polyurethane, the heat gain from the surroundings in kilowatts is the tank surface area (walls and top) in square metres divided by 75. Alternatively, if the tank is uninsulated but inside an enclosed non-cooled winery, the heat gain is the tank area divided by 8. If the tanks are uninsulated but housed in an uninsulated building, the heat gains from the surroundings, fans, people, lights, etc. can be calculated as set out in the section on fermentation cooling in Chapter 8.

Prevention of tartrate precipitation by ion-exchange

Ion-exchange treatment for prevention of potassium bitartrate and calcium tartrate precipitation in wine was developed in Australia and has been in use since 1955, and its application has been of considerable benefit to the wine industry. It employs the same resin and equipment as is used for acidification of must and wine, and Chapter 7 should also be referred to.

An ion-exchange resin is an insoluble gel matrix containing labile ions capable of exchanging with ions in the surrounding liquid, without physical change taking place in the structure of the resin. The resins are divided into two broad groups, cation and anion exchangers, which can be further subdivided into weakly acid or basic and strongly acid or basic, according to their chemical groupings. The resins used in Australian wineries are highly acidic unifunctional cation-exchangers with a polystyrene base and sulphonic-acid groups which contain exchangeable hydrogen atoms. The resins are in the form of little amber-coloured beads, which are more easily handled than the irregularly shaped granules of some other types of resin. They are also resistant to chemical attack.

From the viewpoint of understanding the process of prevention of potassium bitartrate deposition, wine may be regarded as a saturated solution of potassium bitartrate in dilute ethyl alcohol, with other cations, mainly calcium, magnesium and sodium; and anions, mainly malate, succinate, lactate and the inorganic anions. Wine can be stabilised by ion-exchange in three ways:

• By replacing potassium with sodium with a cation-exchange resin in the sodium cycle, forming the soluble sodium bitartrate.
• By replacing the tartrate anion with hydroxyl or other anion with an anion-exchange resin.
• By replacing potassium and tartrate respectively with hydrogen and hydroxyl by a cation and an anion resin, in effect exchanging portion or all of the potassium bitartrate for water.

In practice, the sodium cycle is the most suitable because wine can be stabilised without affecting its flavour and with only slight reduction in acidity. It increases the sodium content of the wine, which may be undesirable for people on a low-sodium diet. If desired, the acidity of the wine can be increased by preparing the resin in the mixed sodium and hydrogen form. This is desirable when treating low-acid dessert wines, since the acidity of the wine can be increased to any desired level concurrently with prevention of potassium-bitartrate precipitation. The resin can also be prepared in the magnesium, or mixed magnesium and sodium form.

When considering the sodium exchange, in which wine passes down through a column of a cation exchange resin in the sodium form so that the potassium in the wine is replaced with sodium from the resin, care must be taken not to oversimplify the process. The resin has a greater affinity for the divalent cations, calcium and magnesium, than for potassium, and as the wine flow progresses the resin column takes up calcium and magnesium preferentially as a top zone, below which is the potassium zone while the remainder of the resin column is in the sodium form.

As the wine continues to pass down, these zones in the resin also extend although far more slowly than the wine, until at the breakthrough point where no more sodium remains on the resin, the potassium zone reaches the bottom of the resin column. Potassium then begins to be released from the resin back into the wine, due to its continued replacement on the resin by calcium and magnesium. If the wine flow continues the situation alters markedly. The resin is then in the combined potassium, calcium and magnesium form and further wine flow will have the effect of displacing potassium from the resin column, so that the effluent wine again becomes prone to potassium bitartrate precipitation.

Method of operation

The recommended flow rates and related details for column operation are set out below. For proper operation of the column a flow meter or gauged vessels are essential.

1 *Regeneration*: 2.5 resin volumes of 10 per cent sodium chloride brine are flowed up through the resin bed in about 20 minutes. This regeneration rate corresponds to 25 kilograms of sodium chloride per 100 litres of resin, and for a column containing 800 litres of resin, for example, 126 kilograms of salt dissolved in 1200 litres of water are required. In the past, down-flow regeneration was carried out but has now been replaced by the more efficient up-flow.

2 *Washing*: About 6 resin volumes of clean wash water are required and this should flow down through the resin bed in about 30 minutes until free from salt. A check with silver nitrate solution will indicate whether any salt remains by forming a white silver chloride cloud. Rain water is best, but if this is in short supply then mains water can be used after passage through the resin, which then acts as a conventional water softener. Untreated mains water can contain appreciable quantities of calcium and magnesium, which will reduce the efficiency of the resin.

3 *Wine flow*: 15 resin volumes per hour are flowed down through the resin until the breakthrough point occurs. This is usually after about 30 resin volumes have been treated, depending on the content of potassium, calcium, and magnesium in the wine. The wine flow is complete in about 2 to 3 hours. A knowledge of the cation content of wines likely to be encountered is important in understanding the reason why the resin does not treat the same quantity of different wines. The range of values of the major cations in Australian wines in milligrams per litre is shown in the following table.

Wine type	Potassium	Sodium	Calcium	Magnesium	Sum of cations
White table	390–1520	12–276	38–112	55–115	495–2023
Red table	730–3000	9–276	40–112	68–180	847–3568
White dessert	702–1560	58–253	30– 70	49–114	839–2027
Red dessert	780–1870	70–276	32– 78	73–132	955–2356

In order to avoid diluting the wine on initial entry to the column, it is best to drain the wash water to waste and then introduce the wine from the bottom until the column is full and the air removed, then reverse the flow so that the wine enters at the top of the column. Upward flow of wine should not be used because channelling occurs resulting in inefficient exchange. To avoid aeration all wine movements should be carried out under inert gas.

It is important to be able to measure the breakthrough point when the resin becomes exhausted of its sodium ions. Since the process principally involves exchange of two similar cations, potassium and sodium, there is no obvious change in acidity or taste at the end of the run, and the progress of the treatment cannot be observed by acidity measurements. The pH of the wine usually rises slightly during the course of the exchange (up to 0.05 pH unit) due to replacement of some of the hydrogen ions in the wine with sodium.

The most desirable method of detecting the breakthrough point is to measure the potassium content of the effluent wine at intervals, so that the breakthrough point can be determined accurately. The measurements can be made quickly with a flame photometer, or by measuring the potassium content chemically with an appropriate reagent, such as cobalt-nitrite. The flame photometer is rapid and accurate, and should be regarded as part of the capital outlay of setting up an ion-exchange plant. It is possible to determine the stage at which potassium bitartrate precipitation reappears in the effluent wine by refrigerating samples taken at intervals, but such a procedure cannot be carried out immediately and does not give an indication of the stage at which the breakthrough point occurs.

4 *Backwashing*: This loosens and resets the bed, and also washes out any particulate matter that may have been introduced during the previous cycle. About 12 resin volumes of water are required and should be passed up through the resin in about 30 minutes, and until the effluent is quite clear. The wine should always be clear before treatment and the resin should not be used as a filter, since a surface coating of colloidal and suspended constituents will reduce the exchange capacity of the resin as well as reduce the flow rate.

Size of ion-exchange columns. When ion-exchange treatment was first introduced the columns used were almost all less than 50 centimetres in diameter, and were eventually found to be too small as wineries treated a larger proportion of their output. Current practice is to build columns with larger diameters, such as one metre, containing about 1000 litres of resin. Assuming a minimum throughput of 30 resin volumes to the breakthrough point, 1000 litres of resin will treat about 30,000 litres of wine, which is a useful size for many wineries and does away with the need for back-blending. The depth of resin in the column should be at least 75 centimetres, otherwise channelling and inefficient exchange will occur.

Inefficiency of batch regeneration. One maker of ion-exchange columns produced a unit mounted on trunnions so that it could be rotated end-over-end in a vertical plane, with the object of mixing the resin with the brine to achieve regeneration as a batch process. This is an inefficient method, because to obtain the most efficient regeneration the brine must pass through a stationery resin bed whereby an efficient exchange takes place with the released cations—potassium, calcium and magnesium—passing to waste with the brine effluent. If the regeneration process is carried out batch-wise the regenerant actually becomes a mixture of sodium, potassium, calcium and magnesium—the last three being released from the resin—and the final charge on the resin is a mixture of the four cations in an equilibrium determined by their concentrations and relative affinities for the resin.

Effect on taste of the wine. Many tests have been carried out on the effect of ion-exchange treatment on the taste of the wine, with the consensus being that the taste of dessert wines is not detectably altered but that of delicate table wines may be. Some winemakers treat their entire make of dessert and table wines, whereas others do not ion-exchange their white table wines. It is unlikely that a trained taster could detect whether a wine has been treated without having the control as a comparison.

Danger of over-running the column and effect of blending. The danger of over-running the column should be stressed. The treated wine up to the stage of breakthrough cannot precipitate potassium bitartrate under any conditions, and can be blended judiciously with a proportion of untreated wine if desired. However, if the column is over-run well past the stage where potassium begins to be released from the resin back into the wine, then the wine will again precipitate potassium bitartrate, and this cannot be corrected by a further passage through regenerated resin since the wine is now high in sodium and the second exchange treatment is ineffective. It should be remembered that an exchange of ions continues as long as wine is passed through the resin, until the resin is saturated with calcium and magnesium.

The danger of over-running the column is related to a situation which can easily occur—viz. the purchase of a parcel of treated wine, perhaps in ignorance that it has been treated, and blending this with other wine which has not been treated to produce a composite blend for bottling. If the final blend is unstable due to the moiety of untreated wine, it may not be able to be stabilised by a subsequent ion-exchange treatment because the wine already contains a considerable amount of sodium from the first treatment. In such cases, it is advisable to ensure that the proposed components of a blend are both ion exchanged before blending.

Storage of resin in the column. Preservation of the resin in the column during the period when it is not in use can present a problem, since removal of the residue of sugar left after treating dessert wines is difficult and the moist resin may grow mould or become stagnant. Various methods have been used, such as storage in brine, sulphurous acid or diluted spirit. The resin should be in the regenerated hydrogen form, and most winemakers prefer to use brine storage although it has a slight corrosive action on stainless steel. Sulphurous-acid storage has the advantage of acting as a mild acid regenerant and removes the metal ions bound to the resin. New resin may impart an initial off-flavour to the wine, and this is best prevented by soaking the resin in fortified wine for a few days and then regenerating it with warm dilute hydrochloric acid before brine regeneration.

Restoration of resin after prolonged use. After long use the resin may partially lose its exchange capacity and progressively treat less wine per regeneration. The reason for this is due to absorption by the resin of a range of polymeric compounds—proteins, tannins, pectins and the like—which reduce the number of exchange sites available. These compounds, together with metals, are not adequately removed by brine regeneration and more drastic action is necessary. The best treatment is to soak the resin in sodium hypochlorite solution containing about 3 per cent available chlorine which will restore its colour and activity. Soaking in hydrogen peroxide is another treatment. If this does not fully restore the resin then a treatment with chromic acid (after removing the resin from the column) will rid the resin of contaminants, but this acid is corrosive and difficult to handle. Cation-exchange resins are resistant to oxidation and can withstand fairly drastic treatment without damage.

Measurement of exchange capacity of resin. The method of checking the exchange capacity of the resin is simple and is given here so that winemakers can test their own resin.

1 Dry the resin in a thin layer in an oven at 105°C for an hour. Weigh accurately 1 gram slurry with water and place in a vertical glass tube about 6 millimetres internal diameter, with the resin supported on a pad of glass wool. The resin bed will be approximately 10 centimetres high. Fit a rubber tube and constricting clip to the bottom of the glass tube so that the flow of liquid down through the resin can be controlled, and mount the tube vertically in a retort stand. Ensure that the resin is free from air bubbles and covered with liquid throughout the determination.

2 Pass down through the resin 10 millilitres of dilute hydrochloric acid (1 part acid and 3 parts water) with the flow rate adjusted so that this takes about 20 minutes. Then pass down distilled water, at a faster rate if desired, until the effluent is less acid than pH 4. Pass down through the resin 10 millilitres of 20 per cent sodium chloride solution in about 20 minutes, followed by 10 millilitres of distilled water, collecting the effluent in a beaker. Add approximately 50 millilitres of distilled water and a few drops of phenol-phthalein indicator to the beaker and titrate with standard sodium hydroxide, either normal or tenth normal. The exchange capacity of the resin in milli-equivalents per dry gram is simply the number of millilitres of normal sodium hydroxide, or one-tenth the number of millilitres of tenth normal used in the titration.

Resins from different makers vary somewhat in their exchange capacities, and the makers' specifications should be referred to, but new resins usually have an exchange capacity of between 4 and 5 milli-equivalents per dry gram.

Removal of trace metals from wine. Copper and iron are present in wine in both ionised and bound forms. The ionised metals are removed by ion-exchange but those bound as non-ionised complexes to the organic acids in wine are not. The extent of complexing is less as the pH falls and this is the reason why metal removal is more effective with acid wines, and best when the resin is used in the hydrogen form for acidification. Ion-exchange treatment does not bring about a significant reduction in the content of lead in wines. It has been found that metals removed from wine tend to accumulate on the resin and are poorly removed by brine regeneration. It is desirable to give the resin a regeneration with acid at intervals to remove these metals.

Comparison with refrigeration. The advantage of ion-exchange treatment is its low cost compared with refrigeration, usually less than 10 per cent. The final result of both treatments is the same as far as prevention of potassium bitartrate deposition is concerned, although refrigeration is claimed to stabilise wine against other cold-unstable materials, which are little affected by ion-exchange. It is sometimes claimed that refrigeration improves a wine, although the danger of oxidation after refrigeration is well known. Also, refrigeration has other uses, such as cooling fermentations during vintage, and ion-exchange may be used in conjunction with refrigeration, for example, when a winemaker does not wish to ion-exchange a delicate white table wine, while the remainder of the wines are ion-exchanged.

In recent years sodium ion-exchange has decreased in use, because wineries have installed refrigeration for temperature control during vintage and then used this later for cold stabilisation. In addition, if the wine is to be exported some countries have a maximum limit for sodium, which precludes the use of sodium ion-exchange for such wines.

Metatartaric acid

One of the valuable recent developments in oenology has been in new methods of preventing potassium bitartrate precipitation when wine is chilled. Metatartaric acid falls into this category—it is a nucleation inhibitor meaning that it prevents crystals from forming. It was first used in Europe in 1955.

When finely ground tartaric acid powder is heated in an oven at 170°C it melts and undergoes a transformation involving release of water vapour, dehydration, esterification and polymerisation. The result is an amorphous deliquescent (absorbs moisture from the air) off-white to light-brown vitreous spongy mass. Its composition is changed to that of a hemipolylactide, where the molecules link to present a polymer-like structure. A purer product is obtained if the heating is carried out in vacuum at a slightly lower temperature, such as 150 to 160°C.

Metatartaric acid is not a precise chemical entity. It depends for its efficiency as a nucleation inhibitor on the degree of esterification, or the amount of the hemipolylactide present. From a quality control viewpoint an esterification index of 40 per cent is desirable, which is more than twice as effective as a product of

30 per cent esterification. Metatartaric acid acts by sheathing the microscopic crystals of potassium bitartrate and calcium tartrate as they precipitate from wine, thus preventing crystal growth and formation of visible crystals.

However, this preventative action is not permanent, since metatartaric acid in solution slowly rehydrates to tartaric acid, losing its property of inhibiting crystal formation. Rehydration is hastened by storing the wine at an elevated temperature, and the effectiveness of metatartaric addition varies from about a month up to several years, depending on temperature. If the wine is stored at 0°C its effectiveness is several years, at 10°C about eighteen months, whereas at 25°C only a few months. These figures are of course relevant to warm Australian storage temperatures. In general, it would be more stable in wine in cooler New Zealand than in Australia. It is legally permitted in both countries.

Consequently, metatartaric acid is most effective in wines for current consumption and stored in a cool cellar, and is used mainly for white wines where crystal formation is unsightly. The dosage rate is normally 100 milligrams per litre, and the product is first dissolved in cold water (hot water hydrolyses it) then is added with mixing to the wine. A concentrated solution in water loses its strength by about 1 per cent per day, so the solution should be used soon after it is prepared. When metatartaric acid is added to wine it sometimes causes a slight opalescence, so addition should be made before final filtration and bottling.

As a matter of interest, Australian annual usage is estimated at approximately 4 tonnes, which is enough to stabilise about 40 million litres of wine—a sizeable proportion of Australia's annual white wine production.

Sorbic acid

Sorbic acid is a fungicide or inhibitor of yeast growth, which can be added to wine up to a legal maximum level of 200 milligrams per litre both in Australia and in New Zealand. It was discovered in 1895, synthesised in 1900 and its antifungal properties verified in 1945. Its use was legalised in France in 1959 and in Germany in 1971, and is permitted in most winemaking countries. Its sole function is to prevent unwanted yeast growth, which it does by inhibition of the yeast's dehydrogenase system. It is not a natural constituent of wine. Sorbic acid is added in amounts between 100 and 200 milligrams per litre, usually as the more soluble potassium sorbate or sorbistat K, which contains 75 per cent sorbic acid and has a solubility in water at 20°C of 56 per cent compared with that of sorbic acid of 0.16 per cent. The proportion of undissociated sorbic acid (in which the fungicidal action resides) in wine depends on pH, being higher in more acidic wines.

Since sorbic acid inhibits the growth of yeast but not bacteria it is added to wines which are prone to yeast spoilage, viz. sweet white table wines. The taste threshold for sensitive tasters is approximately 130 milligrams per litre. It should not be added to wines intended to be made into sparkling wines by secondary yeast fermentation.

Certain yeast, mainly strains of *Saccharomyces bailii* are naturally resistant to sorbic acid and can grow in wine to which it has been added. Consequently, such resistant yeasts have to be removed in other ways, such as filtration or pasteurisation. Yeast species differ widely in their resistance, with *Kloeckera* being among the least resistant and *S. bailii* among the most. Effectiveness of sorbic acid is low when many yeasts are present, thus wine should be filtered to reduce the yeast population before its addition. Low alcohol and high pH levels also reduce its effectiveness. Furthermore, sorbic acid needs to be used in conjunction with sulphur dioxide, but not as a replacement, because unlike sulphur dioxide, it has no antioxidant or antibacterial action.

If added to red table wines low in sulphur dioxide and these wines subsequently undergo malo-lactic fermentation as a result of bacterial growth, serious tainting can occur resulting from bacterial attack on sorbic acid, with the formation of 2-ethoxy-hexa-3:5-diene. This off-character is called geranium taint, so named because it resembles crushed geranium foliage. The aroma is also likened to putrefaction, and it is certainly undesirable. It is described in Chapter 19.

One final point—sorbic acid should not be used to cover up poor wine-making practice.

Dimethyl dicarbonate (DMDC)

For many years winemakers have been searching for a compound which could be added to wine at the time of packaging to prevent the growth of unwanted micro-organisms in the bottle or soft pack. Sulphur dioxide has traditionally been added as an antioxidant and sterilant, but it does not always prevent the growth of resistant yeasts. Sorbic acid is an effective fungicide but, as we have seen, is relatively ineffective against bacteria and can give rise to an undesirable odour ('geranium') due to attack by bacteria.

When diethyl dicarbonate (DEDC), or its synonym diethyl pyrocarbonate (DEPC), was approved in 1963 in the United States and later in Australia and New Zealand, this seemed to be the long-sought perfect sterilant, since it was effective both against years and bacteria and decomposed after addition to ethanol and carbon dioxide—both normal constituents of wine. However, ethyl carbamate, which is reported to have carcinogenic activity, was also formed, and resulted in the legislation being rescinded by the Federal Drug Administration of the United States in 1972 and later in Australia and New Zealand.

In 1973 the Logica International Corporation of Milwaukee, Wisconsin, suggested the possible use of the analogue dimethyl dicarbonate as a suitable replacement. Tests carried out by various laboratories, in particular at the University of California at Davis under Professor C.S. Ough, indicated that this analogue had similar fungicidal and bactericidal properties to diethyl dicarbonate and did not produce ethyl carbamate. It is now permitted for use in soft drinks and juice drinks in Europe and for wine in New Zealand in a maximum level of 200 milligrams per litre. Its use is not, however, legal in Australia.

Dimethyl dicarbonate is a colourless volatile liquid with a specific gravity of 1.26. It is unstable to heat and is best stored frozen. In aqueous solution or in wine it hydrolyses rapidly into methanol and carbon dioxide as shown below:

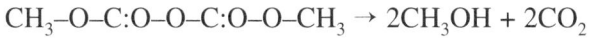

$$CH_3-O-C:O-O-C:O-O-CH_3 \rightarrow 2CH_3OH + 2CO_2$$

Assuming an addition of 200 milligrams per litre, according to the above formula the amount of methanol produced would be 96 milligrams per litre, which is in the range of the normal methanol content of wine (36 to 116 milligrams per litre). Methanol is known to be toxic to humans when taken orally at 340 milligrams per kilogram of body weight, but it has been concluded that the amount of methanol produced from the hydrolysis of 200 milligrams per litre of dimethyl dicarbonate in wine is not toxicologically significant. In addition, methyl carbamate is produced in an amount approximately one-twentieth of the amount of dimethyl dicarbonate added, and has been shown to be non-toxic. Various other compounds are formed or postulated to be formed and apparently these are not toxic.

The dosage of dimethyl dicarbonate required depends on several factors: the number of micro-organisms present (the fewer the number, the more effective the addition); ethanol content (the more ethanol the more effective); and pH (the lower the pH, the more effective). The normal addition is about 100 milligrams per litre, and is dosed into the wine with a special dosing pump before filling into bottles and casks. The dosing equipment can be automated, and the addition has the effect of also eliminating contamination from other sources, such as filling equipment, bottles and closures. The rate of hydrolysis depends on the temperature of the wine—it is completely hydrolysed after 5 hours at 10°C, 2 hours at 25°C and 1 hour at 30°C.

11 Oxidation

Oxidation is one of the major problems in Australian winemaking, particularly in hot areas, and can be prevalent in small wineries and in home winemaking. It is caused by exposure of wine to oxygen (air) under warm conditions, resulting in browning of the colour, loss of vinosity and grape flavour, and development of bitterness. Once a wine is oxidised its quality is permanently impaired, because some of the chemical reactions involved are irreversible.

Accordingly, prevention is much more important than cure, and the key points are summarised below. They are dealt with in detail in other chapters.

Prevention of oxidation

Condition of the grapes
If the grapes are mouldy and hot, the increased rate of activity of the oxidase enzymes produced by the mould can damage the fruit before it is crushed. Therefore, it is important to obtain sound and healthy grapes and process them as soon as possible after harvesting.

Sulphur dioxide
For grapes in good condition, cool and sufficiently acid, only a little sulphur dioxide is required, from 10 to 50 milligrams per litre. More is needed if the fruit is damaged, mouldy and hot. Sulphur dioxide acts as a germicide, an antioxidant and an enzyme inhibitor, but loses its effectiveness during fermentation as it becomes bound to acetaldehyde and other constituents.

Pre-fermentation handling
In spite of statements sometimes made to the contrary, it is best to avoid aeration of must and juice wherever possible. If the juice from healthy grapes is cool (less than 15°C), moderately acid, such as pH 3.0 to 3.3 for whites, with some free sulphur dioxide and ascorbic acid, then it is resistant to oxidation. However, hot low-acid juice without sulphur dioxide oxidises rapidly. Other pre-fermentation treatments, such as pressing whole bunches or including a proportion of stalks, can be carried out. Such treatments tend to respectively minimise or increase the level of phenolics in the resultant wine.

Post-fermentation handling

It is here that oxidation is most damaging and the greatest care needed, not only in handling but also in ensuring that the following important aspects of wine composition are controlled.

Acidity. The desirable pH range for white table wines is 3.0 to 3.4 and for reds 3.3 to 3.7. Malo-lactic fermentation (mainly in reds) raises pH, and subsequent adjustment with tartaric acid may be necessary to ensure that the pH of the wine lies in this range. It is better to rely on pH than titratable acid, because oxidative reactions and microbiological growth are much more closely linked to pH.

Free sulphur dioxide. The correct free sulphur dioxide levels in whites are of critical importance after fermentation, and the aspiration (Rankine) method of measurement should be used, because it is precise and not influenced by antioxidants, such as ascorbic or erythorbic acid. The level of free sulphur dioxide depends on the pH of the wine, with more needed at higher pH (lower acidity). The following is a useful guide for white table wines; pH 3.0 to 3.2, free sulphur dioxide 20 milligrams per litre; 3.2 to 3.4, 30 mg/l; 3.4 to 3.5, 40 mg/l; above 3.5, 50 mg/l.

Temperature. The rate of oxidation is temperature-dependent and approximately doubles for a rise of 10°C. For a rise of 20°C (not unusual under Australian conditions) the oxidation rate is four times as fast. This is the main reason for cooling the various individual operations and storage vessels, so that the wine is maintained at a desirable temperature of below 18°C. Cooling the whole winery is an advantage and cooled Californian wineries in warm areas, for example, are producing significantly better wines than those made without cooling. One further important point is that oxygen is considerably more soluble in cold wine.

Antioxidants. For white wines the addition of small amounts of ascorbic acid (vitamin C) or its cheaper optical isomer, erythorbic acid (with only 5 per cent of vitamin activity) is desirable. As a guide the addition of 20 to 30 milligrams per litre of either antioxidant is desirable before each handling of the wine, so that the level of ascorbic acid in the wine is maintained at 50 to 100 milligrams per litre. Its action is to combine rapidly with any oxygen present so that the antioxidant, and not the wine, is oxidised. Care is still needed not to aerate the wine, and it is essential that a measurable level of free sulphur dioxide is present at all times, otherwise the ascorbic acid can be oxidised to hydrogen peroxide with disastrous results of serious oxidation.

Inert gas. Oxidation results from exposure of wine to oxygen in the air, so the use of inert gas (nitrogen or carbon dioxide) to replace air is desirable whenever wine is moved. The level of oxygen in the headspace above bulk and bottled table wines in storage should be measured with an oxygen electrode, and maintained at less than 1 per cent oxygen.

Winery operations. The following general guidelines are important in prevention of oxidation:

- Handle all juice and wine as cold as possible.
- Ensure adequate sulphur dioxide and ascorbic acid levels before handling.
- Start and stop pumps slowly if possible.
- Fill all lines with inert gas before each transfer by means of a side-valve fitting, and push the wine out of the hose with inert gas.

Bottling

Bottling can be of a serious source of oxidation in table wines if the headspace of the filled bottle contains air, since this dissolves in the wine. Accordingly, the headspace (ullage) should be replaced with inert gas before closing the bottle, and checked to ensure that after closing, the oxygen content of the headspace is below 1 per cent. Various methods of excluding air in the ullage space are available, and some are not as effective as users may believe.

Dissolved oxygen in wine

One of the most important problems facing winemakers in Australia, particularly in warm areas, is loss of aroma and flavour in wine. Two crucial reasons for such losses are excessive heat during making and maturation, and oxidation. The two are coupled. In cold climates like Germany, where the grape temperature is normally quite low and the winemaker may wear an overcoat during vintage, oxidation is less of a problem. However, in Australia it can be of critical importance, because access to oxygen from the air and elevated temperature can damage table wines irreparably. One must be careful, therefore, not to transfer winemaking practices on the Rhine and the Mosel to Australia too literally, and an understanding of the role and importance of dissolved oxygen is particularly desirable in Australia. Because New Zealand is cooler, oxidation is somewhat less of a problem but it still occurs.

The measurement of dissolved oxygen at the various stages during the winemaking process is highly desirable from the viewpoint of obtaining maximum quality. The amount of dissolved oxygen in a wine normally does not remain constant, because it is consumed by the wine and results in oxidation. In freshly crushed grape juice saturated with oxygen (as it usually is) the level of dissolved oxygen falls rapidly to zero, because of the naturally occurring oxidase enzymes in the juice. If the juice is again aerated to its saturation point of dissolved oxygen and allowed to stand, a further rapid reduction in dissolved oxygen takes place, and this process can be repeated many times because fresh juice has a high capacity for utilising oxygen. For wine the rate of utilisation is considerably less, and the dissolved oxygen level in wine in a closed vessel may decrease only slowly with time.

Oxygen can dissolve in juice or wine until saturation is reached. The maximum amount which can be dissolved at any one time at atmospheric pressure is relatively small, of the order of 7 milligrams (5 millilitres) per litre, depending on temperature. Freshly crushed must, for example, is normally saturated with oxygen because of the aerating action of crushing. From the viewpoint of definition, aeration is the physical process of dissolving oxygen in the must or wine, while oxidation is the subsequent chemical process of oxidising the juice or wine constituents. Aeration is greater at a low temperature, whereas oxidation takes place more rapidly at a high temperature, which speeds up the rate of chemical reactions.

The worst situation is thus to aerate the wine (aeration of must is less important) during chilling—a leaking gland on the suction side of a pump will do this—then subsequently store the wine warm, during which the dissolved oxygen brings about oxidation by chemical and sometimes enzymatic changes.

Dissolved oxygen in juice and wine is measured with a dissolved oxygen meter, which actually measures the partial pressure of oxygen in the liquid, although the meter may be calibrated in parts per million or milligrams per litre. The meter is usually calibrated with nitrogen to set the zero reading, and with air (20.9 per cent oxygen) to set the 100 per cent saturation (155 millimetres of mercury at 20°C). These meters are small and portable, and usually powered by batteries. Examples of the readings of oxygen content and their interrelationships are given overleaf in part (a) of the table.

Both alcohol and dissolved solids decrease the amount of oxygen which the liquid can contain at saturation, and temperature markedly influences the amount of oxygen which can be dissolved. The figures given in part (b) of the table are for water, on which the data for wine are based. For grape juice and wine the figures are actually marginally lower, but since they depend on composition the figures for water are normally quoted.

(a)

| | *Air-saturated at 20°C* | | |
	Water	*Table wine*	*Grape juice*
Partial pressure (mm)	155	155	155
Per cent saturation	100	100	100
Parts per million (mg/L)	9.1	7.2	6.5
Millilitres per litre	6.4	5.0	4.6

(b)

Temperature °C	*Dissolved oxygen mg/L*
minus 5	18.0
0	15.0
plus 10	11.4
20	9.1
30	7.7

It is preferable to use the term per cent saturation rather than parts per million, since this is what the meter actually measures. It is meaningful to say that one winemaking operation results in an increase of, say, 20 per cent in oxygen saturation, while another does not increase oxygen saturation. For white table wine 0 per cent saturation is desirable. Some dessert wines may benefit from dissolved oxygen, since their maturation regime is oxidative rather than reductive. The state of oxidation or reduction in the wine is influenced by dissolved oxygen, since the presence of oxygen tends to raise the oxidation-reduction or redox potential of the wine. This is dealt with later.

Gaseous oxygen in the headspace of tanks, bottles and other vessels dissolves in the wine, and the level needs to be known. It can be measured by a dissolved oxygen meter employing a Clark-type polarographic electrode, or by a gaseous oxygen meter which depends on the para-magnetic properties of the oxygen molecule. This latter meter is more rapid and easier to use, but will not measure dissolved oxygen.

It is thus important to be aware of the danger of dissolved oxygen in table wines and to measure it to establish the contributions made by the various winemaking operations, particularly after fermentation. It is essential to ensure as low a level as possible in white table wines at all stages from fermentation until after packaging.

Danger of aerating cold wine

The danger of aerating cold wine is one of the most difficult points to get across to winery workers.

Refrigeration has brought great advantages to winemaking, but has inadvertently introduced an important danger if the wine is aerated after chilling. This is particularly so if the wine is very cold, such as after cold-stabilisation. The reason is that oxygen is considerably more soluble in cold than in warm wine, and when the aerated cold wine is allowed to warm up this greater amount of dissolved oxygen contributes more to oxidative reactions, resulting more rapidly in irreversible oxidation. At minus 5°C, for example, the wine can adsorb twice as much oxygen as at 20°C, and the reader should see the previous section for details.

Avoidance of aeration at low temperature is consequently much more important than at ambient temperature, which in itself is clearly undesirable. Care must be taken to avoid leaking unions, glands and fittings on the inlet side of pumps, as well as exposure to air in other ways. All handling of table wine should be carried out under a blanket of inert gas, containing less than 0.5 per cent oxygen.

In addition, it should be emphasised that the proneness to oxidation of white table wines is minimised by ensuring that the pH, free sulphur dioxide and ascorbic acid content are in the correct range, as follows:

pH   3.1 to 3.4
free sulphur dioxide   15 to 35 milligrams per litre
ascorbic acid   50 to 100 milligrams per litre

The higher the pH within the above range, the more free sulphur dioxide is required.

Oxidase enzymes

Historically, winemaking in Australia and New Zealand has undergone a profound change in the past thirty years, with the move from oxidative winemaking of dessert fortified wines to reductive winemaking of table wines, particularly whites. This has meant a new approach to the basis of winemaking, in avoiding oxygen and oxidation rather than encouraging it. With this change has come realisation of the importance and undesirability of the group of enzymes known as the oxidases. These are distinct from other enzymes, such as pectinases or pectin-splitting enzymes, which are legally permitted additives.

Oxidases are naturally occurring enzymes which catalyse the transfer of oxygen to the colourless phenolic substrates and result in browning, astringency and coarseness. Two enzymes are involved: tyrosinase and laccase. They have different properties and origins, which are set out below.

Tyrosinase is known by various synonyms—polyphenoloxidase, catecholoxidase, catecholase, phenolase, phenoloxidase and o-diphenoloxidase. It is widespread in fruits and is the enzyme responsible for browning a freshly cut apple. It occurs regularly in sound grapes in the chloroplasts of the berries, and is responsible for the browning of unsulphited juice of warm, low acid, sound grapes. It is poorly soluble in juice and wine, rapidly destroyed by sulphur dioxide, oxidises relatively few phenols and is unstable in wine. Its susceptibility to sulphur dioxide is of particular oenological importance.

Laccase or p-phenoloxidase, on the other hand, is more dangerous. It derives from the mould *Botrytis cinerea* and not from the grape berry itself. It is soluble in juice and wine, resistant to sulphur dioxide, oxidises many phenols, is stable in wine, and can bring about serious and permanent browning and oxidation. The browning problems associated with oxidised red table wines made from mouldy grapes are largely due to laccase.

Control of oxidation resulting from oxidase enzymes is one of the important developments in modern winemaking. The obvious prevention of laccase damage is not to use mouldy grapes, but this is not always possible. Sulphating reduces the effect of oxidases, whereas bentonite removes only little of them. Heating the must to 65 to 70°C destroys the oxidases, which, being proteins, are denatured at this temperature, but heating can introduce other problems. Preventing contact of the must with air certainly helps, since crushing saturates the must with oxygen, which needs then to be removed by sulphur dioxide and ascorbic acid.

Temperature control is of basic importance. Oxidase activity is greatly increased by high temperatures, thus starting with cold grapes (15°C or below) and cooling all winemaking operations to this temperature greatly inhibits their activity. This is an essential part of oxidation control, since the rate of enzymatic oxidation is about three times faster at 30°C than at 10°C. Prompt addition of sulphur dioxide and ascorbic or erythorbic acid at or before crushing inhibits oxidase activity, binds its phenolic substrates and removes oxygen from the must. Inert gas blanketing from crushing to the beginning of fermentation assists by preventing access of atmospheric oxygen to the must and juice. The phenolic substrates are largely bound to particles of grape flesh, so that clarification of the drained juice assists in reducing oxidase activity. Finally, the activity of oxidases is much more rapid at high pH levels, so the lower the pH the slower the rate of oxidase activity.

Oxidation-reduction potential

The oxidation-reduction or redox potential is a summation of all of the oxidative and reductive reactions existing in a wine at a particular time. It is not a constituent of the wine, but a measure of the *state of oxidation or reduction*. The higher the value, the more oxidised is the wine. It is measured by immersing replicated platinum electrodes in the wine in the absence of air and measuring the electrical potential generated, compared with that of a calomel half-cell of known potential (249 millivolts at 20°C). The wine is forced by nitrogen or carbon dioxide into a vessel containing the electrodes, which is connected to the reference half-cell. The potential is measured on a pH meter reading in millivolts.

The figures so obtained range from approximately 50 to 550 positive millivolts (0.05–0.55 volts), and are higher in musts than in wines. Crushing the grapes with resultant aeration raises the potential by up to 80 millivolts from approximately 400 to 480. Fermentation, on the other hand, is a strongly reductive process which rapidly reduces the potential to between 50 and 100 millivolts at its peak. After fermentation the potential gradually rises to some intermediate value, usually between 200 and 350 millivolts, then slowly diminishes as the wine becomes more reductive during maturation and in bottle. If wine handling involves aeration the potential rises. Bottled wines eventually reach an equilibrium between 100 and 150 millivolts.

Sometimes redox potential is linked to pH and the result expressed as rH, using a scale of 0 (most reduced) to 28 (most oxidised). The validity of this expression is suspect on theoretical grounds, and measurements nowadays are usually expressed as millivolts at a particular pH value. Examples at pH 3 are:

Redox potential in millivolts	rH
0	6.0
100	9.3
200	12.7
300	16.0
400	19.3
500	22.7

At pH 7, for example, the relationship is different.

The important point, of course, is what does a knowledge of the oxidation-reduction potential and its numerical values mean in relation to winemaking and wine quality? Much work has been carried out at the University of Bordeaux and elsewhere on this, and the redox concept has considerable theoretical importance. However, with our present knowledge it has little significance to the practical winemaker, and the values appear to give little more information than can be gained by tasting the wine. Clearly, the higher the value the more oxidised the wine, but the best wines do not always have the lowest values.

However, the redox potential does help us to understand some of the haze problems in wine. Wine normally contains traces of iron and copper which catalyse various chemical reactions, and, if present in sufficient amount and in the required state of oxidation or reduction, will precipitate as a haze. Iron needs to be in the oxidised or ferric form and its half-oxidised potential is 750 millivolts, so that the proportion which is oxidised (less than half in wine) can precipitate. Copper, on the other hand, needs to be reduced to the cuprous form, and its half-oxidised potential is 170 millivolts. This is why copper haze or *casse* forms in bottled wine, because the redox potential slowly decreases converting the copper from cupric to cuprous ions.

The oxidation-reduction systems in the wine which collectively are represented by the redox potential are not all understood. We know that polyphenolics, anthocyanins, tannins, ascorbic acid, sulphur dioxide and various other constituents are involved, but we do not yet know the relative importance of all of the various oxidation-reduction reactions which can occur. In my own study of redox potential in wine, hundreds of measurements were made with triplicate platinum-foil electrodes in an attempt to relate the redox potential to wine quality, but no reproducible correlation was found. So advice to winemakers is not to consider it seriously until we understand it better.

Inert gas

The use of inert gas is a major development in Australian and New Zealand winemaking, and has contributed much to the improvement in quality of table wines. The two gases used are carbon dioxide and nitrogen, both separately and as mixtures in various proportions. Argon and combustion gas, the latter produced by the controlled burning of natural gas, are also used occasionally overseas. Modern wineries have either or both carbon dioxide and nitrogen reticulated throughout the winery, with tapping-off points at appropriate locations.

Inert gas is used for two basic purposes, viz. to reduce the possibility of oxidation of table wines by preventing access to air (oxygen content 20.9 per cent) and to prevent the growth of spoilage yeasts and bacteria on the surface of wine. Carbon dioxide is also used for other purposes, such as in the production of sparkling wines by providing counter-pressure during transfer and bottling.

Although nitrogen and carbon dioxide are widely used, they have in part separate functions because of their different solubilities. Nitrogen dissolves in water at atmospheric pressure to the extent of 19 milligrams per litre (15.5 millilitres) at 20°C, whereas carbon dioxide is far more soluble at 1.7 grams per litre (878 millilitres). Solubility of these gases in wine is of a similar order of magnitude to their solubility in water, but depends somewhat on the composition of the wine, particularly with respect to carbon dioxide. Whether to use one or other of these gases, or a mixture of the two, depends on the particular requirements. Carbon dioxide is applied more to white table wines, whereas nitrogen is more suitable for red table wines.

Still table wines require between approximately 0.4 and 1.0 gram per litre of dissolved carbon dioxide for palatability, depending in the wine. More is required in white wines than red, but above 1.2 grams per litre the gas tends to force the corks out of bottled wines. A mixture of gases over the wine can be used to regulate this amount. For a dry red wine to contain 0.6 grams per litre of carbon dioxide (35 per cent of the saturation level) a gas mixture of 2 parts nitrogen and 1 part carbon dioxide is appropriate. For white wines a 1:3 ratio is desirable.

Fermentation produces copious amounts of carbon dioxide, between 35 and 50 times the volume of the juice fermented, depending on the initial sugar content. If fermentation is carried out in a closed tank, the carbon dioxide can be ducted to where it may be used as an inert gas, e.g. crushers, presses, drainers, gassing empty tanks and so on. This is common practice in many of the co-operative wineries in South Africa.

The main use of inert gas is in replacing air in the ullage or expansion space above table wines in closed vessels. Sometimes vessels may be linked together so that the gas is passed through the head spaces of a series of tanks. When no oxygen, or a maximum of 0.5 per cent (the level required to prevent growth of film-forming micro-organisms) emerges at the end of the series of tanks, it can be assumed that the gassing is effective. Detection of oxygen is carried out with an oxygen meter. In this example, the paramagnetic oxygen detector is most suitable because of its speed of measurement.

Another use of inert gas is in sparging wine to remove dissolved oxygen. Sparging involves blasting fine bubbles of nitrogen through the wine in a column or hose at a rate of 0.3 to 0.8 litres of nitrogen per litre of wine. The oxygen in the wine tends to diffuse into the bubbles of inert gas, according to Dalton's extension of Henry's law (the amount of any one gas dissolved from a mixture of gases is proportional to its partial pressure, when the gas has come to equilibrium with the liquid). The nitrogen also tends to dissolve in the wine and the wine issuing from the pipeline with the froth of nitrogen bubbles is richer in dissolved nitrogen and poorer in dissolved oxygen than it was before sparging. Nitrogen is used for sparging because of its low solubility.

Sparging is moderately effective in removing oxygen but has the disadvantage in that it tends to remove some of the volatile aroma compounds important to wine quality, particularly if the wine is warm. It is better to apply inert gas to prevent the entry of oxygen into wine rather than to endeavour to remove it once it has entered.

Use of inert gas can be particularly beneficial during bottling, where oxidation resulting from air in the ullage space in the filled bottles can be serious and irreparable. To remove air, the bottles can be purged with inert gas before filling (relatively wasteful of gas and rather inefficient in removing the air in the bottle), and the headspace in the filled bottle evacuated or replaced with inert gas. A combination of both is more effective. Replacement of air in the headspace in the filled bottle has a further advantage in conserving the free sulphur dioxide content of white table wines. For example, if the headspace contains 10 millilitres air, i.e. 2 millilitres or 2.8 milligrams oxygen, then 11.2 milligrams of free sulphur dioxide are required to combine with this oxygen (4 milligrams of sulphur dioxide combines with 1 milligram of oxygen). This represents a significant loss of free sulphur dioxide.

In all operations involving inert gas it is important to keep the gas laws and their implications in mind. The gas should be free from oxygen, since any oxygen present exerts its own partial pressure. Furthermore, inert gas flushed rapidly and continuously over the surface of wine in a closed tank tends to remove some of the more volatile aroma compounds.

Dangers of inert gas

Winery staff need to be aware of the danger inherent in using inert gas in confined spaces. For example, carbon dioxide generated by fermentation has to be dissipated—during fermentation of the must from 1000 tonnes of grapes of 11° Baumé no less than 27 million litres of carbon dioxide are released. The legal maximum limit of carbon dioxide in air for continuous work is 0.5 per cent by volume (5000 ppm or 9000 milligrams per cubic metre). In any vessel containing fermenting must or lees there is a real and invisible danger, since there will be no air above the liquid in the vessel. The danger of carbon dioxide resides in its displacement of oxygen in the air, causing unconsciousness or death by asphyxiation. The percentage of oxygen in the air, normally 20.9 per cent by volume, should not be reduced below 19.5 per cent. A lighted candle is not a good indicator, because it will remain burning until the oxygen content in the air falls below 16.5 per cent. Some wineries now automatically monitor the oxygen content of the air, and raise an audible and visual alarm if the level falls below 19.5 per cent.

Carbon dioxide has a density at 0°C of 1.52 compared with 1.00 for air, and thus is 52 per cent heavier than air. When carbon dioxide and air are mixed in a closed empty vessel, the carbon dioxide does not form a permanent lower layer, as its higher density would suggest. Due to molecular movement of the gases, the carbon dioxide becomes uniformly distributed throughout the confined space in a matter of hours. However, if carbon dioxide is continually generated it will eventually remove all the oxygen.

Dry ice or solid carbon dioxide is a useful source of inert gas, and is used in vessels to exhaust air. One kilogram releases 500 litres of carbon dioxide. It is used in closed vessels as either a block of dry ice floating on a buoyant raft or intermittent dosing of the gas into the ullage space. If dry ice is simply thrown onto the surface of wine in a vessel, a layer of water ice forms around it which impedes the release of carbon dioxide.

Practical recommendations

Small volumes of wine are more easily aerated than large volumes during wine-making operations, and this applies especially to small wineries. In addition to the direct use of inert gas, oxygen contact with the wine can be avoided by the following practices:

* Storage vessels should be kept full.
* Containers should be filled from the bottom.
* Pumps and suction lines should be air-tight.
* Air pockets in pipes and hoses should be avoided.
* Agitators should not be run any longer than necessary.
* If working with compressed air the pressure should be lowered to atmospheric before prolonged breaks in operation, such as overnight.

Ascorbic and erythorbic acids

Ascorbic and erythorbic acids are antioxidants and have found an important place in winemaking. As we know, many wine-growing areas in Australia are warm to hot by European standards, and the possibility of oxidation during winemaking is always present. White table wines are most prone, because of their low phenolic content, light colour and delicate flavours. One of the ways to prevent oxidation is to use antioxidants, and both ascorbic and erythorbic acids and their salts (as well as sulphur dioxide) are permitted by law for this purpose. This is a recent development, and prevention of oxidation by the combined use of antioxidants, cooling and inert gas, has resulted in a marked increase in the overall quality of Australian table wines.

Ascorbic acid is better known as vitamin C and is marketed under at least fifty synonyms. It is widely distributed in the plant and animal kingdom and was first isolated from nature in 1928 and synthesised in 1933. Its main commercial use is as an antioxidant and antimicrobial agent in foodstuffs, while therapeutically it is administered to correct vitamin C deficiency and for treatment of the common cold. In winemaking we are essentially concerned with its antioxidant properties. It is a white crystalline powder, has a sharp acidic taste, is stable on storage when dry, soluble in water and wine (a 5 per cent solution in water has a pH between 2.2 and 2.5), and is a strong reducing agent.

Erythorbic or iso-ascorbic acid is the optical isomer or epimer of ascorbic acid, and is marketed under at least eleven synonyms. It has the same empirical formula, but structurally is the mirror image of ascorbic acid, and has only 5 per cent of the vitamin C activity. It is usually purchased as the soluble sodium salt, the aqueous solution of which has a pH of between 5 and 6, but when added to wine it converts to the acid because of the low pH value of wine. Sodium erythorbate is currently about half the price of ascorbic acid, and both perform the same function in wine. One hundred milligrams per litre of ascorbic or erythorbic acid is equivalent to 123 milligrams per litre of sodium erythorbate.

From the oenological viewpoint both ascorbic and erythorbic acids function as antioxidants and oxygen scavengers, due to their strong reducing properties resulting from their ene-diol (double-bond) structure. They are preferentially oxidised and prevent or minimise oxidative flavour and colour deterioration. Because of this property they should be handled with minimum contact with air or iron or copper equipment. Solutions should be prepared immediately before use.

Sodium erythorbate and ascorbic acid are used widely in Australian white table winemaking—the former more than the latter because of cost. They are added to the grapes along with sulphur dioxide (usually as PMS or potassium metabisulphite) as well as after fermentation. Ascorbic acid occurs naturally in grapes in amounts between 10 and 100 milligrams per litre, but rapidly disappears after crushing and the associated aeration, due to enzymic oxidation of phenols followed immediately by reduction by ascorbic acid (which is itself oxidised) of the quinones back to the phenols. On present evidence the most desirable practice in making white table wines is to add 50 to 100 milligrams per litre at the crusher and maintain a level of between 50 and 100 milligrams per litre from the juice stage to bottling, with the level checked by analysis and additions made if necessary after each racking or handling. If analyses are not carried out, the usual practice is to add 20 to 30 milligrams per litre before each movement.

The wine must have the normal level of free sulphur dioxide present (between approximately 15 and 35 milligrams per litre, depending on the pH of the wine), because if all the ascorbic or erythorbic acid is oxidised to its oxidation product dehydro-ascorbic acid and then further oxidation takes place, hydrogen peroxide and other oxidation products can be formed with disastrous results of irreparable browning. Sulphur dioxide prevents this from happening, since it helps to control oxidised flavour development and prevent enzymatic and non-enzymatic browning. It has the added advantage of being an antiseptic, preventing the growth of bacteria and some yeasts, which ascorbic and erythorbic acids cannot do. Thus the two latter antioxidants supplement sulphur dioxide but do not replace it, although they are more rapid and effective oxygen scavengers. Since dry red wines are low in free sulphur dioxide content or may contain nil, ascorbic or erythorbic acids should not be added to them.

Pinking in white wine

Pinking refers to the development of a pink colour after fermentation in white wine in bulk or in bottle. It is not related to the use of red grapes taken off-skins to produce white or pink wine. The pink colour obscures the natural green or light yellow colour of the wine and gives the impression of oxidation, which is characterised by brown tinges in the colour. Oxidation is a separate phenomenon but both pinking and oxidation result from the exposure of the wine to oxygen after fermentation.

Pinking is most likely to occur after fermentation when the level of dissolved carbon dioxide falls, and where the wine is exposed to oxygen. The problem is largely one of appearance, since the aroma and taste of the wine are usually not altered. Over time the amount of pinking usually decreases.

The phenomenon occurs with a range of grape varieties and young white wines differ in their susceptibility. It basically occurs in wine with a low level of free sulphur dioxide and can be detected both by sight and by spectrophotometric measurement, where an increase in optical density occurs at 500 nanometers. Pinking can be induced by the addition of hydrogen peroxide (15 milligrams per litre), which can be used as a test to indicate a wine's proneness to this problem. It is encouraged by a lack of oxygen during the early stage of fermentation, high storage temperature, low free sulphur dioxide, and exposure to light and air.

The treatment to remove pinking is a fining with polyvinyl-polypyrrolidone (PVPP), which is better than either casein or nylon powder. This fining removed the pink colour and lowers the content of the precursors leading to it. The appropriate preventative measures are to maintain an adequate level of free sulphur dioxide in the wine, minimise the exposure of the wine to oxygen, remove the precursors with a small fining of PVPP, and ensure an adequate level of ascorbic or erythorbic acid.

The material comprising the pink colour in the wine is not a single monomeric anthocyanin in the same way as these comprise the colour of red and rosé wines. The actual nature of the pinking compounds has not been completely elucidated but they appear to be formed from proanthocyanins. It is interesting to note that the occurrence of pinking is related to modern technology in the production of white table wines. The wines which are most prone are those made by the use of cold fermentation with inert gas and under reductive conditions. If such wines are exposed to oxygen after fermentation then they have a greater tendency to develop a pink colour.

Measuring the temperature of a grape load. (S. Smith & Sons Pty Ltd, Angaston, SA)

Grape receival hopper (Renmark Growers Cooperative Ltd)

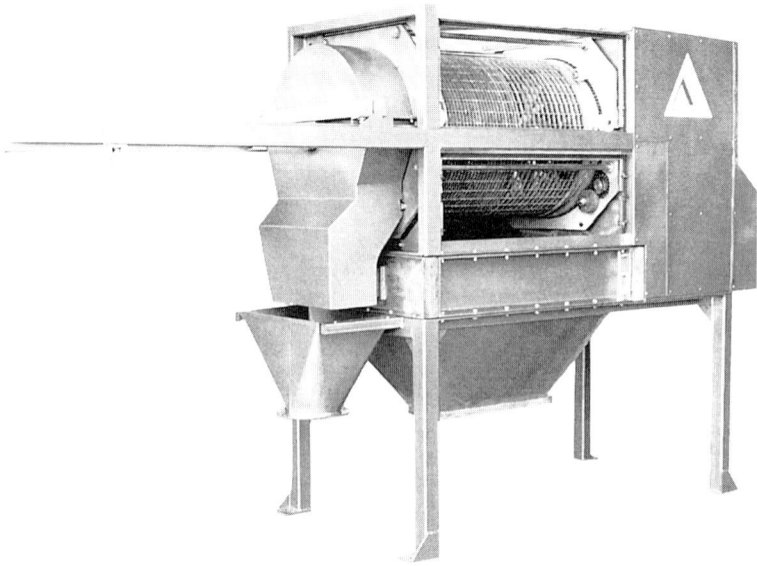

Miller stainless-steel destemmer/crusher with moulded rubber rollers. It has a capacity of 35 tonnes per hour. The cover has been removed to show the destemmer. (F. Miller & Co., Adelaide)

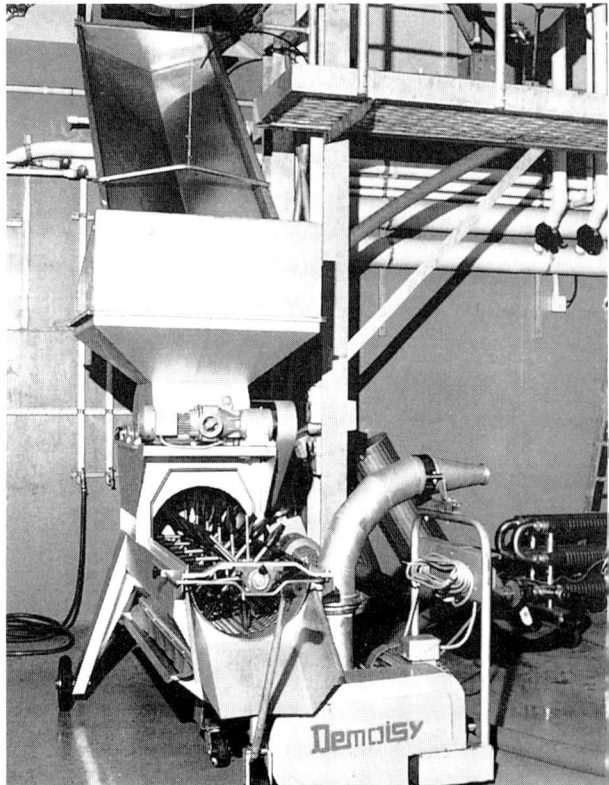

Demoisy D8 stainless-steel crusher and integral must pump at Mountadam Winery. The destemmer cover has been removed. (Industrial Supplies Pty Ltd, Adelaide)

The Willmes TP6 tank press at Tim Knappstein Wines Pty Ltd, Clare, SA (Industrial Supplies Pty Ltd)

Chilled stainless-steel draining tanks over a Willmes UP 5000 Universal pneumatic press (left) *and a Willmes TP4 tank press* (right) *at Petaluma Pty Ltd* (Industrial Supplies Pty Ltd, Adelaide)

Miller CO$_2$ pressure drainers, each with 20-tonne capacity, at Seppelts Chateau Tanunda Winery (F. Miller & Co., Adelaide)

Miller inclined stainless-steel drainers, 500- and 300-mm diameter, at Krondorf Winery (F. Miller & Co., Adelaide)

A rotating 28-tonne Vinimatic wine fermenter/drainer (A. & G., Griffith, NSW)

A small winery centrifuge, with hermetic sealing and automatic desludge, at Roseworthy Agricultural College.

A Westfalia centrifuge with hermetic sealing and automatic desludging (APV Bell Bryant Pty Ltd/Westfalia Separator AG)

Variable capacity stainless-steel tanks. Note the removable lids and cooling jackets. (David Wynn, Mountadam)

Tall stainless-steel multipurpose tanks (McWilliams Wines Pty Ltd, Hanwood, NSW)

Wine fermentation vessels (450 hectolitres) with automatic temperature and pressure control (G. Gramp & Sons Pty Ltd, Rowland Flat, SA)

Alfa Laval Rosenblat spiral heat-exchanger (Rosemount Estates Pty Ltd, Hunter Valley, NSW)

Spiraflo stainless-steel tubular heat-exchanger. Note, curved ends removed for cleaning. (Petaluma Pty Ltd, Piccadilly, SA)

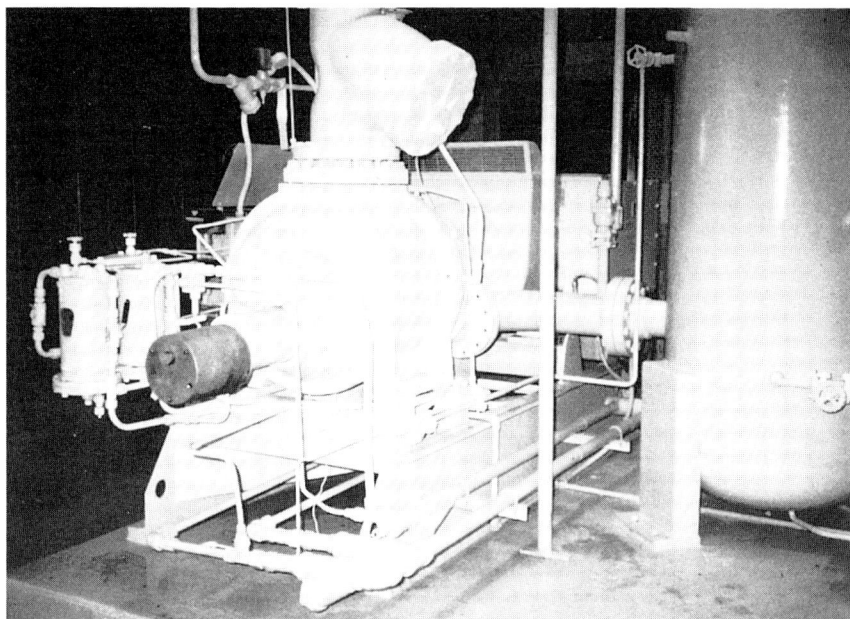

Refrigeration screw compressor (Lindeman Wines Pty Ltd, Karadoc, Victoria)

Integrated wine refrigeration plant (White Refrigeration Pty Ltd, Adelaide)

Bank of four tube ultra-coolers operating with liquid ammonia refrigerant (Lindeman Wines Pty Ltd, Karadoc, Victoria)

Riddling machines for bottle-fermented sparkling wine, each with a 504-bottle capacity (A. & G., Griffith, NSW)

Ion-exchange plant: the treatment column (left) *and regeneration vessel* (right) (G. Gramp & Sons Pty Ltd, Rowland Flat, SA)

Brimstone juice desulphiting unit (A. & G., Griffith, NSW)

Bulk storage of liquid nitrogen and carbon dioxide (Renmark Growers Cooperative Winery)

The 2-inch, stainless-steel Mono pump. It has variable speed drive, forward and reverse, and a capacity of 2300–14,800 litres per hour. (Mono Pumps (Aust.) Pty Ltd)

Jabsco stainless-steel flexible impeller pump (All-Pumps Supplies, Adelaide)

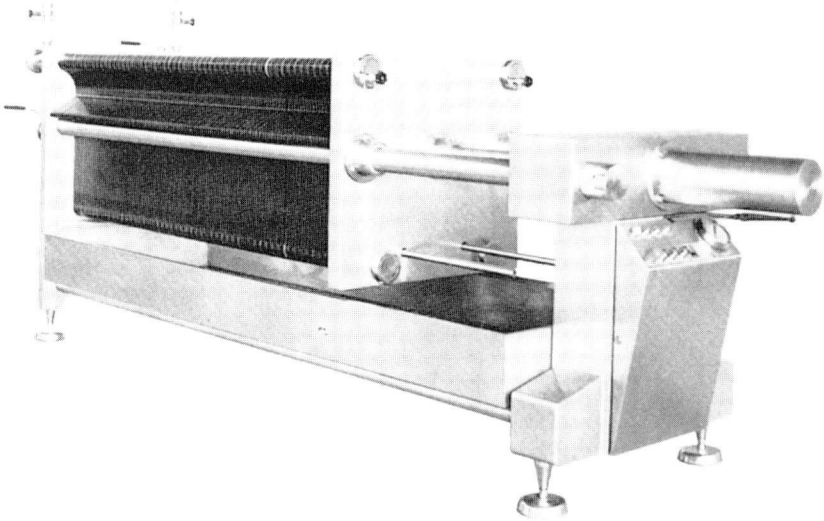

Plate and frame filter press, for use with filter sheets, filter cloths and diatomaceous earth (J.B. MacMahon Pty Ltd, Adelaide)

Alfa Laval rotary drum vacuum filter at Peter Lehmann Wines Pty Ltd in the Barossa Valley (Alfa Laval Pty Ltd)

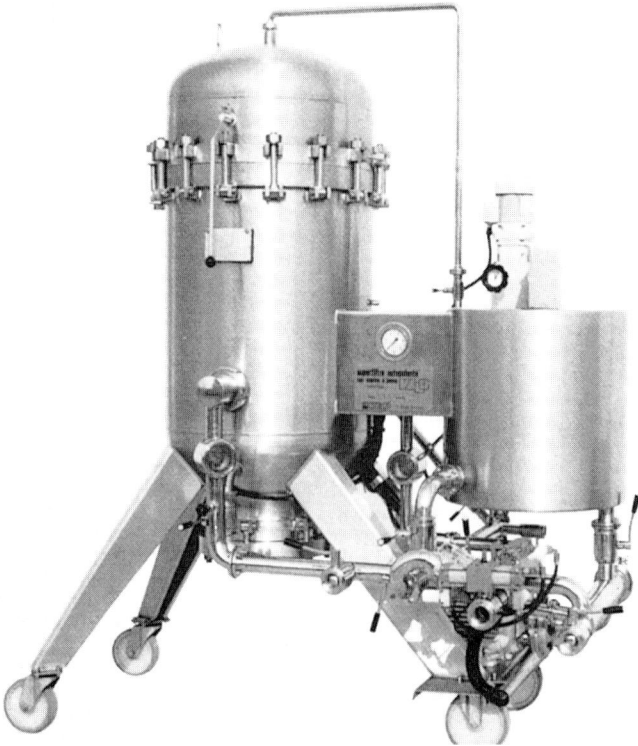

A Velo 20-square-metre stainless-steel, diatomaceous-earth filter (J.B. MacMahon Pty Ltd, Adelaide)

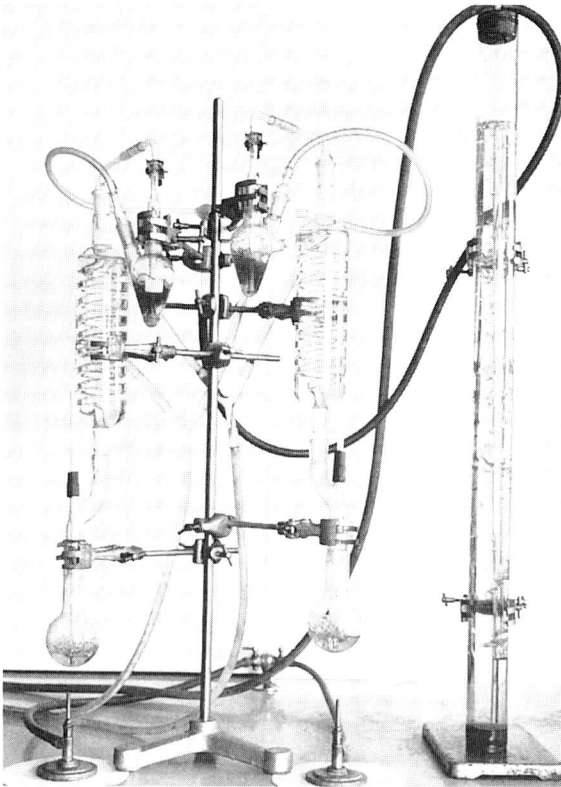

The Rankine SO₂ aspiration equipment

Chromatographic equipment for detecting the occurrence of malo-lactic fermentation in wine

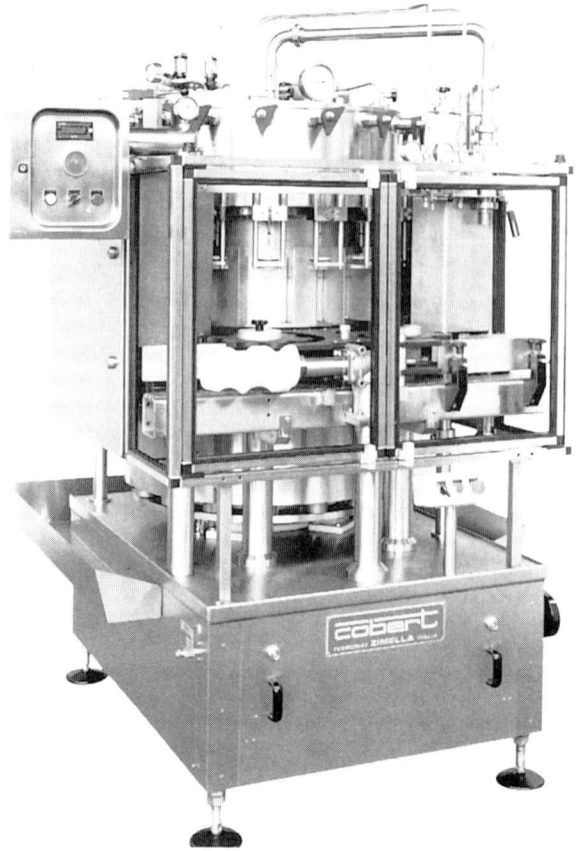

Cobert 16-head counter-pressure filler with pre-evacuation of bottles and self-levelling (J.B. MacMahon Pty Ltd, Adelaide)

'Cask Room' for public relations functions (McWilliams Wines Pty Ltd, Hanwood, NSW)

12 Malo-lactic fermentation

For centuries some red table wines have been observed to become hazy and liberate small bubbles of gas at some stage after their alcoholic fermentation was complete. This curious phenomenon did not seem to harm the wines generally, and in many cases they were improved. This frequently coincided with the rise of sap in the vine, and it was thought that these two phenomena were in some way connected. They were in the sense that both were the result of the onset of warmer weather.

Malo-lactic fermentation is basically the bacterial decarboxylation of L-malic acid in the wine to lactic acid, with the liberation of carbon dioxide, as shown in the following equation:

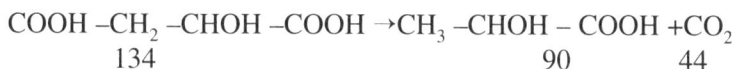

$$COOH-CH_2-CHOH-COOH \rightarrow CH_3-CHOH-COOH +CO_2$$
$$134 \qquad\qquad\qquad 90 \qquad\quad 44$$

Malic acid derives from the grape and, together with tartaric acid, comprises more than 90 per cent of the acidity of grape juice. The fermentation is, however, considerably more complicated chemically than it appears. It is important in practice, not only in Australia but also in most wine-growing areas of the world, and particularly where the wines are naturally high in acid.

A German, P. Kulisch, in 1889 first established its biological nature, although Pasteur had hinted at it earlier, and since that time malo-lactic fermentation, as it came to be called, has been widely studied in various parts of the world. Kulisch thought that the causative organisms were yeasts, but Müller-Thurgau in 1891 showed that the transformation was due to bacteria, and Alfred Koch in 1900 was the first to isolate malo-lactic bacteria and to induce malo-lactic fermentation by inoculating wine with these bacteria. The clarification of the overall malo-lactic equation (malic acid to lactic acid and carbon dioxide) was made by Moeslinger, of blue-fining fame, in 1901.

Occurrence

Malo-lactic fermentation is a characteristic of table wines only. Dessert wines contain too much ethanol to allow bacterial growth, except for the spoilage bacterium *Lactobacillus trichodes* which attacks sugar but not usually malic acid. In table wines the fermentation is more frequent in dry red than in dry white wines, due to the lower level of sulphur dioxide and less acidity in red wines. In Australian table wines approximately two-thirds of the dry red wines and one-third of the dry white wines undergo malo-lactic fermentation in the first six months of age.

The occurrence depends on the winery, which reflects the influence of wine-making practice by individual winemakers, and is related to the type of bacteria present, sulphur dioxide dosage, time of racking and other factors. In some wineries malo-lactic fermentation regularly occurs during or directly after completion of the primary fermentation, while in neighbouring wineries its natural onset may be delayed for months or in some cases years.

The bacteria which bring about malo-lactic fermentation have been found on grapes and vine leaves, as well as in wineries. The practice of some wineries of disposing of marc and lees by spreading it in nearby vineyards could lead to the continued existence of the bacteria in and around the winery, in much the same way as certain yeast strains become established in vineyard areas.

Bacteria involved

Malo-lactic fermentation is something of a misnomer, in that the fermentation is unrelated to the normal alcoholic fermentation of sugar. Indeed, if sugar is present it may not be attacked at all, depending on the type of bacteria present. The bacteria involved belong to the general group of lactic acid bacteria, but their ability to produce lactic acid from malic acid does not have taxonomic significance. The classification of lactic acid bacteria is technically difficult, since some of them have exacting growth requirements and are difficult to grow on defined media, as well as being rather similar both in morphology and in certain biochemical activities.

The genera involved are *Lactobacillus*, *Leuconostoc* and *Pediococcus*. The classical organism of Müller-Thurgau and Osterwalder, *Bacterium gracile*, was probably a *Leuconostoc*. It is likely that the predominant organism in Australian wines is *Leuconostoc oenos*. One difficulty in identification has been the confusion which has arisen in the behaviour and function of the bacteria. Malo-lactic fermentation has been confused with spoilage in wine, in which micro-organisms attack other compounds in wine, such as sugar, tartaric acid and glycerol.

Lactobacillus are short to long rods occurring singly or in chains. They are gram-positive, asporogenous, non-motile, anaerobic or micro-aerophilic, and catalase negative. They convert glucose to lactic and acetic acids, alcohol and carbon dioxide, and also form mannitol from fructose. Some strains attack malic, citric and tartaric acids and glycerol. The facultative anaerobic cocci are important in malo-lactic fermentation, and may be divided into *Pediococcus*, which are homofermentative (producing only lactic acid) and *Leuconostoc*, which are heterofermentative (producing lactic acid, acetic acid and other compounds). Heterofermentation is characterised by gas production from glucose.

The organisms which have been isolated from Australian wines are all heterofermentative, and comprise strains of *Leuconostoc mesenteroides*, *Leuco. oenos*, *Lactobacillus hilgardii*, *Lb. brevis* and *Pediococcus damnosus* and *P. pentosaceus*. Some of the strains of *Leuconostoc* may produce dextran (a mucilaginous gum) from sugar under certain conditions. This imparts a viscous appearance to the liquid and is responsible for 'ropy' wines, but this phenomenon is rare in Australia. Many other organisms have been isolated overseas, and comprise *Lactobacillus buchneri*, *casei*, *delbrueckii*, *fermenti*, *pastorianus*, *planarum*, *leichmanii* and *Leuconostoc citrovorum*, *dextranicum*, *gracile*. Several *Streptococcus* have been reported, but there is doubt as to their correct classification since they do not normally grow in wine.

The cultivation of these bacteria as a prerequisite to their identification and study presents certain problems because of their fastidious growth requirements, particularly the heterofermentative organisms. Synthetic media of defined composition are not always suitable for the most nutritionally demanding bacteria. The complex vitamin requirements are best satisfied by autolyzed yeast or yeast extract, together with amino acid supplement, such as tryptone or peptone. Tomato juice is a desirable addition. Yeasts grow readily in these media and need to be inhibited by such compounds as actidione (cyclo-heximide) or sorbic acid. Diphenyl prevents mould growth.

The method of preparing the medium is important. One batch of medium may support good growth of the bacteria, while the next batch may allow only weak growth. Possibly small differences in time and temperature of heat sterilisation are responsible. The effectiveness of the media also decreases with length of time of storage. However, for obtaining a good inoculum for bacterial inoculation, non-defined media allow excellent growth.

Chemistry

The fermentation is usually represented as a simple decarboxylation of L–(–)malic acid to either L– or D–lactic acid (depending on the strain of bacteria and the substrate attacked), with the carboxyl group appearing as carbon dioxide. D–malic acid is not attacked. However, this is an oversimplification, since different bacteria in fact utilise different pathways. In bacteria which possess 'malic enzyme', malic acid is first converted to pyruvic acid and carbon dioxide in the presence of the co-enzyme nicotine-adenine-dinucleotide, and the pyruvic acid is immediately reduced to lactic acid by lactic dehydrogenase, with the aid of the reduced form of nicotine-adenine-dinucleotide formed from the first reaction. A malic-lactic transhydrogenase has been reported for *Micrococcus*, which converts malic and pyruvic acids to oxalacetic and lactic acids, and it is possible that for some bacteria oxalacetic acid is an intermediate.

Furthermore, in some bacteria the malic enzyme is induced by the presence of malic acid, while in others it is present as a constituent of the bacterial cell.

Some strains of bacteria which have inducible malic enzyme only bring about the malo-lactic fermentation when a high level of malic acid is present, and this has oenological significance. In the presence of these bacteria, wines with a low level of malic acid may not undergo the fermentation.

The transformation of malic to lactic acid and carbon dioxide curiously provides little, if any, energy for the bacteria, and therefore another source of energy is required, which is usually sugar, either hexose or pentose. It is interesting, therefore, to speculate on the purpose of malo-lactic fermentation from the point of view of the bacteria involved. Since the bacteria are living in an acid environment, and malo-lactic fermentation reduces the acidity and renders the medium more favourable, the fermentation probably has survival value.

Carrying out the fermentation

The fermentation can occur naturally or be induced by addition of a bacterial starter culture. If malo-lactic fermentation regularly occurs without inoculation, either during or soon after the primary fermentation, and has no undesirable effect on the wine, then it is best to continue this practice. If not, then bacterial inoculation with a selected strain or inoculation with a wine undergoing the fermentation should be carried out.

There are several options as to the best time to inoculate. The first is to inoculate during the primary fermentation, when the sulphur dioxide has been bound by acetaldehyde and the alcohol level is still low, such as on the second or third day after the fermentation has begun when the mass is warm—most strains will not grow below about 15°C. The second option is to inoculate immediately after the completion of the primary fermentation, before the addition of sulphur dioxide and when the wine is still warm. This places a greater resistance on the bacteria, since they must grow in the full alcoholic strength of the wine. The third option is to use a wine undergoing the fermentation as the inoculum, either during or after the alcoholic fermentation.

The alternative to inoculation is to leave the fermentation to chance, in the hope that naturally occurring bacteria will carry out the fermentation at some stage. This may take weeks or months to commence and the winemaker has little or no control over the strain of bacteria involved.

Thus, the best option depends on the winery and the history of occurrence of the fermentation. If bacterial inoculation is to be used, dried cultures are available commercially. The culture should be reactivated and handled according to the manufacturer's instructions, and added about midway through the primary fermentation, as set out in the first option above. The induction of malo-lactic fermentation by addition of bacteria has developed much in recent years, and several commercial preparations are now available.

The desirable conditions for inoculating red wines are pH between 3.3 and 3.5, total sulphur dioxide below 50 milligrams per litre, temperature 18 to 25°C and before racking. There is an indication that bacteriophage may be present in some red wines, but this seems not to be important. The inoculation rate is of the order of 10 million bacterial cells per millilitre, and a mixed culture appears to have advantages over a single strain.

An example of the progressive changes in pH and the level of malic acid during and after fermentation, when the malo-lactic fermentation takes place after the alcoholic fermentation, are shown diagrammatically in Fig. 12.1.

Benefits and disadvantages

Malo-lactic fermentation has several effects.

Deacidification or the reduction of high acidity. In Australia the pH can increase during malo-lactic fermentation by between 0.05 and 0.45, with a reduction in titratable acid of between 1 and 4 grams per litre. In warm areas, where the wines have a higher pH and lower acidity than their European and New Zealand cool-climate counterparts, this reduction in acidity is undesirable, and malo-lactic fermentation should be avoided because it results in flat insipid wines with little protection against the growth of spoilage bacteria.

The *stability* of the wine is improved, and if all the malic acid is consumed the wine will not undergo a further malo-lactic fermentation in bottle. Sometimes malo-lactic fermentation will stop before all of the malic acid is broken down, and the wine may then undergo the fermentation later. This can occur after a cold snap, inadvertent addition of sulphur dioxide, premature clarification, or blending one wine which has undergone the fermentation with another which has not. To be sure of the completeness of the fermentation, the level of malic acid should be below 0.1 gram per litre and this is best checked by enzymatic analysis. However, it should be remembered that the wine can still undergo other types of bacterial spoilage, such as breakdown of residual sugar.

Fig. 12.1: Changes in pH and malic acid levels during and after fermentation

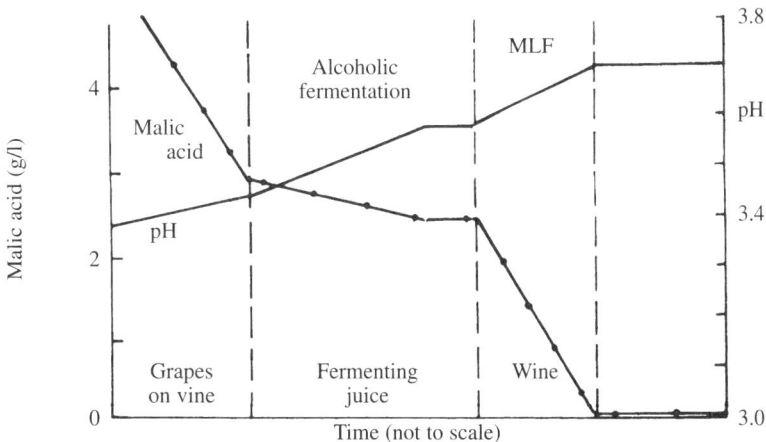

The *quality* of the wine may be improved, but this is not easy to demonstrate unequivocally, and winemakers frequently cannot tell by tasting whether or not a wine has undergone the fermentation. In quality French red wines malo-lactic fermentation is regarded as an integral part of the wine maturation process because of the reduction in acidity, and this concept has carried over into Australian winemaking without proper justification. As stated above, low-acid wines can be reduced in quality by malo-lactic fermentation.

An example of a desirable aspect is the production of moderate quantities of diacetyl during the fermentation. At levels of 2 to 4 milligrams per litre diacetyl adds complexity to the wine flavour, imparting a pleasant buttery character. Above this level its effect becomes overpowering and undesirable, imparting rancid overtones to the wine. The maximum level of diacetyl found in Australian wines is 7 milligrams per litre.

Changes in other acids. Citric acid may or may not be attacked, depending on the strain of bacteria present. Bacteria which can metabolise citric acid use it as an energy source, and not only diacetyl but also undesirable products, such as acetic acid, result from its breakdown. It is unwise, therefore, to acidify dry red wines with citric acid, either before or after malo-lactic fermentation.

Tartaric acid breakdown by lactic acid bacteria in Australian wines is rare, and only occurs in wines with pH values over about 4. This biological degradation should not be confused with the precipitation of potassium bitartrate (thus lowering the tartrate content of the wine), which sometimes occurs during the malo-lactic fermentation, due to change in acidity, brought about by the fermentation. If tartaric acid is broken down the structure of the wine is seriously damaged, because it is the most resistant of the major acids in wine to bacterial decomposition.

The *loss of fruit aroma* following malo-lactic fermentation is a frequent observation, and is sometimes a reason given by winemakers for not wanting malo-lactic fermentation to occur in their red wines. The problem, however, is how to stop the fermentation, because when it becomes established in a winery it usually occurs naturally every year without the winemaker's intervention. Not only is loss of fruit character observed but also reduction in varietal character. In addition, when a wine is undergoing malo-lactic fermentation it may smell quite peculiar and give the impression that its quality is seriously impaired. These off-characters are caused by production of a range of transient volatile compounds, produced by the bacteria, which slowly disappear from the wine.

But other events also take place, one of them being a considerable reduction in certain fruity esters, of which isoamyl acetate is a case in point. This is present in wine and has a fruity aroma reminiscent of bananas. It is broken down during this transformation, and for the wine in question almost 80 per cent of the isoamyl acetate disappeared during malo-lactic fermentation. This provides an explanation for both reduction in fruitiness and development of off-characters which can occur when a red wine undergoes malo-lactic fermentation. If a winemaker has difficulty in preventing malo-lactic fermentation (and most do) then citric acid should not be used to acidify the must or wine, because of the resulting formation of acetic acid and diacetyl.

Detection

The presence of malo-lactic fermentation can usually be detected by observing the evolution of carbon dioxide from the wine, after ensuring that the primary alcoholic fermentation is complete. In certain cool areas in Australia, such as Coonawarra, the malo-lactic fermentation may be so vigorous that it assumes the proportions of a mild alcoholic fermentation.

However, it is rarely possible to taste a wine, free of obvious dissolved carbon dioxide, and state with certainty that it has undergone malo-lactic fermentation. The presence of detectable diacetyl is a good indicator, but if this is absent one cannot be sure. Some dry red wines develop off-flavours when they are undergoing malo-lactic fermentation and the wine seems to be spoilt, but these off-flavours are usually transient and soon disappear after the malo-lactic fermentation is over. It is likely that such transient undesirable volatile products are the result of particular strains of bacteria.

Although malo-lactic fermentation produces a reduction in titratable acidity and an increase in pH, such changes are not positive evidence that the fermentation has taken place, since they can be influenced by other factors. The sure way to detect the occurrence of malo-lactic fermentation is to demonstrate the absence of malic acid, and this is best carried out by a simple paper-chromatographic test (see Chapter 22). The presence of a spot corresponding to lactic acid is not confirmatory proof, because with the chromatographic solvents normally used lactic and succinic acids appear together as a single spot. There are various other methods available—manometric, enzymatic, microbiological—but paper or thin-layer chromatography is an easy and rapid procedure.

13 Oak maturation

Oak cooperage is widely used in Australia and New Zealand for quality red and some white table and dessert wine maturation, but there is not complete uniformity in aging practice. The type of oak is mainly American (*Quercus alba*, together with seven other species) and French oak from the forests of Nevers, Tronçais, Limousin and Alliers, as well as oak from Germany, Yugoslavia and occasionally other European countries. European oaks consist mainly of *Quercus robur* (*pendunculata*) and *sessilis*, together with no less than ten other and less preferred species. All these oaks have more extractable material than American oak, but contribute less 'oakness' per litre of wine. *Quercus* oak is all imported and cask prices depend, among other things, on the prevailing currency exchange rates.

The normal cask size in Australia is the hogshead of approximately 300 litres. Surprisingly, this is confined mainly to Australia, with New Zealand, for example, using mainly barriques and a lesser proportion of puncheons. A wide range of sizes of casks exist in various parts of the world, but it is interesting to note that, apart from Australia, the most commonly used casks for aging of red wine are between 190 and 230 litres capacity, more or less all over the world. Bordeaux barriques of 225 litres fit in here. Puncheons of approximately 500 litres, used in some Australian and New Zealand wineries, cost less per litre than hogsheads and barriques but are rather large for handling.

The surface area per unit volume is a useful indication of availability of maturation and extractable oak surface, and details are set out below.

Capacity in litres	Surface area in square metres	Square centimetres per litre
200	1.8	90
300	2.4	80
500	3.0	60

The relationship between surface area, expressed as square centimetres of surface area per litre of capacity, and volume for vessels of different shape, is also of interest and is set out in the following table:

Volume (litres)	Sphere	Barrel	Cylinder
20	173	195	215
200	83	90	99
2,000	38	42	46
10,000	22	24	27
100,000	10	11	12

In order to achieve oak flavour without cask maturation, oak chips or shavings may be used. The rate of addition depends on various factors, including surface area of the chips, the type of wine and the oak intensity desired. Addition is usually made during fermentation, and the rate is between 1 and 10 grams per litre. Oak extracts may be used and their addition can be more precisely controlled.

Time and temperature of storage (which have to be considered together) of wine in oak depend on the winery. For red wines the time is usually 12–18 months and for whites 2–6 months. Temperature of storage is usually in the range of 18 to 24°C, with the optimum for table tines being 15–20°C.

The number of times a cask may be reused for table wines is between three and six, after which the casks are usually used for storage of dessert wine. Shaving the inside of the cask, removing a millimetre or so of surface wood and exposing a new surface, imparts a longer life to the cask for table wine maturation and is common practice. Shaving a cask which has been used for red wine storage does not enable it to be used for white wines.

Fermentation in casks is sometimes carried out, depending on the winery and the wine type, and is becoming popular for Chardonnay in Australia and New Zealand. The new barrels are normally only rinsed with water beforehand. Opinions differ as to the wisdom of fermenting in wood, since the presence of solids tends to block the pores in the wood. This may be an advantage in that porosity is a problem with cooperage, and if wines are clarified before cask storage the incidence of porosity appears to be greater. Casks tend to show porosity more with wine than with water, and more so with sweet dessert than dry wines.

Storing wine in casks

One of the characteristics of *Quercus* oak casks is that they permit slow evaporation of wine through their staves, with consequent reduction in the volume of wine in the cask. This loss of volume has traditionally been corrected by topping up the casks with some of the same wine kept for the purpose in small containers. As well as replacing wine, topping-up exposes the wine to air, which in table wines encourages the growth of acetic acid bacteria leading to volatile acid formation. These bacteria can grow on the surface of wine exposed to as little as 1 per cent of oxygen in the headspace.

In the case of table wines, if the casks are filled full, hammered with a rubber mallet to dislodge air bubbles adhering to the rough inside of the cask below the wine surface, and bunged tight, the casks may be rolled so that the bung is at 2 o'clock or about 60 degrees from vertical. The cask may then be left for weeks or months without topping up. The wine in the cask still evaporates slowly through the staves, reducing in volume and leaving a space in the sealed cask. If the cask is properly sealed and does not contain porous staves, air does not move in through the staves to replace the wine diffusing out. In fact, a partial vacuum of 100 to 150 millimetres of mercury forms above the wine over a period of time. This ullage consists of water vapour with almost no oxygen, except a minute amount which may be present in the wine and come partly out of solution to reach equilibrium in the headspace.

This partial vacuum means that the wine in the sealed and rolled cask is on ullage, but not in contact with air and thus does not develop volatility. The practice is common in some overseas red wine areas, such as Bordeaux and California, and has been adopted by many winemakers in Australia. The requirements for success are:

- Sound barrels without leaky or porous staves or bung.
- Wine without residual sugar, already having undergone malo-lactic fermentation and been clarified.
- A uniform temperature.

Topping-up of wine in small casks in order to prevent or reduce oxidation may, in fact, do more harm than good. The practice of bunging the filled casks, rolling to about 60 degrees from the vertical and leaving them, is now accepted as an effective and reliable means of aging dry red wines in cask.

Maintenance of oak cooperage

Despite many recent developments in winemaking practices, the traditional storage of red and some white wines in oak casks is still the best way to mature them. Oak cooperage is all imported and expensive, especially French oak at present, and its cost is increasing faster than the rate of inflation. Accordingly, it is of considerable importance to maintain casks in the best manner.

When discussing cooperage we need to know the jargon associated with it, and the following definitions are relevant:

- Cask—any wooden vessel of any capacity having bent sides (but not a plastic bag inside a cardboard carton!).
- Vat—any wooden vessel of any capacity having straight sides.
- Staves—the pieces of timber which form the sides of a cask (in which case they are bent) or a vat. They are not stays, slats or strakes.

- Heads—the flat ends of a cask or vat. The pieces of timber forming the heads are called head staves.
- Bung—the hole through which the cask is filled and emptied. It is positioned at the bilge and in the bung stave. Also the tapered plug of wood, silicone or glass used to seal the bung hole.
- Hoops—metal strips which hold the cask together, and the ends of which are rivetted together.
- Croze—the groove at the end of the stave or cask cut to take the head. The tool used to cut the groove is known by the same name.
- Bilge—the centre of the cask viewed lengthwise where the cask has its widest diameter. It is not the bulge.
- Chime—the end of the staves at the point of the cask's smallest diameter.
- Toasting—the browning or blackening of the insides of the staves as a result of lighting a fire inside the partially assembled cask during making. This is normal manufacturing process and the toasting can be light, medium and heavy.
- Charring—accentuated toasting which ignites the insides of the staves and results in a layer of charcoal being formed. It is traditional in casks used for American whiskey.

Let us assume that the casks (quarter casks, barriques, hogsheads and puncheons of approximately 160, 225, 300 and 475 litres capacity respectively) are to be used for storing dry red wine. The best way to maintain their condition is to keep them full with clarified, stabilised, good-quality wine which has undergone malo-lactic fermentation (if this is desired). Such wine will respond to oak maturation and produce the least deposit during maturation, usually only a small quantity of precipitated pigment (anthocyanins and coloured tannins). Thus the internal surface of the cask will not be coated with precipitated potassium bitartrate, pigments, tannins, yeast, gums, pectins and other precipitated solids which cloudy and unstabilised wines deposit.

When the wine has been in the casks for the desired period of time, which depends on the age of the wood, temperature, type of wine, amount of wood character required and other factors, it should be emptied and the casks washed and refilled promptly with fresh wine.

This is the ideal way to use oak casks for dry red maturation, but is not always possible in practice. It is when casks are left empty that shrinkage, mould and acetic problems arise. Some wineries never leave their casks empty, and if they do not have wine available for refilling they buy some for the purpose.

If no wine is available the winemaker has two alternatives, either to wash the casks with hot water or lightly steam, drain, sulphite and store dry in a cool area, or store filled with water. The water should be acidified to about pH 2.5 with tartaric or sulphuric acid, and sulphur dioxide must be added. The amount depends largely on the prevailing temperature, and should be between 200 and 500 milligrams per litre. As a guide, sufficient sulphur dioxide should be present in the acidified water to be smelt. The important point is that the water must not be allowed to become stale. The sulphur dioxide gradually disappears and when it can no longer be smelt more should be added. But be sure that it is mixed with the water after addition. Aqueous sulphurous acid solution (sulphur dioxide in water) is heavier than water (see the section on sulphur dioxide in Chapter 5 for details) and forms a layer at the bottom of the cask if it is simply poured in through the bung hole without mixing. Storage with water as above is at best a temporary measure.

Casks can be cleaned of deposit left by the wine in several ways—rinsing with recirculated cold water—which is slow (hot water is quicker), or washing and soaking with acid or alkali, such as 0.1 per cent sulphuric acid (1 litre acid in 1000 litres of water) or 2 per cent hot sodium carbonate solution (20 kilograms per 1000 litres of water) followed by a water rinse. Various proprietary products are also available. Acid wash is more effective in that it dissolves potassium bitartrate more rapidly but this argol deposit in the cracks between the staves helps to prevent leakage. This is why sound casks may leak after an acid wash. Sometimes used casks are rumbled with a length of stainless steel chain to help remove the tartrate deposit.

If new casks have been received and are not intended for immediate use, they can either simply be stored in a cool place, or lightly steamed, sulphur dioxide gas added, bunged and stored cool. The advice of the cooper should be sought.

Acetic and mouldy casks need to be watched out for. The former results from the growth of acetic acid bacteria in wine stored in the cask, while the latter arises from residual wine, or diluted wine from insufficient washing, left in the cask. Once a cask becomes acetic or mouldy, restoration is usually not possible.

A further problem can result from sulphuring empty casks by burning sulphur rings. This is an easy way to generate sulphur dioxide, but if drops of molten sulphur fall to the bottom of the casks, these will act as a prolific source of hydrogen sulphide if yeast fermentation takes place subsequently in the cask. Readers are referred to Geoff Schahinger's book *Cooperage for Winemakers. A Manual on the Construction, Maintenance and Use of Oak Barrels*, Ryan Publications, Adelaide, 1992, for more information.

14 Filtration

Filtration should be viewed as part of the overall process of wine clarification. To the present, no single filtration process meets all the clarification requirements of a modern winery, and preparation of wine for bottling—the major but not the only filtration requirement in the winery—normally involves a series of clarification steps. The wine must firstly be stabilised, so that it does not precipitate or become cloudy after bottling. Then it is usual to carry out a preliminary clarification by centrifugation. Advances in centrifugation now make it possible to obtain liquids with a high degree of clarity, which with the most advanced centrifuges may then bypass some, if not all, of the subsequent filtration steps. The partially clarified wine is then usually further clarified to cellar brightness by earth filtration using diatomaceous earth and cellulose precoat, then through sheet (pad) filtration and finally through one or other of a variety of membrane filters.

In considering filtration the following general guidelines apply:

- Filter as little as possible. Each filtration is a cost and the intrinsic quality of the wine may be reduced.
- Clarify before filtration by settling and racking, as this saves time and money.
- When using diatomaceous earth select the coarsest grade of filter earth which will do the job.
- Minimise pressure surges in pad and membrane filtration by starting and stopping the pump slowly.
- Minimise the pressure differential in pad filtration according to manufacturer's recommendations.
- Examine the various items of individual equipment carefully before purchase. Check that the pressure gauges have diaphragms to prevent entry of the liquid into the gauge (with the consequent possibility of yeast infection), avoid metals such as bronze and iron, and ensure that no dead pockets exist to prevent heat sterilisation, along with any other design faults.

Earth filtration

In this process the clarifying medium is added continuously to the juice or wine to be clarified, and forms a filter bed through which clarification is achieved.

Various grades of diatomaceous earth are available, with or without additives and treatments such as electrostatic charge on the particles. Diatomaceous earth filters are of two general types: filter elements in a pressure vessel, and rotary vacuum precoat filters.

The *pressure vessels* contain horizontal or vertical filter elements (plastic or stainless-steel screens), on which a cellulose precoat is applied, by followed by the diatomaceous earth, continuously added to the incoming liquid, which forms the filtering surface. Eventually the flow rate decreases to the point where the filter needs to be cleaned and a new earth layer built up. Cleaning is carried out by backwashing, with or without pressure fluctuations and with the filter elements either moving (rotating or vibrating) or stationary.

Disposal of spent earth constitutes an environmental problem which has led to the development of dry cake discharge, in which the solids content of the cake is increased to between 30 and 40 per cent.

It is possible to purchase plate and frame filters (see below) designed to be used with diatomaceous earth as well as with normal pads or sheets. For small wineries the use of a plate and frame filter with this dual operational capacity is an advantage. The construction material of earth filtration equipment using pressure vessels is stainless steel, whereas plate and frame filters and rotary vacuum precoat filtration may use other construction materials, such as plastics and coated mild steel.

Rotary vacuum precoat filters are used for filtering high-solids juice or wine, tank 'bottoms' (such as the deposit after settling), enzyme and fining lees and centrifuge sludge. They employ a rotating drum partially submerged in a bowl into which is fed the liquid to be filtered together with diatomaceous earth. The liquid is drawn by vacuum through the earth into the interior of the drum, and the filtration surface is continually renewed by a cutting blade, which shaves off a layer of earth containing the solids trapped on and in it. Since vacuum is employed aeration can be a problem and needs to be controlled, but the filter has important application in various recovery operations in the winery.

Earth filtration is the most cost-effective procedure for clarifying young wine to the state of cellar brightness. It is important to ensure efficient utilisation with high throughput per unit of filtration medium used. The ideal of yeast-free filtrate is desirable but, at present, cannot be guaranteed by earth filtration. Rotary vacuum precoat filtration is very effective for high-solids juice and wine where the maximum recovery of product is desired. The equipment is expensive with a high cost of earth usage. It is more expensive than pressure-vessel earth filtration, but precise comparisons are difficult because of the different uses to which both types of earth filtration are put.

Pad filtration

This has been the classical method of clarifying wine and has reached a high level of sophistication. Pads are made in a range of porosities from rough clarification to sterilisation, and manufacturers offer many grades of porosity. Special types of filter pads are produced for specific application, such as pads designed for particular liquids or containing diatomaceous earth, active carbon or other constituents. The initial development of such pads was by the Seitz brothers in the 1880s using cellulose and asbestos, which has been the basis for the subsequent development of pad filtration.

Health concern over the use of asbestos in filtration materials has resulted in the introduction of non-asbestos filter pads, based on cellulose with various additives. It is claimed that non-asbestos pads have the same filtration capacity and effectiveness as those which contain asbestos, but this is not always the case, although non-asbestos pads have a higher initial flow rate than cellulose-asbestos pads.

Filter pads operate on several principles. First of all they have a sieve effect in which large particles are trapped on the surface of the pad; then a depth effect where smaller particles are drawn into the pad and trapped by the tortuous pathways which constitute the fibrous structure of the pad; and, finally, various adsorptive effects based on electrostatic and other charges which bring about adherence of charged particles to the pad. A development is in control of the zeta-potential charge on the pad, claimed to be advantageous in filtration of liquids containing charged particles. Wine contains both positively and negatively charged particles (yeast cells and suspended bentonite respectively are examples) and a charge on the filtration medium assists in retaining suspended particles of the opposite charge by electrostatic attraction, up to the stage where neutralisation of the charge on the filter sheets occurs.

Pad filtration finds a place particularly in clarification before bottling to reduce or eliminate the number of micro-organisms present. The maximum number of micro-organisms permissible in the filled bottle depends on the type and sweetness of the wine, and the finest porosity pads used according to the manufacturer's instructions are able to remove all yeasts and bacteria in the wine.

Membrane filtration

This has been a major development in filtration, and is used mainly as a safeguard after pad filtration to ensure the complete removal of micro-organisms on final filtration before bottling. Membranes are made from a variety of synthetic materials, including cellulose acetate, cellulose nitrate, polypropylene, polycarbonate, polyamide and PTFE. They are available in a range of pore sizes, which in all but polycarbonate membranes are a theoretical concept rather than actual measurable pore sizes.

Most of the membranes are shallow depth filters and all have very little capacity for removing solids. Accordingly, wine needs to be well clarified before presentation to the membranes. Developments in this field have been in the

replacement of flat sheet membranes by cylindrical cartridges, usually comprising two or more membranes integrated into the cartridge and differing in
porosity, with the membrane with the greater porosity acting as a screen for that
of finer porosity. Most of the membranes can be tested for integrity by either
bubble-point or diffusion tests, and automatic equipment for doing so is available. Membranes are capable of withstanding high pressure and can be
heat-sterilised in place, but such sterilisation may reduce the flow rate and life
of the membrane and increase the bubble-point test value. Taints can occur
because of the plastic nature of the membranes, and it is a wise precaution to
precondition membrane filters with acidified hot water before filtration, to prevent any taint arising from the plastic membranes being transferred to the wine.

New membrane materials are capable of repeated steam sterilisation without
loss of filtration effectiveness. Besides being used as final filters before bottling,
the membranes, as small discs of known porosity, can be used as a laboratory
tool to count the number of micro-organisms present in the wine before and after
filtration. The wine is continually sampled and filtered. The cells collect on the
membrane and are grown into micro-colonies and counted, either manually or
electronically, to obtain an assessment of the effectiveness of filtration.

Crossflow microfiltration

So far we have been considering classical or 'dead-end' filtration in which all of
the liquid passes through the filter, with the accumulation of suspended solids
eventually blocking it. With the development of membrane filtration over the
past fifteen years, the application of crossflow techniques, as distinct from 'dead
end', as an alternative to classical clarification has become important and shows
considerable promise.

Crossflow microfiltration was developed originally to produce potable water
in arid areas, and it is now being applied to other industrial processes, including
wine. Crossflow or tangential filtration involves three types, viz.: reverse osmosis, ultrafiltration and microfiltration, based on increasing pore size, and various
types of equipment are available, depending on the pore size of the membranes
used. We are concerned here with microfiltration in which the pore size is
approximately 0.2 microns.

The crossflow technique is such that the liquid to be filtered flows across or tan-
gentially to the membrane filter surface, which consists of many fine-bore tubes.
Some of the steam will pass through the pores of the membrane as filtrate, while
the remainder flows back to the vessel holding the unfiltered liquid and is termed
retentate. This continual crossflow helps to prevent the build-up of particulate matter with consequent blockage of the filtration surface. The particle size involved
ranges from about 0.2 to 12 microns—a yeast cell is about 5 microns in diameter.
The effect is to continuously sweep the membrane surface clean of debris and thus
prevent the solids or cake build-up with subsequent slowing of the filtration rate.

However, the membranes can become blocked or fouled, and this is where the nature of the filtration surface and backwashing techniques are important. The faster the flow rate of the liquid at the surface of the membrane, the less fouling of the membrane occurs and the greater will be the filtration rate. Various backwashing techniques, including gas under pressure, have been developed to minimise the build-up of this contamination layer on the surface of the membrane.

The winemaking applications of this new process are still being developed, and are regarded by the manufacturers as considerable. Already, wines and juices with considerable turbidity can be clarified by crossflow microfiltration. At present there are several units operating in the wine industry, and manufacturers claim to be able to obtain simultaneous clarification and filter-sterilisation without the need of other filtrations of the wine. In addition, the life of the normal membranes (operating on the 'dead-end' principle) used immediately before bottling is considerably extended by microfiltering the wine beforehand.

Some wines are difficult to filter because of the presence of high molecular-weight polymers, and this is dealt with below. It is claimed that these wines can be successfully filtered by the crossflow technique at slow flow rates (about 15 per cent of normal) without the life of the membrane being shortened. Flow rates range from approximately 50 to 600 litres per square metre of filtering surface per hour, depending on the clarity of the product. Preliminary treatment of the must or wine with enzymes increases the throughput.

It is also claimed that sterile filtration of fermenting wine can be carried out with this technique, enabling fermentation to be stopped at any stage to produce a sterile product still containing fermentable sugar. Reports to date indicate that crossflow microfiltration with the present membranes seems to influence wine quality, in that some of the high molecular-weight compounds, such as oak flavour, are partially removed, and the commercial applications at present are in cask and bulk wines. However, the field is developing rapidly and further advances in wine applications are expected.

Other aspects

Dealing with wines which are difficult to filter

Some wines are difficult to filter, and present a problem due to slow filter throughput and expensive blocking of filters. This is usually encountered in membrane rather than plate and frame filters. The wines appear free from visible suspended material, but for no visible reason are hard to filter. This problem is distinct from filter-blockage due to the presence of visible suspended particles, such as yeasts, bacteria and fining residues.

The reason for such wines being hard to filter is the presence of complex long-chain polymers or colloids, soluble in wine and thus not visible to the naked eye. An extreme example is the curious case of ropy beer, which is so viscous that it flows like treacle or thick lubricating oil and yet is visibly quite clear.

In this case the problem is due to the presence of a long-chain dextran polymer which is formed by micro-organisms. One such bacterium, *Leuconostoc dextranicus*, derives its name from its ability to produce these viscous dextrans in liquids in which it grows. Fortunately, its occurrence in wine is rare. The growth of encapsulated *Pediococcus cerevisiae* has recently been reported in France.

These problem polymers in wine usually come from the grapes, especially if they have had mould growth, such as *Botrytis*. The polymers involved are the polysaccharides of various sugars, such as glucose, mannose, galactose, arabinose, fructose and rhamnose. Pectins derived from the grapes and based on galacturonic acid may also be involved, but proteins are not. Yeasts can also produce the sugar-based polymers by breakdown of cell walls.

These polymers can be separated by ultrafiltration and identified. Their levels in wine can be up to 0.3 grams per litre, and those causing the greatest problems are glucan, galactomannan, xylan and carboxy-methyl cellulose. These may be present in considerably lower concentrations than the overall polymer level and still effectively block filters.

It is interesting to note that the gross amounts of these polymers in wine are not the important feature. Some wines with high polymer colloid content can be filtered without difficulty, whereas others with much lower content (less than 10 milligrams per litre) may be difficult to filter—the types of colloids present are more important than the total amount. Yeast glucans, for example, from the yeast cell-wall, and polymers with molecular weights of approximately 250,000. They cannot be removed by normal fining agents, but their presence can be detected by adding 5 millilitres of alcohol to 10 millilitres of wine, and observing the occurrence of a filament-like precipitate. This test detects down to 15 milligrams per litre of glucan, but since lower levels can still influence filterability, the wine needs to be concentrated beforehand. Glucan from *Botrytis cinerea* has been shown to be involved. This polymer has a molecular weight of approximately one million and forms highly viscous solutions. The presence of alcohol enhances the filtration problem.

Filtration rates of wines containing these polymers can be considerably increased by warming the wine to about 40°C, but this is not a practical solution. What is more relevant is the use of newly developed specific glucanase enzymes, which can break down the polymer molecules. One such enzyme is glucanex, a glucanase prepared from the micro-organism *Trichoderma*, produced by Novo Ferment Laboratories. Certain fungi and bacteria are becoming increasingly important as sources of industrial enzymes. Pectin-splitting enzymes, however, cannot break down glucan, and thus do not improve filterability of wines containing it.

Accordingly, a test for filterability is useful for practical winemakers, quality-control personnel and cellar staff. A suitable test is as follows: Filter one litre of wine through a standard 25-millimetre-diameter 0.45-micron membrane, noting the volume filtered at constant pressure in a fixed time. The test normally takes about 10 minutes. The ratio of the number of millilitres filtered between 30 and 90 seconds over that filtered between 120 and 180 seconds should not exceed 1.5. If it does, the wine will be difficult to filter.

Importance of diaphragm pressure gauges for sterile filtration

At first sight it seems curious that a simple pressure gauge should be regarded as important in sterile-filtering table wines before bottling. In fact, it can be of critical importance in contributing to yeast contamination of the bottled wine.

Some years ago I was involved with a winery which was having a serious yeast spoilage problem in its bottled white table wines, especially if the wines contained fermentable sugar. The procedure adopted to find out the source of the contamination was to sample the bottling line at various points from the stage where the wine entered the filter to it being in the filled and closed bottle. This involved hundreds of samplings over a considerable period. The yeast infection was sporadic, and the results clearly showed that it had to come from the filter, since all other possible sources, including the bottles and closures, had been checked and cleared. The filter pads were not letting yeasts pass through, although the incoming wine did contain yeasts. It had to be some part of the filter, and was eventually identified as the pressure gauge on the outlet side of the filter.

Pressure gauges consist of an internal curved Bourdon tube closed at the far end. When the pressure increases the tube tends to straighten, and in doing so transmits its movement via a simple lever mechanism to the pointer on the dial of the gauge. This tube is hollow and cannot be sterilised by steam, because the back pressure prevents the steam from entering the tube. What was happening was that wine had entered the tube, as would be expected to happen with fluctuating pressure, and had become infected and established a breeding ground for the yeast. The infected wine tended to bleed back into the sterile filtrate sporadically, depending on fluctuations in pressure, and the pressure gauge by virtue of its design acted as a continuing source of spoilage yeast.

The remedy was to ensure that wine could not have access to the tube in the gauge by using a flexible diaphragm of either stainless steel or rubber, which transmitted the pressure to the tube via a high-density liquid like glycerine. Various types of diaphragm pressure gauges can be used, providing that they can be steam-sterilised. In the above case, once the faulty pressure gauge was replaced with a diaphragm gauge, the problem disappeared.

Other cases of yeast infection from faulty pressure gauges have subsequently been encountered in Australian wineries. So in buying a pad filter for use in final filtration it is important to ensure that the outlet pressure gauge has a diaphragm and is heat-sterilisable.

Cold stabilisation of wine by filtration

This is an intriguing use of filtration jointly developed in California and Germany. The filter medium is loaded with potassium bitartrate crystals through which the chilled wine is passed. Potassium bitartrate in the wine deposits on the crystals which increase in size, and the filtered wine is thus rendered stable to further potassium-bitartrate crystallisation down to the temperature at which the wine is filtered. In this case the filter acts as a device for precipitating a dissolved constituent and not for removing suspended material.

Lees filters

These filters or presses are physically among the largest filters in use in wineries, and are designed to clarify high-solids materials, such as lees and fining residues. They consist of large plates and frames with a diatomaceous-earth feed and woven pads with, usually, automatic opening, closing and cleaning. They perform the same kind of duty as does the rotary vacuum precoat filter. They have a high capital cost, a low operating cost, low throughput and a high maintenance cost because of the high pressure at which they operate. They cannot be classed as a hygienic piece of equipment.

15 Bottling and packaging

Bottling is a particularly important part of wine production. It requires care and attention to detail, particularly for delicate table wines. Bottling procedures do not improve a wine and the bottling operations must be so carried out as to minimise damage to it. The most common problems associated with bottling are as follows:

- faulty filtration
- faulty pumping
- dirty bottles
- excessive dissolved carbon dioxide
- oxidation
- faulty corks and corking
- capsule and capsuling problems
- labelling problems
- faulty conveyor design.

In this section we will consider the various aspects of bottling and these problems.

Pumps

Pumps in general were dealt with in Chapter 5, and we are concerned here with pumps specifically in relation to bottling. Always check with the manufacturer of the filler as to whether a specific pump type should be used, then purchase the correct model. Check the recommended layouts of pumps, lines, filtration, bypasses etc. to be used and comply with them. The usual pumps are centrifugal which do not build up pressure. Other types of pumps may require relief valves and bypasses.

Wine lines

The pump and filtration system must be able to deliver at constant pressure at least one and a half times the volume of wine flowing out of the filler into the bottles or casks. This is because most fillers do not demand wine continuously. In the case of counter-pressure fillers, in which the wine is filled against a pressure of sterile carbon dioxide or sometimes nitrogen, the wine flow must be sufficient to maintain pressure in the filling bowl.

Wine lines must be at least equal in internal diameter to the filler inlet, without any restriction between the pump and the filler. For example, if the wine line has an internal diameter of 50 millimetres (1960 square millimetres cross-section) and the filter has fittings of 30 millimetres internal diameter (710 square millimetres cross-section), then three filters in parallel are required to enable the wine to flow along the line at the correct volume without pressure fluctuations in the system. Wine lines should be as short as possible with the minimum number of bends, none of them sharp. Check the specifications of the filling machine with respect to the internal diameters of wine-supply lines, their maximum length, and whether they should be rigid, flexible, insulated, etc. Incorrect wine-feed procedures may not affect the rate of filling, but can subject the wine to oxygen absorption, agitation, loss of carbon dioxide and contamination, as well as influencing the effectiveness of filtration.

Sterilisation

Cold (meaning not hot) sterile filling originated with the Seitz-Werke company in Germany and has been carried out in Australia and New Zealand for many years. It provides a sterile product and conserves the quality of the wine more than any other bottling method. It requires all equipment and vessels which the wine contacts to be free from micro-organisms which can grow in wine. The aim of sterilisation is to have no yeast and bacteria present, or as close to none as is achievable.

Bottles directly from the glassworks and freshly shrink-wrapped while still hot are sterile, but can be contaminated on storage. Bottles from overseas or secondhand are not sterile and require treatment. This can be carried out by a jet of sulphurous acid solution, or by immersing the bottles in either sulphurous acid solution or hot water. The last method is the most effective but is expensive. The time required for sterilisation of the empty bottle with a solution of sulphurous acid depends on the strength of the solution as shown in the table on the following page.

After the bottles are rinsed they should be drained before filling to prevent excess sulphur dioxide entering the wine.

Sulphurous acid strength in per cent SO_2	Time in seconds
0.5	60
1.0	45
1.5	30
2.0	5

The wine lines, final filter and filler are sterilised by moist steam at 115°C, which is allowed to circulate through all parts of the equipment for 20 minutes from the time the steam exits from the coldest parts of the equipment. The entire system must be sterilised, including the wine, gas and air lines, filters and all equipment downstream from them. It is important to avoid cold points, dead ends and water boiling within filters. Chemical 'sterilisation' is relatively ineffective and not recommended.

Filtration

This was discussed generally in Chapter 14, but the following points are relevant to the bottling operation. The bottling filters should not perform a 'dirt-removing' task—the wine should be both stabilised and filtered bright before arriving at the final filter. It is important in sterile bottling not to exceed the specified flow rate, which for a 60-centimetre square pad filter is usually 100 to 130 litres per pad per hour, with a pressure drop across the packed filter of not more than 100 kilopascals. Always check the manufacturer's specifications before using any brand of sterile filter pads. In addition, the wine should be introduced to the filter slowly to avoid an hydraulic shock on the pads.

Filling

We will be considering sterile filling here because it is widely carried out and imposes the most stringent demands on the bottling and bag-in-box filling processes. The wine is filtered bright into the final storage tank before filling, and filtration from there to the filling is only a precaution. The filler is the centre of the bottling line, and should be selected with care. It should be made of type 316 stainless steel, with easy cleaning inside and out, good fill accuracy and readily available spare parts. Most filling machines have safety factors, such as non-return valves, slow opening and shutting wine inlet valves, timing devices for automatic inlet-valve control and so on, to protect the wine feed. It is in this area that problems can occur if these features are not properly understood.

There are four main types of fillers used in Australia.

Auto-Syphon ('Trinne'). This filler operates on the syphon principle, in which the syphon is begun and cut off for each bottle by means of carbon dioxide gas injected into the syphon tube. It has the advantages of slow and steady wine flow without turbulence; the carbon dioxide provides a protective gas cover in the bottle; the wine fills from the bottom of the bottle and the filler is easy to sterilise. A disadvantage is that accurate control of fill heights is difficult. This filler is not being manufactured at present, but there are still many in the industry.

Low vacuum. This type is common in Australia and is available from several manufacturers. It has the advantages of simplicity of operation; ease of sterilisation and cleaning; slow and steady wine flow with little turbulence; reliable fill-height accuracy; and the fillers are relatively inexpensive. A disadvantage is that the design does not prevent oxygen pickup. However, with the use of carbon dioxide to prefill the bottle (thus replacing the air which would otherwise fill the central bowl) and either vacuum corking or filling the headspace with carbon dioxide before corking, this oxygen pickup can be reduced. These fillers cannot handle sparkling wines.

Counter-pressure. This type is the best and most expensive, and can handle all types of wine and spirits. It operates on the principle of pre-evacuating the bottle, then pressurising it with carbon dioxide and filling. This is necessary with sparkling wines and desirable with table wines. The disadvantages are that the fillers are pressure vessels and thus expensive; they are mechanically complex with an involved operation; and fill-height accuracy is somewhat variable unless a self-levelling system is fitted.

Bottom-filling counter-pressure. These are mainly used in breweries to counteract foaming problems. The system reduces oxygen pickup but it is mechanically complex and expensive, and little used in the wine industry.

Corks and corking

A natural straight wine cork is a solid cylinder cut from the bark of the cork-oak tree *Quercus suber*. It is thus a natural product and varies accordingly from tree to tree and from year to year. The most common size in both Australia and New Zealand is 44 millimetres long by 24 millimetres diameter or 44 x 24. The size tolerances allowed are plus or minus 1.0 mm for length and plus or minus 0.5 mm for diameter. Four quality ranges are normally available, from no. 1 (top commercial quality) to no. 4 (lowest quality suitable for wine). Cork suppliers may have their own quality designations. Hand-selected corks are also available at extra cost.

Cork quality is of great importance to wine bottlers and has been a recurring problem. Assessing quality is rather subjective and you have to rely on the supplier. The ability of a cork to provide a good seal depends on various factors:

* elasticity or speed of recovery of the compressed cork
* preparation of the cork before treatment
* surface treatment of the cork before bottling
* moisture content of the cork before bottling
* even compression during corking
* the number and type of structural faults in the cork.

It is wise to buy from a reputable cork merchant who treats the corks locally and provides reliable service and consistent quality. Corks should be stored at 15 to 25°C and 60 to 70 per cent relative humidity for a maximum period of 6 months before being used. The moisture content should be between 5 and 8 per cent, as determined by weighing before and after drying in an oven at 105°C to constant weight. If below this moisture level the cells are too dry and the cork can collapse when compressed, and if above it the cork is too soft and spongy and grows mould readily. Finally, cork quality relates closely to price, and economics dictate how much should be spent in relation to the wine in question and how long the cork is likely to remain in bottle.

Sampling of corks for testing is desirable and the Australian Standard 1199–1972 defines the following sample size:

Batch size	Sample size
1,000– 3,000	200
3,001– 10,000	315
10,001– 35,000	500
35,001–150,000	800
150,001–500,000	1,250

For best sealing results, the cork diameter should be 6 millimetres greater than the bottle internal neck size for still table wines. For slightly effervescent wines, and wines intended for long bottle aging, this figure should be 8 mm. The vacuity or space between the cork and the level of wine in the bottle should be between 10 and 13 mm.

A 24-millimetre-diameter cork should be compressed to not more than 15.5 mm for entry into a 17.5-mm bore bottle neck. Such a compression will give 85 per cent size recovery immediately, 95 per cent within 3 hours, 98 per cent within 6 hours and 99 per cent within 24 hours of insertion. The corker should have a cork compression system which applies an even pressure around the cork, otherwise localised collapse can occur along its length. This creates weakened channels along which the wine can seep. Cutting or deforming the cork is caused by poor compression-jaw design allowing for sharp edges, worn or damaged jaws, and broken jaw-return springs. The corker can bring about contamination by wine squirting up over the jaws, by over-lubrication where oil gets on to the cork and into the wine, by cork dust and by corrosion or damage of the jaws.

When a cork is forced into a bottle a considerable pressure develops in the bottle. If a cork 44 millimetres long by 24 mm diameter is inserted into a standard bottle neck of 17.5 mm diameter and the wine is 15 mm below the cork, a pressure of between 15 and 20 pounds per square inch gauge is created by compression of the air space. If the bottle is lying down this pressure will tend to force wine between the cork and the glass while the cork is still expanding after insertion. If air is in the headspace, this will be compressed and will dissolve in the wine with possible consequent reduction in quality.

To obviate this problem a corker should be used which creates a vacuum between the cork and the wine as the cork is inserted, or the gas space above the wine in the bottle replaced with carbon dioxide, either as the gas, liquid or dry ice, just before corking. Carbon dioxide is more easily compressed than air and dissolves readily in the wine.

From time to time a winery will become infested with cork borers which eat into the corks of bottled wine. This is best prevented by removing organic residues which serve as larval food, and spraying with pyrethrum in piperonyl butoxide at weekly intervals in the warm weather.

Bottled wines suffering from a mouldy cork chemical smell and taste began to become apparent in the late 1980s (and after this book was published). This taint has probably existed ever since corks began to be used as bottle closures, but was obscured by the other more noticeable faults reported in chapter 19. Cork taint at present occurs in between 2 and 5 per cent of bottles and is an international problem. The causative agents are mould metabolites formed during the cork growing and making process before the corks come to this country, and its incidence appears to be random. The main causative compound (2,4,6, trichloroanisole) can be smelt in extremely low concentration (a few parts per trillion)—as can the methoxypyrazines that impart the grassy, herbaceous, vegetative grape varietal aroma in wines made from Sauvignon blanc and Cabernet sauvignon. We are presently living with cork taint. Although we know a lot about it (due largely to Australian research), the problem arises where the corks are made in Portugal and Spain.

Tradition presently demands that quality bottled wine must be closed with a cork. However, the best closure is a non-tainting impervious one, such as a crown seal or a Stelvin roll-on pilfer-proof (ROPP) closure. We investigated the use of Stelvin closures in detail in an extended series of trials over some years in conjunction with Australian Consolidated Industries, which made the bottles and closures. Regular tastings by an expert panel consisting of Don Ditter, Bruce Tyson, Peter Weste and myself produced unequivocal results—the range of wines examined (white and red) retained their quality with a Stelvin closure significantly better than with a cork. However, the closure did not take on for other reasons (not cost). It looked cheap and the customer demanded that the bottle should be closed with a cork—an example of consumer preference dictating over a proven technical finding. It is interesting that a time interval of almost 30 years elapsed following release of the evaluators' publications before the screw cap (Stelvin) closure was adopted by the industry. Many of the premium white wines in the Clare district are now closed with screw caps and winemakers in other areas are beginning to use this closure. The application of screw caps for red table wine is proceeding more slowly.

Capsuling

A range of capsules is available on the Australian and New Zealand market:

- PVC—the most economical when all factors are taken into account.

- Lead (lead/tin/lead laminate)—expensive but provides a top-quality presentation.
- Polylaminate—a less expensive substitute for the lead capsule with a lower-quality finish.
- Stelvin closure—a combined closure and capsule. Tests carried out in Australia over many years have shown that Stelvin can be a better closure than cork. However, its public acceptance for quality wines is not as good as it is for cork with a capsule.

A range of roll-on pilfer-proof (ROPP) and other closures is also available.

It is necessary for capsules to be applied automatically at the speed of bottling, and to achieve this they need to be telescopically packed, spaced as widely as possible in the sticks, able to separate easily, and to be packed to prevent damage during transport.

Labelling and packaging specifications

This is a complex and important subject, since labelling is the nerve centre of packaging. Accordingly, it is important to secure a good labelling machine. Labels are available as wet glued and pressure sensitive. The former are presently cheaper and generally easier to apply, with adhesive which can be all-over, band or strip. The all-over glue application is considered best. It is important in preserving the label on the bottle to allow adequate drying time between labelling and packaging. Pressure-sensitive labels are more popular from the marketing point of view, but difficult to apply to cold wet bottles.

Label paper needs to be selected with care, taking note of the grain of the paper, the weight in grams per square metre (80 to 100 is normal), resistance to scuffing, water and ice, and minimum swelling. The storage of labels is important to the performance of the labelling machine, ideal storage conditions being a temperature of 25°C and 75 per cent relative humidity. Labelling of bottles is the most complex, difficult and expensive part of the wine packaging process, and consultation with the label designer and printer is necessary.

Packaging specifications
Various packaging specifications are used in the industry, and those developed by Jeff Clarke at Tidsdall's Mount Helen winery are reproduced below with acknowledgement to serve as a guide. Each packaged product has its own specifications, which are set out on an A4 sheet of paper (see overleaf).

Bottling line services

Providing the necessary services to the bottling line is expensive. Generally the total service costs are about 40 per cent above the cost of the plant, and include the following considerations:

Fig 15.1: Example of packaging specifications

Packaging specifications

Product: _____
Code: _____

Bottle:
Type: _____
Size:_____
Supplier: _____

Cork:
Size:_____
Quality: _____
Supplier: _____

Capsule:
Size:_____
Colour:_____
Typeface: _____
Supplier: _____

Label:
Front Size: _____
Back Size: _____
Paper:_____
Type Faces: _____
Colours: _____
Application:_____
Placement: _____
Art Supplier: _____
Print Supplier: _____
Finish: _____

Carton:
Type: _____
Dedication: _____
Background: _____
Markings: _____
Art Supplier: _____
Print Supplier: _____

Pallet:
Type: _____
Carton Base: _____
Quantity: _____

- flooring—including non-slip surfaces and slope for drainage
- water—cold, hot and sterile
- steam—with the associated traps
- gases—air, nitrogen and carbon dioxide
- electricity—with oversize provision for the future
- maintenance facilities—which need to be nearby
- filtering needs—for water, wine, steam and gases
- forklift provision and distance
- requisites storage
- management facilities
- laboratory—equipment and location
- lighting—natural and artificial. Localised is better than floodlighting.

Bottling line design

This is a specialised field and advice from an expert is desirable. The filler is the heart of the bottling line and the operations on either side of the filler need to be faster, with accumulation zones to smooth out variations in flow rate. Assuming that the filler has a rated speed of 5000 bottles per hour the line would be structured as follows:

- depallatiser—6500 BPH 130 per cent • accumulation zone
- rinser—6000 BPH 120 per cent • accumulation zone
- filler and corker—5000 BPH 100 per cent • accumulation zone
- labeller—6000 BPH 120 per cent • accumulation zone
- packaging—6500 BPH 120 per cent

Bag-in-box packaging

This is a highly specialised packaging system, in which Australia leads the world. It is too complicated and detailed to be described here, but some basic comments on the package are appropriate.

The bag is a complex system of co-extruded layers of different plastics selected for low oxygen permeability (no greater than 0.175 millilitres at STP per litre capacity in 24 hours at 75 per cent relative humidity and 100 per cent oxygen at 23 plus or minus 3°C), tensile strength (not less than 3.0 kilograms per millimetre), high interlayer peel strength (greater than 150 gram per 25 metre at 300 millimetres per minute jaw speed), minimum flex cracking and so on. The recommended headspace volumes range from 2 per cent for a 20-litre-capacity bag to 14 per cent for a 2-litre capacity.

The bag-in-box components should be manufactured in compliance with the provisions of the Australian Standard 2171–1978 Code of Practice for 'The Manufacture of Plastic Items for Food Contact Applications'.

Hot bottling

In recent years developments in wine bottling have been in the area of cold (meaning not hot) sterile bottling using sterile filtration with prior sterilisation of the filling equipment, empty bottles and closures. This procedure has been shown to best conserve the quality of the wine.

However, cold-sterile bottling is a specialised and costly technique needing relatively high technology and effective quality control. The reason is that the wines bottled in this way are usually prone to yeast and bacterial growth, and these micro-organisms must be excluded. Consequently, hot bottling can be an attractive alternative for standard wines, because the heat involved sterilises both the wine and the bottle, and sterile filtration and microbiological testing of the bottled wine are not necessary. For this reason hot bottling has been developed, and it may be carried out in two ways:

1 The wine is filled cold, then the bottle and its contents pasteurised. This is the standard practice for bottling beer. Alternatively, the wine is pasteurised to sterilise it, then filled cold into the bottle, but this is not hot bottling.

2 The wine is filled hot into bottles which are allowed to cool naturally. The heat sterilises the bottle and closure as well as the wine.

This latter procedure is the standard practice for hot-bottling. The wine (usually still sweet table wine) is heat- and cold-stabilised by bentonite and either refrigeration or ion-exchange, and checked for metal stability. A sample is checked in the laboratory by heating at 80°C for 6 hours to ensure that it is heat-stable and will not form a haze in the bottle. The wine is then filtered and heated to between 53 and 55°C in a heat-exchanger against hot water (not steam) and filled at this temperature into bottles, which are then closed and inverted to ensure that the closure is also heated.

Approximately five times as much hot water at 3°C above the desired wine temperature should pass through the heat-exchanger. Temperature of both the hot water and the wine should be continuously monitored. As a matter of interest, fruit juices are usually hot-bottled at 72 to 75°C, compared with wine at 52 to 55°C. The alcohol in wine becomes sufficiently toxic to micro-organisms at this temperature to permit a lower bottling temperature. The term warm-bottling is perhaps more appropriate.

This temperature is adequate to kill the yeasts and bacteria which can grow in wine. They are not heat-resistant nor do they develop heat resistance, and are readily killed by hot bottling followed by slow cooling, usually in a carton which further conserves the heat.

The hot-bottling equipment is designed so that heating is precise and automatically controlled. A bypass is incorporated, so that if the filling machine is stoped the wine flow through the heat exchanger continues and is returned to the original storage vessel. The loss of carbon dioxide should also be minimised, especially for sparkling wines, and a filling machine with a carbon-dioxide counter-pressure system is required. For sparkling wines higher carbon-dioxide counter-pressure is required to prevent loss in gas pressure in the filled bottle.

Heating wine from 20 to 55°C results in an expansion of approximately 1.6 per cent of its volume, depending on the composition of the wine. Therefore the bottles are filled sufficiently that a contraction in volume of approximately 12 millilitres can be anticipated. Bottle closures must be heat-resistant and so specified when purchased. The time taken for hot-filled bottles to reach room temperature depends on the size of the bottle, the room temperature, whether bottles are stored in cartons, and other factors. The time of cooling is usually from 4 to 22 hours.

Care is needed to avoid contact of the wine with air, either before or during heating. Solubility of oxygen is greater in cold wine, but the rate of oxidation (as distinct from aeration) is much faster in hot wine. Therefore, for wines prone to oxidation, it is important that they should not contain dissolved oxygen at the bottling stage.

The points for and against hot-bottling are summarised as follows:

1 Points in favour:

- Lower investment cost for plant—bottles, equipment and closures do not need to be sterile and the danger of secondary infection is avoided.
- Lower running cost—bottling is more reliable, expensive rebottlings due to microbiological growth in the bottle are eliminated and overall production costs are lower.
- The quality of certain wines which benefit by warming may be improved. Heat results in a slight aging effect which softens and rounds out some wines.
- Labelling is easier as the bottles are warm and dry.
- Despatch delays are avoided as sterility tests, apart from routine intermittent checks, are not required.

2 Points against:

- Loss of freshness—hot wine loses carbon dioxide rapidly if handled incorrectly and particularly if a vacuum-filling machine is used.
- Special temperature-control equipment is required to ensure that the wine is at the required temperature when filled, and not subjected to this temperature for longer than necessary.
- Loss of heat energy occurs when the filled bottles are cooled, without being able to recuperate this heat. This results in higher energy costs.
- Heat-resistant bottle closures are required, for example, corks should not have a layer of low melting-point wax.

Foaming and gushing

Foaming and gushing are nuisances in sparkling wine bottling and can be expensive. There are several causes and consequently the occurrence can be sporadic.

Gushing when the bottle is being opened at a restaurant or home will damage the product's reputation and sales, as well as wasting much of the bottle's contents. The usual cause of foaming during filling is the presence of gases other than carbon dioxide being present. Solubility of air or nitrogen in the wine is so low that when pressure is released by removing the cork these gases come out of solution rapidly as fine bubbles, which then induce the rapid release of dissolved carbon dioxide resulting in foaming. When the wine is being sparkled by tank fermentation, the operator needs to ensure that all of the air initially in the tank is removed by carbon dioxide before the tank is closed to allow gas pressure to build up.

Rough handling of the bottles during filling and before corking can induce foaming. Striking an opened bottle a sharp blow with a heavy metal object can result in spectacular gushing, which can produce a jet of foam a metre or more high. A rough passage of filled bottles to the corker can also result in foaming to a lesser extent. Particles in the bottle or in the wine, or bottle imperfection such as hair cracks can also result in foaming. Particles such as bitartrate crystals, diatomaceous earth, carbon and cork dust have been identified as contributing. Sharp internal bottle imperfections can serve as nuclei for bubble formation, and sometimes a particular batch of bottles induces foaming.

Effect of glass colour on bottled wines

There is ample evidence that sunlight has a detrimental effect on wine resulting in bleaching and general reduction in quality, more so with white table wines than red. This is influenced by the colour of the glass from which the bottle is made, and the range of glass colours available ranges from colourless through various shades of green to amber.

The wavelengths of light transmitted by the various glasses are important, since the high-energy ultraviolet and near-ultraviolet light have the most undesirable photochemical effect on wine. The wavelength range of visible light is approximately 400 to 700 nanometres (nm), while the wavelength range of ultraviolet and near-ultraviolet light—the most damaging radiation—is approximately 200 to 420 nm.

Amber bottles exclude wavelengths below about 450 nm, effectively excluding the damaging ultraviolet rays. In fact, 2 millimetres of glass transmits only about 5 per cent of the light falling on it. White and light-green glass transmit wavelengths down to about 330 nm, and with both green and white glass 2 millimetres transmit more than 80 per cent of the light falling on them. Sunlight emits more high-energy ultraviolet light than fluorescent tubes, and thus is more harmful to wine. Warm-white flourescent tubes give little energy below 420 nm and are accordingly relatively unimportant.

It is problematical how important is the colour of the bottle from a practical viewpoint. Most bottled wines are probably stored under dull light conditions or, if in cartons or cupboards, in the dark. However, modern bottled wine displays in retail outlets and supermarkets are generally well lit. Bottled wine exposed to direct sunlight and heat in shop windows can certainly be damaged depending on colour of the glass, intensity of the sunlight and time of exposure.

While there is ample evidence that amber glass protects table wines from photochemical deterioration much more than green or white glass, the overriding factor is not the colour of the glass but the commercial presentation, cost and sales appeal of the bottle. The proportion of dark amber glass bottles used now is less than formerly, and green glass considerably more. The trend away from amber bottles to green is clearly made on the basis of presentation and customer appeal.

Amber glass is widely used for beer bottles, because of the susceptibility of beer to photochemical deterioration caused by light, resulting in development of what is termed 'sun-struck' flavour. This light-induced change is caused by the action of sunlight on isohumulones (hop resins) and thiols forming methyl-butene-thiol compounds, which give rise to the sun-struck flavour. These isohumulones do not exist in wine and wines do not exhibit sun-struck flavour.

Storage of red wines in bottle

The question of how long red wines should be stored in bottles is frequently asked by consumers and wine marketers. The short and rather unsatisfactory answer is that it depends on the wine. However, there is more to the question, since it also relates to how long the winery should store bottled red wines before release and how long the customer should cellar the wine.

One feature of wine, as distinct from most other foods and beverages, is that certain wines improve with age and thus become more valuable. In fact they become articles of trade—so long as they remain unopened. The classical example is selected Bordeaux reds, which in the past have improved in bottle for twenty or more years. With these wines price reflects actual and potential quality fairly accurately. Features which aid bottle maturation are firm acidity (pH 3.2–3.5), a favourable tannin balance and, of course, fruit character. Certain grape varieties lend themselves more to producing long-lived wines—Cabernet Sauvignon, Cabernet Franc and Merlot in Bordeaux are examples, along with Cabernet Sauvignon and Shiraz in certain areas of Australia.

Vintages in Bordeaux, for example, are much influenced by the weather during grape maturation on the vine, with warm years producing the best wines. The extent of such variation is considerable, ranging from mediocre (e.g. 1974) to outstanding (e.g. 1975) wines. This is reflected in the prices asked, and vintage charts are widely used as a general guide to the area and year. These apply to overall assessments at an early age but may not of course relate to a particular maker or bottle.

In Australia vintages differ much less in most winegrowing areas and vintage charts are consequently of less value. Also, methods of winemaking are changing—

acidity of red wines is increasing as winemakers recognise the value of pH control, and this is favouring quality and longevity. So differences in wine quality from the same grapes from one year to another may relate not only to the climate but also the technology of making.

From time to time we are able to evaluate wines from the same maker and vineyard over a period of years and we can learn much from this. Certain makers have gone to the trouble and considerable expense of withholding bottled stocks for later release. I recently tasted a range of newly released old reds from the Lindeman Rouge Homme winery at Coonawarra, which was a rewarding experience. These wines came from grapes grown in two individual vineyards— Limestone Ridge and St George—and showed the development of the wines and the styles over a number of years. They were all fine wines with some being outstanding. The 1980 St George, for example, which won the 1981 Jimmy Watson Trophy in Melbourne and subsequently other awards, was superb.

The point of this exercise, and what has been written earlier, is that well-made and properly balanced old red wines are much more complex, richer and basically better than when young. Then why do we not drink more of them? There are several reasons for this—young wines attract media attention as new releases. Wine shows tend to favour younger wines, and older wines are, of course, more expensive to buy. However, for red wine lovers with limited resources there is a way—buy a case of each of several wines which show promise and come from wineries with a good track record. Then, at intervals of a few months, open a bottle and note for future reference the evaluation of the wine. Compare these evaluations from one tasting to the next and so plot the curve of development of the wines over a period of some years. This can be a rewarding experience as well as educational fun.

Many Australians and New Zealanders unfortunately do not know the taste of old well-matured reds. We have many fine red wines, and cellaring in a cool and even temperature not exceeding 20°C can permit them to develop to their full potential.

Ultraviolet light and wine sterilisation

Ultraviolet light is used commercially for sterilising water and air, and it is logical to consider its use for sterilising wine. The germicidal property of ultraviolet light (damage to intra-cellular DNA) results from radiation at a wavelength of 254 nanometres which is not visible to the naked eye. Micro-organisms differ widely in their resistance to ultraviolet radiation. Sporing bacteria are the most resistant but do not grow in wine. Wine yeasts, including spores, and bacteria are not particularly resistant. However, the problem is to obtain sufficient penetration of the radiation into the wine. Several examples may help: penetration into solids (such as the inside of the walls of casks) is virtually nil with the treatment only being effective on the directly exposed surface. Penetration into liquids is greater but this depends very much on the liquid. In rain water, about 50 per cent of the radiation energy is lost at a depth of 5 centimetres. In tap water (particularly in Adelaide) it may be lost in 1 centimetre, while in milk significant penetration is limited to 0.2 centimetre.

When we consider wine the situation is different. Both white and red wines, particularly the latter, contain many compounds (mainly phenolics) which strongly absorb ultraviolet light. A convenient method of comparison is to rate wines against water in their relative resistance to penetration of ultraviolet light, using 50 per cent reduction in irradiation intensity as the yardstick. Comparisons of average values as follows: rain water 5 centimetres, tap water 1 cm, white wine 0.04 cm, red wine 0.004 cm. From these figures it is clear that wine is so opaque to ultraviolet irradiation that virtually no penetration takes place, the effect being restricted to the surface. It is for this reason that ultraviolet light is not effective as a sterilising agent.

Other uses are possible, such as prevention of surface film yeast or bacterial growth on wine in ullaged vessels by mounting an ultraviolet lamp in the vessel above the wine. This is effective if the micro-organisms only grow on the surface. Both film yeasts and acetic acid bacteria can grow in the wine as well as on the surface, and if they do then surface irradiation will not kill them.

One further aspect should be noted—ultraviolet lamps normally generate ozone, which can be smelt near the lamp. Ozone is a powerful oxidising agent and harmful to those wines which may be damaged by oxidation. Therefore, surface irradiation of such wines can promote oxidation.

Volume change of wine and juice with temperature

Heat affects wine and juice in various ways, and we are concerned here with the change in volume as they are warmed or cooled. This is important to the winemaker and juice technologist, whether dealing with these products in large or small bulk containers, bottles or soft packs. From the consumer's point of view the influence of temperature in the bottle and soft pack is of the most importance.

When temperature changes occur in a filled bottle of wine, four effects cause the internal volume and pressure to alter.

1 As the thermal expansion of wine is much greater than that of glass, a temperature rise will cause the wine to occupy a larger space in the bottle (with a corresponding decrease in the density of the wine). Accordingly, the gas in the headspace is compressed into a smaller volume. This becomes important when the wine is charged with carbon dioxide, or in the case of the soft pack when the wine is filled under a cover of carbon dioxide.

2 The rise in temperature of the gas itself causes it to exert a greater pressure.

3 There is a change in the vapour pressure exerted by the wine (in addition to the change in the partial pressure of the gas or gases). This is the pressure caused by the evaporation of some of the liquid into the ullage space of the bottle.

4 A change in the capacity of the bottle itself resulting from the change in temperature (approximately 0.5 millilitre per litre increase over the range of 20 to 40°C), as well as the distortion of the bottle under pressure. However, the latter effect is so small relative to the others that it can be ignored.

The rate of volume change with temperature is neither linear nor constant for all beverages, since it depends on composition. With fruit and vegetable juices which may be filled hot the thermal rate of contraction is particularly important, and more information is available on this than for wine. For example, the expansion volume for apple juice is as follows:

Temperature range °C	Volume of expansion ml/l
20–30	3.0
20–40	7.0
20–60	17.0
20–80	25.3

A comparable figure for a vegetable juice from 20 to 80°C is 29 millilitre per litre.

Wine expands with increase in temperature in a predictable way which depends on its alcohol and, to a lesser extent, solute (dissolved solids) content. Alcohol expands about four times faster than table wine depending on the temperature, so the higher the alcoholic content, the greater is the expansion rate. This change in volume is a natural characteristic, and since wine is virtually incompressible such expansion must be allowed for in the container.

Various measurement have been made on the thermal expansion of wine, particularly over the temperature range of 20 to 40°C, as follows:

Wine type	Alcohol % v/v	Sugar g/l	Volume of expansion of ml/l
Table wine	10.00	2	7.3
,, ,,	12.0	2	7.7
,, ,,	14.0	2	7.9
,, ,,	14.0	100	8.6
,, ,,	11.8	–	6.9
,, ,,	12.0	–	6.5
,, ,,	12.2	–	7.6
Fortified wine	18.0	100	10.7

These kinds of figures are used to decide on bottle fill-height and vacuity or head space volume. The volume accepted as a working standard in Australia for expansion of packaged table wine over the temperature range of 20 to 40°C is

6.5 millilitre per litre. As the alcohol and/or sugar content becomes greater so does the increase in volume. Some wine is also hot-bottled, and the contraction in volume as the wine cools after filling from 55°C, the temperature at which the wine is usually bottled, to 20°C, is approximately 16 millilitre per litre, depending on the alcoholic strength. The comparable figures for water, apple juice and alcohol (95 per cent v/v) are 13, 14, and 52.

Alcoholic strength has the greatest influence on thermal expansion of wine. This is demonstrated particularly with brandy, which at an alcoholic strength of 37.5 per cent v/v has a rate of thermal expansion of 3.5 millilitre per litre for a 5°C change from 20 to 25°C. the European Economic Community has published tables showing the increase in volume of water/alcohol mixtures at different temperatures. The figures have been rounded and accordingly are not so precise, but give an indication of the influence of alcohol content. Examples from the tables for the temperature range from 20 to 40°C are as follows:

Alcohol % v/v	Volume of expansion ml/l
10	6
20	7
30	9
40	12

An apple wine (alcohol content unspecified) had a quoted expansion rate slightly higher than that for table wine, as follows:

Temperature range °C	Volume of expansion ml/l
20–40	7.0
20–60	17.0
20–80	25.3

As far as water is concerned, the effect of temperature on its coefficient of thermal expansion is as follows:

Temperature °C	Coefficient of thermal expansion per °C
4	0.00000
20	0.00021
40	0.00038
60	0.00051
80	0.00062

The various figures above are important for several reasons, one of which is the temperature to which packaged wine and juice can be exposed. As an example, the interior of a motor car with its windows closed on a hot day can reach 80°. If we assume that packaged products in a car reach this temperature the volume would increase from that at 20°C by approximately 18 millilitres in a 750-millilitre bottle and 120 millilitres for a 5-litre soft pack. It is little wonder that corks are forced out of bottles and soft packs swell under these conditions.

16 Hazards in the winery

Noise

With the advent of high-speed bottling equipment, centrifuges, hydraulically operated machines and similar noise-producing equipment, the problem of noise in modern wineries and bottling halls is becoming serious, and legislation on maximum permissible noise levels now exists. Let us consider a few fundamental aspects of noise.

Nature and measurement

What is sound? Sound is the sensation produced through the ear resulting from fluctuations in the pressure of the air. These pressure fluctuations can be set up in many ways, but the most common is by some vibrating object. The motion of the surface of the vibrating object produces pressure fluctuations, in the form of alternate compressions and rarefactions, in the air adjacent to the surface. These spread out into the surrounding air, and are interpreted by a listener as music, noise or sound, depending on whether the impressions are good, bad or indifferent.

Levels and decibels. The magnitude of these pressure fluctuations in the air determines the loudness of the noise which we hear. The energy content of a sound wave is actually proportional to the square of the pressure fluctuations in the air, to which the human ear responds, and this is the quantity which we want to measure. When we consider the actual sound pressures involved in common noises, some problems arise. The quietest sound that most young people with good hearing can hear has a sound pressure of about 0.000,02 or 20×20^{-6} Pascals (0.000,003 pounds per square inch gauge pressure). On the other hand, a very loud sound, such as a jet aircraft taking off 50 metres away, might have a sound pressure of about 64 Pascals (9.2 psig) or 3,200,000 times the quietest audible sound. The square of each of these sound pressures becomes 0.4×10^{-9} and 4000 Pascals respectively, or a ratio of 10^{13} between them.

To avoid the difficulties involved in expressing such large numerical ratios, a logarithmic scale is used where the unit is called the bel. An increase of one bel is a tenfold increase in intensity, so the increase of 10^{13} mentioned above is 13 bels. The bel is a very large unit, so for convenience is split up into tenths called decibels. The increase of 13 bels is then 130 decibels, often written as 130 dB.

Combining levels. Rarely do we get a single sound source acting alone, so we need to know how sound pressure levels add to each other. One must beware of the trap of saying that two sources each of 90 dB combine to give 180 dB—in fact they give 93 dB. Despite the fact that adding two identical sounds together produces an increase of 3 dB in the sound pressure level, an increase of 3 dB in the sound pressure level of a noise does not make it sound twice as loud. In fact, an increase of 1 dB is not detectable by ear, an increase of 3 dB is just detectable under good listening conditions, and an increase of 10 dB makes a noise sound about twice as loud. Hence, it can be seen that the human ear is not a particularly accurate or sensitive sound level meter.

Effects of distance. As sound spreads out more or less spherically from a sound source, sound intensity is proportional to the reciprocal of the distance from the noise source. If the distance is doubled, the sound pressure level is reduced by 6 dB. For example, a noise source with a sound pressure level of 76 dB at 2 metres will have a sound pressure level of 70 dB at 4 metres, 64 dB at 8 metres and so on, i.e. 6 dB reduction for each doubling of distance. This only applies in a 'free field' situation, in the absence of nearby reflecting surfaces.

Frequency. We need to know two quantities in order to describe a sound. One is the sound pressure level, and the other is its frequency, or pitch. A vibrating surface is performing a repetitive motion at some certain number of times per second, and causing the same number of compressions and rarefactions per second in the adjacent air. This property is called the frequency, and is measured in cycles per second, called Hertz (abbreviated to Hz). The human ear can hear sound in the range from 20 Hz to 20,000 Hz (20 kilo-Hertz or kHz). As examples, the lowest and highest notes on the piano keyboard are at 28 Hz and 4200 Hz (4.2 kHz) respectively, with middle C at 256 Hz. The hum from a fluorescent light ballast is at 50 Hz, and the ABC radio time 'pips' are at 1000 Hz.

Frequency weighting. Although the human ear can detect sounds over a wide range, it is by no means equally sensitive to all frequencies—sounds at 100 Hz and 1000 Hz with the same sound pressure level do not sound equally loud. It would be desirable to have a sound level meter which 'weights' sounds at different frequencies in a similar manner to the human ear. Most meters now incorporate an electrical adjustment known as the A-weighting network.

This network approximates to the frequency response of the human ear, so that sounds with the same A-weighted sound pressure level in decibels (written as dB(A)) sound equally loud. The A-weighting is internationally standardised and widely used in noise measurement. Table 16.1 shows the A-weighted sound pressure level of some common noises.

A variety of sound-level meters are available, which give direct readings of sound pressure level. These range in price from about $600 for a simple survey meter reading only dB(A), to more than $6000 for a precision sound-level meter capable of measurements over a wide range of frequency bands, and with a range of accessories for various specialised acoustic measurement.

Table 16.1: Typical A-weighted sound pressure levels dB(A)

Jet takeoff, 70 metres	130	
	120	
	110	
Pneumatic drill, 3 metres	100	
	90	Boiler room
	90	Printing plant
Pneumatic drill, 15 metres	90	
	80	City street at peak hour
Freight train, 30 metres	80	
	70	Vacuum cleaner at 3 metres
Male speech, 3 metres	60	Busy office with typewriters
	50	
	40	Quiet private office
Soft whisper, 2 metres	30	Quiet garden at night
	20	Recording studio
	10	
Threshold, acute hearing	0	

Let us now examine the effect of noise on the person and the damage to hearing which can occur.

Effect on people
Physiological effects. The main physiological effect of excessive exposure to noise is noise-induced hearing loss, which usually first occurs at a frequency of about 4.6 kHz. This is often accompanied by a ringing in the ears persisting after the noise exposure, and the subject may notice a slight dulling of the hearing at the end of the exposure or working day. This loss is usually temporary, and hence is known as temporary threshold shift. Removal from the noise usually leads to complete recovery within 24 to 48 hours if the exposure has not been too severe.

If the noise exposure is severe, or is repeated sufficiently often, a permanent noise-induced hearing loss may accrue. This loss also occurs initially around 4 to 6 kHz, but as the hearing loss increases, it spreads to lower and higher frequencies. As nerve cells within the inner ear are damaged, the process is not reversible, and recovery of hearing will not occur even over many years (apart from recovery of any temporary hearing losses).

Damage risk criterion. An acceptable criterion for 8 hours per day for broadband steady-state noise exposure is 85 dB(A). Such exposure is likely to lead to a 25 dB average hearing loss in about 15 per cent of exposed persons after 10 or more years, with about 1 per cent of the exposed population incurring sufficient hearing loss to cause some degree of social handicap.

More complex noise exposure patterns may be assessed using the equal energy principle—converting the time exposure at each noise level into an equivalent acoustic energy, summing the results, and then calculating the equivalent continuous noise level, which should not exceed 85 dB(A). Practical methods for this are given in Australian Standard 1269–1976, 'Code of Practice for Hearing Conversation'.

In some circumstances, it may not be practical to measure noise exposure with conventional sound-level meters. This could occur where people move from one area to another, or are exposed to very variable or impulsive noise. In such cases, pocket noise dose meters or other specialised equipment may be required.

Legislation is now in force relating to noise in industrial premises. Taking South Australia as an example, two Acts deal with noise at work—the *Workmen's Compensation Act* and the *Industrial Safety, Health and Welfare Act*. Similar acts exist in most other states, and you should consult these Acts for further information.

Sources of noise

Various noise sources occur in wineries and we will now consider the most important ones.

Air and refrigeration compressors. These compressors are of two types—reciprocating piston and screw. The reciprocating compressor is usually relatively quiet; some high-frequency broad-band noise may be generated by gas flow through valves, but is not usually a problem. The screw compressor is inherently more noisy, and has gained a bad reputation from the early unlubricated screw compressors. The advent of oil-flooded screw compressors, and attention to the noise problem at the design stage, has substantially reduced the noise. For example, some makes of compressors now have a double-wall stator, which helps to reduce noise.

Refrigeration screw compressors are mainly direct-driven by two-pole (3000 rpm) electric motors, when the main noise source is usually the motor and not the compressor. Standard screw compressors will generally have sound pressure levels at 1 metre in the range of 75 to 95 dB(A), depending on size. However, with attention to design and use of low-noise motors, it is possible to keep noise down to 85 dB(A) at 1 metre.

Pneumatic equipment. Noise from pneumatic equipment can be a serious problem, particularly exhausts from air-operated valves and pistons on machinery (such as some pneumatic bottling machinery). Noise from these exhausts is usually of a sharp impulsive nature, with peak levels in the 90 to 110 dB(A) range. All pneumatic exhausts should be fitted with miniature mufflers, which are readily available in a range of sizes from most manufacturers of compressed air fittings and equipment. These mufflers can reduce exhaust noise by 5 to 15 dB(A), for the price of a few dollars each.

Electric motors. There are three main noise sources in electric motors: fans and air flow, bearings and magnetic effects. Unless there is something wrong with the motor bearings, fan noise usually far outweighs the other two. Historically, the design of fans in electric motors has been unusually crude—in many cases it would be more apt to describe the device as an air stirrer rather than a fan.

More sophisticated fan designs have recently found their way into electric motors, resulting in lower fan-noise levels, more efficient fans and hence overall motor efficiency. For example, an Australian manufacturer has recently released a new range of totally enclosed fan-cooled (TEFC) motors which are about 7 to 15 dB(A) quieter than the standard TEFC motors, and also significantly more efficient, for a price premium of about 10 per cent. Standard 4 pole TEFC motors range in noise from 70 to 90 dB(A) at 1 metre for 10 to 100 kW motors. Drip-proof motors are generally quieter than TEFC by 5 to 10 dB(A).

Bottling equipment. One major noise source in bottling equipment is compressed air exhausts mentioned previously. The other is impact between the bottles. The sound pressure peaks from bottle impacts commonly reach 110 to 115 dB(A). Impact noise of this type is potentially damaging to hearing, but does not sound particularly serious to the ear, and cannot be correctly measured with conventional sound level meters, as they cannot respond sufficiently rapidly to the sharp noise peaks. A special impulse sound-level meter is required for measurement of this type of noise.

Centrifuge operation. Centrifuges are now frequently used in wineries and the trend is towards self-desludging units, which desludge while the rotor is spinning at normal operation speed. The noise of desludging, akin to a piercing howl, can be a serious source of intermittent noise in the winery. Noise levels of 80 to 100 dB(A) can be expected at 1 metre from these machines.

Noise control

The most efficient and effective way to solve a noise problem is to reduce the noise at the source, usually by re-design. However, it is difficult or impossible to do this once a piece of equipment has been delivered to the winery. The place for noise reduction at the source is at the design and construction stage by the manufacturer. It can be achieved for the winery by suitable clauses in the purchasing specification, e.g. 'Noise shall not exceed 85 dB(A) at any point 1 metre from the machine, or at the position of the operator's ears, under normal operation'.

When it is not possible to purchase equipment with inbuilt noise control, the noise source can often be isolated by enclosing it in a noise-attenuating material. Reductions of 7 to 15 dB(A) are possible with relatively simple enclosures. High reductions are possible, but may require specialised design techniques, particularly if ventilation of the enclosure is required. Even relatively small openings can almost completely negate the effects of an otherwise good enclosure, and attention should be paid to sealing at edges of inspection panels, doors or other openings. Acoustically absorbent linings in enclosures add to their effect by preventing high noise levels building up inside the enclosure. At least 50 per cent of the surface inside an enclosure should be lined with an acoustic absorbent, such as plastic foam or mineral wool, at least 25 millimetres thick, and a 50-millimetre thickness of mineral wool protected by a chicken wire facing, is an effective and cheap lining for plant room walls.

Isolation of the receiver of the noise is a similar principle to enclosing the source, but interrupts the noise transmission path near the receiver, rather than near the source. Examples are placing a high noise-reduction wall between a plant room and an office area, or (where other methods have failed) providing personnel in high-noise areas with earmuffs. Earmuffs are not a satisfactory long-term solution to noise problems, due to difficulties of getting people to wear them. Nevertheless they may be used as a temporary measure until other solutions are found, or for short-term noise problems.

The following practical aspects of noise prevention may be of help:

Noise in the bottling hall. Much of the noise is generated by pneumatic machinery (the use of inexpensive mufflers has already been mentioned) and bottles clinking together. Design of conveyor belts, rotating accumulation tables and the like encourages bottles to strike each other. A recent development is to erect a tunnel over the conveyor line and over unscrambling and accumulation tables using thick (10 mm) transparent perspex. Movement of bottles can be observed and the thick plastic absorbs much of the contact noise. Inclusion of some acoustic absorbent, such as thick foam or mineral wool, on a wall or roof of the tunnel will substantially improve its effectiveness.

A sound-protection booth of the same plastic can be built around noisy equipment, such as corking machines, in a manner which allows observation of the equipment in operation together with quick removal for servicing or other attention. Furthermore, plastic guide rails on bottle conveyors help to prevent noise generated by bottles striking the metal conveyor guides.

The use of sound-absorbing walls, floors and ceilings does much to lower sound levels, but since these usually absorb water as well as sound, splashing and high humidity need to be avoided. However, some materials are available which combine acoustic adsorption and water resistance.

Isolation of noisy equipment. A development is to house noisy equipment, particularly centrifuges, in a separate room built for the purpose with high-density materials such as bricks, and without windows or other openings. Particular attention must be paid to doors and the sealing around them. This is very effective in noise reduction and the denser the construction material, the more effective is the sound insulation. This is the reason why sheet lead, for example, is a very effective sound barrier. Developments in design of multiple-leaf walls (plasterboard, cavity brick etc.) can provide an economic solution to severe noise problems, but the advice of an acoustic specialist should be sought.

Positioning of other noisy equipment, such as condensers for refrigeration equipment, compressors and so on, outside the building is desirable if possible, provided that it is not going to create a noise nuisance to neighbours.

Other practical aspects. Various pieces of mobile equipment produce noise, and shrouding or enclosing may not be a practical solution. Mounting on rubber wheels (e.g. pumps) is desirable to prevent contact of vibrating metal with a concrete floor. The use of low-noise electric motors has already been mentioned and shielding of rapidly moving air created by fans also reduces noises.

Foam or mineral wool insulation on walls and ceilings has a double benefit in that it absorbs noise as well as minimises temperature variations. Quietness is particularly desirable in the tasting room where important decisions are made on formulation of blends, purchase of bulk wines, checking winemaking procedures and so on. The tasting room should desirably be separated from other rooms, such as laboratories or offices, and be equipped with sound-absorbing material, such as an acoustic ceiling.

When and where to go for help. A large number of noise problems can be solved by common sense combined with an understanding of noise. However, this may not be sufficient to solve every noise problem, and help from a specialist should then be sought. These can be found in the phone book Yellow Pages, under 'Noise Control Equipment' or 'Acoustic Consultants'. Noise control equipment suppliers will generally give free advice, but are naturally biased towards their own products. Their expertise, particularly in the case of companies who are only agents or distributors, may be limited. Professional consultants do not give cheap advice, but it is usually backed by experience and some qualifications. However, they only measure and design (for a fee) and you are left to find your own builder. Whether to approach equipment suppliers or consultants depends on the problem involved, but major new projects should include some thought for the noise aspects at the design stage.

In conclusion, excessive noise in the winery can have a real cost, in fines, compensation payouts and loss of efficiency. A few of the more serious noise problems may require specialist help, but once noise is understood, many of the more common noise problems can be solved, and costs minimised by application of some simple commonsense measures.

Gases, vapours and liquids

Various gases, vapours and liquids are used or produced during winemaking, and some of these can be hazardous if used in the wrong way or in ignorance of their possible dangers. We must consider them and the most important are discussed below.

Carbon dioxide

The volume of carbon dioxide produced during alcoholic fermentation of grape juice is surprisingly large. It amounts to about forty times the volume of grape juice fermented, depending on the level of sugar in the juice. For example, 1000 litres of grape juice will and must release about 40,000 litres of carbon dioxide during complete fermentation. The rate of evolution is directly related to the rate of fermentation, which is a function of temperature, strain of yeast and other factors. Provision for dispersion of this large quantity of carbon dioxide is necessary in order to prevent accumulation to dangerous levels.

Carbon dioxide acts mainly as an asphyxiant (interferes with respiration), and its toxicity results from exclusion of oxygen in the air to the point where there is insufficient to support life. This is accentuated by the fact that carbon dioxide also increases the breathing rate, e.g. 3 per cent by volume in the air doubles the rate of breathing, while 5 per cent increases the rate four-fold with consequent overloading of the respiratory system. The signs and symptoms are those which precede asphyxia, namely headache, dizziness, shortage of breath, drowsiness and ringing in the ears. If the person can be removed from exposure in time, recovery is rapid.

The normal concentration of carbon dioxide in air is 0.03 per cent by volume and the recommended maximum limit for continuous exposure is 5000 parts per million (0.5 per cent by volume) or 9000 milligrams per cubic metre. The presence of carbon dioxide at low concentrations at the normal oxygen level in the air (20.9 per cent by volume) is not particularly harmful and its main effect is to stimulate respiration. For example, the health of submarine crews exposed continuously to 3 per cent of carbon dioxide is only slightly affected, provided that the oxygen content is maintained at normal concentration, and mixtures of carbon dioxide and oxygen are used medically.

Deaths from carbon dioxide asphyxiation usually result from exposure to levels above about 10 per cent by volume in air, which produces unconsciousness in a few minutes. This is the result of asphyxiation due largely to reduction in the level of oxygen in the air. A level of 18 per cent by volume of oxygen in the air (partial pressure 135 millimetres of mercury) is regarded as the minimum acceptable level even for short periods.

Sometimes a lighted candle is used as an indicator of the level of oxygen in the air inside a winery vessel, and it is assumed that when the candle will not burn there is not sufficient oxygen present. This is not correct because the candle will not burn in an atmosphere containing less than 16.5 per cent oxygen by volume, significantly below the accepted minimum level of 18 per cent. The use of a naked flame can also be a fire hazard and is extremely dangerous if spirit is stored in the vicinity.

The best method of checking the suitability of the air in a tank is to use a portable polarographic or paramagnetic oxygen meter and lower the probe of the meter into the tank. If it reads below 18 per cent oxygen, the tank should be vented with a blower or the worker should wear breathing apparatus.

Carbon dioxide has a specific gravity at 0°C of 1.52 compared with 1.00 for air, and is thus 52 per cent heavier than air. When carbon dioxide and air are mixed inside a closed empty vessel the carbon dioxide does *not* form a permanent lower layer, as its higher density would suggest. Due to molecular movement of the gases the carbon dioxide becomes uniformly distributed throughout the confined space in a matter of hours.

However, if carbon dioxide is continually generated, as in vessels containing fermenting grape juice or marc during vintage, its concentration is greatest at the surface of the fermenting liquid. In fact, in closed fermenters with only a top manhole, the gas above the fermenting liquid usually consists entirely of carbon dioxide. Also, carbon dioxide may continually 'spill over' from an open-topped tank in fermentation to an adjacent empty tank and will accumulate at the bottom of the tank. In such cases the molecular dispersion rate of carbon dioxide into the air is slower than the feed rate of the gas into the empty tank.

Fatalities in the wine industry due to carbon dioxide asphyxiation have usually occurred when a worker has entered a vessel containing a layer of fermenting material. Since carbon dioxide is not readily detectable by the senses, the worker usually becomes unconscious without warning and thus cannot give an alarm. Accordingly, the oxygen content of the air in such vessels should be routinely checked and appropriate action taken. A legal requirement is that the person in the tank should be connected by a waist rope to an observer outside the tank.

Modern winemaking technology involves the use of large quantities of inert gas, either carbon dioxide or nitrogen or a mixture of the two, frequently supplied from bulk liquid storage under pressure, and operators need to exercise care when using it to displace air in vessels and other operations. Dry ice (solid carbon dioxide) is sometimes used as a source of carbon dioxide, and one kilogram releases 500 litres of the gas on vaporisation. Contact of dry ice with the skin can cause frostbite.

Oxygen-alarm equipment is available which can monitor air continuously and sound a visual and audible warning when the oxygen level falls below a preset value. This is a less expensive alarm system than that which monitors carbon dioxide by infrared detection, and it measures the important constituent, oxygen, rather than the diluent gas.

Nitrogen
The same general comments apply to nitrogen as to carbon dioxide, except that nitrogen is less dense (specific gravity 0.97) and less soluble in wine. By displacing oxygen in air (in which nitrogen comprises 78 per cent by volume) it can produce asphyxia in the same way as carbon dioxide and the same precautions need to be observed in its use.

Sulphur dioxide
Sulphur dioxide is a heavy (specific gravity 2.3), highly toxic colourless gas or liquid (under pressure) which can cause serious eye injury and damage to the

upper respiratory tract. The gas is so suffocating and irritating that, unlike carbon dioxide, it provides its own warning of toxic concentrations. A level of 100 parts per million in the atmosphere is considered to be the maximum permissible concentration for an exposure of 60 minutes, and 500 parts per million is dangerous to life. The recommended maximum continuous level is 5 parts per million or 13 milligrams per cubic metre.

Accidents involving sulphur dioxide in the wine industry have been caused by brief exposure to very high levels of liquid or gaseous sulphur dioxide, usually resulting from malfunction of sulphitometers used for dosing liquid sulphur dioxide in grape juice or wine. These have been due to leaking or blocked valves or incorrect operation of the equipment. Sulphitometers should be filled in the open air and the operator should stand up-wind of the equipment. It is far better, however, to wear respirator equipment which also protects the eyes. Liquid sulphur dioxide transfer from one vessel to another under pressure, and dosage into wine, should best be carried out by a person trained and equipped for the purpose. It is important that the correct filling procedure should be used. The empty weight of the cylinder should be measured, and the quantity of sulphur dioxide filled into it determined by weight, which should not exceed 1.23 times the actual water capacity of the cylinder, as prescribed by Table 3 of the Australian Standard CB4 of 1969.

The pressurised cylinders in which sulphur dioxide is supplied to wineries have been known to burst as a result of heat during exposure to the summer sun, and accordingly should be stored in the shade and preferably in a locked cage and handled by a trained operator (see Other gases and vapours, overleaf).

The curious belief exists among some winery workers that since sulphur dioxide is added to wine, and wine is an article of human diet, then sulphur dioxide is harmless and can be handled with impunity. Regrettably, this is far from true, and sulphur dioxide in its pure and undiluted form is a dangerous and hazardous chemical. The instructions in safety textbooks relating to handling, and particularly transfer from one pressure vessel to another, should be rigidly observed.

Ammonia

Many wineries have ammonia refrigeration plants and the characteristic smell of ammonia resulting from leaks in the pressure system is frequently encountered. Ammonia is a toxic chemical and inhalation of concentrated vapour causes oedema of the respiratory tract, spasm of the glottis and asphyxia. Treatment must be prompt to prevent death.

At least one case exists in the wine industry where a refrigeration plant has exploded, filling the winery with toxic fumes of ammonia and rendering it uninhabitable. The lower limit of human perception of the gas is between 20 and 50 parts per million and 35 milligrams per cubic metre is the maximum recommended concentration for continuous exposure. Noticeable eye irritation occurs at about 100 parts per million, and this and other effects become severe above about 700 parts per million.

Alcohol vapour

The inhalation of alcohol fumes during wine handling may cause damage to health, but this applies particularly to fusel oil (mixed amyl alcohols) and methanol, rather than ethyl alcohol, or ethanol. The maximum recommended limits of continuous exposure to ethanol vapour are 1000 parts per million or 1900 milligrams per cubic metre of air; to methanol 200 parts per million or 260 milligrams per cubic metre; and to iso-amyl alcohol 100 parts per million or 360 milligrams per cubic metre.

Ethanol is the alcohol present in greatest concentration in wineries, and exposure to vapour concentrations of 5,000 to 10,000 parts per million results in irritation of the eyes and mucous membranes of the upper respiratory tract, as well as stupor and drowsiness. The health hazard with ethanol vapour is basically minimal and the effects of high concentrations for prolonged periods leads to virtual intoxication. It should be noted that a combination of carbon tetrachloride and ethanol is a toxic mixture.

The most dangerous hazard of alcohol vapour is, of course, its fire danger, and serious explosions and fires in the wine industry have resulted from ignition of vapour by sparks or faulty electrical equipment. Continual policing of the safety requirements by the winery safety officer is essential. The flash point of alcohol vapour is low (12°C) and the explosive minimum level in air is 3.3 per cent by volume.

Other gases and vapours

Exhaust gases from internal combustion engines burning petrol or diesel fuel can also be hazardous in confined spaces, and certain other gases and vapours, such as hydrogen sulphide from yeast lees and acetaldehyde from distillation heads, are possible health hazards.

Gas cylinders are frequently used in the wine industry. Although accidents caused by their misuse are not common, the hazards associated with them are not always appreciated. A suitable form of stable cylinder trolley should be used for moving portable cylinders. Cylinders should not be dropped or allowed to strike against each other. They should be stored upright, out of direct sunlight, in a cool position. To avoid confusion, full cylinders should be stored apart from empty ones. There should be three separate areas—for oxygen, inflammable gases and poisonous gases. This precaution will reduce the hazard should a fire occur. Cylinders should be handled with care in the appropriate way, and safety handbooks set out the relevant details. Statutory requirements are laid down and the Industrial Code also includes a section on gases used in welding.

Hot water and steam can be hazardous, and accidents resulting in scalding are generally due to bursting hoses, so these should be reinforced and in good condition. Kinking results in pressure increase and possible blowout.

Strong acids, alkalies and peroxide need to be handled with care. Materials which constitute the greatest hazard are sulphuric and hydrochloric acids and caustic soda. They cause burning of the skin and blinding if splashed in the eyes. Sulphuric acid generates much heat when mixed with water and can even explode. The concentrated acid should be slowly added to the water, never the other way around. Hydrogen peroxide used to reduce the level of sulphur dioxide in juice and wine is a strong oxidising agent. It will attack the skin and eyes and needs to be handled with care with the user wearing safety glasses.

In conclusion, certain gases and vapours in wineries can cause severe and sometimes fatal accidents. The most serious hazard, however, is ignorance or lack of attention on the part of the operator, and all wineries should have a continuing policy of instruction and education on this and other safety aspects.

17 Winery sanitation and waste disposal

Sanitation

Wine is a beverage for human consumption, and thus by law and consumer expectations must be made under hygienic conditions. Because of its high acid and alcohol content, wine will not support the growth of pathogenic (disease-producing) bacteria, which doubtless prompted Pasteur's oft-quoted comment in the late nineteenth century that 'Wine is the most healthful and hygienic of beverages'. Nevertheless, the presence of contamination, whether microbiological or otherwise, during making and maturation can result in a lowering of quality. Consumers demand and are entitled to wines made from sound grapes (with the exception of grapes infected with the 'noble rot'—botrytis) in a clean winery with clean equipment and with good manufacturing practices as recognised by the industry.

Some aspects of winery sanitation are related to winery construction. Floors should be constructed of acid-resistant concrete, epoxy resins or materials of similar resistant composition. Draining must be effective from any point and rounded gutters are preferable to those with right-angled corners. Avoid any construction areas where rodents can nest, such as double or hollow walls, and avoid structural traps and pockets, ledges, dark corners, etc. Furthermore, the direct contact of grapes or wine with copper, iron, aluminium, zinc or alloys containing these metals should be avoided.

The basic principles in winery hygiene and sanitation are:

- Keep the winery clean and free from refuse inside and out.
- Inspect the premises and equipment regularly.
- Remove insects, rodents and micro-organisms.
- Use water (sparingly), together with cleaning and sterilising aids.
- Keep equipment in good repair, especially that which contacts wine.

One of the main sanitation problems in a winery is the presence of *Drosophila* or vinegar fly, which is attracted to the grapes, fermenting must, lees and wine on which the larvae feed. Preventing involves removing such food sources, together with regular cleaning and the use of pyrethrum-based sprays. Much of the vinegar-fly problem is brought to the wineries from the vineyard, and elimination of waste fruit in adjacent vineyards does much to reduce the problem. Specific recommendations are as follows:

- Remove the marc from the winery premises and nearby before it becomes a breeding ground for vinegar flies and other insects.
- Remove stems as vinegar flies multiply in stem piles. If not removed, spray the piles with pyrethrum.
- Spread marc and stems in a thin layer in the vineyard away from the winery so that they will dry quickly. Stems may be burnt when dry.
- Eliminate all conditions under which vinegar flies can multiply, particularly leakage of wine and uncleaned equipment.
- Wash all grape transport bins after each delivery.

All equipment which comes into contact with wine in a winery must be maintained in a clean and sanitary condition, using a range of products which do not affect the wine, the processing equipment or storage vessels. All of these products are used in an aqueous solution, so that the quality of the water is important.

Water is the most important cleaner used in a winery. Many water-soluble deposits can be cleaned without the use of any product except water, which can come from various sources, such as mains, rain and bores. Depending on the source, the water may need filtration to reduce suspended solids and chlorination to kill bacteria. Water hardness should be checked regularly so that suitable chemicals can be used, since the hardness reacts to form complexes which lower the efficiency of cleaning materials being used. In South Australia, for example, the hardness of mains water varies from 50 milligrams per litre (ppm) from the River Murray at its best to 600 milligrams per litre in other areas. Bore water is often considerably harder. River Murray water in South Australia over a recent five-year period varied in hardness from 50 to over 200 milligrams per litre. One grain per gallon equals 14.3 milligrams per litre.

Water hardness can be overcome by using sequestrants—chemicals which combine with metal ions in solution to form water-soluble complexes. Sequestrants are sometimes referred to as chelating agents and EDTA (ethylenediamine tetra-acetate), sodium hexametaphosphate (calgon) and tetrasodium pyrophosphate (tspp) are normally used.

An important deposit in the winery is potassium bitartrate and sometimes calcium tartrate, and caustic-based cleaners, such as sodium hydroxide, are normally used. Occasionally, sodium hydroxide is used on its own but in areas with hard water the addition of sequestrants and surfactants results in faster and more efficient cleaning. Caustic soda dissolves proteins but has poor dispersing, wetting and rinsing properties. The normal concentration is 1–2 per cent solution of sodium hydroxide, and the solid is quite corrosive (hence its name) and dangerous, as well as forming sticky lumps on storage.

Surfactants or surface-active agents have the property of altering surface tension and improving the wetting and emulsifying properties of cleaners. The best surfactants are polyoxyethylated alcohols, which combine good cleaning ability with low foaming. The normal concentration is 0.2 to 0.5 per cent. A useful mixed cleaner is 1.5 per cent sodium hydroxide, 0.25 per cent of a wetting agent, and 0.1 per cent EDTA, either for hot soaking or cold circulation.

On some surfaces, such as wood, unlined concrete and certain older lined tanks, caustic-based cleaners may be too corrosive for normal use, and an alkaline but less caustic cleaner is normally used. The main cleaners are sodium carbonate, metasilicates, phosphates and surfactants. Sodium metasilicate is not dangerous to the user at less than 65°C in solution, it is easily rinsed off surfaces and moderately stable when stored in sealed dry containers. Sodium carbonate has poor rinsing properties but is stable on storage.

The cleaning process is a multistage operation and the most effective sequence is as follows:

1 Pre-rinse with cold or luke-warm water.

2 Detergent wash.

3 Hot rinse.

4 Acid rinse.

5 Water rinse.

After cleaning, the surfaces contacting wine are normally sanitised to remove microbial contamination. Sanitisers are germicides, but may not kill all of the micro-organisms present because some, such as bacterial spores, are resistant to cold sterilisation. Cold sanitisers cannot be relied on to sterilise fillers and bottle lines, where heat is required to penetrate crevices where micro-organisms may lodge.

The main sanitiser used in cleaners is chlorine, which is available as sodium and calcium hypochlorite, products containing an organic chloride base, and mixed halogen sanitisers containing both chlorine and bromine.

Sodium hypochloride is the cheapest form of chlorine available, and the liquid contains 12.5 per cent available chlorine. Hypochlorite releases chlorine into solution immediately (as distinct from organic chlorine compounds) and loses strength on standing. The diluted form is not stable and loses strength, particularly in hot water. Accordingly, the product should be checked for available chlorine before use, and 100 to 200 milligrams per litre of available chlorine is recommended for about five minutes contact period as a chemical sanitiser. If sodium hypochlorite is used, it is wise to order on a regular basis and make sure that the stock is rotated, as well as being stored in a cool place.

Calcium hypochlorite contains approximately 70 per cent available chlorine. It is stable in the dry form and less expensive than organic chlorine solutions. It has the disadvantage of containing between 3 and 5 per cent of insoluble matter, and is also rather difficult to dissolve.

Organic chlorine compounds are mainly based on sodium dichloroisocyanurate. This is available as a pure compound containing 60 per cent available chlorine, and it may be incorporated as well in other preparations. Organic chlorine compounds release chlorine in aqueous solution at a slower rate than inorganic compounds, and are used in swimming pools for this purpose. These chlorine solutions are more stable and may be kept for some time without significant chlorine loss. They are soluble in water and quite stable to storage in the undiluted form. Their main disadvantage is higher cost.

Mixed halogen sanitisers are usually a blend of constituents which release hypochlorite and hypobromite ions in solution. These act synergistically to provide sanitation at a lower level of halogens than provided by either chlorine or bromine alone. Their main advantages are that, because of the lower concentration required, corrosion is reduced, as is the risk of tainting if rinsing is not carried out properly.

Sanitising solutions should only be used on clean surfaces, since they are not efficient in the presence of dried organic matter. Chlorine is normally used in a concentration of 200 milligrams per litre available chlorine for sanitising tanks and wine lines, and at this concentration a contact time of three minutes is sufficient. In all cases the lines should be rinsed with water to remove all traces of chlorine. Chlorinated compounds can be corrosive even to type 304 stainless steel and high chlorine levels, long residence times and incomplete drainage can all lead to corrosive attack on metal. Such attack is greater if poor quality water with a high dissolved salt content is used.

The best sanitiser is steam or hot water at a temperature of 85°C or higher. For the sterilisation of equipment for the sterile filling of table wines, heat sterilisation is essential. The best sterilising method is to use moist steam at 115°C for 20 minutes, making sure that it contacts all parts of the equipment. This heat sterilisation will kill all of the micro-organisms likely to grow in wine. Hot water at 85°C to 95°C is an alternative, but because of the lower temperature requires a longer holding time of 30 minutes. The advantage of moist steam is that the latent heat of condensation provides more energy content than is available from hot water. The temperature of water-saturated steam is proportional to the pressure, e.g. 0.7 atmospheres (10 psig) 115°C, 1 atmosphere 121°C and 2 atmospheres 134°C.

Housekeeping

Housekeeping is orderliness and cleanliness outside the wine tank, and is an index of a winemaker's attention to detail. Examples of good housekeeping are as follows:

- Crushing equipment cleaned up promptly after use.
- Hose fittings stored clean and in their proper places, and hoses stored neatly in sloping racks to drain when not in use.
- Warehouse reworks and broken cases kept up-to-date and orderly.
- Laboratory glassware clean and put away, and laboratory solutions properly identified and marked with the date of preparation and/or standardisation.

- Wood cooperage tight, leaking wine cleaned up promptly, and cellar aisles free from spills and mould growth.
- Bottling equipment and change parts put away clean.

Waste disposal

Wineries have a legal obligation to dispose of their waste solid and liquid effluent in a hygienic and approved manner. State and local laws define waste disposal requirements, and such disposal is an essential part of winery design and operation. Waste disposal techniques are usually associated with the requirements of Health Commissions and Environmental Protection Agencies. The disposal of winery waste costs money which cannot be recouped, so it is one of the non-productive costs in winery construction and operation.

Solid waste can be carted away to disposal dumps and pits or burnt if combustible or, in the case of stalks, spread out in the vineyard. Liquid waste is generally more difficult and may require treatment. Disposal of distillation effluent containing yeast and grape solids in suspension is the most difficult because of its high level of organic matter, and pH adjustment with aerobic and anaerobic digestion may be required. Disposal in the municipal sewer is a simple solution providing that the authorities approve, but the high level of organic matter in distillation effluent (high biochemical oxygen demand or BOD, expressed as 5 days at 20°C) of the order of 15,000 to 30,000 milligrams per litre tends to unbalance a waste treatment plant if added in sufficient quantity. The seasonal nature of this effluent adds to the difficulty of disposal.

Liquid wastes are best separated into low, medium and high levels of contamination. The least polluted is water used to rinse dust from bottled wine and which has been stored in bins to mature. Likewise, water used to cool the outside of stainless-steel tanks and from cooling towers falls into this category. The modern trend is to minimise the amount of this water which goes to waste.

General cleaning is the biggest user of water in the winery, since hygiene is paramount in producing quality wines. This is wash water which has been used to clean wine storage and fermentation tanks, grape crushing and handling equipment, and general floor areas about the winery. It is often contaminated with detergents and sanitisers. The volume of this water varies from 0.3 to 2.0 kilolitres per tonne of grapes processed, and the degree of pollution is highest during the vintage season which may last about three months. Well-designed wineries restrict the volume of cleaning water by using high pressure and low volume. It is important to monitor and use the minimum quantity of water, and keep in mind at all times the axiom that *dilution is no solution to pollution*. Installing automatic shut-off valves on all water cleaning hoses and using low-volume high-pressure cleaning equipment help greatly in proper effluent control.

Moderately polluted wastes are derived from general cellar wash-water. The level of dissolved and suspended organic load is usually highest during the vintage season, when some grape-juice, skins and seeds are inadvertently discharged into the waste system. The average composition is about 3700 milligrams per litre BOD, pH 4.8, total inorganic carbon 2000 milligrams per litre and total dissolved solids 1000 milligrams per litre. This kind of liquid waste can be disposed of in various ways, one of which is shallow lagoons under aerobic conditions in the same way as for distillation effluent or stillwash, but not necessarily requiring pH neutralisation. Where disposal in the municipal sewer is possible this is a simple solution.

Heavily contaminated liquid waste is the most difficult to handle, and the best method is to screen out coarse suspended solids, neutralise the liquid to pH 7 with calcium carbonate or sodium hydroxide, and evaporate it in shallow lagoons. These must be remote from residential areas since the waste rapidly becomes anaerobic and generates offensive odours. Californian practice is to use a series of shallow ponds in rotation, in which 1000 kilolitres per hectare per day are discharged to 0.5-hectare ponds. The liquid depth is kept below 10 centimetres and the plots allowed to rest and dry for a week while other plots are being irrigated. The rate of evaporation is naturally greater in the summer months, and if operations continue into the winter months of the year the area of land required is of the order of 10 hectares per 1000 kilolitres.

Success has been achieved in Australia with spray irrigation of liquid effluent on to pastures and under trees. In this way the loss by evaporation is high, the effluent remains aerobic, and smell due to anaerobic reduction processes are largely absent. It is necessary to remove as much as possible of the suspended solids to avoid blocking the jets of the sprinklers.

Waste disposal has a special significance to the small winery. It competes for capital badly required to finance stock and equipment improvements. It also competes for the time and effort of the owner/operator at the time of greatest production activity. Consequently, waste disposal is a non-productive exercise involving effort and cost and in direct competition with the production activities of the winery.

The wastes can be divided into those associated with vintage and the others. Non-vintage waste includes solid materials, such as packaging wastes, office, laboratory and sales paper, cardboard and plastic. This collective waste can be containerised and either burnt on site or dumped into municipal dumping sites. Toilet and kitchen wastes can usually be disposed by a septic tank system or the municipal sewerage system. Vintage wastes have already been mentioned generally. They consist of solid material, such as skins, seeds and stalks, and the more bureaucratically important liquid wastes, such as wash water, detergents and the high-solids fining residues, yeast lees and so on. In general the magnitude of the disposal problem is proportional to the volume of water used, and a desirable low usage figure is 500 litres of washwater per tonne of grapes processed.

18 Sensory evaluation of wine

Methods

The ability to evaluate wine by sensory methods (tasting) is essential for anyone seriously involved or interested in the subject. From the winemaker's point of view a crucial part of winemaking, particularly during vintage, is the continual assessment of the fermentations and the young wines. Laboratory analyses can only set general guidelines and detect certain faults, and analytical data cannot usually distinguish between a sound standard and a sound premium wine.

There are certain features which one needs to know.

How perceptive is one's palate? In training students to be winemakers and winemarketers at Roseworthy Agricultural College, considerable time was spent in evaluating their palates before they evaluated wines. This involved assessing their ability to detect known levels of acids, sugars, sulphur dioxide, volatile acidity, hydrogen sulphide, oak character, diacetyl and various other constituents. It is important that people dealing with wine know the strengths and weaknesses of their palate, and techniques are now available to enable them to do this (see references). If you cannot detect volatile acid, for example (and some cannot), this need not be your fault. But you should know about it, and enlist the help of other tasters who can detect it to help in this aspect of evaluation.

It is important to know what faults wine is heir to and able to recognise them promptly. You must be able to recognise coarseness, oxidation, volatility, lack of balance, microbial spoilage, bitterness and related faults and how to prevent and correct them. The best way to learn about this is to do a formal course in sensory evaluation, and taste as many wines as possible in company with tasters of proven ability. There is no substitute for this kind of repetitive tasting experience. Cases are known where winemakers working in isolation have developed such 'cellar palates' that they have not been able to recognise that their wines are faulty.

You should be able to recognise quality and rank wines accordingly. This takes a perceptive palate, practice and a good memory. To serve as a steward (associate judge) on a wine show judging panel is excellent experience, and most shows have a policy training people in this way. This experience helps tremendously in understanding what is quality and what are the quality requirements of the various classes. This is particularly desirable if you want to win prizes at shows.

Learn to describe wines in words in the most meaningful way. This involves developing a good wine vocabulary in order to be able to describe and summarise wines succinctly and record these descriptions for future reference. The glossary of wine terms is included for this purpose. Remember that you are evaluating the wine in the glass—not the label on the bottle. Endeavour always to use words which have specific connotations, and are meaningful to other people. There is so much rubbish talked about wine that you should not add to it.

Follow a routine procedure in evaluating wine by dividing the assessment into three distinct and separate parts:

- Examine *colour and clarity*. The wine should have the colour (tint and hue) appropriate for its style, and if in bottle it should be brilliantly clear—exceptions are old red and occasionally white wines.
- Assess the *aroma and bouquet* by putting your nose well into the glass and taking deep sniffs. Evaluate the amount or volume of nose, varietal character, sulphur dioxide and other volatile constituents. Remember that a wine must have a 'nose'. If the wine has been chilled, allow it to warm to between 12 and 18°C.
- Assess the *taste or palate* by taking a sizeable amount (10 millilitres) into the mouth, rolling it about with the tongue and sucking air through it. Do not hesitate to make slurping noises, because this aspirates the warm wine in the mouth and enhances the evaluation. Then spit out the wine. Look for flavour, acid balance, sweetness, fruit and any faults, such as bitterness (which is evident on the end of the palate).

All this should be the winemaker's stock in trade, since quality evaluation lies at the basis of winemaking. For the wine-lover, the broader implications are that wine is one of mankind's great luxuries and joys, and is worthy of your best efforts in evaluating it.

Setting up a tasting room

One point should be emphasised about a tasting room for quality control—it is (or should be) an integral part of the winery's production facilities, and not be part of the laboratory nor the wine sales or entertainment area. It is a room set aside for the specific and serious purpose of evaluating wines for blends, adjustments, bottling, wine show entries and so on—from which the public should be excluded. While this kind of wine evaluation can be enjoyable, it is essentially work and not fun. As we have seen, critical tasting is an essential part of winemaking, because it is the final arbiter of quality. No machine or analytical instrument can as yet substitute for the trained human palate.

A tasting room has several desirable features.

Quietness without interruptions and if possible sound-insulated. No telephones, loudspeakers, talking or other sources of noise which may distract the taster. (As a matter of interest, these conditions in some wine shows leave something to be desired.) The room should preferably have only one door, so that it is not a passage to somewhere else, and should not be part of the laboratory, although it can be adjacent.

Good *lighting* is essential. Tasters differ somewhat on what kind of lighting they find best but agree on a high level of light intensity. South-facing daylight, free from direct sunlight which may heat the wines unevenly, is preferred. Otherwise white fluorescent tubes, 6500° Kelvin, give the best white light. If incandescent lights are used select blue-tinted bulbs to cut out the red-orange part of the spectrum. A candle is romantic but useless, except possibly to check on haze. To evaluate clarity set up a permanent microscope lamp, which with its associated lens system produces a narrow strong parallel beam of white light, which shows up any haze or deposit in the glass instantly. This is the Tyndall beam, which is the basis of nephelometry or the measurement of haze.

The best *colour* for the room is matt or semigloss white for walls, ceiling, benches and floor. Correct observation of the colour and appearance of wine is essential for proper evaluation, and it is not possible to do this against a coloured background. Viewing the wines against a sheet of plain white paper slanted towards a south-facing window to give maximum reflection of white light from the paper is also helpful.

Benches and fittings. Tasters usually work best comfortably seated at either a bench (91 cm or 3 ft high) or a table (76 cm or 2 ft 6 in high). They should work alone and come to decisions without consultation. White-painted tasting booths are a good idea, with built-in spittoons with running water, as in a dentist's surgery. Booths are desirable to enable tasters to concentrate without interference. They need to be large enough to have room to set up a line of glasses and to write down tasting scores and notes as the tasting proceeds.

Short-stemmed thin-walled tasting *glasses* of colourless flawless glass are necessary. Many prefer the international tulip-shaped wine tasting glass of 215 millilitres (see Fig. 18.1), somewhat larger than the normal tasting glass. Some tasters prefer smaller thistle-shaped glasses (slightly flared at the top). Washing glasses can be a problem—they are best washed in hot water then rinsed in distilled or rain water and allowed to dry. They should not be placed upside down on paper, because of possible taste pickup from the sizing in the paper. Used teatowels are suitable. All glasses should be smelt before the wine is poured into them.

Temperature. The room should be climatically comfortable in the range of 20 to 23°C, but if air-conditioning is used the noise should be unobtrusive and the air draft minimal. White table wines are best evaluated at about 10 to 14°C, reds 15 to 18°C. If the wine is too cold the aroma is lessened; if too hot the alcohol predominates.

Tasting times. This has to fit into the work programme of the staff but the best

Fig. 18.1: International wine-tasting glass

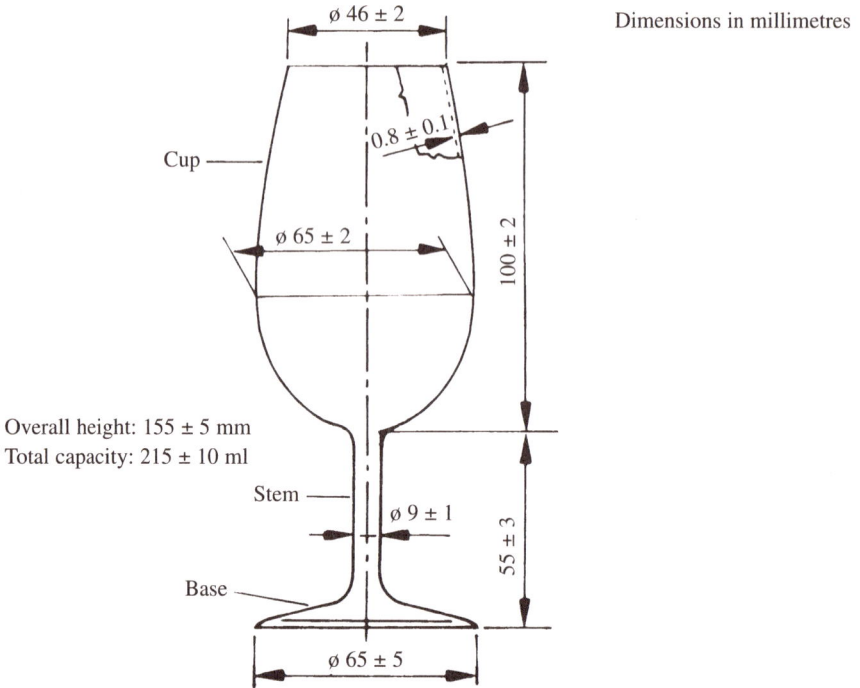

Dimensions in millimetres

ø 46 ± 2

0.8 ± 0.1

Cup

ø 65 ± 2

100 ± 2

Overall height: 155 ± 5 mm
Total capacity: 215 ± 10 ml

Stem

ø 9 ± 1

55 ± 3

Base

ø 65 ± 5

times from the physiological point of view are late morning and late afternoon, when the taster is hungry and palate perceptiveness is at its highest.

Wine evaluation is essentially a serious business by which the quality of the winery's wines and their preparation are assessed and important decisions made. As said earlier, it is work, not fun. A basic condition is that the wines should be anonymous and presented blind (no labels), preferably using two or three code random numbers. Tasters need to be assessed as to their competency, and tests are now available to do this. As well as the technical and sales staff, other people, such as office staff, laboratory assistants etc., can be included, because the perceptiveness of the human palate differs so much between people. Some years ago, I carried out a series of critical tastings with statistical control on the taste threshold of diacetyl (butter-like aroma) and certain other constituents in wine. The most sensitive taster for diacetyl was a young female laboratory assistant, who did not even drink wine.

The taster needs to know the jargon and the words to use which most clearly express the appearance, nose and palate impressions. The Wine and Food Society of Australia has an official glossary of tasting terms (set out below), which can be used in this connection.

Finally, the tasting comments and point scoring (if carried out) should be recorded in the same way as analytical figures are recorded. Some wineries have their own wine-scoring sheets designed to suit their specific requirements. Also either a wine show score sheet or the Roseworthy Agricultural College score card can be used with advantage.

Variations in tasters' perceptions of wine

You will notice the emphasis I have placed on critical wine assessment and its importance, the reason being that the human palate is the final arbiter of wine quality. Modern analytical procedures reveal a wondrous array of constituents (approximately 900 have so far been identified) but these do not indicate wine quality except in quite broad terms. Even the best analytical data cannot normally distinguish between a sound standard and a premium wine. So we must rely on the subjective assessment of the human palate, which has integrative powers superior to the best analytical procedures, and which must be provided with the optimum conditions in which to operate.

Both professional and amateur wine tasters differ in sensitivity to a wide range of constituents, and in their ability to describe them meaningfully. They also respond to experience which helps them to recognise their acuities and deficiencies, as well as to establish a memory base, and acquire a clear idea of quality standards. We know that age affects sensitivity, and that certain aroma and taste blindnesses or deficiencies can occur.

However, we are concerned here with why it is that tasters may respond differently to the same wine on different days, as well as at different times during the same day. It is well known that tasters can have 'off-days' when their perceptive ability is lessened, and we know some of the reasons for this. One's state of health clearly has an important effect, and temporary ailments of various kinds are clearly responsible for lowered sensory perception. Having a cold is an obvious reason, since the heavy mucous secretion blankets the nasal olfactory epithelium resulting in lowered olfactory perception. Other ill-defined and possibly related viral complaints resulting in a fuzzy head are doubtless contributors, and in general any ailment which impairs sensory perceptions and brain activity reduces the taster's acuity.

Experience with students over some years has shown that they perform best when hungry (almost a permanent state with some students!), and tasting classes are accordingly held before meals rather than immediately afterwards. This heightened acuity is well recognised in the wine industry, where it is customary for critical tastings in wineries to be held in the mornings before lunch. There is a sound physiological basis for this. Food digestion diverts blood flow from the brain to the stomach and intestines. Also, during digestion neuropeptides are produced which have a sedative effect on the brain. This means that after meals, particularly heavy ones, the brain operates at a significantly lower level of activity, which is reflected in reduced sensory perception.

We know also that the constancy of sensory perception can vary for other reasons, such as motivation and concentration—illustrated by the following account related by a wine educator in California, who knew that he was scheduled to taste an important and expensive range of wines (Bordeaux reds). He prepared himself psychologically by reading the background to the wines (area, climate, grape varieties, style, etc) and anticipating the event in detail, then during the tasting devoted himself wholly to the task, ignoring all else including his fellow tasters. By this preparation he found himself to be particularly perceptive, and considered that he gained much more from the tasting than he would have, had he approached it without the preparation and intense concentration.

With this kind of experience in mind I have always tried to prepare students beforehand for each tasting sessions by giving them the appropriate background to the wines presented—a brief history, grape varieties, viticultural and oenological details, styles, market requirements, and precisely what to look for in the wines. This tends to prepare them psychologically and whet their appetites for what they are about to taste. Then during the tasting they are required to concentrate on the wines to the exclusion of all else.

We well know the effects of adaptation in which prolonged exposure to wines (and other sensory stimuli) results in considerably reduced sensory response. This is particularly evident with highly flavoured wines, such as muscats. We could furthermore predict that if we were required to taste wine critically when woken from a deep sleep in the middle of the night when the senses have shut down, the results would be rather uncritical. It is also likely that individual differ in the precise times of the day (or longer time interval) when their senses are most discerning.

All of this is relevant to wine evaluation and of critical importance in securing the best and most consistent response from your palate. For further information read *Tasting and Enjoying Wine. A Guide to Wine Evaluation for Australia and New Zealand* by Bryce Rankine, Winetitles, Adelaide, 1990. This book describes in detail the wine sensory evaluation course developed over many years at Roseworthy College and contains suggestions for evaluating one's palate.

Glossary of wine tasting terms

Belonging to a Wine and Food Club enables many people to enjoy and appreciate wines in convivial company. A problem associated with this is being required to speak about a wine to one's peers, and groping for the words which accurately convey one's palate impressions. Communication in wine tasting depends on just this—using words which convey the subjective nose and palate impression of the wine. In order that one wine tasted by several tasters should be reported in the same way, it is necessary for the tasters to use the same words for the impression which the wine creates.

Accordingly, at the request of the Wine and Food Society in Australia, I have compiled the following tasting terms which now constitute the Society's official list of tasting terms. Some foreign terms which have become part of Australian wine nomenclature are also included. Extensive lists of tasting terms exist, particularly in the French language, and various overseas lists of tasting terms contain a preponderance of French terms. Some of these do not have precise Australian and New Zealand counterparts and are not used in these countries for serious tasting. For example, the often-used French term *souple* does not mean 'supple' or 'pliant', as the dictionary would indicate, but 'smooth' or 'harmonious'. Many of the terms listed below are featured in more detail elsewhere in the book.

Where possible, terms have been quantified by using the results of threshold taste measurements. Similarly, particular chemical constituents of wine are listed against certain of the tasting terms, together with legal maximum limits were appropriate. The description has been augmented by indicating whether the particular term relates to sight (appearance of the wine), smell (aroma and bouquet), and/or taste, as indicated:

S   = sight
Sm = smell
T   = taste

acetic Sm T	The smell and taste of a mixture of acetic acid and ethyl acetate, reminiscent of vinegar and also called volatile or pricked. The legal maximum limit for acetic acid in wine is 1.5 grams per litre in Australia and 1.2 in New Zealand. The taste threshold depends on the wine and is about 0.8 grams for acetic acid and 150 milligrams per litre for ethyl acetate. Big highly tannic wines can tolerate higher levels.
acidity T	Used to indicate the quality of tartness or sharpness to the taste; the presence of agreeable fruit acids—the main acids in wine are tartaric and malic. Balanced acidity is desirable and gives crispness in white wines. Sour and tart are synonyms.
amontillado S Sm T	A Spanish term for a type of sherry not as pale as fino, with more bouquet and characteristic sherry flavour and usually older; usually slightly sweet.
amoroso S Sm T	A Spanish term for full-bodied, dark and sweet sherry, lighter in colour and body than oloroso.
aperitif	A French term for appetiser, taken before meals to stimulate the appetite, e.g. dry sherry, vermouth, Champagne and, surprisingly, Sauternes.
aroma Sm	The smell of a wine. If no particular aroma is present, the wine is described as vinous. Aroma and bouquet are

	sometimes used synonymously, but more correctly aroma relates to the smell of the grape and bouquet to the smell of the wine acquired during fermentation and maturation. Some grapes and the wines made from them are aromatic, e.g. Muscat, Gewürtztraminer.
aromatic Sm	The strong scented smell of a wine; not the same as aroma.
astringency T	Detected by a puckering, tactile sensation in the mouth due to high tannin content (absorbed from the skins and seeds); sometimes indicating that the (red) wine will be long-lived. Harsh, rough and tannic are related terms.
balance T	Harmonious taste balance of wine constituents whereby no one characteristic of a wine is predominant; harmonious is a synonym.
Baumé	An old French term used to indicate dissolved solids (mainly sugar) in wine and grape juice. One degree Baumé is equivalent to 1.8 per cent sugar and by fermentation converts to approximately 1 per cent alcohol by volume in a dry wine made from mature grapes; thus grapes picked at 11° Baumé will on fermentation produce approximately 11 per cent alcohol by volume. Details are given in Chapter 5.
beeswing S	A filmy sediment which occurs in old bottled ports.
big T	A tasting term—usually excessive body, often fruity and refers to high extract content.
bitter T	A fault in some wines in which the after-palate has a lingering bitterness, not to be confused with acidity in red table wines. Detected late on the palate.
body T	Consistency, thickness or substance of the wine. Refers to extract content—full-bodied wines are more alcoholic than wines less so.
bottle-aged Sm T	Denoting that the wine has been stored in bottle for a prolonged period, resulting in a mellow matured character. In white wines the colour becomes golden and the fresh grape flavour and aroma is replaced by a more mature and complex vinosity. Some wines, notably vintage ports, require bottle-age for their full development. On the other hand, fino sherries, for example, do not benefit from bottle-aging.
bouquet Sm	The part of the fragrance of wine which originates from the fermentation and aging.
bright (brilliant) S	Absence of suspended or colloidal matter in the wine. Also refers to brilliance of colour as well as clarity.

brut T	A French term describing the driest classification of Champagne, containing usually less than 0.5 per cent sugar. Increasing degrees of sweetness are extra-sec, sec and demi-sec. Originally brut Champagne was unsweetened.
character Sm T	Combination of vinosity, balance and style; refers more precisely to the style of wine, e.g. port or sherry character.
clean Sm T	Freedom from any foreign (or 'off') odour or flavour, but not necessarily indicating high quality.
cloudy S	Colloidal haze and particulate matter.
cloying T	An excessively sweet wine with insufficient acidity.
coarse Sm T	Indicating oxidation and incorrect handling of the wine, particularly excessive skin contact, use of pressings and exposure to air. Characterised by a harsh acidic taste with bitter after-palate. Not the same as the French term *corsé* meaning full-bodied.
condition S	Refers mainly to the clarity of a wine. A cloudy or hazy wine is referred to as being out of condition.
corked, corky Sm T	The off-flavour in wine derived from a defective or mouldy cork.
crust S	Sediment adhering to the inside surface of bottles of old wine, usually red. Consists mainly of pigment and tartrate crystals.
demi-sec T	Seen on Champagne labels, meaning that the wine is medium sweet.
dry T	Denotes absence of sugar and opposite of sweet. Dry wines contain less than 0.2 per cent sugar, but wines containing up to about 0.5 per cent usually still taste dry.
dull S	A definite colloidal haze, easily revealed by passing a strong beam of light through the wine whereby the path of the beam is revealed by light reflected from the suspended particles.
finish T	The taste remaining after the wine leaves the mouth; designated as short, medium and long.
fino S Sm T	A Spanish term for a delicate dry sherry made by the flor-yeast process.
flat T	A sparkling wine which has lost its gas or a low-acid still wine which has lost its freshness.
flowery Sm	The aroma reminiscent of flowers contributed by certain aromatic grape varieties.
foxy Sm T	The methyl and ethyl anthranilate odour of *Vitis labrusca* grapes and wines made from them. Rarely encountered

in Australian wines, occasionally in the past in New Zealand wines.

fruity Sm T — The pleasant aromatic taste of a young wine with strong varietal character. The taste sensation derived from a combination of sugar, acid and grape flavour.

gassy S Sm T — A wine charged with carbon dioxide; *see* spritzig.

geranium Sm T — An unpleasant smell occasionally encountered in red table wines containing sorbic acid in which bacteria have grown. Claimed to be similar to the smell of crushed geranium leaves. The causative compound is 2-ethoxy-hexa-3, 5-diene.

green T — Term applied to a young wine which is unbalanced because of excess acid (largely malic) and made from immature grapes. Can also refer to the greenish colour of certain young white wines, due to chlorophyll from the grapes.

hard, harsh T — Strong tannin taste without harmony and a fault in red wines. Refers also to acidic white wines lacking vinosity.

hydrogen sulphide Sm — The smell of rotten eggs occasionally found in table wines and resulting from the reduction of sulphur dioxide or elemental sulphur. Less than 1 part per million is detectable.

lees Sm T — The odour of wine stored too long on the lees or sediment deposited after fermentation; also solids deposited during racking and fining.

light Sm T — Lack of body, otherwise pleasant.

limpid S — Crystal clarity, synonymous with brilliant.

maderised S Sm T — Oxidative change in white wines brought about by prolonged hot storage under oxidising conditions so that the colour and flavour resemble Madeira.

mellow T — Soft, ripe, well matured; designates sweet sherry as distinct from medium and dry sherry.

mercaptan Sm — An onion-like aroma in wine, due to the presence of ethyl mercaptan and ethyl sulphides and derived from hydrogen sulphide; sometimes referred to as organic sulphide smell.

metallic T — Not quite bitter—certainly a hard finish and a flavour of metal, usually iron or copper.

mouldy Sm T — Off-flavour derived from mouldy grapes or storage in a mouldy cask.

mousy T — An undesirable flavour and persistent taste resulting from bacterial growth in sweet dessert and table wines. Is most evident after the wine leaves the mouth.

neutral Sm T	A wine lacking distinctive or recognisable character; related to vinous.
nose Sm	Characteristics as assessed by smell.
nutty Sm	Characteristic pungent flavour of sherry due in part to wood age and the presence of acetaldehyde above approximately 100 milligrams per litre.
oloroso S Sm T	A Spanish term for old, rich, semi-sweet to sweet, full-bodied sherry.
oxidised S Sm T	A wine which has been exposed to oxygen, resulting in loss of flavour and development of coarseness. Oxidised wines usually contain higher levels of acetaldehyde.
poor Sm T	Not necessarily faulty but of little merit.
precocious Sm T	Suggesting rapid (and unhealthy) development.
pricked Sm T	Having excess volatile acidity arising from the growth of acetic acid bacteria, and containing more than about 150 milligrams per litre of ethyl acetate.
pungent Sm	Very aromatic—often earthy.
rancio Sm T	Distinctive smell of old oxidised dessert wines and associated with warm storage.
residual sugar T	Applied usually to wines which are not quite dry. Sugar (glucose and fructose) above about 5 grams per litre can usually be tasted.
rough T	Astringent, coarse, tannic taste in red wines, indicating lack of balance and maturity.
round T	A well-balanced wine showing body and fruitiness.
rubbery Sm	A peculiar aroma resulting from hydrogen sulphide and related to organic sulphides.
sec T	French term meaning dry; usually applied to sparkling wines containing a small but detectable quantity of sugar.
soft T	Wine with a pleasing finish, without being hard or aggressive. Usually applied to wines low in acid and slightly sweet.
sour T	Disagreeably acid, but not a term used for wines showing volatile acid. Opposite is flat.
stemmy Sm T	The aroma and taste of red wines which have been made in contact with stems damaged during crushing. Stalky is a synonym.
spritzig S Sm T	A German term indicating the presence of some carbon dioxide bubbles in the wine, but insufficient to produce any froth in the glass. Corresponds to a level of about 2 grams per litre. The approximate French equivalent is *petillant*, the Italian *frizzante*.

sulphide Sm	The disagreeable odour of hydrogen sulphide and mercaptans—evident above about one-tenth of a milligram per litre.
sulphur dioxide Sm	A suffocating sulphurous smell resulting from too much being added to the wine. Sulphur dioxide added to wine separates into free and chemically bound, and only the free can be smelt, usually at levels of above about 40 parts per million, depending on acidity of the wine.
sulphury, Sm sulphurous	Smelling of sulphur dioxide
sweet T	More than fruity, distinctly sweet due to the presence of sugar.
tannin T	A complex organic constituent of wine occurring in greater quantities in reds than in whites. Plays an important part in the self-clearing of young wines after fermentation. Has an important influence on the palate impression of the wine. Conveys fullness of body and astringency (grip) in dry reds while in sweet wine it helps to balance the sugar, giving a desirable palate. An excess of tannin in light dry whites is undesirable as such wines are then too big in body and too coarse. The period of maturation is related to the tannin content of the wine; a full-bodied red wine high in tannin requires a longer period than a lighter-bodied wine in order to obtain the same degree of harmony.
tart T	Too high in acid, but high-acid wines balanced by residual sugar do not taste tart.
tawny S	Applied to wines which have turned from red to brownish during maturation; also a style of port matured in cask.
terroir T	French for earthy, particularly refers to flavour. Has also a broader environmental meaning not related to tasting.
thin T	Lacking in body, almost watery.
vinosity T	The characteristic of wine made from grapes but not exhibiting varietal character. Vinous is a synonym.
weeper	A bottle showing signs of a leaky cork.
woody Sm T	The presence of oak (*Quercus*) aroma and flavour in a wine. Sometimes hardwoods are used which leave an undesirable character.
yeasty Sm T	Containing materials which smell or taste of yeast, particularly acetaldehyde. Applies especially to the aroma of wines spoilt by oxidative yeasts.

How to seek awards at wine shows

This may appear to be an unlikely topic for a book on winemaking, but success in marketing a wine can be helped by its success in wine shows. The simple answer on how to win awards is to make good wines—but there is more to it than this.

Wines are exhibited in separate and defined classes, and the exhibitor nominates in which class or classes the entries are to be judged. So first you must learn the requirements of the classes. Entry of a fine wine in the incorrect class is unlikely to win an award. Judges may have the discretion to transfer an entry in an obviously incorrect class to the appropriate one if they wish to, but this may not be done in a show with hundreds of entries. There are several ways to learn the requirements of the class—study the schedule of classes prepared by the wine show society, in which class descriptions are usually included; attend tasting days at wine shows and taste the wines winning awards in the classes of interest; discuss the entries with an experienced judge before entering them, to check that they fit the requirements of the class.

The next point is to ensure that the wines are technically sound. If a wine has a fault it is downgraded early in the judging (nowadays judges have so many entries in some classes that they are anxious to cull out faulty wines). Examples vary with the classes but the following faults result in low scores: yeastiness, oxidation, hydrogen sulphide, haziness, excess sulphur dioxide, volatility, bacterial taints, corkiness, and off-odours and tastes of various other kinds. In wine shows we meet most of them. If the exhibitor is unable to detect a specific fault, e.g. hydrogen sulphide, then help should be sought from someone who can. No palate is perfect so you should try to evaluate the wines, before entering them for shows, with someone else with an experienced palate.

Another point to be aware of is that wines are judged on appearance, nose and palate, and points are given to each—3, 7 and 10 totalling 20 points. If the wine lacks aroma and bouquet, i.e. does not have a nose, points will be deducted even before the wine has been tasted. Aroma and bouquet result from a combination of many factors—grape variety and maturity, method of making and maturation, temperature of storage and so on. It is not possible to be specific here, but many wines lose their nose by being stored too hot, handled excessively and exposed to too much air. Details are given elsewhere in this book.

Finally, avoid being too critical of the judges—they have a difficult and arduous task (for which they are not paid), and in large classes they are overloaded. Also, the judging facilities are usually less than ideal, although the wine show societies do as much as they can to provide appropriate judging venues.

19 Faults in wines

In view of its complex chemical nature and the microbiological changes involved, wine is heir to various faults. The winemaker and the quality control officer need to be aware of these and how to cure them and, more importantly, how to prevent their occurrence. We will consider below metal haze in wine, and other hazes and deposits and their identification will be discussed in Chapter 21.

Metal haze

Haze caused by traces of certain metals used to be one of the most serious problems in bottled wine, and is still encountered sporadically. The main metals are iron and copper, and occasionally aluminium. The surprising feature is how small a quantity of metal is necessary to form a haze—only a few milligrams per litre (parts per million) are required, depending on the wine.

Metals in wine derive essentially from contamination with metallic equipment—the metal content of washed grapes is much too low to contribute to haze. Historically, iron equipment and pipelines were used widely in wineries, later to be replaced with copper, bronze and brass. By doing this, iron contamination was replaced with copper, which resulted in a more serious and insidious problem. Subsequently stainless steel, plastics and glass were introduced, and their use has resulted in the virtual disappearance of metal hazes.

One of the main sources of iron contamination is the use of uncoated iron grape bins and hoppers, which can result in a level of more than twenty times that which causes haze in wine. White juices containing this amount of iron turn grey to dark brown. Much of the metal contamination is removed by the yeast during fermentation, but enough remains after such heavy iron contamination to result in a haze in wine. Iron contamination can also arise from contact with iron equipment generally, as well as bentonite and unwashed filter pads. Iron haze is caused by ferric phosphate or, in red wines, ferric tannate, and aerating the wine hastens formation by converting ferrous ions to ferric. In fact, the haze forms poorly or not at all under reducing conditions. Also, the more acid the wine, the more likely that iron haze (sometimes called casse) will form.

Copper contamination is not usual in grape-handling, and normally arises from copper-containing winery equipment contacting the wine after fermentation. Unwashed filter pads can also be a source of both copper and iron, which are taken up by the first run of wine through the pads. Thus, bottles from the beginning of a bottling run may contain enough metal to cause a haze. Copper haze forms under reducing conditions and is insidious, in that it appears some time after the wine has been bottled when the oxidation-reduction potential has fallen. It forms most readily if the wine contains some protein, because the deposit consists of a cuprous-sulphide-protein complex. If the wine is free from protein it can tolerate a higher copper content before forming a haze.

Maximum tolerance limits for iron and copper depend on the wine type and its composition, but a rule-of-thumb guide is a maximum level of 0.5 milligrams per litre for copper and 6 milligrams per litre for iron. Measurement is relatively simple and can be carried out chemically, or more rapidly by atomic-absorption spectroscopy. Removal of metals in wine is usually achieved with potassium fer-rocyanide, which precipitates them as blue floccules. This treatment should only be carried out by a qualified oenologist or chemist, and prevention of metal con-tamination is much better than trying to remove the haze once it has formed.

Although aluminium haze is rare, a brief comment is appropriate. Aluminium is by no means an inert metal and can produce an intractable haze in wine. Alu-minium and its alloys are moderately resistant to corrosion by wine, and this has been taken to indicate that they are satisfactory for use in winery equipment. However, this is not correct and all aluminium equipment and surfaces which come into contact with wine are potential sources of haze, unless treated with a permanent and durable coating. Besides haze formation aluminium has other undesirable effects. It can impart a metallic taste, and is one of the metals which can form hydrogen sulphide in wine from sulphur dioxide by reduction with nas-cent hydrogen. It also has a bleaching effect.

As far as sources of aluminium in wine are concerned, grapes contain only traces. The problem arises when must or more particularly wine contacts alu-minium surfaces, which corrode and aluminium dissolves. Contact with grapes and grape juice is less serious than contact with wine, because up to 90 per cent of alu-minium in grape juice is removed by the yeast during fermentation. For this reason aluminium buckets and other utensils are sometimes recommended for grape trans-port, but this is unwise. Some grape mills have aluminium alloy rollers but the contact is too brief to impart sufficient aluminium to the must. Fining materials are also a source of aluminium, especially bentonite which is an aluminium-silicate clay mineral. Bentonite fining can increase the level of aluminium in wine up to 2 milligrams per litre. Other fining materials and some filter aids are possible sources.

The appearance of aluminium haze in wine can range from faint opalescence to a cloud with deposit, depending on the extent of contamination. Microscopi-cally, it appears as rather uniform amorphous particles about 1 to 2 microns diameter. The haze dissolves on addition of hydrochloric acid but is unaffected by addition of hydrogen peroxide or hydrosulphite. In this way it can be distin-guished from iron and copper hazes. It does not give a positive test for protein, and heating or chilling the wine does not influence haze formation.

It is possible to set an approximate upper limit for aluminium in wine at 1 milligram per litre. Aluminium is not an essential nutritional element in grape juice or wine, nor does it play a role in fermentation biochemistry. Wines differ in their tolerance to aluminium and pH is important—maximum haziness occurs at pH 3.8, and the higher the acid level present, the more the aluminium is complexed and not available to form a haze.

One of the main sources of aluminium contamination in wine (as distinct from must) is from aluminium alloy equipment, particularly plate and frame filters, where the inert coating is damaged or absent. So if one is concerned about the possibility of aluminium haze, which incidentally cannot be removed by blue fining, then make sure that any aluminium surfaces contacting the wine are properly coated.

Protein haze

A typical practical example illustrates the nature of protein haze. A winery has bottled some white table wine and stacked it for later labelling and packaging. Imagine the concern of the winemaker when a haze is observed in the contents of the bottles on the top of the stack, and, as time passes, the bottles lower down the stack begin to show this haze. The haze slowly settles as a light amorphous deposit which is soluble in sodium hydroxide, when examined by the methods set out later.

This is protein haze, and is the result of the wine containing heat-unstable grape protein, which slowly denatures and precipitates as the wine is warmed. Due to natural temperature stratification (as described in Chapter 8), the warmer bottles on the top of the stack develop the haze first. Protein haze is more common in the hotter areas of Australia, where the grapes are higher in soluble protein. The grape varieties most frequently involved are Muscat Gordo Blanco, Traminer and Semillon; the extent depending on climate and grape maturity—with the more mature grapes containing more protein.

The proteins involved have molecular weights in the range of 40,000 to 200,000 with iso-electric points between pH 4.8 and 5.7. There are many other nitrogenous compounds in wine, such as amino acids and peptides, but these are not involved in protein haze. As a matter of related interest, protein is also linked with copper haze, which involves a cuprous sulphide-protein complex, and tin, although the latter is rare in Australian wine.

Protein haze is mentioned in various places in this book. It is referred to in the sections on Bentonite and protein stabilisation (Chapter 10), stability tests (Chapter 21) and Identification of hazes and deposits (Chapter 21).

Hydrogen sulphide

Hydrogen sulphide (H_2S or rotten-egg gas) can best be described as one of the nuisances of winemaking. It can come from more than one source, which is confusing and is the reason why the occurrence is sometimes sporadic and difficult to understand and predict.

Hydrogen sulphide itself is a reactive gas which, when formed in wine, changes into other very smelly substances, such as mercaptans, organic sulphides and thiols, which can impart garlic or onion-like smells to wine. These are liquids with relatively high boiling points, and thus are much more difficult to remove than hydrogen sulphide. Therefore, if hydrogen sulphide is detected it should be removed as soon as possible, before it changes into these other compounds.

Hydrogen sulphide can be formed in several ways.

If elemental sulphur is present during the yeast fermentation hydrogen sulphide is almost an inevitable outcome, due to reduction of the sulphur to hydrogen sulphide. The elemental sulphur can come from sulphur dust used in the vineyard to prevent fungus infections, or from sulphur residues from burning sulphur discs or wicks in casks to sterilise them. For this reason the latter practice is not recommended. The alcoholic fermentation is strongly reductive with the oxidation-reduction potential less than 100 millivolts at the peak of fermentation. This encourages the reduction of sulphur to hydrogen sulphide.

All fermenting yeasts appear to be able to reduce sulphur to hydrogen sulphide, but they differ in the amount formed. The smaller the sulphur particles (i.e. the greater their surface area), the more hydrogen sulphide is formed. Vineyard sulphur dusting to prevent powdery mildew (Oidium), if applied close to harvest, is an important cause of hydrogen sulphide, because it leaves a residue of finely divided particles of elemental sulphur on the leaves and fruit. These are carried over into the fermentation on the grapes and hydrogen sulphide is formed. Therefore, it is important not to dust or spray vines with dusting sulphur within about four weeks of harvest.

Certain yeasts can reduce sulphur dioxide to hydrogen sulphide during fermentation. A lesser number can even reduce sulphate in grape juice, although this occurs less readily because more chemical reduction steps are required. A yeast should be selected which will not reduce sulphur dioxide or sulphate.

If the grape juice does not contain enough inorganic nitrogen to meet the nutrient requirements of the yeast, some of the grape proteins naturally present in the juice are broken down by the yeast to provide this nitrogen. The sulphur-containing amino acids of the proteins, such as methionine and cystine, can give rise to hydrogen sulphide as a by-product of this protein breakdown. For this reason diammonium phosphate is added before fermentation to increase the available inorganic nitrogen and, incidentally, to provide phosphorus which the yeast also needs. This nitrogen addition usually prevents hydrogen sulphide formation, providing that the other sources are absent. The amount of diammonium phosphate needed depends on the amount of inorganic nitrogen (FAN or free amino nitrogen) naturally present in the juice. Unless this is measured it is not possible to state how much diammonium phosphate should be added. The usual addition rate before fermentation is 100 to 200 milligrams per litre irrespective of the juice.

Certain metals, such as zinc, can produce hydrogen sulphide in wine by direct chemical reduction. The metal reacts with tartaric and malic acids in the wine to produce 'nascent' hydrogen which reduces sulphur dioxide to hydrogen sulphide. This is not an important source, because zinc or zinc-coated equipment does not normally come into contact with wine. However, it is possible for hydrogen sulphide to be produced from stainless-steel vessels if they are not acid-rinsed beforehand. Manganese sulphide forms on the surface of the stainless steel and liberates hydrogen sulphide when the acidic wine contacts it. A preliminary rinse with citric or tartaric acid removes this sulphide layer, thus preventing it from contacting the wine.

Of the various ways of removing hydrogen sulphide from wine, the simplest and quickest is a small addition of copper as copper sulphate solution—up to about 1 milligram per litre of copper, depending on the hydrogen sulphide content of the wine. A laboratory trial is necessary, using a range of levels of copper addition and selecting the lowest level which removes the hydrogen sulphide smell. A stock solution of 400 milligrams of copper sulphate in a litre of water is appropriate, and 1 millilitre of this solution added to 100 millilitres wine corresponds to an addition of 1 milligram of copper per litre of wine. In the winery an addition of 4 grams of blue copper-sulphate crystals per 1000 litres of wine corresponds to an addition of 1 milligram per litre of copper. The crystals are dissolved in a little water and added slowly with stirring to the wine. The hydrogen sulphide combines with the copper to form insoluble copper sulphide, which settles to the bottom of the vessel as a fine brown dust. The amount formed is so small that no further steps to remove it are necessary.

In some French winemaking practices, for example, where one would expect hydrogen sulphide to be present it is not, and winemakers affirm that they are rarely trouble by it. When one examines their wineries in detail the reason becomes apparent—there are always pieces of brass equipment in use (taps, pipelines, pumps etc.). Where the brass contacts the wine it is invariably black, due to deposited copper sulphide. What is happening is that hydrogen sulphide is being formed then removed by brass equipment, which in principle has the same effect as the current practice of adding copper sulphate. There is a lesson for us here.

Volatile acidity

Volatile acidity or volatility is a jargon term indicating that the wine (usually dry red) has been infected with acetic acid bacteria, or possibly lactic acid bacteria or certain yeasts, which oxidise alcohol to acetic acid and to its ester, ethyl acetate. The level at which these constituents become detectable to taste varies with the style of wine, but the generally accepted maximum limits in practice are about 0.8 grams per litre for acetic acid and 0.15 grams per litre for ethyl acetate. Big alcoholic wines tolerate higher levels of volatility than light thin wines.

Under Australian law acetic acid in wine has a legal maximum level of 1.5 grams per litre, while in New Zealand the limit is 1.2 grams per litre. There is no legal limit for ethyl acetate. Volatile acidity is an age-old problem in red table wines, and its occurrence means that the winemaking process needs to be examined. Once a wine becomes volatile it is not possible to remove or cure the fault without seriously damaging the wine, so prevention is important.

The detection of volatility is carried out by tasting (smell of vinegar) and chemically by measuring the acetic acid present, which constitutes more than 96 per cent of the acids in wine which are volatile in steam. Ethyl acetate is more important from the taste viewpoint, but difficult to measure and thus not usually determined. Ethyl acetate is usually produced concurrently with acetic acid and in the same relative proportion, although this depends on the type of micro-organisms involved. Some *Saccharomyces* yeasts produce significant levels of acetic acid but almost no ethyl acetate, so the wine may have a high level of volatility analytically, but this is not apparent on the palate. Measurement of acetic acid by steam distillation is not the simple determination it is made out to be, and the enzymatic method is an alternative.

From the winemaker's point of view the conditions contributing to the development of volatility are as follows:

- Presence of spoilage micro-organisms—usually these are present in small numbers and will only grow if the conditions set out below prevail.
- Warm temperature—growth and formation of volatility by acetic acid bacteria is twice as fast at 23°C as at 18°C and four times as fast at 28°C.
- Presence of air—acetic acid bacteria need contact with air (they are aerobic although they can sometimes be found growing in the body of the wine). Thus, they can grow on ullaged red wine, on damaged grapes prior to crushing and in the dry cap of skins during fermentation.
- Low sulphur dioxide.
- Low acidity (high pH)—encourages the growth of lactic acid and to a lesser extent acetic acid bacteria.
- Low alcohol—encourages growth of bacteria generally. However, in practice this is not very effective in preventing volatility because approximately 14 per cent alcohol by volume is needed before significant reduction of bacterial growth occurs.

Some methods of preventing volatility are:

- Use effective sanitation during making and clarification of wine.
- For red wines in open-top tanks, keep the cap of skins immersed during fermentation.
- Keep wines cool and (for table wines) out of contact with air. For red wines top-up regularly or bung tight and roll the casks to 60° and maintain the

correct pH and sulphur dioxide content. Recommended levels are set out in Chapter 5.

Casks which have contained volatile wine should be treated with a hot 1 per cent solution of sodium carbonate, followed by a 1 per cent solution of tartaric or sulphuric acid, then rinsed out and sulphited. Inert gas should be used to displace air above table wines in ullaged vessels, and the oxygen content of headspace should be less than 0.5 per cent to prevent the growth of aerobic micro-organisms.

Mousiness

Mousiness is a curious term which applies to microbiological spoilage of certain wines, resulting in a particularly undesirable smell and taste reminiscent of mice. It is an infrequent problem these days but in the past was not uncommon. Few people appear to be able to detect this character, but those who do find it very unpleasant. It is one of the most serious examples of microbiological spoilage and is associated with advanced cases of lactic spoilage, usually in dessert wines. The mousy taste becomes apparent late in the evaluation after the wine has left the mouth, and persists for some time.

The causative organisms are certain lactic acid bacteria and/or *Brettanomyces* yeasts. The bacteria may work symbiotically with the yeasts. Both of these groups are inhibited by sulphur dioxide, and prevention of mousiness is achieved by proper sanitation and effective use of sulphur dioxide. This involves an understanding of winemaking practice as it influences microbiological growth in white wines—specifically pH control, early racking and maintaining a level of free sulphur dioxide between 20 and 40 milligrams per litre for white table wines and about half this for dessert wines for the life of the wine. It is also important to relate the free sulphur-dioxide level to pH, in that the higher the pH, the more free sulphur dioxide is required.

Until recently the chemical nature of mousiness was unknown. It was (and sometimes still is) referred to as acetamide, which has a somewhat mouse-like smell when impure, but in fact no smell at all when pure. The contaminant giving rise to this smell is a trimethyl triazine, but this has not been found in mousy wines. The causative compound rejoices in the name 2-ethyl-delta 1-piperideine. When pure its odour is hemlock-like (it is chemically related to hemlock), but when oxidised by exposure to air produces a powerful mousy smell, persistent and difficult to remove from any surface with which it comes into contact. This means, of course, that mousiness is accentuated if the wine is oxidised.

The amino acid lysine is involved if the causative organism is the yeast genus *Brettanomyces*, but lysine may not be involved with bacteria. The essential requirements for production of mousy wines are presence of certain spoilage bacteria and/or yeasts, alcohol and air. Consequently, prevention of microbiological growth in the wine is a prerequisite for preventing mousiness.

One final and disconcerting feature of all this is that when a wine becomes mousy it is a permanent affliction and cannot be removed without further damaging the wine. The lesson here is that prevention is far better than cure.

Geranium smell

This unusual smell and taste occasionally encountered in dry red wine is one of the worst misfortunes which can happen to a wine. The smell has been variously described as putrid, vile and reminiscent of crushed geranium leaves—whence its name derives. The wine is usually unsaleable and the smell is difficult to remove. It arises from the bacterial decomposition of sorbic acid, which may be added to wine as a fungicide, meaning that it kills yeast and moulds. It is also used in various foods. Because of this desirable property the addition of sorbic acid is permitted in wine, and almost wholly confined to white table wines containing fermentable sugar. Sorbic acid is not a bactericide, and in the amounts added to wine, bacteria can still grow. They actually metabolise sorbic acid and convert it into other compounds, one of which is 2-ethoxy hexa-3, 5-diene, an unsaturated compound having the smell found in wine with geranium character.

Since the growth of lactic acid bacteria and the presence of sorbic acid are the two requirements for formation of this geranium character, prevention is achieved by inhibiting bacterial growth and not using sorbic acid in red table wines. Sorbic acid should only be added to sweet white table wines, and then only when free sulphur dioxide (20 to 30 milligrams per litre) is present to prevent bacterial growth.

Yeast spoilage

Yeast spoilage can be one of the most serious technical problems confronting the bottler of table wine. It occurs in all winemaking countries and usually happens unexpectedly. The winemaker is suddenly confronted with a stock of bottled wine which has become cloudy without warning, or bag-in-box packages that distort due to gas pressure. When the cloud is examined microscopically it is seen to consist of budding yeast cells. In view of its importance the problem will be considered in some detail. See also Chapter 15, Bottling.

Repercussions of yeast spoilage can range from a nuisance up to a problem of disastrous proportions. Financial loss can be considerable, since the wine has to be disgorged, perhaps treated in some way, sterile-filtered and rebottled into washed and sterilised bottles. All this rehandling is a complete waste of time and money, and the wine is usually lowered in quality.

Nature of spoilage

Yeast growth occurs more often in white than in red table wines and can be separated into two broad types. If the wine contains residual sugar, carbon dioxide is usually evolved and the cloudy wine becomes charged with gas. The pressure of carbon dioxide may force the cork out of the bottle or swell the bag-in-box to resemble a football. This type of spoilage is a refermentation of sugar and, depending on the yeast strain involved, may or may not be accompanied by formation of off-flavours.

If a non-fermenting yeast is present or the wine is free from fermentable sugar, a haze and/or deposit will form without noticeable formation of gas. This type of spoilage is less commonly encountered, but if a resistant strain of non-fermenting yeast is involved, spoilage can also be quite serious. It is frequently accompanied by off-flavours, due to formation of acetic acid, ethyl acetate and other undesirable metabolic products.

Appearance of the bottled wine may or may not be indicative of yeast spoilage. The deposit can range in appearance from a fine sandy deposit, which readily disperses to a haze on shaking, to discrete globular particles which settle to the bottom of the bottle and do not disperse on shaking. In all cases the haze or deposit appears under the microscope (about 600 diameters magnification) as yeast cells, either round, ovoid or cylindrical. If other material is present besides yeast, the spoilage may have more than one cause, such as protein, metal haze and so on.

Yeasts involved

Many yeasts have caused spoilage of table wines in Australia and the nature of the spoilage is generally related to the characteristics of the yeasts involved. Usually the yeasts are species of *Saccharomyces*, the most common being *S. cerevisiae*, *S. bayanus*, *S. bailii*, *S. capensis*, *S. bisporus* and *S. rouxii*. Of these, *S. cerevisiae* and *S. capensis* are extensively used for primary fermentation and flor sherry production respectively. In fact, the yeasts isolated from spoiled wine are frequently identical to the yeast which carried out the primary fermentation.

In addition to *Saccharomyces* species, spoilage may be caused by poorly or non-fermenting yeasts, such as *Pichia membranaefaciens, Torulopsis bacillaris, Rhodotorula rubra, Candida mycoderma, C. sake, C. valida* and *C. parapsilosis*. Surprisingly *Brettanomyces*, which has been reported as causing spoilage in other countries, appears to be rare in Australia. Sometimes yeasts have been isolated, particularly those forming pink colonies such as *Rhodotorula* spp, that do not appear to multiply in wine and are thus of little significance.

Characteristics of spoilage yeasts

Yeasts isolated from spoilt bottled wine show wide differences in their ability to grow under different conditions. The alcohol tolerance can range up to about 17 per cent v/v, sulphur dioxide in excess of 200 milligrams per litre, sorbic acid up to 200 milligrams per litre, sugar concentration 0 to 10 per cent and temperature range 15 to 30°C. The main food for the yeasts is sugar, but some are able to grow on other carbon sources, such as tartaric, citric, malic, lactic and succinic acids and glycerol. The most resistant yeasts to a range of fungicides are strains of *S. bayanus* and *S. bailii* (*S. acidifaciens*). The latter yeast is sometimes referred to in the literature as *Z. bailli*.

Whether a contaminating yeast will or will not grow in bottled wine depends on many factors, such as the strain (not only the genus and species), the number of cells present, temperature and the amount of alcohol, sugar, sulphur dioxide and other fungicides, growth factors and various nitrogenous compounds present. Wines may effectively sterilise themselves in time, while others may maintain a low level of viable yeasts, of no apparent practical significance, for some time. Yet others encourage the growth of yeasts and rapidly become cloudy. Accordingly, it is not possible to say what is the maximum number of yeast cells which may be tolerated at the time of packaging without knowing more about the yeast and wine involved. Some bottlers regard 10 cells per bottle as a rule-of-thumb maximum, but this depends on the yeast and the wine, and the ideal to aim for is zero count.

While the presence of fermentable sugar generally encourages the growth of yeasts, certain strains can readily grow in wine containing only non-fermentable pentose amounting to about 0.1 per cent. They do this by using other wine constituents, such as acids, as a source of carbon by oxidative growth. *S. bayanus, S. bailii* and *Pichia membranaefaciens* are well known in this regard. Various other yeasts, such as *Brettanomyces*, reported in South Africa and Europe, require thiamine and biotin in the wine as growth factors. If the wine is deficient in these two B-group vitamins, *Brettanomyces* contaminants will grow only slowly or not at all.

Yeasts, as a group are not particularly heat-resistant when compared with sporing bacteria, for example. In general, they are killed by exposure to 70°C moist heat for 20 minutes, and heat sterilisation of filling equipment is so arranged as to expose all parts of the equipment which contact wine to this temperature or above for at least 20 minutes.

Sources of spoilage yeasts

Although yeast contamination can come from various sources, such as the air, empty bottles, corks, bottling equipment and so on, most spoilage yeasts come from the wine itself and are not sufficiently removed by pre-bottling filtration. The types of yeast involved are listed above, and where *Saccharomyces* strains are involved it is probable that they are in the wine as a residue from the primary fermentation.

Prevention of yeast growth

Since yeast spoilage in packaged wine is caused by growth of yeasts after packaging, prevention is best achieved by sterile filtration, hot bottling or the use of appropriate fungicides. Other sterilising procedures have been proposed in various parts of the world, such as dielectric heating, radio frequency, ultraviolet irradiation and alternating current, but are not alternatives.

Sterile filtration

This section should be read in conjunction with Chapter 15. Sterile-grade filter pads deliver wine free from yeast providing that they are used under the operating conditions specified by the manufacturer. These conditions are adequate heat sterilisation, filtering below a maximum pressure differential, avoiding pressure surges and not using the pads for too long—preferably for one day only. With most of the sterile-grade filter pads currently available the maximum recommended pressure drop is 21 psig (1.46 kilograms per square centimetre, 15 metres water pressure or 145 kilopascals). Any action which flexes the filter sheet is undesirable because of possible pad fracture. This can occur with pressure surges due to a variety of causes, such as stopping or starting filtration too suddenly, running wine or water suddenly into a steam-filled filter causing a partial vacuum by steam condensation, or by stopping the filling operation without having an effective recirculation of filtered wine. These pressure surges need not be large to cause damage and makers advise that filter sheets may be damaged by rapid pressure changes of approximately 11 psig.

Apart from discrete pressure surges the retention capacity of the pads may be impaired by sudden and repeated surges caused by filling with rapid action on-off valves. These produce a vibrating action on the pads which can eventually result in leakage of yeast cells. The presence of air or carbon dioxide coming out of solution can also help to fracture pads, and adequate counter pressure to retain dissolved carbon dioxide is needed in bottling sparkling wines.

In considering sterile filtration it is important to appreciate the numbers of yeasts which have to be removed. White table wines, for example, may appear clear or brilliant, but normally contain considerable numbers of yeasts. Makers of sterilising-grade filter pads recommend that wine before sterile filtration should not contain more than 500 cells per millilitre.

The plate and frame filter with pads in place needs to be heat-sterilised by steam or hot water circulated via the outlet side of the filter until the steam or hot water issuing from the coldest draining point of the filter is above approximately 70°C. Circulation is continued for at least 20 minutes after this temperature is reached. The coldest outlet on the filters is the bottom drain-cock. Filters differ in the amount of steaming required and two different makes of filters required 25 and 45 minutes steaming respectively before the condensate from the coldest drain of the filter exceeded 70°C. Instructions for steam sterilisation of packed filter presses are supplied by manufacturers and should be followed closely, bearing in mind the above comments.

All equipment downstream from the filter, including the membrane filter and bottling equipment, needs to be heat-sterilised. With rotary bottle fillers designed for heat sterilisation this is best carried out using steam with empty bottles in place in all filling heads so that steam is passed through all the ducts in the filler. Bottles can be a source of sporadic yeast infection and should be checked. Bottles packed in shrinkwrap plastic envelopes under conditions of industrial cleanliness, including treatment with formaldehyde at the glass works, have been found to be oenologically sterile, providing that the shrinkwrapping is not broken. However, new bottles stored in shrinkwrap envelopes exposed to the weather have been demonstrated to be non-sterile due to splits in the envelope and condensation in the bottles. Washed second-hand bottles can be more contaminated with micro-organisms after washing them before, and treatment with sulphur dioxide gas or solution is desirable, followed by a sterile air blast or a sterile water rinse. Corking machines can be a secondary source of infection, in that they can transmit yeasts from one bottle to another via spillage of wine on the jaws of the corker. This occurs particularly when the bottles are overfilled. Heated jaws are a useful feature providing that the corks are not damaged by the heat.

One of the important sources of infection can be pressure gauges of the non-sanitary type, in which wine can enter the pressure-sensitive Bourdon tube of the gauge. This was referred to in Chapter 14. Contamination can occur in dead pockets, such as side branches to safety valves, pressure gauges and thermometer probes. Unless the side branch has a vent cock to ensure that steam can pass through the pipe during sterilising, such dead pockets have been shown to result in irregular contamination of the product.

Membrane filtration has become important in sterile filtration as a final filter after the usual sterile-grade filter pads. Provided that the membranes have a maximum pore size guaranteed to be smaller than the smallest yeast cell, then the filtered wine will be sterile at that stage. Infection at a subsequent stage can still take place. The advantage of membrane filtration after sterile pad filtration is that it is a safeguard against yeast contamination after pad failure. The wine must be brilliant before membrane filtration because membranes have no depth capacity and are easily blocked. In fact rapid blockage of a membrane filter is indicative of filter pad breakthrough.

It is wise to have sampling ports (rubber diaphragms) in the wine line at accessible positions after both the sheet and membrane filters. Wine samples can be drawn aseptically at regular intervals with an hypodermic syringe and examined for presence of yeast by laboratory membrane filtration. By this means the effectiveness of the filtration equipment can be checked routinely.

Sulphur dioxide cannot be relied on to inhibit fermenting yeasts and some yeasts have a high tolerance to it. The levels of alcohol and sugar influence the tolerance of yeasts to sulphur dioxide and cases of yeast spoilage in wines containing up to 600 milligrams per litre sulphur dioxide have been found. An actively growing strain of *Torulopsis bacillaris* has been isolated from fermenting black currant juice containing 1200 milligrams per litre of sulphur dioxide, including over 100 milligrams per litre in the free state.

Sorbic acid is largely effective in preventing yeast growth at or below the maximum legal limit of 200 milligrams per litre (measured as sorbic acid and not as potassium sorbate, the more soluble salt in which form sorbic acid is usually added to wine). However, yeasts can ferment in the presence of a sufficiently high level of sorbic acid to influence the taste of the wine. Sorbic acid has no significant inhibitory action on bacteria in amounts added to wine, and the bacterial growth may produce undesirable off-flavours when growing in the presence of sorbic acid (see the section above on geranium taint). Accordingly the presence of free sulphur dioxide is necessary when sorbic acid has been added. Therefore, the cold sterile filtration at filling is the best method presently available to remove spoilage micro-organisms and preserve the quality of the wine during the process. Its practicability has been widely demonstrated, but the equipment is expensive and its correct use, coupled with competent microbiological control, is necessary.

Some winemakers believe that airborne yeasts are responsible for at least some of the yeast spoilage in bottled wine, but the numbers of these yeasts capable of growing in wine have been insignificant. While a bottling room with sterilised air under positive pressure is a good safeguard against contamination and assists in providing hygienic bottling conditions, from the viewpoint of possible airborne yeast infection this kind of provision is probably unnecessary. It does have the advantage of serving as a wind barrier and keeping personnel away from the filtering, bottling and the corking equipment until after the bottles are stoppered. Usually only a few people are allowed in the room, and while they may have no formal microbiological training, they appreciate the rather special requirements of the process.

Sterile bottling requires sterile closures and the sterilisation of a naturally porous bark cork presents certain problems. Wineries formerly sterilised their corks by immersion in sulphur dioxide solution, and this is still practised, along with the use of pre-sterilised corks. Recommendations by various cork and bottling equipment suppliers do not agree as to the best concentration of aqueous sulphur dioxide to use for how long and at what temperature. Concentrations of sulphur dioxide solution recommended range from 1 to 2 per cent, times from 10 minutes to overnight and temperatures from ambient up to 49°C. In general terms corks should not be soaked hot and the concentration of sulphur dioxide should be kept low to avoid making the cork brittle. A few hours at room temperature in 1 per cent sulphur dioxide containing a little glycerol and in the absence of iron is a general recommendation. Pre-sterilised corks are widely used in Australia, supplied in plastic bags which are only opened when the corks are to be used. The advantage of pre-sterilised corks is that they are intended for use without further treatment. Corks treated by gamma irradiation are sterile and this process is used commercially.

Quality control procedures
In the bottling of table wines, particularly those containing fermentable sugar, some form of quality control is essential in order to detect the presence of yeast.

The use of membrane filtration has been a boon, since the small membranes can be directly laid onto nutrient medium and the appearance of yeast colonies noted after a period of incubation. Unfortunately this procedure takes at least overnight (if microcolonies are to be counted) and a rapid and foolproof method of detecting yeast cells, of the order of 10 cells or less per bottle, is needed. If a check can be made in less than an hour, this would be of great help in preventing yeast spoilage on a large scale. Various types of staining techniques and the use of ultraviolet light microscopy hold promise here.

To conclude, yeast spoilage of bottled table wines can be a serious problem, particularly if the wines contain fermentable sugar. A wide range of yeasts are involved, both fermenting and non-fermenting, and some of them are resistant to the present legally permitted germicides—sulphur dioxide and sorbic acid. Sterilising-grade filter pads used according to the maker's instructions provide wine free from yeasts. Infection can occur subsequently from such sources as non-sanitary-type pressure gauges, contaminated bottles and corking machines. Airborne infection appears to be relatively unimportant. Microbiological quality control procedures applied routinely are essential for detecting yeasts in bottled wine, and these procedures, coupled with sanitary and well designed filtration, filling and corking equipment, are necessary for sterile filling.

Other taints and off-flavours

Various other taints and off-flavours can occur in wines, resulting from contamination by trace amounts of foreign substances, and we are concerned here with those regarded as the most serious. Fortunately for the wine consumer, these problems rarely find their way into the packaged wine, but they can provide difficult problems for the winemaker to rectify.

One serious cause of tainting is contamination by chlorophenols. These compounds in very low concentrations can impart medicinal, disinfectant, phenolic or antiseptic off-odours and flavours to foods and beverages. Chlorophenols are most likely to be produced in wines by the reaction of chlorine-based sterilants on phenols which may be present in the juice, must or wine. These phenols can be inadvertently picked up during the winemaking operation by contact of must or wine with certain rubber products, paints and resins. The need to prevent chlorophenol formation is highlighted by the fact that certain chlorophenols can be up to 10,000 times more effective as tainting agents than the free phenols from which they are derived. In some cases, e.g. 6-chloro-ortho-cresol, these compounds can contaminate the foodstuff or beverage in such low amounts that they elude analytical detection.

Recommendations to help avoid chlorophenol contamination of wines involve assessments of the 'tainting potential' of winery equipment made from or coated with organic resins. Resinous linings, paints, rubber or plastic hoses and gaskets, etc., should be treated with the normal chlorine sanitising agent and careful attention paid to the generation of any of the 'disinfectant-like' odours during the treatment. Should any problem odours arise the use of chlorine-based sanitisers should be discontinued.

Another source of tainting is the contamination of bottled wine by naphthalene present as a contaminant in the corks. Corks are a common cause of such problems due to their adsorptive properties. Corks kept in close proximity to certain chemicals during storage or shipping can absorb the vapour of the chemical and pass the contaminant into wine after bottling.

More easily recognisable and hopefully more avoidable problems have involved contamination with adhesives or oil. The latter can be introduced into wine from leaking machinery gear-boxes during filtration and from hydraulic lines on mechanical harvesters. Many other taints are encountered, such as contaminated water used for diluting brandy to bottling strength, contaminated carbon dioxide, leaking refrigerant and so on. Details are available from the Australian Wine Research Institute.

Often a taint is not recognised until the wine is bottled, and this can be expensive. Furthermore, tainting is commonly caused by such low concentrations of contaminants that treatment procedures may be ineffective. Accordingly, it is important for the winemaker to be aware of and eliminate the likely sources of tainting.

Also see corkiness.

20 The composition of wines

Wine is the product of the alcoholic fermentation of the juice of grapes, and is a complex natural product. Its composition depends on that of the grapes, together with changes brought about by fermentation and subsequent winemaking treatments and maturation. Grapes differ widely in composition, depending on the variety, the climate and soil in which they are grown, their maturity and soundness. Because of the chemical complexity of the fermentation process, many volatile and non-volatile compounds are formed which are not present in the grapes.

Consequently, wine is chemically a very complex beverage. More than 900 constituents have been identified, and as analytical procedures continue to improve, we can expect this number to increase. Although the proportion of table wines produced is high in Australia and New Zealand, considerable quantities of dessert wines are still made, and their chemical composition differs in several important respects from that of table wines. This is due to the addition of fortifying spirit to the wine, the effect of this dilution on the other constituents present, methods of maturation and other factors. This has been taken into account in the data given below.

The amounts of certain wine constituents, such as alcohol and sugar, are directly related to the types of wine, and in general terms these are:

- Dry table wines—red, white and rosé, alcohol 8 to 14 per cent by volume, sugar less than 7.5 grams per litre.
- Sweet table wines—mainly white and rosé, alcohol 8 to 14 per cent by volume, sugar up to about 10 per cent.
- Dessert wines—red and white, alcohol 17 to 20 per cent by volume, sugar up to about 20 per cent.
- Sparkling wines—red, white and rosé, alcohol 8 to 12 per cent by volume, variable amounts of sugar and dissolved carbon dioxide.
- Sherry—alcohol 17 to 20 per cent by volume, sugar 0 to 15 per cent. Dry sherries are high in acetaldehyde.
- Flavoured wines (Vermouth, Marsala etc.)—alcohol 17 to 20 per cent by volume, sugar 0 to 15 per cent with herbal and other flavours.

The basic subdivision is into table wines, with an alcoholic content of 8 to 14 per cent by volume, and fortified dessert and aperitif wines, in which the alcoholic content has been increased by addition of grape spirit. Coolers which are made with a wine base are not included.

The various compounds in wine may be grouped into broad classes as follows:

water	70 – 90 per cent (V/V)
ethyl alcohol	8 – 20 per cent (V/V)
sugars	0.1 – 20 per cent (W/V)
acids	0.3 – 1 per cent (W/V)
bases	0.1 – 0.3 per cent (W/V)
phenolics, tannins – up to	0.4 per cent (W/V)
volatiles – up to	0.2 per cent (W/V)
other non-volatiles	0.5 – 1 per cent (W/V)

Table of wine composition

Details of wine composition are given in the following tables, which have been collated from world oenological literature and analyses of Australian wines. So far as is known, this is the only compilation available which has taken into account the composition of Australian wines. Where reliable and comprehensive data are available, a range of values has been given, otherwise mean values are listed.

The data are for normal wines. Special wines made in certain parts of the world may have components which lie outside the range listed, e.g. wines made in restricted areas in Europe from grapes infected with *Botrytis* may contain up to 9 grams per litre of gluconic acid, and certain special wines contain very high amounts of sugar. Certain wine treatments, such as ion-exchange and some clarification procedures, modify the composition of wines treated, but these have been taken into account in preparing the table.

Acids

	grams per litre
Tartaric	2 – 5
Malic	tr. – 5
Citric	tr. – 1
Succinic	0.5 – 1.5
Lactic	0.4 – 3
Formic	0.05
Acetic	0.3 – 1.5
Propionic	tr.
Butyric	0.02
Pyruvic	tr. – 0.13
α-Ketoglutaric	tr. – 0.12
pH (units)	3.0 – 4.3

Approximately sixteen other acids have been detected in low concentration. Ascorbic acid is present in grapes, but is largely destroyed by fermentation.

Sugars

	grams per litre
Glucose	tr. − 100
Fructose	tr. − 100
Arabinose	0.3 − 1
Xylose	tr. − 0.05

Small quantities of twelve other sugars have also been detected. Sucrose is normally present only in traces, but is permitted for sweetening sparkling wines in which it may be present in variable concentrations, depending on the amount of sweetness desired. When added to wine it is hydrolysed to glucose and fructose.

Alcohols

	grams per litre
Methyl	tr. − 0.6
Ethyl	60 − 160
n-Propyl	tr. − 0.01
iso-Propyl	tr. − 0.25
iso-Butyl	tr. − 0.1
iso-and act-Amyl	0.1 − 0.6
2-Phenethanol	tr. − 0.08
n-Hexanol	tr. − 0.01

Small quantities of eighteen other alcohols have also been detected. The propyl, butyl and amyl alcohols are collectively known as higher alcohols or fusel oil, and are sometimes reported as such.

Esters, carbonyls, aldehydes

	grams per litre
Ethyl acetate	0.05 − 0.15
Acetaldehyde	0.02 − 0.4
Acetyl methyl carbinol	tr. − 0.08
Diacetyl	tr. − 0.007
Acetal	tr. − 0.01
Hydroxymethyl furfural	tr. − 0.3

Approximately eighty other esters and seven other aldehydes have been detected. The esters are combinations of the acids and alcohols listed above.

Polyols

	grams per litre
Glycerol	1 – 15
2:3 Butandiol	0.1 – 1.6
Inositol	0.2 – 0.7
Sorbitol	tr. – 0.1

Anions

	grams per litre
Tartrate	0.5 – 4
Sulphate	0.1 – 3
Chloride	0.02 – 0.4
Phosphate	0.05 – 1
Bisulphite	0 – 0.3
Fluoride	tr. – 0.005
Bromide	tr. – 0.002
Iodide	tr. – 0.0002
Borate	tr. – 0.1

Small quantities of various other anions have also been detected.

Cations

	grams per litre
Potassium	tr. – 2.5
Sodium	0.02 – 2.5
Calcium	0.01 – 0.15
Magnesium	0.01 – 0.2
Iron	tr. – 0.015
Copper	tr. – 0.002
Aluminium	tr. – 0.005
Zinc	tr. – 0.005
Manganese	tr. – 0.001
Arsenic	tr. – 0.0001
Lead	tr. – 0.0005

Traces of fifteen other metals have also been detected.

Phenolics

	grams per litre
Anthocyanins	0 – 1
Tannins	0.2 – 4
Other phenolics	0.1 – 1

Other phenolics comprise a wide range of catechins, flavones, flavonols, cinnamic acids and related compounds. Australian dry red wines have been shown to contain the anthocyanins cyanidin, delphinidin, malvidin, peonidin and petunidin as their 3-glucosides and acylated with coumaric and caffeic acids. Malvidin-3-glucoside is the major constituent. The amounts of these constituents decrease as the wine ages.

Nitrogenous compounds

	grams per litre
Proteins	tr. – 0.04
Amino Acids:	
Alanine	0.07
Aminobutyric acid	0.03
Arginine	0.02 – 0.1
Asparagine	0.05
Aspartic acid	0.01 – 0.1
Cystine	0.01 – 0.1
Glutamic acid	0.09 – 0.4
Glutamine	0.03
Glycine	0.01 – 0.07
Histidine	0.005 – 0.04
Leucine and isoleucine	0.01 – 0.06
Lysine	0.02 – 0.07
Methionine	0.002 – 0.05
Phenylalanine	0.01 – 0.03
Proline	0.05 – 0.7
Serine	0.01 – 0.07
Threonine	0.02 – 0.4
Tryptophane	tr. – 0.005
Tyrosine	0.005 – 0.04
Valine	0.01 – 0.08

The total nitrogen content of wines ranges from 0.15 to 0.9 gram per litre, and the nitrogenous compounds comprise proteins, polypeptides, oligopeptides, peptones, amides, amino acids and other constituents. The amino acids listed above are present in the free state.

Vitamins

	milligrams per litre
Thiamine	tr. – 0.01
Riboflavin	tr. – 0.3
Pantothenic acid	0.5 – 2
Pyridoxin	0.2 – 0.8
Nicotinic acid	1 – 3
Biotin	tr. – 0.002
Mesoinositol	200 – 700
Choline	17 – 40
p-Aminobenzoic acid	tr. – 0.2
Pteroylglutamic acid	tr. – 0.004

Various other compounds are present in wine, such as pectins, gums, terpenes, certain histamine-like compounds which have physiological activity, traces of volatile sulphur compounds and dissolved gases.

Glycerine in wine

There is currently considerable interest in the glycerine (glycerol) content of wine, and it is frequently a topic of discussion with winemakers and in wine and food clubs.

Glycerine is a major and important constituent of wine. The amounts present vary from one wine type to another and range from about 1 to 10 grams per litre (0.1 to 1 per cent), except for wines made from botrytised grapes which can be considerably higher. In fact, in some wines it can be, after alcohol and water, the constituent present in greatest abundance—a fact not commonly recognised. Australian dry red wines usually contain 7 to 10 grams per litre (mean 7.8), white wines 4 to 8 (5.5), tawny ports 3 to 9 (6.7) and fino sherries 1 to 8 (3.4) grams per litre.

Glycerine influences wine quality by conferring smoothness and viscosity. In its pure form, it is a clear, sweet-tasting viscous liquid. In some wines made from mouldy grapes the glycerine content can be remarkably high—up to 3 per cent. This is because it is performed in the grapes as a result of metabolism by the mould *Botrytis cinerea* responsible for noble rot. It then passes into the must, survives the fermentation and ends up in the wine. The particularly oily viscous consistency of the classical French Sauternes and the German Auslese, Beeren-auslese and Trocken-beeren-auslese wines is due in part to glycerine, as well as to high sugar.

In wines from sound grapes glycerine is formed by yeast as a byproduct of the fermentation of sugar into alcohol. It actually forms via a side pathway early in the fermentation, deriving from glyceraldehyde phosphate formed from phosphorylated sugar. This sounds complicated but the salient points are that glycerine comes from sugar, its amount depends largely on the sugar content of the must and the strain of yeast, and is formed early in the fermentation.

Since yeasts are involved we may expect them to differ in the amount of glycerine which they form—and this they do. The strain of yeast has a considerable effect on the amount of glycerine formed. In one comparative experiment with different yeasts under controlled conditions the amounts of glycerine formed ranged from 5.5 to 9 grams per litre in the same must, depending only on the yeast.

Other factors are also involved: the more sugar in the grapes the more glycerine is formed, and the more sulphur dioxide, the higher the glycerine level. In fact, in World War I in Germany, glycerine was made industrially for explosives manufacture by yeast fermentation of sugar in a highly sulphited alkaline medium.

As far as Australian wine types made from sound grapes are concerned, as we have seen, more glycerine is present in red than white table wines, while the level in flor sherry is quite low, since the flor yeast partially metabolises it. The highest levels are present in wines from grapes infected with botrytis, and since these are now being encouraged in Australia and New Zealand we will be seeing more wines with a higher glycerine level.

Glycerine can be measured in wine in several ways. The chemical method by periodate oxidation is rather tedious and not very accurate. The enzymatic method is precise and rapid. It requires an ultraviolet spectrophotometer and specific enzymes. High-pressure liquid chromatography (HPLC) measures glycerine quickly, along with various other constituents.

Finally, the 'tears of wine' on the sides of a wine glass are caused by alcohol, sugar and other constituents including glycerol—but they are not composed of glycerol.

21 Quality control

Quality control is an essential requirement of modern winemaking, as the reader will be aware from previous chapters. It commences in the vineyard and concludes when the packaged wine reaches the consumer. Its purpose is to make the most efficient use of the available resources—grapes, facilities and people—to produce products of an agreed standard. Looking at the Australian and New Zealand wine industries generally, quality-control practices vary widely from effectively very little to highly efficient operations. In general, lack of proper quality control is correlated with poor wines and variable and unpredictable quality.

Quality control lies at the basis of winemaking and is involved in all operations—not just some of them. In the establishment of standards of production and packaging, the technical procedures are set by production, with quality control ensuring that they are carried out in conformity with these standards. Ideally, quality control should be a state of mind for all personnel, rather than a department or a person in a white coat. Every member of the winery should be a quality-control officer within the framework of his or her particular duties. An analogy here is in motor-vehicle production in Japan, where we are informed that any worker on the production line can stop the line if the quality of the product is not correct.

Winemaking

We will now examine the various aspects and responsibilities of quality control.

Quality control has the responsibility for ensuring that the products and operations conform to specifications established by the company. It has the power to stop a bottling line, for example, thus alerting production and management to a problem. In principle, production seeks maximum output at acceptable quality, whereas quality control seeks acceptable quality without lowering output.

The development of test procedures is another aspect of the responsibilities of quality control. Procedures must be available to measure every quality attribute and production variable which the company considers necessary. These test procedures must meet the prevailing requirements of the Food and Drug, Customs and Excise, and Packaging Acts and Regulations.

Sampling procedures are an important part of the quality-control function, since 100 per cent inspection is rarely feasible or desirable, and their development is a quality-control function. Sampling plans for Acceptance Quality Levels are available, and reference should be made to the latest edition of the Australian Standard Sampling Procedures and Tables for Inspection of Attributes (AS 1199–1972).

Recording and reporting results is a further quality-control operation. Tabulated charts are frequently used, which enable out-of-control situations to be promptly checked.

Trouble shooting is an important part of the quality-control function. It should not be outside a section's operations to identify problems, diagnose the faults and apply corrective measures. This also relates to special problems involving a multidisciplinary approach. As a matter of principle, quality control should be the continuing assessment of current situations, while research and development is the search for something new or different. The two may with advantage be combined, if appropriately trained personnel are available, but it should be remembered that one person does not make a research team.

An essential part of the quality-control function is to prepare technical communications and instructions for the company's operations. This is usually carried out in conjunction with production. All winemaking instructions to cellar operators, for example, should be in writing on an appropriate form and signed by the responsible production person. On completion of the operation the form is countersigned by the operator and/or the foreman and returned to the winemaker, with a copy to the quality-control department together with a properly labelled sample for checking by the laboratory.

A coordinated quality-control programme requires a commitment on the part of management. In order to ensure that the system functions properly, a clear management structure of the personnel in the system and their responsibilities is required. The definition by a company as to these responsibilities serves to show how widespread is the quality function in the company and, more importantly, that it is not just the preserve of the quality controller. When setting up a quality-control operation it may be necessary to modify the existing management structure, but care must be taken to allow other functions to fulfil their own roles. Quality control cannot be added on as such but must be integrated into the overall structure.

The quality-control operation should be responsible to management, not to production. Various charts showing lines of authority exist in the literature on quality control, with the essential feature that quality control should not be subservient to production. It must of course work with (not for) production and marketing, but its responsibility is to management.

The laboratory is essential to the winemaking operation and is an important part of quality control. Basically, it puts a value, number or approval (or rejection) on something, usually a measure of composition, so that the item or product conforms to specifications. In carrying out such tests the procedures used by the laboratory should be above reproach and be checked for accuracy at regular intervals.

Let us look briefly at an example of quality control in the important field of bottling, in which the following sequence of operations is desirable:

1 The production and marketing departments decide on the package, such as the wine, bottle size, shape, mould number, closure, labels, cartons, and so on. All of the materials used should be approved by quality control at purchase, before payment is made. The wine must be approved by quality control before bottling.

2 The quality-control department ensures that bottling proceeds as it should, such as the correct wine is bottled, the bottle fill-height, clarity and packaging are correct and so on. This is carried out by regularly sampling and checking at pre-determined intervals, using a procedure designed for the purpose.

3 In a large winery the quality-control inspector reports either verbally or in writing to the foreman of the bottling line and the quality-control supervisor, and a quality-control chart is filled in for each bottling programme. This chart identifies all of the necessary data involved with bottling, the number of samples checked in a given time, the nature of these checks and any departures from established norms. The chart is retained as a record.

Customer complaints are important because they give an indication of the quality, or departure from it, of a product as perceived by the purchaser. Formal customer complaints are estimated at less than 10 per cent of total complaints. These complaints should be handled by the quality-control manager, who monitors the performance of the company's products and checks their public reaction and acceptance. Furthermore, customer complaints enable quality control to check on established standards with a view to assessing their suitability. Finally, all complaints should be answered in writing with restitution being made where appropriate.

Many quality-control forms for recording information are in use in the wine industry for a wide range of technical operations. Such forms are usually in-house documents prepared by the winery for its own use. Regardless of the size of the winery, it is important that documentation is established to enable quality-control operations to be carried out and to acquire a documented history of the company's operations and products.

Finally, if quality-control fails, profitability will fall and the company may go out of business—it is as important as this.

Laboratory

As we have seen, the laboratory is an essential part of quality control, in that it puts a value or number on something. Chemical analysis of wine, for example, is now one of the most powerful tools in modern wine production, and every aspect of modern winemaking should be monitored by the appropriate chemical and physical tests.

The size and complexity of a winery laboratory depends on the type and number of analyses to be carried out. The minimum analyses required in wine-making are set out in Chapters 22, and these may be increased, but preferably not reduced, depending on the requirements of the winery. Where many of the same analyses are to be carried out the use of automatic or repetitive analytical equipment may be justified.

The accuracy of the individual determinations depends on the circumstances; for example, the measurement of free sulphur dioxide content of a white table wine in bulk storage is less precisely required than at bottling. The measurement of pH is usually required with an accuracy of plus or minus 0.02 of a pH unit. Analytical data are required not only for winemaking operations but also for legal purposes, examples being alcohol, sulphur dioxide, volatile acid, and to check that any compounds prohibited by law are absent. Finally, chemical analyses should fulfil a need, not because they 'look good' on paper. In the following sections we will be describing the various basic laboratory operations.

Wine stability tests

The consumer expects wine (except aged red wine) to be bright and stable with a reasonable shelf-life under a range of storage conditions. To produce these wines in bottle in Australia, where the wines may travel long distances between the point of bottling and the consumer, and be subjected to a range of temperature, requires sound quality-control procedures for checking the stability of the wines before bottling. Similar checks are also required for bulk or bottled wines intended for export, particularly to such cold countries as Canada where stringent cold stability is required.

The various kinds of stability tests considered suitable in assessing the anticipated shelf-life of wines are set out below. They take into account practicability and cost of treatment, with the understanding that striving after a particularly stringent degree of stability may involve unjustified costs of processing. Wine stability is a relative term, and few wines will remain stable indefinitely under all conditions. For practical purposes a stable wine will now show undesirable physical or organoleptic changes under normal conditions in bottle or in bulk transport and storage for a reasonable time. The operative words here are 'normal' and 'reasonable', and these depend on the type and style of wine and the market for which it is intended.

A new wine is basically unstable. It is usually saturated or even supersaturated with potassium bitartrate. It contains greater or lesser amounts of proteins and other high molecular-weight materials in colloidal solution, and a range of microbiological and non-living particles in suspension. The wine undergoes spontaneous clarification by simply being left alone—suspended particles deposit, tartrates crystallise and unstable colloids precipitate and settle. These changes may be hastened or impeded by heat, cold, exposure to air, uptake of tannin from oak casks and pick-up of metals from metallic equipment. As a result of these precipitations and coagulations, the wine becomes clear and acquires a measure of stability. It is usually, but not always, further stabilised by the winemaker, who rightly regards excessive stabilisation as undesirable from a quality viewpoint. However, if the wine is still unstable when bottled or exported in bulk, these changes will continue and may present serious instability problems.

The increasing importance of wine stability is due to the demand for brilliant clarity by the consumer, the trend towards early bottling, particularly with white wines, storage in domestic refrigerators, and the marketing of wine in a climate different from that in which it was made and matured. Hence the need for stability tests to ensure that the wine is stable to the main sources of normal instability.

It is important that stability checks are carried out on the final blend, not on individual components of the blend, because although these components may all be stable, the blend of them may not. This applies particularly to potassium bitartrate deposition.

Cold stability

This is concerned mainly with precipitation of potassium bitartrate as a crystalline deposit when the wine is chilled. The deposit is harmless, but customer reaction may not be. Calcium tartrate may sometimes be involved, but its solubility is not greatly influenced by temperature. Precipitation of colour or other polyphenolic materials may also take place, although these deposits may redissolve on warming.

The most stringent cold-stability test is to seed the wine in a nearly filled bottle with about 1 milligram of powdered potassium bitartrate, then freeze it overnight at about minus 12°C. Next morning transfer the bottle to a normal refrigerator to allow the contents to thaw, but not to warm up unduly. If crystals are present the wine is unstable. This test involves an artificial set of conditions, except for exports to cold countries like Canada. As an alternative, the wine can be placed in the freezer compartment of a normal refrigerator at about minus 5°C for two days, then inspected for crystal formation. A normal domestic refrigerator at about plus 3 to 5°C is not cold enough to give a reliable test for cold stability over a short period.

The mini-contact process can be used to check on cold-stability. To determine whether or not a wine requires cold-stabilisation, analyse the wine for tartaric acid, then chill 100 millilitres to 0°C, add 0.4 grams of powdered potassium bitartrate and shake or stir mechanically for two hours at 0°C. Filter while still cold then analyse for tartaric acid. A wine is considered stable if the decrease in tartaric acid does not exceed 100 milligrams per litre. A more simple alternative is the change in conductivity with chilling. This involves the addition of 2 grams per litre of potassium bitartrate to a sample of chilled wine and stirring for 20 minutes. If the conductivity drops by more than 5 per cent the wine is unstable. This test is simple and rapid, and shows promise as a routine check on cold stability.

Prediction of potassium-bitartrate stability in wines by analytical means alone can be done by the use of appropriate analytical figures. The concentration product of potassium bitartrate is calculated, and if below a certain empirical figure, which is based on experience, then the wine is considered stable. This procedure is not widely used in Australia and more data are needed to make an assessment of its reliability.

Mention may be made of cold stability for brandy and other spirits. Many spirits are unstable to cold and a haze may be formed when the spirit is chilled in the domestic or hotel refrigerator. Potassium bitartrate is not involved and the haze usually consists of tannin materials extracted from the wood during maturation. The most suitable stability test for spirits is to store them overnight at about minus 5°C, then examine for haze. This applies more to trade brandies than to old liqueur brandies which are not usually chilled.

Heat stability

The major cause of heat instability in wine is the presence of grape protein, and a wide range of heating temperatures and times have been used to assess heat stability. The most effective test is to filter the wine through a membrane, then heat in an oven, covered water bath or microwave oven at 80°C for six hours. Addition of 0.5 grams per litre of tannic acid makes the test more stringent in simulating cork contact. If no haze forms on cooling, the wine is heat-stable. Protein instability is more frequent in white wines, particularly those made from Muscat Gordo Blanco, but some red wines may show this fault, if they have been over-fined with gelatin or other protein fining agent.

An alternative procedure for testing protein stability in white wines is to use the Bentotest reagent (a proprietary preparation of phosphomolybdic acid). This is a rapid chemical test which provides somewhat more stringent results than the heat test. The procedure is simple: add 1 millilitre of Bentotest reagent to 10 millilitres of wine and examine the solution for haze. If no haze forms, the wine is stable to protein.

Several other chemical tests may be applied, such as the trichloracetic acid test, which is used in some wineries. This test takes longer to perform and requires a nephelometer (haze meter) for its proper evaluation. On the basis of ease of operation, cost and time-saving, either the heat test or Bentotest are currently recommended.

Metals

Copper and iron are the two most important metals causing haziness and deposit in wine, and aluminium and calcium may occasionally be involved, along with zinc and tin in spirits. Copper forms a reddish-brown haze and deposit, consisting of a cuprous-sulphite-protein complex, in white wines. It forms only under reducing conditions, and usually some time after the wine has been bottled. On the other hand, iron forms a haze of white ferric phosphate in white wines and blue ferric tannate in red wines under oxidative conditions.

Both of these metals occur in wine as a result of contamination from such sources as grape-handling and winemaking equipment, bentonite (mainly iron), filter pads and other sources. The maximum amount of copper and iron which a wine will tolerate before forming a haze depends on its type, composition and to some extent conditions of storage, and maximum limits of 0.5 milligrams per litre for copper and 6 milligrams per litre for iron are recommended. These tests can be carried out chemically or by atomic-absorption spectrophotometry.

Proneness to oxidation

Some wines contain oxidase enzymes which cause them to turn brown rapidly on exposure to air. A simple test is to place a small quantity of wine, e.g. 30 to 50 millilitres, in a partly filled clear-glass bottle, stopper and leave in a warm sunny place for a few hours. The wine should not turn brown, as assessed by comparison with a non-ullaged control. This test can also detect iron haze, which is encouraged by warm oxidising conditions. If a haze forms the wine needs to be checked for iron contamination.

Microbiological stability

The presence of yeasts or bacteria in certain bottled wines can bring about serious instability, and membrane-filtration tests should be carried out during bottling to check that the bottled wine contains no micro-organisms. The wine is passed through a small membrane filter, which is then placed on sterile nutrient medium contained in a petri dish and incubated. The yeast and/or bacterial cells grow into small colonies which are counted to provide an assessment of the numbers of micro-organisms in the wine. Alternatively, the micro-organisms can be counted directly on the filter after appropriate staining, although this is laborious and electronic methods of counting can be used. Details are too complicated to be included here, but are available from membrane-filter supplies.

Polysaccharides

A range of carbohydrate polymers can exist in wine, and the main one causing problems with filtration is glucan, resulting from the growth of *Botrytis cinerea* on the grapes. These polysaccharides are soluble in wine and can influence filtration and the stability of other constituents at quite low concentration, of the order of a few milligrams per litre. The test for their presence is as follows:

Mix 10 millilitres of wine with 10 millilitres of 96 per cent alcohol, allow to stand for 30 minutes, centrifuge, decant and discard the supernatant, redissolve the deposit in 2 millilitres of water and add 1 millilitre of 96 per cent alcohol. A precipitate indicates the presence of polysaccharide. A less sensitive text is to add 3 millilitres of 96 per cent alcohol to 2 millilitres of wine. A precipitate indicates the presence of polysaccharide in a concentration of about 10 milligrams per litre. Removal of glucan from wine is achieved by the addition of glucanase.

Other analyses

Certain other analyses give an indication of the future stability of the wine, such as sulphur dioxide (coupled with pH), reducing sugar and malic acid. Inadequate levels of sulphur dioxide are still a major reason for oxidation in white table wines, and the recommended levels of free sulphur dioxide are given in the section on sulphur dioxide in Chapter 5.

If residual sugar and malic acid are present in table wines (the latter in dry red wines), the wines are prone to yeast and bacterial growth respectively. The filtration and bottling processes need to be checked to ensure that no micro-organisms are present in these wines after bottling.

The size of the samples of wine used for these stability tests depends on the size of the refrigerator and other equipment used and the convenience of the operator. Some wineries handling large numbers of samples use 30-millilitre McCartney screw-capped bottles, but these are rather small and a larger bottle is recommended. Whatever size bottle is decided on it should be used uniformly for all tests and should be scrupulously clean before the wine is placed in it, otherwise any deposit taken up from unclean bottles may give misleading results.

Identification of hazes and deposits

Since the customer now demands wine in brilliant condition, with the exception of old red wines, the identification of hazes and deposits in wine leading to their correction and prevention is important in winemaking. Since wine is such a complex beverage it is prone to a wide range of what are called 'condition' problems, consisting of haziness, clouding or occurrence of crystalline, microcrystalline or amorphous deposits.

Lack of clarity is usual in bulk wines at stages during making (suspended yeasts after fermentation, presence of finings, etc.), but bottled wine which is 'out of condition' can be an expensive problem for the winemaker. If faulty wine reaches the market the result can be serious to the maker in damage to reputation, cost of recall and subsequent treatment or disposal. The most frequently occurring types of unwanted haze and deposit are protein instability, microbiological contamination and metal hazes. Pigment precipitation in old red wines is usual and is not included as a problem. Set out below are the recommended procedures for the identification of these 'condition' problems.

Equipment and materials

In order to identify hazes or deposits in wine the following laboratory equipment is required:

A laboratory centrifuge capable of holding four to six 15-millilitre glass centrifuge tubes and rotating at speeds up to 4000 revolutions per minute. A swing-out head is preferable to a fixed angle head, because the deposit is confined to a smaller area in the centrifuge tube. This is particularly useful when a faint haze is being examined, so that the material comprising it can be concentrated sufficiently to collect enough for identification. Glass centrifuge tubes with conical ends are preferable for concentrating the deposit.

A filtration assembly capable of holding 47-mm-diameter membrane filters. Two types are available: plastic and glass, both of which have the same function. The wine is poured into a top funnel connected by a clamp mechanism to a membrane filter which fits into a lower collecting pressure-flask attached to a vacuum line.

A microscope comprising a binocular head, 15x eye pieces, 10x and 40x objective lenses (100x is useful but not essential) and phase contrast illumination, which enables the sample to be viewed without staining. Microscope slides and cover slips should be clean and free from scratches. The microscope should be permanently set up on a small table (not a bench) so that the user can be seated, and covered with a dust cover when not in use. The microscope and membrane-filter assembly are used for routine microbiological testing.

Other miscellaneous items such as glassware, burners, reagents etc.

Examination of the wine

The wine should be examined visually and tasted, and the following points noted:

Colour and appearance of the haze or deposit. If the haze is fine and dispersed it may be metallic or biological. If coarse and crystalline it is usually potassium bitartrate or calcium tartrate. An amorphous non-crystalline deposit suggests either bacterial, yeast, protein or metallic contamination. Check the presence of carbon dioxide, which may indicate fermentation resulting from microbiological action. Either yeast or lactic acid bacteria may be present in wines, both capable of producing carbon dioxide as a fermentation product.

The *aroma and taste* of the wine should be noted. Bacterial spoilage is indicated by mousiness and other bacterial off-odours, particularly in fortified wines, and yeastiness suggests refermentation in table wines containing residual sugar. An investigation of the history of the wine may help to indicate the nature of the problem. Exposure to metallic equipment other than stainless steel (copper, brass, iron and aluminium) during the winemaking, handling and bottling processes can result in metal hazes. Storage in unlined cement tanks can result in calcium contamination; insufficient protein stabilisation can result in the wine still containing unstable protein and so on.

Preparation of the deposit for examination

The wine is either centrifuged or membrane-filtered to obtain the deposit, which is then examined. If the wine is hazy with no precipitate, centrifugation for up to 20 minutes at 4000 rpm is necessary to produce sufficient deposit for examination. However, if the bottle contains a deposit the wine is simply carefully decanted leaving the deposit, which can be filtered or centrifuged to separate it from the remaining wine if necessary. Filtration completely removes the deposit, and tests are carried out on the residue collected on the membrane filter. The deposit may be removed from the membrane with a spatula or rinsed into a centrifuged tube with filtered water.

Examination of deposit

Microscopic examination should be carried out initially to indicate the general nature of the deposit. Place a small portion of the deposit on a clean microscope slide, add a drop of filtered water and apply a cover slip. Examine under a magnification of approximately 600 times, which enables the general nature of the deposit to be ascertained. Deposits can be divided into microbiological, crystalline or amorphous.

Microbiological deposits will be yeast, bacteria or, rarely, mould. Yeasts, lactic and acetic acid bacteria are the only micro-organism capable of growing in wine. Mould can grow in wine which has been diluted with water, such as in a filter which has been rinsed and left standing, or in an ion-exchange column. Yeasts and bacteria are initially identified by their shape and size, but identification of species is specialised and not usually carried out by a winery laboratory.

Yeast cells are round, oval ellipsoidal, lemon-shaped or cylindrical. Sometimes a group of cells gives the appearance of a branch-like structure. Sizes vary from 2 to 10 micrometre (1 micrometre or µm equals 0.001 millilitre). The majority of actively growing yeasts multiply by producing buds, although one group of yeasts not usually found in wine (*Schizosaccharomyces*) multiples by splitting into two.

Bacterial cells are smaller than yeasts, with cell shapes and sizes varying from rods (2 to 10 µm × 0.4 to 1.2 µm), coccobacilli (1 to 2 µm × 0.6 to 0.8 µm) and cocci (spheres about 0.6 to 0.8 µm diameter). The cells occur singly, in pairs, tetrads or groups, or in short or long chains. *Acetobacter* can be distinguished from *Lactobacillus* as short rods of variable shape with rounded club-shaped ends.

If the deposit consists of regularly shaped particles with angular corners, it is *crystalline*. In this case, wash the deposit with cold water or a dilute (10 per cent V/V) aqueous alcohol solution. Recentrifuge or filter, then dry at approximately 80°C. Crystals in wine are usually potassium or calcium salts, and the deposit is analysed as follows:

1 Dissolve a small portion of the crystalline deposit in a few millilitres of glacial acetic acid and add several drops of a saturated solution of oxalic acid in water. Formation of a white precipitate of calcium oxalate indicates the presence of calcium in the deposit.

2 Dissolve the deposit in water and introduce into a non-luminous flame of a bunsen burner on a piece of nichrome or platinum wire. Calcium produces a brick-red colour, potassium a lilac colour.

3 Add a few drops of sulphuric acid (1 + 9 water) to the crystalline deposit, warm to dissolve, then cool. Formation of crystals indicates calcium sulphate (potassium sulphate is soluble).

4 Place a small drop of sulphuric acid (1 + 9) on portion of the crystalline deposit which has previously been washed with a small quantity of cool water. Apply a drop of 3 per cent sodium metavanadate solution: if tartrate is present, a yellow-orange colour will appear.

Amorphous deposits are characterised by their small and irregular shape and size. Some deposits showing these characteristics may, however, be microcrystalline, i.e. have a crystalline microstructure which may not be apparent on visual examination. A solubility test usually indicates the general nature of the deposit. Take four centrifuge tubes each containing the deposit, from which the supernatant has been removed, and add a few drops of the following filtered reagents to separate tubes: distilled water, 50 per cent V/V alcohol, hydrochloric acid (1 + 3 water) and 2 normal sodium hydroxide. Shake the tubes and examine under a strong light at right angles to the direction in which the liquid is viewed. This highlights suspended deposits and is a rapid means of checking whether the deposit is soluble or insoluble. The solubility tests are interpreted as follows:

Soluble in 50 per cent V/V alcohol—polyphenolics (pigments and tannins)

Soluble in hydrochloric acid—metals

Soluble in sodium hydroxide—protein

The deposits may be composed of individual components or mixtures, and confirmatory tests are applied to the deposit in order to characterise its nature.

Pigments and tannins: Add 1 millilitre of concentrated sulphuric acid to a small amount of deposit in a centrifuge tube and warm gently. If tannin compounds are present the solution will turn bright red. Another check is to add a drop of Folin-Ciocalteau reagent (available from chemical suppliers) diluted 1 to 10 with water. Tannin or colouring matter will partially dissolve and form a grey-blue to dark-blue solution.

Metal haze: Dissolve the deposit in a few millilitres of hydrochloric acid (1 + 3) and add concentrated ammonium hydroxide solution drop by drop. A blue colour indicates the presence of copper. To a solution in hydrochloric acid, add a few drops of a mixture of 1 per cent potassium ferrocyanide and 1 per cent potassium ferricyanide solution. A blue or green colour indicates iron, a red-brown colour indicates copper, a white colour indicates zinc. The hazy wine itself may be examined for the presence of metal contamination by simply adding a few drops of 30 per cent (100 volume) hydrogen-peroxide solution. If the wine clears this indicates that copper is present. If the haze increases iron is indicated. Add a small amount of sodium dithionite on the tip of a spatula to the cloudy wine in a test tube, shake to dissolve and note the appearance. If the wine becomes more cloudy this indicates copper, if less cloudy it indicates iron.

Protein: Add a few drops of 2 normal sodium hydroxide solution to dissolve the centrifuged deposit, and heat a wine known to contain protein to 80°C for

6 hours and separate the deposit formed on cooling. Dissolve this deposit in a small amount of sodium hydroxide to produce a standard protein solution with which the unknown solution may be compared for identity.

To do this, place a drop of each of the solutions in separate places on a filter paper, dry the spots with a hair-dryer, place the paper in a dish containing nigrosine stain (125 milligrams of nigrosine in 1 litre of a solution consisting of methanol 483 millilitres, glacial acetic acid 86 millilitres and water 430 millilitres) for 15 minutes. Pour off the stain and flood the paper with destaining solution (methanol 50 millilitres, glacial acetic acid 10 millilitres and water 50 millilitres) for 10 minutes. Remove this solution and soak for a further 5 minutes with more of this solution until the paper is almost white. Dry the paper in a well-ventilated area and then observe. If the deposit is protein, the spot on the paper will be blue-grey—this is compared with the colour developed on the standard protein spot.

Another protein test is to filter the deposit in the wine through a polycarbonate membrane filter and wet the membrane with a staining solution consisting of 0.2 grams amido black 10B (naphthalene black 12B) dissolved in 10 millilitres of a 9:1 methanol/acetic acid mixture. After 10 minutes reapply vacuum and rinse the filter membrane with the 9:1 methanol/acetic acid solution until all the colour is removed. Protein will stain black or dark-blue.

Other types of deposit

The methods described above should be sufficient to identify the commonly occurring deposits in wine. If, however, a deposit or haze remains unidentified by these procedures, more sophisticated examination needs to be applied, such as infra-red analysis, X-ray diffraction, gas chromatography and mass-spectrometry, and nuclear magnetic resonance. These techniques are specialised and expensive for a winery laboratory, and the samples should best be sent to a consulting laboratory. The deposit may be broadly differentiated into organic or inorganic by simply placing a small amount on a metal spatula and heating gently over a small flame. If the material chars it is organic, if not, it is inorganic. Wineries are encouraged to use these kinds of tests on problem wines, and usually the identity of hazes and deposits can be resolved.

22 Wine analysis

As we have seen, wine is a complex natural product containing at least 900 known constituents. It is normal practice to measure a few of these as a guide to overall composition and quality control. In the present state of our knowledge it is not possible to measure wine quality chemically, because far too many components are involved and they and their interactions are far too complex. Quality evaluation requires organoleptic examination or tasting, supplemented where appropriate by analysis.

A knowledge of the amounts of certain of these constituents is desirable to establish a basic quality-control programme. These comprise total soluble solids, pH, titratable acidity, sulphur dioxide, acetic acid, reducing sugar, alcohol and paper chromatography (to monitor malo-lactic conversion). Other constituents may also be measured. Recommended levels for the above constituents are dictated both by chemical principles and by winemaking experience. It is important to realise that decisions are dictated by circumstances, and that not every wine will fit ideally into certain analytical parameters and some compromises may be necessary. Since the values obtained by these chemical analyses form the basis for any decisions, it is important that the correct analytical methods are chosen, and that they are performed accurately.

Each of the chemical analyses making up a winery quality-control programme will be described from the point of view of chemical concepts, which help to define recommended values for each analysis, and practical approaches to assure the accuracy of each analysis.

Total soluble solids

The measurement of total soluble solids in musts gives an approximate indication of the sugar content, since sugar represents 90 to 94 per cent of the total soluble solids in the juice of mature grapes. The predominant sugars in musts are glucose and fructose (both reducing sugars) and a very small amount of sucrose (non-reducing).

Total soluble solids may be measured by hydrometry, pycnometry and refractometry. There are termed physical methods and are only estimates of sugar content. An accurate measure of reducing sugar can only be obtained by chemical analysis, such as the Lane and Eynon (described below), Rebelein or enzymatic analysis method.

Hydrometry offers the most convenient and rapid method for determining the approximate sugar content in musts. Hydrometers indicate the specific gravity of a liquid, which for musts relates to the total soluble solids content. They may be calibrated in specific gravity (or Oeschlé), degrees Brix, Balling or Baumé, or some other scale at a specific temperature, usually 20°C. If measurements are made at a different temperature, a correction is required and this is set out below. The definition, background and interrelation of these hydrometer units were given in Chapter 5.

The recommended soluble solids values cover a range, depending on the pH, titratable acidity and flavour development of the juice. At the later stages of grape ripening, the sugar levels may change only slightly whereas flavour levels may increase considerably. Provided that the pH and sugar levels are not so high that acidity adjustments are compromised, or where the resultant wine will be too alcoholic, then flavour intensity should be a prime consideration when deciding on the date of harvest.

Hydrometry measurement

Fill a suitable-sized measuring cylinder to about 10 centimetres from the top with juice free from coarse suspended solids, gently lower the hydrometer into the cylinder and give it a spin to remove air bubbles. Read the indicated graduation on the hydrometer at a level corresponding to the bottom of the meniscus. Insert a thermometer into the juice and measure the temperature. Apply the appropriate temperature correction to the indicated reading as follows:

- For Baumé hydrometers—for every degree C above or below 20°C add or subtract respectively 0.03° Baumé to or from the indicated value.
- For Brix or Balling hydrometers—for every degree C above or below 20°C add or subtract respectively 0.06 degrees to or from the indicated value.

Errors may occur due to:

- Faulty hydrometer—check by immersing in an aqueous sucrose solution of known concentration at the temperature at which the hydrometer is calibrated. For example, a 20° Brix solution is prepared by mixing 20 grams of sucrose (cane sugar) with 80 grams of distilled water and mixing to dissolve.
- Failure to measure the temperature of the juice and apply the appropriate temperature correction.
- Hydrometer not floating freely—due to suspended solids in a must or juice sample which has not been adequately settled, or a measuring cylinder in which the hydrometer fits too snugly.

Reducing sugar

In the grape varieties of *Vitis vinifera* the predominant sugars are glucose and fructose, with minor amounts of sucrose and other sugars. In some varieties of *Vitis labrusca* and its hybrids, which are not grown in Australia but some are still planted in New Zealand, sucrose may comprise as much as 25 per cent of the total sugar. During fermentation, grape sugar is converted to alcohol and carbon dioxide, as well as many other compounds in lower concentration. As the juice ferments, the alcohol formed affects the hydrometer reading by lowering the specific gravity. Thus a wine near the completion of fermentation will read below zero degrees Brix or Baumé or 1.000 specific gravity. Completion of fermentation is shown by the constancy of the hydrometer reading with time. Truly dry wines contain less than 0.1 per cent reducing sugar and much of this is non-fermentable pentoses. The taste threshold for sugar depends on the wine, and ranges from about 0.4 per cent for low-alcohol white table wines to 1.0 or more per cent for red wines. In winery operations the sugar is measured to determine the completeness of fermentation, to conform to legal or commercial requirements, in quality control, and in the cuvée (base wine) for sparkling wines.

The Lane and Eynon procedure

This frequently used procedure is based on the reaction of reducing sugar with alkaline copper sulphate solution, using a sugar solution of known concentration for standardisation. The procedure is as follows.

The following solutions are required:

- Glucose solution 0.5 per cent: dissolve 5.00 grams of glucose (accurately weighed) in distilled water and make to volume in a 1 litre volumetric flask.
- Fehlings A: Dissolve 36.64 grams cupric sulphate (Cu SO_4 5H_2O) in distilled water and make to volume in a 500-millilitre volumetric flask.
- Fehlings B: Dissolve 173 grams sodium potassium tartrate (Rochelle salt) plus 50 grams sodium hydroxide in about 400 millilitres of distilled water (take care as the solution of sodium hydroxide will generate heat on dissolving), cool and make to volume in a 500-millilitre volumetric flask.
- 1 per cent methylene-blue indicator: Dissolve 1 gram of methylene blue in 100 millilitres of distilled water.
- Decolourising charcoal.

To prepare the sample for analysis, measure 100 millilitres of wine accurately into a 100-millilitre volumetric flask and transfer quantitatively to a 250-millilitre beaker. Add a boiling chip and boil to about half its volume to remove the alcohol. If the wine has any red colour add about 0.5 gram of activated (decolourising) charcoal to the beaker before boiling. Cool and filter through Whatman no. 5 filter paper. Transfer the dealcoholised and decolourised wine sample quantitatively to a 100-millilitre volumetric flask and make up accurately to the mark with distilled water and mix.

To standardise the Fehlings solution, pipette 10 millilitres of both Fehlings A and Fehlings B into a 250-millilitre conical flask. Add 2 to 3 boiling chips or a small spatula tip of pumice powder to the flask. Bring to the boil* and immediately start titrating with the 0.5 per cent glucose solution from a burette. The solution will now be blue. While boiling keep titrating with glucose solution until only a faint blue colour remains, then add 5 drops of 1 per cent methylene blue indicator. The blue colour will intensify. Continue titrating,* still with the solution boiling, until the blue colour in the solution is dissipated. A precipitate of cuprous oxide is formed which imparts a brick-red colour to the solution, but when this settles the solution is clear and colourless. This is difficult to recognise at first and is easier if the solution is viewed through the edges for the disappearance of the blue colour. This is the end-point.

To determine the reducing-sugar concentration of the wine, pipette 10 millilitres of both Fehlings A and Fehlings B and 20 millilitres of the dealcoholised, decolourised wine sample into a 250-millilitre conical flask. Add some boiling chips or pumice powder to the flask and titrate with 0.5 per cent glucose as before, observing the 3-minute time-period. Record the number of millilitres used in the titration.

Calculation: when the volume of the wine sample is 20 millilitres the reducing sugar content in grams per litre equals the difference between the two titration figures multiplied by 0.25. For different sample volumes the calculation is altered accordingly.

Errors may occur due to:

- Incorrect concentration of 0.5 per cent glucose solution. The 0.5 per cent glucose is unstable and needs to be prepared freshly. A bulk supply may be accurately prepared and smaller portions frozen in plastic bottles (e.g. 200-millilitre lots) and then thawed for use as required.
- Stale mixed Fehlings solution—do not prepare the mixed Fehlings A and B until required as the mixture is unstable.
- Incorrect heating time—the reaction conditions need to be standardised to heating for 3 minutes.

Acidity

In the past winemakers customarily measured titratable acidity rather than pH in wine, because it was easier and less expensive to do so and the values obtained gave some indication of acidity. Even when pH meters became readily available,

---

* Timing is critical. From the start of boiling until the end point is reached should take 3 minutes. Record the number of millilitres used in the titration (standard titre).

winemakers still tended to think in terms of titratable acidity. However, as acidity and its importance became better understood, the overriding significance of pH came to be recognised. Its measurement is now one of the most important analytical measurements in wine, and every winery should have a reliable pH meter and know how to use it.

The notion of pH as an expression of wine acidity is initially confusing, because it is a concept and not a constituent—you cannot buy a kilogram of pH as you can buy a kilogram of tartaric acid. In addition, the lower the figure, the more acid the wine—as distinct from titratable acid. We are dealing with only a small difference in values (most wines lie between pH 3 and 4). Strong mineral acids, such as sulphuric and hydrochloric, have low pH values in the range of 0 to 1, and strong alkalies, such as sodium hydroxide, in the range of 13 to 14, depending on concentration. Blood has a pH of about 7.3 or near neutrality (pH 7.0—representing the mid-point between the extremes of 0 and 14), and milk is usually between 6 and 7. Beer is about 4.

Understanding the difference between titratable acidity (sometimes incorrectly called total acidity) and pH invokes the theoretical concept of partial dissociation of weak acids in wine. These acids, such as tartaric, malic, succinic and lactic, are weak, in that they do not liberate nearly as many hydrogen ions or protons as strong acids. The acid exists as two forms—undissociated, where the acid is simply dissolved, and dissociated, where the hydrogen ions separate from the acid and may be measured separately.

The number of hydrogen ions in a solution is an indication of its real or active acidity. This is what the pH meter measures—hydrogen ions. The definition of pH by S.P.L. Sorensen in 1909 is the negative logarithm of the hydrogen ion concentration. Thus the pH range from 0 to 14 is logarithmic, which means that a wine with a pH of 3 is ten times as acid in terms of hydrogen ions as a wine of pH 4.

Titratable acidity, on the other hand, measures both the free and bound hydrogen ions together, without distinguishing between the two, and is determined by the amount of alkali used to neutralise them. The result is arbitrarily expressed as grams per litre of tartaric acid (in France as sulphuric acid), and the normal range of values is between about 4 and 9 grams per litre without relating it to a particular acid, but this is not normally used in commercial wine analysis (one gram per litre as tartaric acid is equivalent to 13.3 mill-equivalents per litre). The acid taste of wine is related both to titratable acidity and pH.

Another aspect of the imprecise nature of titratable acid, is that it measures both free and bound hydrogen and all acids in wine (tartaric, malic, lactic etc.) as tartaric acid. To obtain the precise total acidity each acid needs to be measured separately. As a result of all this, titratable acidity is of less oenological importance than pH. To illustrate, a strong acid is completely dissociated or ionised whereas the weak acids (those in wine) are only about 2 per cent dissociated. The pH of solutions of a strong and a weak acid, e.g. sulphuric and tartaric, of the same titratable acidity, are different, with the strong acid having the lower pH.

Accordingly, titratable acid is not directly related to pH, except in a general sense that the higher the titratable acidity the lower (more acid) the pH. It is not possible to say that a wine with a titratable acidity of 6 grams per litre, for example, has a specific pH. The various acids and buffering systems in wine are too complex to permit such a simple relationship.

During fermentation the pH of white wines usually does not change significantly, whereas in red wine fermentation a considerable rise in pH can occur. Factors contributing to this effect are decreased ionisation of the organic acids due to accumulation of alcohol, conversion of malic acid to weaker acids, and the extraction of potassium from solid parts of the grape. Monitoring and adjustment of pH should be carried out at various stages of fermentation, e.g. during the skin-contact period for reds, after primary fermentation, after malo-lactic fermentation and at bottling.

pH

The pH is measured by a pH meter with an accuracy of ± 0.02. the meter should be calibrated with two standard buffers covering the pH range of wines. Suitable buffers include saturated potassium-bitartrate solution (pH 3.55 at 20° or 3.56 at 25°C), potassium hydrogen phthalate (pH 4.01 at 20°C) and a commercial buffer of pH 7.00. The determination is carried out on the settled grape juice or wine without dilution.

To standardise the pH meter, the two-buffer adjustment is carried out as follows:

1 Temperature adjustment—set the temperature control to that of the standard buffer solution (normally room temperature).

2 Set the sensitivity (or slope) control to the 100 per cent position.

3 Initial adjustment—immerse the electrode in pH 7.00 buffer contained in a small beaker, stir slowly and adjust the buffer control so the digital display shows pH 7.00.

4 Sensitivity (slope) adjustment—immerse the electrode in the stirred pH 4.01 buffer (or another standard buffer in the range of 3.00 to 4.01) contained in a small beaker, and adjust the sensitivity or slope control so that the digital reading shows the standard buffer value on the display.

5 Final adjustment—immerse the electrode again in the pH 7.00 buffer and adjust the buffer control so that the digital display shows pH 7.00. Rinse the electrode with water after immersion in a buffer or wine.

6 When not in use, store the electrode immersed in storage solution as recommended by the manufacturer.

To measure pH in grape juice or wine:

1 Standardise the pH meter as above.

2 Rinse the electrode with a small portion of the sample to be analysed. The sample temperature must be the same as the temperature of the standard buffers.

3 Immerse the electrode in the sample contained in a small beaker and slowly stir the solution. The pH value of the sample will be shown on the digital display. Allow time for the display to stabilise.

4 Rinse the electrode with distilled water and return it to the storage solution. Errors may occur due to:

- Unsuitable pH meter—a pH meter with the following features is necessary:
  — accuracy of plus or minus 0.02 pH units.
  — repeatability of at least plus or minus 0.02 pH units.
  — buffer or calibrate adjustment, sensitivity (or slope) and temperature controls.
  — digital display.
- Incorrectly standardised pH meter—the meter may be checked by preparing a saturated buffer solution of potassium hydrogen tartrate as follows: add 0.5 grams of solid potassium hydrogen tartrate to 100 millilitres of distilled water until no more will dissolve. Add a little more, warm the solution and then allow it to return to room temperature. Solid potassium hydrogen tartrate will settle out on standing. Filter and use the clear solution for the pH buffer. This should read pH 3.56 plus or minus 0.02. This standard buffer solution should be prepared fresh every few days, and may be used as an alternative to the pH 4.01 buffer.
- Faulty buffers—buffers should be stored in tightly capped glass or plastic vessels in the refrigerator. Take a small portion of the stock buffer solution and allow it to reach room temperature before using to standardise the pH meter. If using the same standard buffer solution over the period of a day cap or cover the small beaker containing it with plastic film.
- Incorrect temperature correction—the temperature dial should be set to the temperature of the standard buffer solutions and the must or wine sample should be at the same temperature as these solutions.
- Insufficient stirring during measurement—stirring is best achieved with a magnetic stirrer, although careful rotation of the beaker containing the sample by hand should achieve adequate stirring.
- Worn or insensitive electrode—if adjustment of the sensitivity control cannot achieve the correct buffer setting, this indicates that the electrode has lost sensitivity. It is worth trying to recondition the electrode by soaking in dilute hydrochloric acid (0.1 molar) for 24 hours followed by soaking in pH 4.01 buffer for a further 24 hours, then check the standardisation procedure. If this fails the electrode should be replaced.

Titratable acidity

The juice or wine needs to be degassed to remove dissolved carbon dioxide which will interfere with the measurement. Pour about 100 millilitres of wine into a 250-millilitre Buchner thick-walled flask. Fit a rubber bung, connect to a vacuum source and gently shake the flask under vacuum for 3 minutes. The determination is carried out on the degassed sample using a pH meter and titrating to pH 8.4. The procedure is as follows:

1 Standardise the pH meter, rinse the electrode with distilled water, and add sufficient distilled water to a small beaker to ensure that the electrode bulb will be covered when it is lowered into the solution.

2 Lower the electrode into the distilled water and adjust the distilled water pH to 8.4 by adding drops of 0.1 molar sodium hydroxide solution with a fine pipette. Stir the solution while adjusting the pH. This operation corrects for any acidity present in the distilled water.

3 Pipette accurately 10 millilitres of degassed wine into the adjusted distilled water.

4 Titrate with the standard sodium hydroxide solution from a burette into the beaker until the pH of the solution is pH 8.4. Stir the solution during the addition and wait a short period after each addition to allow adequate mixing and reaction. Near the end point add the sodium hydroxide solution drop by drop.

5 Record from the burette the number of millilitres of standard alkali used in the titration.

6 Calculation—when a 10-millilitre wine sample and 0.1 molar sodium hydroxide solution are used, the titratable acidity in grams per litre as tartaric acid equals 0.75 times the number of millilitres of standard alkali used.

Errors may occur due to:

• Incorrectly prepared standard sodium hydroxide solution—this needs to be accurate and is best prepared from commercial standard solutions.
• Failure to remove carbon dioxide by degassing prior to measurement.

Determination of sulphur dioxide

Sulphur dioxide in must or wine acts as an antioxidant and an inhibitor of microbial growth. It exists in two forms, free and bound, as shown in Fig. 22.1.

Fig. 22.1: Free and bound sulphur dioxide

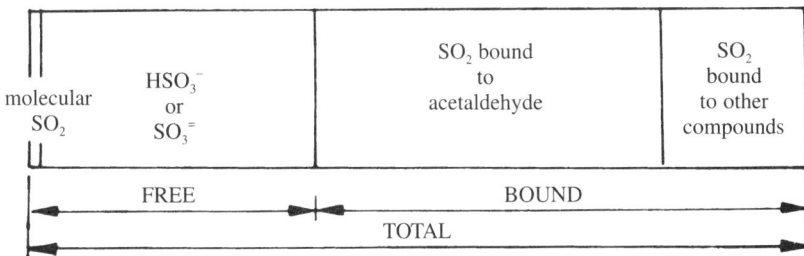

When sulphur dioxide is added to white table wine, for example, an equilibrium takes place between the three forms—molecular, bisulphite and sulphite. All these forms represent free sulphur dioxide, with the amounts of each depending on pH. In wine the major portion of free sulphur dioxide exists as bisulphite, with only a small portion as molecular sulphur dioxide and none in the sulphite form. The proportion of molecular to free sulphur dioxide depends on pH as shown below.

pH	Percentage of SO_2 as molecular
3.0	6.0
3.3	3.0
3.6	1.5
4.0	0.5

The molecular form of free sulphur dioxide exhibits the greatest toxicity towards yeast and bacteria, e.g. 0.8 milligrams per litre of molecular sulphur dioxide inhibits the growth of spoilage yeast (*Brettanomyces* species) and lactic acid bacteria in white wine. An important oenological principle for white winemaking is that free sulphur dioxide levels should be adjusted regularly to maintain at least 0.8 milligrams per litre of molecular sulphur dioxide at all stages of processing.

The relationship between pH and the amount of free sulphur dioxide necessary to achieve this critical level of molecular sulphur dioxide is set out in the section on sulphur dioxide in Chapter 5. At low pH values, less sulphur dioxide is required to achieve effective protection. In fact, free sulphur dioxide is one of the most important measurements in winemaking.

When sulphur dioxide is added to white must or white wine part is bound to sugar and acetaldehyde. At the end of fermentation the sulphur dioxide present is all bound strongly to acetaldehyde. The higher the addition of sulphur dioxide at the crusher, the higher the amount bound at the end of fermentation. At this stage (immediately after fermentation) it is critical to adjust free sulphur dioxide levels in the wine to the required level, the aim being to obtain the correct free level with the lowest possible total. During cellar operations (e.g. racking) sulphur dioxide can be decreased by oxidative reactions and thus free sulphur dioxide levels should be checked before and after such operations and adjusted accordingly to the guidelines above.

Ascorbic acid addition is often used in conjunction with sulphur dioxide. In this case it is critical that free sulphur dioxide is present to scavenge any hydrogen peroxide resulting from the oxidation of ascorbic acid, thus preventing any further oxidative reactions due to hydrogen peroxide. This reaction between hydrogen peroxide and sulphur dioxide also depletes the free sulphur dioxide level in the wine, thus the latter should be monitored and adjusted accordingly.

In red wines sulphur dioxide is bound strongly to acetaldehyde and lightly to anthocyanins. Free sulphur dioxide measured by the aspiration method (as well as other methods in use) includes that portion lightly bound to anthocyanins, and thus overestimates the true free level.

The aspiration (Rankine) method for measuring sulphur dioxide is set out below. It is based on the removal of sulphur dioxide from the wine sample by aspiration through a condensing column (to trap any volatile acid) into a solution of hydrogen peroxide to oxidise the sulphur dioxide to sulphuric acid, which is then titrated with standard sodium hydroxide. Aspirations of cold wine yields free sulphur dioxide, while aspiration of hot wine yields total sulphur dioxide.

The following reagents are required: 0.3 per cent hydrogen peroxide (store cold), 25 per cent orthophosphoric acid, 0.01 normal sodium hydroxide prepared from an ampoule of the standard reagent, mixed indicator (0.1 gram methyl red plus 0.05 gram methylene blue made up to 100 millilitres with 50 per cent alcohol).

To measure free sulphur dioxide:

1 Set up the apparatus as shown in Fig. 22.2 and check that the flow rate of the air through the two flasks is approximately 1 litre per minute.

2 Add 10 millilitres of 0.3 per cent hydrogen peroxide to the pear-shaped flask, then 3 drops of mixed indicator and titrate to an olive-green colour with 0.01 normal sodium hydroxide. Reconnect the flask.

Fig. 22.2: Determination of sulphur dioxide in wine

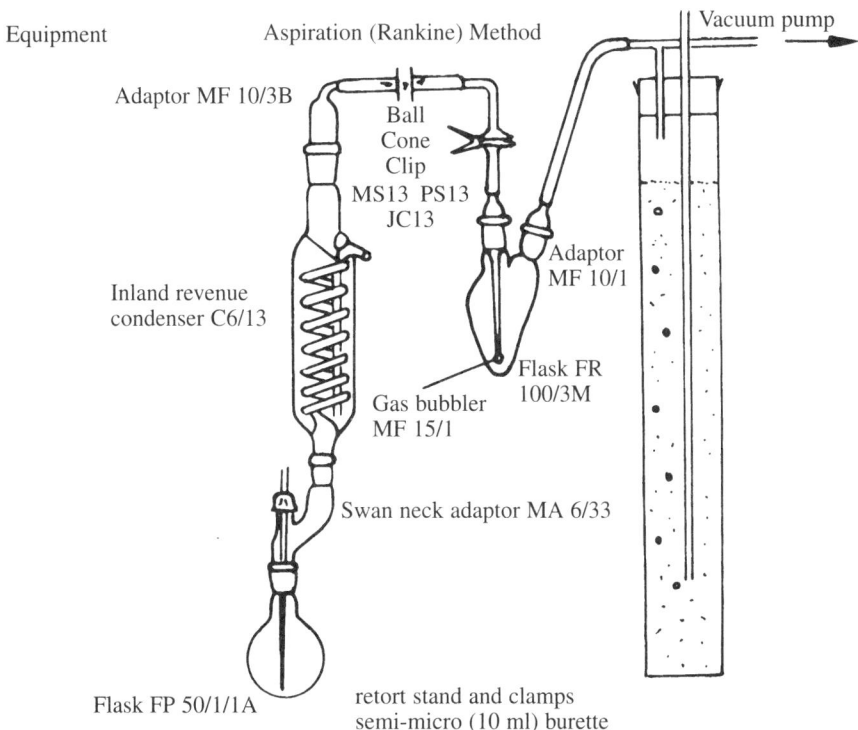

Equipment Aspiration (Rankine) Method Vacuum pump

Adaptor MF 10/3B

Ball
Cone
Clip
MS13 PS13
JC13

Inland revenue
condenser C6/13

Adaptor
MF 10/1

Flask FR
100/3M
Gas bubbler
MF 15/1

Swan neck adaptor MA 6/33

Flask FP 50/1/1A   retort stand and clamps
semi-micro (10 ml) burette

3 Add 10 millilitres of phosphoric acid and 20.0 millilitres of wine to the round-bottom flask, reconnect and aspirate the flask with air at the flow rate set out above for 12 minutes.

4 Remove the top pear-shaped flask with the bubbler, rinse the latter with distilled water and titrate the solution and rinsings with 0.01 normal sodium hydroxide to the olive-green colour obtained before.

To measure bound sulphur dioxide:

1 After completing the titration in step 4 above, replace the top flask or attach a fresh one prepared as in step 2.

2 Check that the air flow-rate is correct (step 1) then, with the same bottom flask in place from the determination of free sulphur dioxide, turn on the water flow in the condenser and heat the bottom flask to boiling with a microburner. Aspirate for a further 10 minutes.

3 Turn off the burner, remove the top flask and titrate with 0.01 normal sodium hydroxide as before. If the total sulphur dioxide only is required then omit aspiration in the cold.

4 The calculation is as follows:

Free sulphur dioxide (milligrams per litre) = millilitres of 0.01 normal sodium hydroxide $\times$ 16

Bound sulphur dioxide = same calculation

Total = free plus bound sulphur dioxide

Errors may occur due to:

- Incorrect concentration of sodium hydroxide. The solution should be prepared fresh weekly.
- Stale hydrogen peroxide—0.3 per cent hydrogen peroxide should be stored in the refrigerator and renewed monthly.
- Incorrect aspiration flow rate or time (standardise the equipment). To establish the aspiration time for the particular apparatus, carry out a series of measurements on the same wine with different aspiration times, selecting the least time of aspiration which provides the maximum recovery of sulphur dioxide.
- Incorrect determination of end-point.

Determination of alcohol

Alcohol in wine results from fermentation of the natural grape sugars, which usually represent about 15 to 24 per cent by weight of the must. Fortification increases the alcohol content. During fermentation approximately half the weight of the sugar is converted to alcohol, the balance being respired as carbon dioxide. In Australia and New Zealand it is customary to express the alcohol content in per cent by volume, regardless of the method used for the determination. Expression of alcohol content at 20°C instead of 15.56°C (60°F) conforms to the ruling from the Australian Customs Laboratory that the ethyl alcohol content of all beverages be expressed in terms of per cent ethanol by volume at 20°C as from 1 July 1972. The alcohol content is required for both technical and legal reasons.

Determination of alcohol by distillation and hydrometry

The alcohol content of the wine is separated from the non-volatile constituents by distillation, and its concentration in the distillate is measured by an alcohol hydrometer at a known temperature and with reference to tables.

The following materials are required: distillation apparatus (see Fig. 22.3), 250 millilitre volumetric flask, constant-temperature water bath, alcohol hydrometers (0–10 per cent v/v, 10–20 per cent v/v), tables relating specific gravity to alcohol content, if specific gravity hydrometers are used, thermometer, hydrometer cylinder and miscellaneous glassware.

The determination is carried out as follows:

1 Fill a 250-millilitre volumetric flask to just above the graduation mark with wine, and bring the contents to 20°C by allowing the flask to stand in a water bath at 20°C for 20 minutes. Adjust the volume accurately by drawing off the excess with a fine pipette. Pour the entire contents of the flask into the distillation flask, rinsing several times with water (using about 200 millilitres of water), and adding the washings to the distillation flask.

2 If the volatile acidity of the wine exceeds 1 gram per litre and/or sulphur

**Fig. 22.3: Equipment required for the determination of alcohol by
distillation (Quickfit catalogue numbers)**

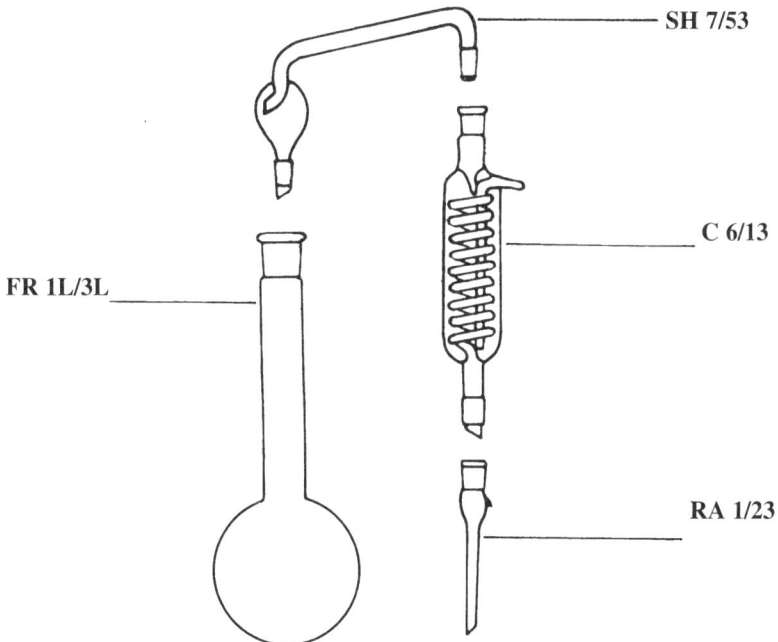

SH 7/53

C 6/13

FR 1L/3L

RA 1/23

dioxide exceeds 200 milligrams per litre, neutralise with sodium hydroxide solution. Add some pumice powder or boiling chips to prevent bumping during heating, and connect the distillation flask to the assembly, as shown in Fig. 22.3. Ensure that the adaptor reaches well into the neck of the receiving flask, which should be packed in ice. Secure all joints and heat slowly.

3 Collect about 220 millilitres of distillate, rinse off the outside of the delivery tube into the distillate with a small amount of water, ensuring that the contents of the flask do not exceed the graduated volume. Place the flask in the 20°C water bath for 20 minutes and then adjust the volume accurately with water at the same temperature using a fine pipette. Mix the contents of the flask thoroughly by repeated inversion.

4 Rinse a suitable hydrometer cylinder or measuring cylinder with a small portion of the distillate and then carefully transfer the distillate to the cylinder. Gently lower an alcohol hydrometer of the appropriate range into the liquid, ensuring that the hydrometer floats unobstructed in the liquid by giving the stem of the hydrometer a gentle spin. These instruments are expensive and should be handled carefully. Read the alcohol content on the hydrometer at the point corresponding to the level of the meniscus, ensuring that the temperature is the same as that at which the hydrometer is calibrated.

Errors may be due to the following:

- Incorrect volume measurements—make sure that the wine distillate volumes are made up at the same temperature. Use the same volumetric flask for wine measurement and distillate collection.
- Incorrect distillation technique—make sure that the glass joint are not leaking, and that the delivery end of the condenser is under water in the collecting volumetric flask. The volumetric flask should be surrounded by iced water.
- Failure to measure temperature and correct the hydrometer reading to 20°C.

Determination of alcohol by ebulliometer
This measurement of alcohol determination is based on the principle of the depression of boiling point by alcohol. The ebulliometer is a device for accurately measuring the boiling point of a liquid (see Fig. 22.4) and the difference between the boiling points of the wine and pure water indicates the alcohol level for dry wines. For sweet wines, in which the sugar influences the boiling point, a correction is made.

The following materials are required: ebulliometer, special thermometer and burner, tables relating ebulliometer degree to per cent alcohol by volume, tables for sweet wine correction (Churchward), thermometer, Baumé hydrometer (0–10°), measuring cylinders.

The method of determination is as follows:
1 Rinse the boiling chamber of the ebulliometer with a small amount of the

Fig. 22.4: Dujardin and Salleron ebulliometer

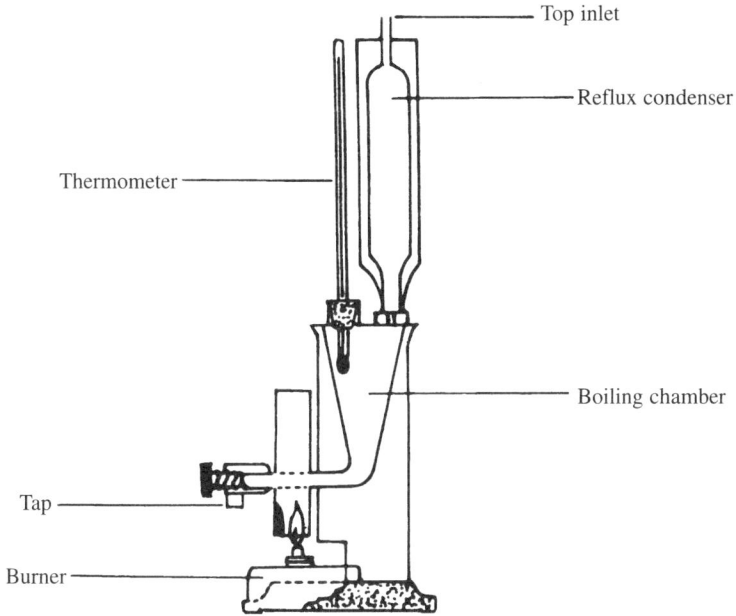

wine to be tested, drain completely through the outlet tap and close the tap. Pipette 50 millilitres of the wine into the boiling chamber, and insert the thermometer. Fill the reflux condenser with cold water, and apply heat to the projecting tube with the burner supplied.

2 When boiling commences, watch the mercury column of the thermometer until it remains stationary for at least 30 seconds, then read and record the temperature to the nearest 0.02°C. This degree of accuracy is required for both table and dessert wines.

3 Using the same thermometer, carry out a similar test using distilled water in placed of the wine sample. Rinse the boiling chamber carefully, drain and pipette 50 millilitres of distilled water into the chamber. During this test the reflux condenser may be left empty. Allow the water to boil until steam issues freely from the top of the condenser, and read the temperature as before.

4 The difference between the two temperature readings in degrees C is the 'ebulliometer degree'. In the case of wines with an hydrometer reading of less than 0.5° Baumé the alcohol content is read directly from Table 22.1. In the case of sweet wines, in which the Baumé exceeds 0.5°, the apparent alcohol content obtained from Table 22.1 is multiplied by the correction factor for the measured Baumé from Table 22.2 to give the true alcohol content.

In using the ebulliometer, it is important to observe the following points. On removing the thermometer from the hot liquid place it carefully on a soft pad to cool. Renew the wick of the spirit lamp when it becomes charred. Periodically

Table 22.1: Ebulliometer degree (wine) table by Churchward (*ACI Jnrl. & Proc.* January 1940)

Ebull. Deg.	% v/v Alcohol	Ebull. Deg.	% v/v Alcohol	Ebull. Deg.	% v/v Alcohol	Ebull. Deg.	% v/v Alcohol	Ebull. Deg.	% v/v Alcohol
6.15	7.4	8.50	11.4	10.85	16.5	11.82	19.1	12.76	22.0
6.20	7.5	8.55	11.5	10.90	16.6	11.84	19.2	12.78	22.0
6.25	7.6	8.60	11.6	10.92	16.7	11.86	19.2	12.80	22.1
6.30	7.6	8.65	11.7	10.94	16.7	11.88	19.3	12.82	22.2
6.35	7.7	8.70	11.8	10.96	16.8	11.90	19.4	12.84	22.2
6.40	7.8	8.75	11.9	10.98	16.8	11.92	19.4	12.86	22.3
6.45	7.9	8.80	12.0	11.00	16.9	11.94	19.5	12.88	22.4
6.50	7.9	8.85	12.1	11.02	16.9	11.96	19.5	12.90	22.4
6.55	8.0	8.90	12.2	11.04	17.0	11.98	19.6	12.92	22.5
6.60	8.1	8.95	12.3	11.06	17.1	12.00	19.6	12.94	22.5
6.65	8.2	9.00	12.4	11.08	17.1	12.02	19.7	12.96	22.6
6.70	8.3	9.05	12.5	11.10	17.2	12.04	19.8	12.98	22.7
6.75	8.3	9.10	12.6	11.12	17.2	12.06	19.8	13.00	22.8
6.80	8.4	9.15	12.7	11.14	17.3	12.08	19.9	13.02	22.8
6.85	8.5	9.20	12.8	11.16	17.3	12.10	19.9	13.04	22.9
6.90	8.6	9.25	12.9	11.18	17.3	12.12	20.0	13.06	22.9
6.95	8.7	9.30	13.0	11.20	17.4	12.14	20.1	13.08	23.0
7.00	8.8	9.35	13.1	11.22	17.4	12.16	20.1	13.10	23.1
7.05	8.8	9.40	13.2	11.24	17.5	12.18	20.2	13.12	23.2
7.10	8.9	9.45	13.3	11.26	17.6	12.20	20.2	13.14	23.2
7.15	9.0	9.50	13.4	11.28	17.6	12.22	20.3	13.16	23.3
7.20	9.1	9.55	13.5	11.30	17.7	12.24	20.3	13.18	23.3
7.25	9.2	9.60	13.6	11.32	17.7	12.26	20.4	13.20	23.4
7.30	9.3	9.65	13.8	11.34	17.7	12.28	20.5	13.22	23.5
7.35	9.3	9.70	13.9	11.36	17.8	12.30	20.5	13.24	23.6
7.40	9.4	9.75	13.9	11.38	17.9	12.32	20.6	13.26	23.6
7.45	9.5	9.80	14.0	11.40	17.9	12.34	20.6	13.28	23.7
7.50	9.6	9.85	14.2	11.42	18.0	12.36	20.7	13.30	23.8
7.55	9.7	9.90	14.3	11.44	18.0	12.38	20.8	13.32	23.8
7.60	9.8	9.95	14.4	11.46	18.1	12.40	20.8	13.34	23.9
7.65	9.8	10.00	14.5	11.48	18.1	12.42	20.9	13.36	23.9
7.70	10.0	10.05	14.6	11.50	18.2	12.44	20.9	13.38	24.1
7.75	10.0	10.10	14.7	11.52	18.3	12.46	21.0	13.40	24.2
7.80	10.1	10.15	14.8	11.54	18.3	12.48	21.1	13.44	24.2
7.85	10.2	10.20	14.9	11.56	18.4	12.50	21.2	13.46	24.3
7.90	10.2	10.25	15.1	11.58	18.4	12.52	21.2	13.48	24.4
7.95	10.4	10.30	15.2	11.60	18.5	12.54	21.3	13.50	24.5
8.00	10.5	10.35	15.3	11.62	18.5	12.56	21.3	13.52	24.5
8.05	10.6	10.40	15.4	11.64	18.6	12.58	21.3	13.54	24.6
8.10	10.7	10.45	15.5	11.66	18.7	12.60	21.4	13.56	24.7
8.15	10.8	10.50	15.6	11.68	18.8	12.62	21.5	13.58	24.7
8.20	10.9	10.55	15.8	11.70	18.8	12.64	21.6	13.60	24.8
8.25	10.9	10.60	15.9	11.72	18.8	12.66	21.7	13.62	24.9
8.30	11.0	10.65	16.0	11.74	18.9	12.68	21.7	13.64	25.0
8.35	11.1	10.70	16.1	11.76	19.0	12.70	21.8	13.66	25.0
8.40	11.2	10.75	16.3	11.78	19.0	12.72	21.8	13.68	25.1
8.45	11.3	10.80	16.4	11.80	19.1	12.74	21.9		

Table 22.2

Baumé	Factor	Baumé	Factor	Baumé	Factor	Baumé	Factor
0.1	.998	3.3	.950	6.5	.902	9.7	.854
0.2	.997	3.4	.949	6.6	.901	9.8	.853
0.3	.995	3.5	.947	6.7	.899	9.9	.851
0.4	.994	3.6	.946	6.8	.898	10.0	.850
0.5	.992	3.7	.944	6.9	.896	10.1	.848
0.6	.991	3.8	.943	7.0	.895	10.2	.847
0.7	.989	3.9	.941	7.1	.893	10.3	.845
0.8	.988	4.0	.940	7.2	.892	10.4	.844
0.9	.986	4.1	.938	7.3	.890	10.5	.842
1.0	.985	4.2	.937	7.4	.889		
1.1	.983	4.3	.935	7.5	.887		
1.2	.982	4.4	.943	7.6	.886		
1.3	.980	4.5	.932	7.7	.884		
1.4	.979	4.6	.931	7.8	.883		
1.5	.977	4.7	.929	7.9	.881		
1.6	.976	4.8	.928	8.0	.880		
1.7	.974	4.9	.926	8.1	.878		
1.8	.973	5.0	.925	8.2	.877		
1.9	.971	5.1	.923	8.3	.875		
2.0	.970	5.2	.922	8.4	.874		
2.1	.968	5.3	.920	8.5	.872		
2.2	.967	5.4	.919	8.6	.871		
2.3	.965	5.5	.917	8.7	.869		
2.4	.964	5.6	.916	8.8	.868		
2.5	.962	5.7	.914	8.9	.866		
2.6	.961	5.8	.913	9.0	.865		
2.7	.959	5.9	.911	9.1	.863		
2.8	.958	6.0	.910	9.2	.862		
2.9	.956	6.1	.908	9.3	.860		
3.0	.955	6.2	.907	9.4	.859		
3.1	.953	6.3	.905	9.5	.857		
3.2	.952	6.4	.904	9.6	.856		

Note: Baumé must be expressed at 20°C.

clean out the boiler with hot dilute caustic soda solution, followed by thorough rinsing, and do not introduce suspended solids into the boiler.

Errors may be due to the following:

- Failure to correct for the sugar content of sweet wine.
- Incorrect temperature measurement—the temperature of the boiling points of the wine and distilled water must be read as soon as the thermometer reading becomes stable.
- Failure to observe the following procedural points: The same quantities of all liquids, including the water-blank, must be taken for each test. The same thermometer must be used for both water and sample. After each test empty the

condenser and refill with cold water when wine is being tested. When making a series of tests determine the boiling point of distilled water every hour, as an undetected barometric movement of 4 millimetres in atmospheric pressure will cause an error of 0.5 per cent by volume of alcohol.

Determination of volatile acidity

Volatile acid is formed mainly by acetic acid bacteria which convert alcohol to acetic acid and ethyl acetate. Its measurement refers to acetic acid, and the amount formed during fermentation with a pure yeast in the absence of bacteria is usually less than 0.5 grams per litre. Higher amounts may be formed by bacterial or oxidative yeast activity during and after fermentation. Ethyl acetate is produced concurrently with acetic acid, usually in the ratio of about 5 parts of acetic acid to 1 part ethyl acetate. Ethyl acetate is more readily detected organoleptically than is acetic acid but considerably more difficult to measure.

High volatile acidity is objectionable and indicates spoilage and incorrect handling of the wine. It is one of the few constituents in wine for which a legal maximum limit (1.5 grams per litre as acetic acid in Australia and 1.2 in New Zealand) exists. Monitoring changes in volatile acidity is important to detect the onset of spoilage, particularly during wine storage where ullage may be involved.

Volatile acid is measured by steam-distilling the wine to separate the acetic acid and titrating this with standard alkali. The method is as follows:

1 Three-quarters fill the 5-litre flask (see Fig. 22.5) with distilled water and boil for 10 minutes to remove dissolved carbon dioxide before starting the distillation.

2 Degas the wine samples by shaking gently under vacuum for 3 minutes.

3 Prepare a 250-millilitre receival flask containing about 50 millilitres of distilled water, 2 drops of phenolphthalein, titrated to the palest permanent pink colour with 0.01 normal sodium hydroxide.

4 Pipette 10.0 millilitres of degassed wine into the still (A in Fig. 22.5) and add 1 millilitre of 0.3 per cent hydrogen peroxide solution (1 millilitre of 30 per cent hydrogen peroxide (100 volumes) in 100 millilitres of distilled water) to oxidise the sulphur dioxide. Rinse in with a small amount of distilled water.

5 Steam-distil rapidly about 100 millilitres into the 250-millilitre flask, ensuring that the delivery adaptor is below the surface of liquid in the flask.

6 Remove the flask before interrupting the steam supply, and titrate the distillate with 0.01 normal sodium hydroxide to the palest permanent pink colour.

7 Repeat the procedure from step 4 until concordant results are obtained.

8 Repeat the procedure with 10 millilitres of distilled water instead of wine to determine the blank titration value.

9 To calculate the results first subtract the blank titration value from that of the wine sample.

Volatile acidity as grams per litre of acetic acid = (sample titration minus blank titration) × 0.06

Fig. 22.5: The Markham still

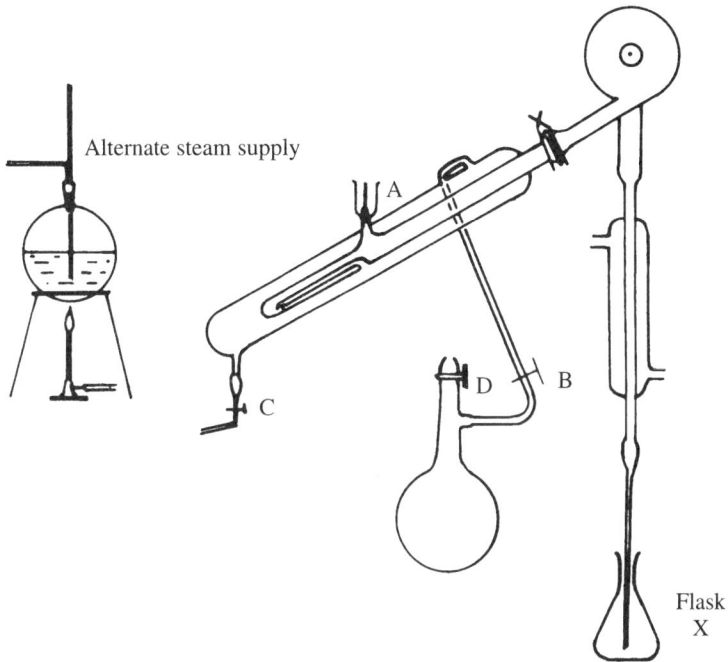

Errors may occur due to:

- Failure to add hydrogen peroxide—thus not eliminating the interference with sulphur dioxide.
- Failure to remove carbon dioxide.
- Failure to neutralise the distilled water in the receival flask.
- Failure to run a blank determination using distilled water.
- Difficulty in detecting the phenolphthalein end-point.
- Incorrect concentration of 0.01 M sodium hydroxide. Prepare fresh solutions every week and store in tightly closed plastic bottles.
  The procedure for operating the Markham still (see Fig. 22.5) is as follows:
- Steam preparation—open D, close B, boil water for 10 minutes.
- Initial washing—open B, close D, place 10 millilitres of water in vessel A, when the still is hot admit water by opening A, close C, pass steam through for a short time, open D, close B, open C to drain.
- Sample addition—open B, close D, pipette sample into vessel A, open A then rinse inlet with a few millilitres of distilled water.
- Sample distillation—close A and C.
- Displacement of sample—open X, open D, close B and after the contents have syphoned out open C to drain.
- Washing—close C, add distilled water through A, close A, open C.

Monitoring malo-lactic fermentation by paper chromatography

Malo-lactic fermentation essentially involves the conversion of L-malic acid to L-lactic acid and carbon dioxide, brought about by lactic acid bacteria either naturally present or added to the must or wine. This results in an increase in pH of between 0.05 and 0.45 pH units and a decrease in titratable acidity, the extent depending on the initial pH and the amount of malic acid in the wine before conversion.

Red wine colour decreases during malo-lactic fermentation, due to this increase in pH as well as to the metabolism of acetaldehyde by certain bacteria. Any sulphur dioxide bound by acetaldehyde is then released into the wine and binds with the coloured anthocyanins producing colourless forms. The effectiveness of sulphur dioxide in the wine is also reduced due to the rise in pH during the conversion. Red wines of high pH and low malic acid content do not benefit from malo-lactic fermentation and it is best to prevent the conversion from taking place. In general, red wines should be adjusted to pH 3.5 or below prior to malo-lactic fermentation.

The paper-chromatographic procedure set out below is simple and can be carried out by a laboratory assistant without expensive equipment.

1 *Solvent preparation.* Place in a 100-millilitre separating funnel a mixture of 33 millilitres of n-butanol, 33 millilitres of distilled water, 3.6 millilitres of formic acid and 5 millilitres of 1 per cent aqueous brom-cresol green indicator solution. Shake the mixture thoroughly for a few minutes, then allow it to settle and separate into two layers. Run the lower aqueous layer down through the tap to waste. Filter the remaining (top) solvent layers through several fluted filter papers to remove traces of water, which adsorb on to the paper, and store in a stoppered glass container in the refrigerator.

2 *Spotting the paper.* Place a piece of Whatman number 1 chromatography paper with dimensions about 50 centimetres by 25 centimetres on a clean bench, holding only the top corner with the fingers. Draw a pencil line from side to side 2 centimetres from the bottom of the long dimension of the paper, and mark cross lines at 2.5 centimetres intervals along this line. Write in pencil the names of the respective standards and wines below the cross lines, which serve as markers for location of the spots.

Raise the bottom of the paper above the bench by supporting it on a glass rod or pencil, and using either a capillary tube or nichrome loop, keeping the spots as small as possible, spot the wine samples and aqueous malic and lactic acid standards (2 grams per litre) four times exactly on the respective pencil cross and drying with a hair-drier between each application. Use a fresh capillary tube for each different sample. If using a loop, clean by washing in distilled water, flaming and drying before each application. When the spots are dry, curl the paper into a cylinder and clip or staple the sides together at the top only.

3 *Setting up the chromatogram.* Place sufficient solvent in the chromatography jar (a covered fish tank or large jam jar will suffice) to provide a layer about 0.5 centimetres deep. Lower the prepared paper into the jar, being careful not to touch the side of the tank. Place the lid on the jar and leave until the solvent front has risen up the paper about 20 centimetres. This will take about 3 hours.

4 *Assessing the chromatogram.* After this time remove the paper and allow to dry in a well-ventilated area, away from contaminating acid or alkaline vapours. The paper will develop yellow spots on a green background. Observe the position of each spot and identify the acids present in the tested wine sample by comparison with the position of the standard spots. This is illustrated in Fig. 22.6, in which wine 1 has not undergone the fermentation whereas wine 2 has, as shown by the absence of the spot for malic acid.

Lactic and succinic acids are produced during the primary fermentation of yeast, hence their presence in the chromatogram is not conclusive evidence for a malo-lactic conversion. The criterion for malo-lactic conversion is the absence of a spot in the position of malic acid and a more intense spot in the position corresponding to lactic acid.

Points to observe:

- The chromatography solvent can be reused several times. With time, water will come out of solution and the solvent needs to be rejuvenated by adding a few drops of formic acid, returning it to the separating funnel, and carrying out the procedure for separating the water and filtering the solvent as before. The solvent should last at least a month.
- The presence of water in the solvent can be assessed from the appearance of the chromatogram. A large yellow zone at the bottom of the paper indicates

Fig. 22.6: Assessing the chromatograph

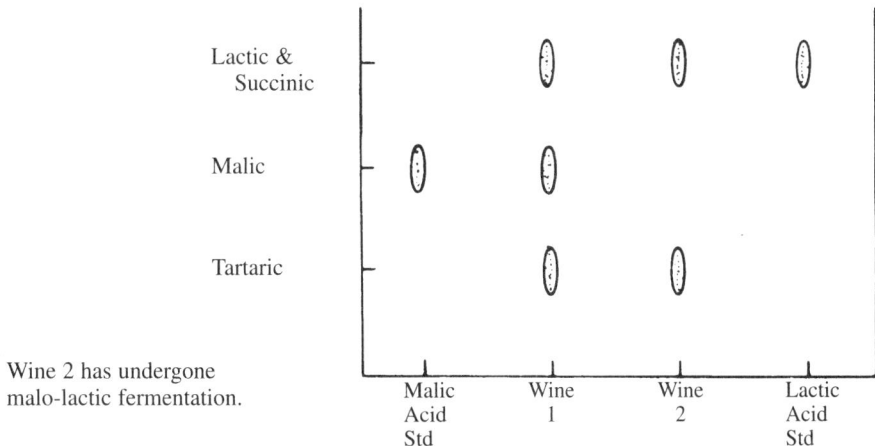

Wine 2 has undergone malo-lactic fermentation.

that the solvent contains too much water. Poor development or separation indicates that the solvent needs to be replaced with a new preparation.

• The blue spots near the baseline are produced by pigments in the wine.
• The chromatographic tank needs to be clean and dry before use.
• Be careful not to contaminate the capillary tubes or the loop between samples.

23 Overseas wine visits

Since Australia and New Zealand are remote from other major winegrowing countries and make many wine types, it is important for winemakers, and fascinating for wine lovers, to know what is happening overseas and to taste overseas wines where they are made. A well-prepared and organised tour can be of great interest and benefit, whereas one which is poorly prepared can be unrewarding and a considerable waste of money. From time to time various public 'wine tours' are organised and can be well worthwhile, providing that they meet the requirements of the traveller and have a properly informed guide.

The best places to go are western Europe, western United States and South Africa. The former is the home of classical wine types (which can be quite expensive, especially in France) while the latter two countries have climate and wine styles similar to our own, as well as a common language.

Here are some suggestions and recommendations:

It is important to be clear in your mind as to what is the purpose of the trip and what are the priorities. What do you want to find out? What particular wines do you want to taste? With whom do you want to talk? What things do you want to see? Make a list of the key questions.

If you are not going on a tour organised by someone else, obtain a few good contacts for each place to be visited. Write advising them of the visit, its anticipated date and duration, and intended purpose, about two months beforehand. Confirm nearer the date of arrival and advise any change in plans promptly. It helps to include a brief written statement listing your interests, experience, qualifications and any other information which will enable your hosts to arrange the most suitable meetings or visits.

If visiting non-English speaking countries, try to learn something of the language beforehand. This is an immense help in establishing communication and rapport. Good interpreters who know the technical jargon are not easy to find, and non-specialist tour guides usually cannot help here.

Arm yourself with some background of the countries you intend to visit, such as their grape area, wine production and wine types, consumption trends, markets and historical background. Consult Hugh Johnson's *World Atlas of Wine* and other references. Carry maps of the various places you intend to visit. Michelin guides (red and green) are excellent in France.

Similarly, become familiar with the various aspects of the Australian and/or New Zealand wine industries and, preferably, note the relevant statistics for quick reference. If you can, take the latest annual reports of the Australian Wine and Brandy Corporation and the Winemakers Federation of Australia Inc. (or the New Zealand equivalent) for reference.

If planning your own tour make use of travel agents in planning the itinerary. They can help to plan the trip in the most economical way, both in time and money, and can usually make helpful suggestions. They need to be told specifically where you want to go and can advise you of the best way to get there, as well as arranging accommodation and car hire. However, a note of caution about driving in Europe in August—it is the holiday season and the roads are crowded. A Eurail train ticket is a useful alternative.

Arrange for flexibility in the itinerary and, if possible, allow one working day in each week unallotted. Especially allow some free time at the end of each visit for checking back. Where possible, use weekends for travelling and settling in.

Two heads are better than one—try to join up with someone else with similar or complementary interests. This is particularly useful when travelling in non-English-speaking countries.

If possible, stay a longer time in fewer places, rather than cram in many short stops, with a short time in each. Allow a day to settle in after a long flight.

Travel as light as possible and wear 'non-iron' clothing. As literature collects, post it home. a portable roll-up clothes line is useful.

If a report is required write it each night as you go. Use small sheets of loose-leaf paper in a pocket ring binder and put only one idea on each sheet. Later, sort the sheets into subjects and the report begins to take shape. Take photographs to illustrate points and as memory aids. A flat pocket-sized camera with a flash attachment is convenient and easy to carry. A lightweight tape recorder can be useful. The tapes can be posted home and dealt with later, but this takes time.

Ask the meaning of words. Ask to be shown the item under discussion. This applies particularly in foreign-language countries, and even in different parts of the English-speaking world words have different meanings.

If possible, check back with your host or guide before leaving. Ask: Is my understanding correct and properly balanced? Have I missed any important points? There may be something misinterpreted or overlooked which would modify your assessment or recommendation.

Use the social niceties—advise your hosts in good time, write thanking them for their help. If the occasion demands, arrive with a small gift. A gift of flowers to your hostess indicates your courtesy. Remember that you are representing more than just yourself.

On return, complete your report quickly, if you have to write one, while it is still fresh in your mind and, if possible, before your return to work. Include a brief summary presenting the salient points and recommendations. Set out details in the body of the report or in appendices.

Finally, if you intend to claim tax deductions get expert advice and keep all records and receipts.

Index